Contributions to Philosophy
(From Enowning)

Studies in Continental Thought

Martin Heidegger

Contributions to Philosophy
(From Enowning)

Translated by
Parvis Emad and **Kenneth Maly**

Indiana University Press
Bloomington & Indianapolis

Publication of this work was supported by funding from Inter Nationes, Bonn.

This book is a publication of

Indiana University Press
601 North Morton Street
Bloomington, Indiana 47404-3797 USA

www.indiana.edu/~iupress

Telephone orders 800-842-6796
Fax orders 812-855-7931
Orders by e-mail iuporder@indiana.edu

Published in German as *Beiträge zur Philosophie (Vom Ereignis)* edited by Friedrich-Wilhelm von Herrmann © 1989 by Vittorio Klostermann, Frankfurt am Main

English translation © 1999 by Indiana University Press

The paper used in this publication meets the minimum requirements of American National Standard for Information Sciences—Permanence of Paper for Printed Library Materials, ANSI Z39.48–1984.

Manufactured in the United States of America

Library of Congress Cataloging-in-Publication Data

Heidegger, Martin, 1889–1976.
[Beiträge zur Philosophie.   English]
Contributions to philosophy : from enowning / Martin Heidegger :
translated by Parvis Emad and Kenneth Maly.
p.   cm. — (Studies in Continental thought)
Includes bibliographical references.
ISBN 0-253-33606-6 (cloth : alk. paper)
1. Philosophy.   I. Title.   II. Series.
B3279.H48B44513   1999
193—dc21   99-34597

1 2 3 4 5   04 03 02 01 00 99

Contents

I. Preview

viii   Contents

Translators' Foreword

With this publication of *Contributions to Philosophy (From Enowning)*, Martin Heidegger's second major work, *Beiträge zur Philosophie (Vom Ereignis)*, becomes available for the first time in English. Known in philosophical circles as *Beiträge*, this work had been awaited with great expectation long before its publication on the centennial of Heidegger's birth in 1989. *Beiträge zur Philosophie (Vom Ereignis)* opens the third division of Heidegger's *Gesamtausgabe*, which is devoted to the publication of book-length manuscripts and treatises.

Contributions to Philosophy (From Enowning) was written almost a decade after *Being and Time*. Like *Being and Time*, it is a treatise that was not originally presented as a university lecture course. But unlike *Being and Time*, it is the first treatise whose maturation and unfolding are not reflected in any of the lecture courses of the years 1919 to 1937. Even the university lecture text *Basic Questions of Philosophy: Selected "Problems" of "Logic,"* though it was written at the same time as *Contributions*, involves some of the same language, and also deals with the question of truth, *still* does not reveal anything of the maturation and unfolding of *Contributions*. Thus, as far as the interrelation of Heidegger's treatises and university lecture texts is concerned, *Contributions to Philosophy (From Enowning)* stands alone. Perhaps the "prolonged hesitation" spoken of in the epigram to *Contributions* reflects the inaccessibility to *any* form of publicness—and not only the publicness of the university lecture course setting. That is, perhaps the thinking that goes on in this work could not find a proper hearing anywhere—until now.

The singular importance of *Contributions to Philosophy (From Enowning)* consists in its being Heidegger's first fundamental work in which so-called "being-historical thinking" is enacted. In six "joinings"—not to be mistaken for "chapters"—called "Echo," "Playing-Forth," "Leap," "Grounding," "The Ones to Come," and "The Last God," Heidegger enacts "being-historical thinking" as a thinking that is enowned by being in its historical unfolding. Whether we consider the echo of being, the way in which the first Greek beginning of thinking plays forth *into* the other beginning, the manner in which thinking leaps into the essential swaying of being, or how this thinking is engaged in the grounding of this swaying as the ones to come who receive the hints of the last god—in any case we witness the gradual, systematic, cohesive, and closely interrelated unfolding of a thinking that presents *Contributions* as a work which—as no other work of Heidegger's—shows the active character of "being-historical thinking." If we fail to consider this active character and if we do not question the traditional pattern that structures a philosophical work (a presupposed thesis, its development and demonstration), we may be misled into assuming that *Contributions to Philosophy (From Enowning)* is a collection of "aphorisms" or that it presents Heidegger's "working notes." Both assumptions are wrong.

The appearance in the text of *Contributions* of a number of sentences that, seen from the outside, look like "notes" should not mislead us into believing that Heidegger is making certain notes to himself. The sentences in *Contributions* that look like "notes" are virtually all formal indicators of the paths to be taken or paths that have already been taken in the course of "being-historical thinking." When, for example, close to the end of *Contributions,* and after a focused discussion and analysis of the work of art, Heidegger lays out a series of questions and issues and addresses the views of the Berlin architect K.F. Schinkel—questions and issues that at first glance look like "notes"—he shows in a formal-indicative manner that each and every word used by Schinkel is open to a "being-historical" interpretation.

Moreover, Heidegger's own understanding of and relation to *Contributions* is such as to leave no doubt that he did not consider this work to be a collection of "aphorisms" or "notes." Indicating that "be-ing and only be-ing *is* and that a being is *not,*"[1] Heidegger makes clear that statements made on behalf of "being-historical thinking" are not to be confused with assertion as "a subsequent expression in the language of a re-presentation."[2] Rather, these statements emerge from and return to what shows and manifests itself, i.e., ἀπόφανσις of be-ing. Thus, Heidegger's own understanding of this work comes from the non-representational apophantic origin of "being-historical thinking." A characterization of *Contributions* as a collection of "aphorisms" or as "working notes" is only possible when we ignore what defines this work and structures it, namely be-ing's self-showing and manifesting.

Heidegger's concern with the cohesive character of *Contributions* is clearly manifest in the close attention that he paid to the process of the typing of the manuscript, in his checking the typed copy against the handwritten original, and, equally importantly, in the meticulous cross-references throughout the *Contributions.*[3] When carefully followed through, these cross-references show the path that thinking has traversed or is about to traverse. Cross-references are given in order to facilitate the engagement of thinking in what is formally indicated: They are not there for demonstrating what a preceding stage of discussion has already established.

As translators of this work, we had to face the necessity of reflecting its singularity. We also had to be constantly aware of its unusual syntax, remaining always fully aware of the source from which this translation receives guidance and directive.

In our attempt to let the singularity of *Contributions* be reflected in its English translation, we tried to keep in mind that "being-historical thinking" is not a thinking *about* being. For being is not an object and cannot be treated as a delimitable and objectifiable topic. For us as translators this meant that we could not use an objectifying approach to the language and word-structure of this work. Throughout *Contributions to Philosophy (From Enowning)* — in the course of a "preview," six "joinings," and a concluding section entitled "Be-ing" — Heidegger takes a new approach to the question of being by enacting a thinking that is "enowned by being." The singularity of this work comes through in translation when translation mirrors "being-historical thinking" as a thinking that is "enowned by being." It has been one of our goals to let this happen throughout the translation.

It is the enactment of this thinking that molds the unusual syntax of *Contributions*. Translating this work into English, we faced the necessity of coming to terms with this syntax, since we realized that it is only by understanding and interpreting this syntax that the singularity of this work can come through in translation. We were thus called upon to characterize and appraise this syntax.

A careful reading of the *Contributions* shows that its unusual syntax is neither extraneous to the work nor an insurmountable obstacle. Thus the unusual syntax cannot be set aside as having no impact on translation. The unusual character of this syntax shows itself in two ways: in the incompleteness of some sentences and in an occasional ambiguity with respect to German grammar. We found that both must be accounted for in our translation. We came to terms with the unusual syntax of the work by making minor additions to the text (they appear within square brackets [ ]). These additions are meant to enhance the readability of the text. What we have added to the text within square brackets is in each case either an interpretation of a certain punctuation mark or derived from the immediate context. This device leaves the reader free either to use or to ignore the additions. The reader who opts for the latter needs only to overlook what stands between the square brackets.

We decided to implement this device in spite of the fact that Heidegger opted for leaving the syntax of the *Contributions* intact. Indeed, the enactment of a new approach to the question of being, which is what *Contributions* is all about, does not depend on a detailed unfolding of its syntax. In a note written at the same time as *Contributions*, Heidegger points out:

> In its new approach this *Contributions to Philosophy* should render manifest the range of the question of being. A detailed unfolding here is not necessary,

because this all too easily narrows down the actual horizon and misses the thrust of questioning.[4]

He was clearly aware of both the incompleteness and the grammatical ambiguity of some passages as they determine the present shape of the *Contributions*. And yet he saw an improvement on this score as unnecessary and perhaps not useful because, in his own mind, a more detailed unfolding of the syntax of this work would distract thinking from the thrust of questioning.

Seen in this light, our few parenthetical remarks are meant to enhance readability as well as to acknowledge that here and there the English needs (can make use of) additions that are less necessary or useful in the German. Sometimes the *context* relieves and releases the text in German in ways that do *not* occur in English. Given these deliberations, it should be pointed out that our parenthetical additions do not pretend to be equal to Heidegger's own "detailed unfolding"—had it occurred—first, because we do not know how he would have actually carried out such an unfolding, and second, because our additions to the text are only indications showing how we as translators understood and interpreted the text. Thus our parenthetical additions are intended only to enhance the readability of the translation and to present the full scope of our interpretation—an interpretation that is inherent in *any* translation.

What is the source from which we drew guidance and directive for carrying out this translation? To respond to this question, we must characterize the act of translating the text of the *Contributions* as an act of disclosing the orienting power of "being-historical words" as this power shapes the cohesive, systematic, and closely interrelated "joinings" of be-ing as enowning. However, this is a power that undermines mere lexicography—the one-to-one correspondence of the German words to their English counterparts. The cohesive, systematic, and closely interrelated "joinings" of Heidegger's "being-historical thinking"—which comes "alive" only in enactment—presents the translation process with the possibility of rethinking, revising, and eventually combining English words in a new way.[5]

Thus the source from which this translation received directive and guidance was not primarily the lexicographical settlement of the relation between Heidegger's German and the English words. It was rather the cohesive, systematic, and closely interrelated "joinings" of "being-historical thinking" that guided this translation toward disclosing the orienting power inherent in the key words of *Contributions*. We see clearly how such a disclosing occurs when we discuss our specific choices for rendering into English the key philosophical words and phrases of the *Contributions*. This discussion forms the core of the Translators' Foreword. (The reader who reads this work for the first time will do well to return to this Foreword in order to bear in mind the reasons that support our renditions of the key words of *Contributions*.)

In preparing this translation and in consulting with scholars in the field, we—as they—have discovered that this text, even in the original, is not readily accessible to its readers. This is true even for those readers who are well read in Heidegger. If this is the case for those reading the *Contributions* in its original German, it is all the more true for anyone who wants to appropriate the text in English. Given the groundbreaking character of *Contributions,* reading this work demands an exceptional scrutiny and precision. Individual words and punctuation marks often carry an even greater weight than normal—even in "normal" Heidegger. Often words and punctuation marks must be read within the context that is *both* prospective *and* retrospective. A case in point is the rendition of *Seinsentwurf* as *projecting being open,* where the danger of imputing this "projecting" to a "subject" is avoided by reading "projecting-open as thrown" within "projecting being open."

Thus we advise readers of this English text that it requires some getting used to, just as does the German text itself. This is a groundbreaking work of thinking, one that opens pathways to the thinking of being that (a) have never been opened before and (b) require a profoundly renewed way of listening to and active engagement with the text. This is true regardless of one's philosophical persuasion and regardless of which current "movement" in philosophy one adheres to.

In what follows we shall do three things. First, we shall discuss families of words that gather around one central German word—families that are recognizable in their phenomenological kinship. Second, we shall address the special case of the large number of words in *Contributions* that carry the prefix *er-*. Third, we shall clarify certain technical aspects of the translation.

I. The Group of Words That Gather Around One Single Word

1. *Ereignis* and Related Words

We considered the possibility of leaving the word *Ereignis* untranslated, since we were aware of Heidegger's own view, corroborated by our understanding of *Contributions*, that *Ereignis* is "as little translatable as the guiding-Greek word λόγος and the Chinese Tao . . . and is . . . a *singulare tantum*."[6] And yet we opted for translating *Ereignis* rather than leaving it untranslated, for three reasons: (1) Leaving the word *Ereignis* untranslated in the text requires an explanation, which involves an interpretation of this word, which in turn constitutes translating it. That is, leaving *Ereignis* "untranslated" is itself a translation. Thus translating this word becomes unavoidable. (2) Leaving the word *Ereignis* untranslated would make it practically impossible to translate the family of words that are closely related to *Ereignis*, such as *Ereignung, Eignung, Zueignung, Übereignung, Eigentum, ereignen, zueignen, übereignen, eignen.* (3) Actually translating this word does not resolve the problem of the untranslatability of *Ereignis*. Thus, what is called for is an English rendition of *Ereignis* that approximates the richness of the German word *without pretending to replace it.* (Heidegger shows that such approximation is possible, e.g., with his own rendition of the Greek λόγος.) In the case of *Ereignis*, feasibility of an approximation is foreshadowed by the way in which the *er-* in *Ereignis* has the function of stressing and putting forth the movement of *eignen* in *-eignis*.

We found a good approximation to *Ereignis* in the word *enowning.* Above all it is the prefix *en-* in this word that opens the possibility for approximating *Ereignis*, insofar as this prefix conveys the sense of "enabling," "bringing into condition of," or "welling up of." Thus, in conjunction with *owning*, this prefix is capable of getting across a sense of an "owning" that is not an "owning of something." We can think this owning as an un-possessive owning, because the prefix *en-* has this unique capability. In this sense owning does not have an appropriatable content.

We found that none of the existing English translations of Heidegger's word *Ereignis* is capable of showing the movement that runs through the *en* and the *own*, as *enowning. Enowning* approximates the movement of *er-* that runs through *eignen* and the *eignis* in *Ereignis*. Part of this movement is a "going all the way into and through" *without possessing*. We consider it a significant confirmation of the appropriateness of the word *enowning* that this word provides a unique possibility for bringing into English what Heidegger does, at important junctures of *Contributions*, when he hyphenates *Ereignis*. By sometimes hyphenating this word, he draws special attention to *er-* as an enabling power and as naming the always ongoing movement "in" and "through" without coming to rest in a "property" or "possession." We found that the en- of "enowning" is capable of doing this.

The existing options in English for translating *Ereignis*, i.e., "event," "appropriation" (sometimes as "event of appropriation"), and "befitting" are totally mute when it comes to the movement that runs through *Ereignis*. None begins with the prefix *en-*, with its specific indication of "enabling" and "thorough moving unto." None approximates the *er, eignen,* and *eignis* the way *en, own,* and *owning* do. It is also clear that none of these words is capable of showing this movement by way of hyphenation. Let us take a closer look at each option.

The first word, *event*, does not even remotely approximate *Ereignis*, because "event" immediately evokes the metaphysical notions of the unprecedented and the precedent that are totally alien to *Ereignis*. Moreover, as born out by sections 238–242 of the *Contributions*, "event" cannot live up to the demands put on it by *Ereignis* because "event" emerges from within "time-space" and as such is *itself* enowned by *Ereignis*. This means that "event" must be understood from within *Ereignis* and cannot function as its approximation.

After carefully examining "appropriation," we came to the conclusion that this word also does not approximate *Ereignis*, for at least three reasons: First, "appropriation" is more static than the German *Ereignis* in Heidegger. This English word conveys a sense of stability that is foreign to the vibrancy of *Ereignis*. Second, and more important, "appropriation" brings to mind the act of seizing something without negotiating, which would misconstrue *Ereignis* as an active agent, as one highly bent on ruling and dominating. "Appropriation" proved not to be a viable option because it strengthens the misconception of *Ereignis* as agency of seizing, ruling, and hegemony. Third, "appropriation" lacks a prefix that is necessary in order to reflect the hyphenation of *Er-eignis*. We found that this prefix puts extra demands upon translation, since at highly crucial junctures of *Contributions* the German prefix *"Er"* in *Er-eignis*—when hyphenated by Heidegger—functions with the autonomy of a full word. To have opted for "appropriation"—disregarding other reservations—would have amounted to depriving the English translation of reflecting what goes on in *Contributions* with the aid of the prefix *"Er."*

Finally, we rejected "befitting" as an option because this term runs the risk of misinterpreting *Ereignis* as something self-subsisting that is destined to fit another self-subsisting thing. In other words, "befitting" would dichotomize *Ereignis*. Moreover, the prefix "be" in "befitting" conveys the sense of a "completion" rather than an enabling process.

These reservations about "event," "appropriation," and "befitting" were strengthened by the realization that none of these three terms presents translation with the possibility of reflecting the phenomenological kinship—so central to an understanding of the *Contributions*—that exists on the one hand between *Ereignis* and *Ereignung, Eignung, Zueignung, Übereignung*, and on the other hand between *Ereignis* and *ereignen, eignen, zueignen*, and *übereignen*. We found that this phenomenological kinship must at all costs be reflected in the English translation in order for this translation to belong to the domain of phenomenological thinking. The three terms—*event, appropriation*, and *befitting*—have the added disadvantage that none is equipped with a prefix to indicate that, with *Ereignis*, an enabling power comes to the fore that extends itself into words like *Ereignung, Eignung, Zueignung, Übereignung, Eigentum, eignen, ereignen, zueignen, übereignen*—all words surrounding *Ereignis*.

It is this same dynamic at work in *Ereignis* that guides our translation of *vom* as "from": from Enowning. Rather than merely referring to enowning as a topic ("on" or "of" enowning), the *vom* here is to be understood as indicative of a thinking that is enowned by being, being as enowning. Thus: from Enowning.

Having decided for *enowning* as the translation of *Ereignis*, we found that the way was opened for translating *Ereignung* with *enownment*, *Eignung* with *owning*, *Eigentum* with *ownhood*, *Zueignung* with *owning-to*, and *Übereignung* with *owning-over-to*.

2. *Sein* and Related Words

Near the end of *Contributions* Heidegger remarks that, by writing *Seyn* instead of *Sein*, he wants to "indicate that [*Sein*] here is no longer thought metaphysically."[7] Thus he elucidates the specific way in which these words, *Sein* and *Seyn*, with their frequent appearance throughout *Contributions*, are to be understood. But how do we reflect this understanding in translation?

Heidegger uses the eighteenth-century orthography of *Sein*, i.e., *Seyn*, in order to indicate that, when he writes *Sein*, he means the way *Sein* is grasped metaphysically and, when he writes *Seyn*, he means the way *Sein* is no longer grasped metaphysically. In both cases, then, he is dealing with one and the same *Sein* and not, as it were, with *Sein* differentiated from *Seyn*: He intends no opposition. Accordingly, to use two different words for translating *Sein* and *Seyn*—e.g., "being" and "beon"— would increase the danger of carrying too far a simple orthographic device.[8] It suggests too much of a "division." Thus we realized (a) that translating *Seyn* with a new English word is misleading, in indicating too great a delineation, and (b) that, if available, an orthographic device is enough for drawing attention to *Seyn*.

Considering the fact that both *Sein* and *Seyn* are pronounced in exactly the same way and that the difference between these words is noticeable only in writing, we decided to use the English word "being" for translating *Sein* and to hyphenate the same word as "be-ing" for translating *Seyn*. In this way we have two English words, *being* and *be-ing*, that, like *Sein* and *Seyn*, are pronounced in the same way but written differently. Thus we are able to avoid using a "new" word for *Seyn*—like *beon*—which could be misunderstood as standing in opposition to "being." For, distinguishing *Seyn* from *Sein* is not the same as creating an opposition between them. (It should be noted, however, that, as F.-W. von Herrmann writes in the Editor's Epilogue, "The alternating spellings "*Seyn*" and "*Sein*" ["be-ing" and "being"] were left unchanged, even where the matter at hand is "*Seyn*" ["be-ing"] and not "*Sein*" ["being"] and where Heidegger here and there, apparently during the writing, did not consistently maintain the different spelling."[9] We have made the same decision and consistently translated *"Seyn"* with "be-ing" and *"Sein"* with "being.")

Regarding words that are related to be-ing and being, we found that they fall into two groups: (1) the group in which be-ing and being are directly present, (2) the group of words derived from be-ing and being.

From the first group we must discuss our choices for rendering *die Geschichte des Seins, Seinsgeschichte,* and *seinsgeschichtlich.* Focusing on the "being" component in these words and deciding to translate *Geschichte* with "history," we rendered these words as "history of being," "being-history," and "being-historical." But how to reflect in translation the important difference between *Geschichte* and *Historie*?

Our translation needs to reflect the difference between *Geschichte* as what is enowned by being and *Historie* as the discipline of historiography. This differentiation is of paramount importance for understanding *Contributions* because, as Heidegger points out near the end of this work, "enowning" is the "origin of history."[10] "History" here is quite different from history as a discipline or as historiography. The happenings that constitute *Geschichte* are quite different from the events that make up *history.* The German word *Geschichte,* more so than the English word *history,* implies: unfolding, issuance, and proffering. Given this difference and considering the sheer impossibility of using two different words in English, one for *Geschichte* and one for *Historie,* we decided to use the same word *history* for both but to demarcate *Historie* by using two parenthetical devices. Whenever the context makes it clear that *Historie* is meant, the reader will find the word *history* followed in brackets either by the word *Historie* or the words "as a discipline."

Belonging to the second group are words such as *das Seiende, das Seiendste, seiender,* and *seiend.* Whereas *das Seiende* appears quite frequently in the text, other variants of this word appear infrequently. An unsurpassable philosophical precision in translation—if such were ever achievable—would demand that we uniformly render *das Seiende* with "a being." However, realizing that such precision is not achievable in translation, we exercised two options. For those cases where the philosophical meaning would be otherwise totally compromised, we opted for translating *das Seiende* with "a being." In all other cases we translate *das Seiende* with "beings" in order to maintain a uniform level of readability. But the reader should bear in mind that throughout this translation "beings" is used as a word whose point of reference is "a being's restoration in the other beginning," which is to say that our choice of "beings" is not to be taken as a generalization of all "beings."

When Heidegger uses *das Seiendste, seiender,* and *seiend* in *Contributions,* he does not assume a chain of beings and its inherent hierarchy. Although these words bring to mind the Platonic ὄντως ὄν and the Thomistic *maxime ens,* what is to be disclosed by them is called in the

Contributions "restoration of beings." Thus our renditions of these words with "most being" and "more being" are to be taken *not* in the sense of a series of superlatives but as indicating restoration of beings.

3. *Wesen* and Related Words

One might perhaps say that the words *Wesen* and *Wesung* are *the most* crucial words for translating *Contributions*. Therefore, when translating *Wesen* and *Wesung* into English, it is of paramount importance to convey the richness, complexity, and subtlety that these words have in German. No other word in the entirety of *Contributions* offers as varied a possibility for the translator as the word *Wesen*. Whether *Wesen* refers to something specific—e.g., language, history, truth—or appears in the context of the first Greek beginning or exercises its disclosive power in conjunction with being and be-ing, each time *Wesen* comes through with a demand for a different way of being translated. The varied possibilities for translating this word range from a rather simple rendition of it as "essence," when the context is that of the first Greek beginning, to a more difficult rendition when this word says something directly and specifically about being and be-ing and thus borders on untranslatability. In short, as a central being-historical word, *Wesen* in *Contributions* defies a uniform English rendition.

When *Wesen* appears in the context of the first beginning, which, among other things, is distinguished by the questions τί ἐστιν (what a being is) and ὅτι ἔστιν (that a being is) and by a discussion of ἰδέα, οὐσία, κοινόν, etc., we consistently translate *Wesen* as "essence." We do so because, in the context of the first beginning, Heidegger uses the word *Wesen* as the German rendition of *essentia,* in English: *essence.* But it should be pointed out that this is more than simply using a traditional and available word. For Heidegger's returning to *Wesen* as the German rendition of *essentia* cannot be understood as simply picking up a German word that happens to be available to him as he thinks *essentia.* The return to *Wesen* as *essentia/essence* occurs in the context of a being-historical decision which shapes the entirety of *Contributions.* This is the decision for opening up and disclosing that unprecedented and monumental unfolding in the thinking of being that *is* the first beginning. Thus, *Wesen* is always situated within a broader context, one that the word *essence* cannot convey.

Thus, sometimes the word *Wesen* simply means "essentia" or "essence." As a "being-historical word," however, it also discloses a profound and comprehensive occurrence that *is* the first beginning and in which the word *Wesen* is not *simply* a rendition of *essentia* (essence). In order to convey that occurrence, Heidegger now uses the same word *Wesen* but with a significant twist. This "twist" is of paramount importance for the translation of *Contributions.* He uses *Wesen* as a word derived from the verb *wesen,* with meanings such as "swaying," "enduring," "abiding," "whiling," and the like. He sees in this "swaying" the originary, profound, and comprehensive occurrence that in the first beginning he calls "being." Thus, in order to translate *Wesen* properly when this word appears in conjunction with being, we were required to account fully for this originary, profound, and comprehensive occurrence.

It should be clear that the rendition "essence of being" is not an option at all, since "essence" refers to a multiplicity of things and being is neither multiple nor a thing. Moreover, the expression "essence of being" misconstrues the originariness of the occurrence of being in the first Greek beginning by reducing this occurrence to one of its offshoots, i.e., the constancy and accessibility of essence. We found other options such as "presence of being" or "coming to presence of being" misleading because, as Heidegger shows in *Contributions,* presence is only one modification of that vibrancy which he calls *das Wesen des Seins.* Moreover, "presence of being" and "coming to presence of being" have the added disadvantage of attributing to being the status of something that *is* before it becomes present or before it comes into presence. These renditions encourage misunderstanding being as a substance. What was needed was an English word that leaves intact its possible modifications and determinations.

In order to translate the word *Wesen* as it reflects the originary, profound, and comprehensive vibrancy called being, we might have translated *Wesen* as "abiding, enduring sway" or "in-depth-sway." Given the awkwardness of "abiding, enduring, in-depth-sway," we allowed *Wesen* to be translated as "essential sway." This is possible only because the English word *essential* has a broader usage than simply its connection to and derivation from "essence." So that "essential" can mean "carrying the whole within itself," "inherent," "through," "belonging inherently to," "inmost"—perhaps even, "in-depth."

Thus rendering *Wesen* as "essential sway" is less than ideal (since there is an etymological hint at a connection with the word *essence,* a connection that is completely inappropriate in *Contributions*), though perhaps acceptable, given the connotations of the word *essential:* carrying the whole sway within itself, inherent sway, inmost sway, belonging inherently to sway, or: in-depth-sway. This fact allowed us to translate the adjective *wesentlich* as "essential."

"Essential sway" has nothing to do with "essence" and everything to do with what inheres within the sway of being in its originary, profound, comprehensive vibrancy and resonance. Using the word *essential* while calling on the reader to ignore the word's etymological rootword, *essence,* is a risk that we had to decide to take.

In attempting to translate *Wesung,* another word that appears in conjunction with being and be-ing, we were guided by Heidegger's return to the word *Wesen* in its power to say what is utterly other than "essence." In this respect *Wesen* and *Wesung* say the same thing. However, since Heidegger uses *Wesung* mostly—and, it should be said, inconsistently—in conjunction with be-ing *(Seyn)*, differentiation in the translation was necessary. Gathering all of these aspects together, we have consistently translated *Wesen* as "essential sway" and *Wesung* as "essential swaying"; *Wesen des Seins* as "essential sway of being" and *Wesung des Seins* as "essential swaying of being"; and *Wesen des Seyns* as "essential sway of be-ing" and *Wesung des Seyns* as "essential swaying of be-ing."

Further, the word *Wesen* in *Contributions* sometimes serves yet another function, appearing in the context where identifying the specificity and peculiarity of certain things is at issue, for example, language or modernity. Here Heidegger uses the word *Wesen* as denoting *das Eigenste einer Sache,* what is ownmost to something.[11] In cases such as these we translated *Wesen* consistently with "what is ownmost."

In contrast to the prevailing practice of translating *Wesen* in these cases also as "essence," its rendition with "what is ownmost" is a philosophically more correct and viable rendition. Thus, considering the expression *das Wesen der Sprache,* we find that this expression can be brought into English accurately with *what is ownmost to language* rather than with *the essence of language.* Here *Wesen* does not name what is "common" to all *languages,* i.e., to a multiplicity, and cannot be translated with "essence," i.e., with a concept whose philosophical viability, like the Greek κοινόν, is predicated upon a multiplicity. Accordingly, we translated *das Wesen der Sprache* as "what is ownmost to language."

Furthermore, we opted for "what is ownmost" rather than "essence" because we realized that this expression opens up a domain that is not the same as the domain opened up by "essence," i.e., the domain of universality. For example, what is ownmost to Dasein is "existence," which is not the domain of the universality of essence because, unlike "essence," existence of Dasein is a matter of experience and enactment. And this means that existence of Dasein is as little an *essentialist* determination of Dasein as Dasein's existentiality is an *existentialist* determination of it.

Finally, *Contributions* presents certain cases where *Wesen* indicates neither "essence" of something nor "what is ownmost" to something nor "essential sway," but "a way of being" of something. Heidegger has in mind, for example, "a people's way of being" when he talks about a *"Volk . . . unbestimmt genug in seinem Wesen."*[12] We translated this sentence as "the people . . . however undetermined in its way of being," because here *Volk* is at issue and not *Völker* and because *Volk* does not immediately refer to the first beginning and because *Volk* as "undetermined" precludes application of a determination to it as "what is ownmost." To elucidate: The singularity of *Volk* circumvents the applicability of "essence"—which is always predicated upon a multiplicity. Further, *Volk* does not—at least not immediately—refer to the first beginning, which means that *Wesen* here is not used as the German rendition of *essentia*. Finally, *Wesen* here does not refer to what is ownmost to something (people), because what is ownmost to something is a determination that cannot be said to be undetermined. Thus *Wesen* here is translated as "way of being."

Having proceeded in this way with regard to *Wesen*, we found that translation of *Unwesen* needed to avoid the variants of the word *essence*. Thus we translated *das Unwesen der Wahrheit* as *what is not ownmost to truth*. Rendition of *Unwesen* with "what is not ownmost" is philosophically more accurate than the available options such as "non-essence," "negatived coming to presence," and "disessence." First, this rendition is based on a clear distinction between "essence" and "what is ownmost," which allows an understanding of the specificity and peculiarity of individual things without assuming in advance that these things must have an essence and must fit into the constancy of essence. (There is a significant difference between assuming that truth has an essence and searching for what is ownmost to truth. When we say, for example, that correctness is not what is ownmost to truth, we say that what is ownmost to truth cannot be determined in terms of correctness. We are *not* saying that truth has an essence that can be determined by discarding and rejecting correctness.) Secondly, this rendition is based on the realization that the word *Wesen* in the word *Unwesen* is not the German translation of *essentia* but rather an indication of peculiarity and specificity of things in terms of what is ownmost to them. Accordingly, this translation of *Unwesen* avoids the complicated and misleading route of using a negative form of essence.

These varied ways of translating *Wesen* determined our approach to the problem of translating the words that are related to *Wesen*. These appear in *Contributions* in the form of compounds whose translation requires that the segment *Wesen* in the compound be translated in the specific ways that this word is translated when it appears alone in the text. Depending then on what the word *Wesen* indicates, the compounds are variously rendered. This is another way of saying that here, too, a uniform rendition cannot be achieved. Whereas, for example, the compound *Wesensmöglichkeit* is translated as *essential possibility*, the compound *Wesensmitte* is translated as *swaying mid-point*. Likewise, the context makes clear that *Wesensgewinnung des Menschen* needs a rendition such as *gaining of man's way of being* because the context makes clear that *Wesen* in this compound indicates *way of being*.

4. *Werfen* and Related Words

The root-word for the phenomenological kinship among the words *entwerfen, loswerfen, Entwurf, Entwerfer, Entworfenes, Werfer, Wurf, Gegenwurf, Loswurf,* and *Geworfenheit*—all of which put forth the being-historical thinking of *Contributions* as an enactment-thinking—is *werfen*. The orienting power of this word as a being-historical word is unmistakably at work in this family of words and should be preserved in the English translation. When Heidegger calls the main task of the *Contributions* an *Entwurf*, he alludes to the role that the word *werfen/throwing* plays in the entirety of this work.[13]

We use "throw" and "throwing" to translate all of the above variants of *werfen*, except for *Entwurf*, which we translate as "projecting-open," (occasionally also as "projecting-opening") and *entwerfen*, which we translate as "to project-open."[14]

In an effort to preserve the phenomenological kinship among *werfen* and related words and to find appropriate words for rendering *entwerfen* and *Entwurf*, sections 122, 182, 183, 203, 262, 263, and 264 of the *Contributions* prove to be crucial. These sections bring together *entwerfen*, *loswerfen*, *Entwurf*, *Entwerfer*, *Geworfenheit*, *Gegenwurf*, *Loswurf*, *Wurf*, and *Werfer* in such a way as to leave no doubt that what is at stake in *entwerfen* and *Entwurf* is an act of opening and disclosing which, as enowned by be-ing, does not occur in the domain of subjective choice and decision. We found that the prevailing renditions of *entwerfen* and *Entwurf* with *projecting* and *projection* fail to avoid a subject-oriented misinterpretation and mistranslation of *entwerfen* and *Entwurf* and do not fully and clearly account for the activity of opening and disclosing. Thus, in translating *entwerfen* and *Entwurf*, we decided to avoid both failures in that we modified *projecting* by indicating that it is one that opens up. Thus for *entwerfen* we chose to say: *to project-open*. This rendition is necessary if we want to differentiate *entwerfen* from such subjective manners of acting as planning, designing, scheming, etc., i.e., from the familiar meanings of *projecting*. Let us take a closer look at this rendition.

The English word *open* differentiates "to project-open" from the familiar translation of *entwerfen*, namely "to project," in that the word *open* accounts for the significant impact of the German prefix *ent-* upon the infinitive *werfen* in *entwerfen*. Since one of the functions of the prefix *ent-* is to unfold the action of the verb to which it is attached, we attend to this function by adding the word *open* to "projecting." Thus "to project-open" as a rendition of *entwerfen* indicates that *this* projecting is distinguished by an opening, which differentiates it from what happens as planning, designing, scheming, plotting, etc.

We prefer this rendition to *projecting* by itself because "projecting" by itself can mislead the reader into thinking that *entwerfen* is entirely under the jurisdiction of the thinking subject. The English word *projecting* has not only a psychoanalytic connotation, it also implies planning, scheming, programming, designing—involves strategy and control. Neither the connotation nor the implication is appropriate here. More importantly, by placing itself under the command of the thinking subject, *projecting* fails to account for *entwerfen's* being enowned by be-ing. We find that it is "projecting-open" rather than "projecting" that is capable of reflecting the fundamental insight of *Contributions,* according to which thinking, as being-historical, is above all *enowned* by being and is thus not a matter of strategy and control.

The decision to translate *entwerfen* as "to project-open" determined our rendition of *Entwurf.* We decided to translate this word with *projecting-open,* sometimes with *projecting-opening,* as these renditions meet two demands of the original: First, these renditions allow for carrying into English the meaning of *Entwurf* when the word is hyphenated, i.e., *Ent-wurf.* Second, these renditions bring into English the unfolding of *throwing* in that the first part of the compound, "projecting," unfolds what goes on in its second part, "open" (or "opening"), and thus indicates that thinking cannot forego its allotted exertion (which does not mean control). When used alone, the English word *project* meets neither of these demands. When *project* is hyphenated, i.e., *pro-ject,* the meaning of *Wurf* is lost.

Moreover, in translating *Entwurf,* we must not use the word *project* alone, because this word by itself can mislead the reader into thinking that *Entwurf* has something to do with a "perspective." As Heidegger alerts us in *Contributions,* perspective has nothing in common with *Entwurf* and must be clearly distinguished from it:

> Here [*Entwurf*] . . . is not a "perspective. . . ." For every *per*-spective always lays claim to what is passed *through* for its point of view.[15]

Seen in this light, *Entwurf des Seins,* as enacted in *Contributions,* is a *projecting open of being* (sometimes *projecting being open*), which does not rely on a point of view since it projects being open as that into which this very same *Entwurf* is thrown.

We translate *Werfer* in such a way that its connection with *werfen* continues to be preserved. We realized that the word *Werfer* must be translated in a way that reflects its phenomenological kinship with *entwerfen* as well as with *Entwurf* and *Geworfenheit.* We translated *Werfer* as *thrower*—which clearly preserves the relationship of *thrower* to *thrownness,* i.e., *Geworfenheit.* This relationship would be totally lost if we translated *Werfer* with *projector.* We found *projector* unsuitable for rendering *Werfer* into English because in its current as well as archaic use, *projector* indicates either an agent who is in charge of a project or an instrument used for projecting, both of which do not reflect the *Werfer* as one who is *thrown into and thus enowned by being.* Moreover, the word *projector* in this context is extremely awkward.

By translating *Werfer* as *thrower,* we preserved the relationship between *Werfer* and *Geworfenheit* as a relationship between *thrower* and *thrownness.* Thus the interconnection of words like *Werfer, Entwurf,* and

Geworfenheit, and the relationship so vital to an understanding of *Contributions,* between *Entwurf* and *Geworfenheit*—obvious in German—are
preserved. This also resolves the issue of translating *der geworfene
Entwurf.* We rendered this technical term with *thrown projecting-open.*
(An option in current use, "thrown projection," preserves all the disad-
vantages of "projection" and is generally inadequate.)

By translating *Werfer* with *thrower,* we paved the way for translating
Entwerfer and *das Entworfene.* The context in which *Entwerfer* appears
makes clear that *Werfer* and *Entwerfer* are the same. Thus for *Entwerfer* we
also say "thrower." And we translate *das Entworfene* as "what is thrown."

Having translated *entwerfen, Entwurf, Werfer, Entwerfer,* and *das
Entworfene* in such a way as to preserve the connection with *throwing,*
we rendered *Wurf* into English as "throw." Translation of *Wurf* with
throw further determined our rendition of the compounds *Gegenwurf*
and *Loswurf,* which we translate with *counter-throw* and *free-throw.* In
the same vein we rendered *loswerfen* with *throwing free.* Renditions of
Gegenwurf, loswerfen and *Loswurf* with *counter-throw, throwing free,* and
free-throw capture the being-historical movement in the context of
ἰδέα.[16]

5. *Grund* and Related Words

The clue to translating words such as *Abgrund, Ungrund, Urgrund,
gründen, Gründer,* and *Gründung*—all of which directly pertain to being's
sway—is given in the word *Grund.* Thus, when Heidegger asks, "Why is
Da-sein the [*Grund*] and [*Abgrund*] for historical man . . . and why
should he then not continue to be the way he is?"[17] he alludes to the
proximity of *Grund* to *Abgrund. Grund* can be clearly brought into
English with *ground,* and this word guides and "grounds" the compounds of *Grund: Abgrund, Ungrund,* and *Urgrund.* Any English word
that fails to preserve the connection that these words have to *ground* is
misleading and inappropriate.

Analyses in *Contributions* that are carried out under the title *Gründung*—and specifically those devoted to "time-space" and "the last
god"—rely directly on what Heidegger, using all the force of hyphenation, calls *Ab-grund.* The significance of this word in Heidegger's eyes
becomes unmistakably clear when we come upon his crucial pro-
nouncement in section 242: "Der *Ab-*grund ist Ab-*grund.*"[18] Stressing
either the prefix *ab-* or the noun *Grund,* Heidegger puts forth the entire
context in which space and time are lodged, i.e., determined by an
Ab-grund. However, he cautions us not to misunderstand *Ab-grund* as
something negative. He says *Ab-grund* "is not . . . simply pulling back
and going away,"[19] but a *staying away.* In *staying* away *Ab-grund* somehow *is.* Considering what goes on in *Contributions* regarding "time,"
"space," "ground," and "god," we realized that *Ab-grund* cannot be

translated with "abyss," or "non-ground" because neither of these renditions reflect that *Ab-grund* is a ground that prevails while *staying away*. It is the element of *staying* in *staying away* that the words *non-ground* and *abyss* are incapable of reflecting. Thus these existing options for the rendition of *Abgrund*—namely *non-ground* and *abyss*—fail to reflect the sense in which *Abgrund* does *not* say dissipation and disappearance of *ground*. We realized that, in order to reflect the sense in which *Abgrund* shows the staying power of the *ground,* we need an English word other than *non-ground* or *abyss.*

The word we were looking for had to meet the following requirements: (a) it had to be equipped with a prefix that would allow the translation to reflect the movement of *staying away* in the *ab-* of *Ab-grund,* (b) it had to preserve the word *ground* as the rendition of *Grund,* (c) it had to be structured in such a way as to provide the possibility of receiving an emphasis that is placed either on *ab-* or on *Grund*. We found such a word in *abground.*

The prefix *ab* in English reflects the movement of "staying away from something" and enables the translation to convey what Heidegger has in mind when he uses the German prefix *ab-*. When this prefix is attached to the word *ground,* it conveys the sense of a *ground* that *stays away* and in staying away somehow *is*. Putting *ab* and *ground* together, we arrive at a word in translation that reflects what goes on in *Ab-grund.* The word *abground* then provides a fitting translation of *Abgrund.*

Renditions of *Grund* and *Abgrund* with *ground* and *abground* easily lead to translation of *Ungrund* and *Urgrund:* as "unground" and "urground." Prefixes such as *un-* and *ur-* in English facilitate these renditions. These renditions readily allow for hyphenated forms of these words.

Gründung, the name of one of the six "joinings" of *Contributions* is a special case. Seen in the light of being-historical thinking, *Gründung* indicates a "ground" that is *urground, abground,* and *unground* at the same time. The reader must keep in mind the significant and subtle difference between *Gründung* as "grounding" that goes straightaway for a ground as the ground and a "grounding" that involves a *ground* which is simultaneously *urground, abground,* and *unground*. We translate *Gründung* as "grounding," while advising the reader that here in *Contributions* it is always the latter sense of the word *grounding* that is meant.

The same considerations apply to the verb *gründen. Gründen* works with a "ground" that is simultaneously "urground, abground, and unground." Here a happy coincidence—rare in this translation work!—emerges: two English words overlap and interweave in their etymology and disclosive power: *founding* (from the latin *fundus*) and *grounding* (from the German *Grund*). Whereas they are not so close together in their noun forms—"foundation" and "ground"—their verb-forms show great affinity: "To found" and "to ground." We translate *gründen* as either "to ground" or "to found," depending on the context. In either case it says fundamentally the same thing. In the same vein, *Gründer* is "founder."

6. *Bergen* and Related Words

The phenomenological kinship in *Contributions* between words such as *bergen, Bergung, verbergen, Verbergung, Sichverbergen, Sichverbergende,* and *Verborgenheit* is a kinship of critical importance to understanding and translating this work since these words hint at the core of the question of being, namely, its self-showing and manifesting. In translating these words we were concerned with reflecting the subtle difference between *bergen* as sheltering-preserving and *verbergen* as sheltering-concealing. While we render *bergen* and *Bergung* with *shelter* and *sheltering,* we account for the difference between *bergen* (or *Bergung*) and *verbergen* (or *Verbergung*) in that we render *bergen* with *sheltering* and *verbergen* with *sheltering-concealing.* This also applies to the variants of *bergen* and *verbergen.*

7. *Besinnung* and Related Words

How we translate the words *Selbstbesinnung, Reflexion,* and *Selbstreflexion* depends largely on how we bring the word *Besinnung* into English. By paying close attention to what Heidegger says about *Besinnung*—for example, with regard to *self, history, the first beginning,* and *science*—we can come upon an interpretation of *Besinnung* which will guide us in translating this word. Here is what Heidegger says about *Besinnung* and *self:*

> [*Besinnung*] is . . . so originary that it above all asks how the *self* is to be grounded. . . . Thus it is questionable whether through *reflection* [*Reflexion*] on "ourselves" we ever find our *self*. . . .[20]

We come upon this same characterization of *Besinnung* in the context of the *first beginning, history,* and *science.* It turns out that *Besinnung* is (a) originary, (b) concerns matters whose treatment through *reflection* is inadequate, and (c) is not the same as *reflection.* This means that, regardless of whether *Besinnung* concerns the *self* or any other being-historical theme, it is an originary way of awareness that is always exposed to the threat of a crushing reflection. In order to bring into English this originary awareness, we translated *Besinnung* with *mindfulness*—except in those cases where the word *Besinnung* indicates normal German usage; then we translate *Besinnung* as "consideration" or "deliberation." Mindfulness comes from *mindful,* which carries the connotations of open, attentive, aware, heedful, care-ful.

Translating *Besinnung* with "reflection" or "meditation" does not bring into English the originary awareness that is *Besinnung.* The word *reflection* is inadequate to this task because the activity to which this word refers

and the assumptions that go along with it constantly bypass the awareness which is *Besinnung*. When reflection sets in, there begins a process
of continual rebounding and recoiling that is bent on nothing other than
refinement of the reflection itself. The rebounding and recoiling, as well
as the ensuing refinement, easily bypass *Besinnung* as an awareness that
cannot be achieved through refinement of reflection. Given the Cartesian background of the word *meditation,* this word also proved inadequate to this task because it maintains a close proximity to reflection.
But the awareness that is *Besinnung,* as *mindfulness,* is unobtrusive and as
such is at the service of what *Contributions* calls "sheltering."

Rendering *Besinnung* with *mindfulness* opens the way for translating
Selbstbesinnung with *self-mindfulness, Reflexion* with *reflection,* and *Selbstreflexion* with *self-reflection.* Translating *Besinnung* as "reflection" would
have offered no possibility at all for differentiating *Selbstreflexion* from
Selbstbesinnung, because both words would be translated as "self-
reflection." By contrast, *mindfulness* presents the possibility of differentiating *Selbstreflexion* from *Selbstbesinnung* with the word *self-mindfulness.*

8. *Rücken* and Related Words

The phenomenological kinship among words that gather around *rücken,*
namely *entrücken, verrücken, Rückung, Entrückung, Verrückung, Ruck,
berücken,* and *Berückung,* provides an important clue for bringing into
translation the enactment-character of being-historical thinking. The
word *rücken* can be brought into English with *move* or *remove.* And this
means that *rücken* can be readily translated with variants of *move* and
remove. However, discussion of *Zeit-Raum* in sections 238–242 makes it
clear that understanding the enactment-character of being-historical
thinking and reflecting this understanding in translation depends on
the success of the translation in accounting for the difference between
moving and *removing* in *rücken.* We heeded this difference in our translation by rendering *entrücken* with *"to remove unto,"* *Entrückung* with
"removal unto," *rücken* with *"moving,"* and — depending on the context —
sometimes with *"shifting."* However, we rendered *verrücken* and *Verrückung* with *"displace"* and *"displacing,"* or *"displacement,"* because both German words manifest the movement that occupies the core of the
experience of man as he is *dis-placed* into Da-sein: these words stand for
the profound recasting and transformation of man.

We faced an altogether different situation in attempting to render
berücken and *Berückung* into English. Guided by what Heidegger accomplishes in section 242, "Time-Space as Ab-ground" — one of the most fascinating sections of *Contributions* — and understanding his being-
historical analysis of "time," and "space," we reflected his understanding
in our translation by rendering *berücken* and *Berückung* with *moving that
charms* and *charming-moving-unto.* This compound reflects the orienting

power which, as *Berückung,* comprises the core of Heidegger's analyses of "space" and "spatiality"—inseparable as these analyses are from those of "time" and "temporality" in the context of being-historical thinking. We decided that "charming" was the most appropriate English word to carry the crucial nuances of "captivating," "fascinating," and "alluring"—all of which inhere in *Berückung.* The other two words in this family of words, i.e., *Ruck* and *Rückung,* we rendered with *shift* and *shifting.*

The manner in which *Contributions* makes use of the word *Auseinandersetzung*—a word as often used in German academic philosophy as perhaps the words "discussion," "dispute," and "argument" in English academic philosophy—requires that we discuss our renditions of this word in connection with the preceding deliberations on *rücken* as a related word. The main reason for including *Auseinandersetzung* in the present discussion of *rücken* and related words is *not* that *Auseinandersetzung* is a member of this family of words. Plainly it is not. The main reason for this inclusion is that, *as Heidegger uses Auseinandersetzung* here in *Contributions,* there is a phenomenological kinship between *Auseinandersetzung* and *rücken* as well as *verrücken* and *Verrückung.* It is our understanding that when *Auseinandersetzung* appears in several sections of "Playing-Forth" and elsewhere in *Contributions,* the word assumes an orienting power that is purely being-historical, which the word does not have in its "normal" usage. When Heidegger talks about *Auseinandersetzung* in connection with the "first" and the "other beginning," he does not primarily and exclusively have in mind a "debate" or an "argumentative relation" between these "beginnings"—as if these "beginnings" were "events" that are extant and accessible to historiography. Rather, the word *Auseinandersetzung* indicates a specific manner in which philosophical thinking gets *dis-placed,* is *moved unto* and *shifts into* these beginnings. In order to reflect this understanding in our translation, we decided to render *Auseinandersetzung* with "contention," "setting into perspective," "setting apart," "coming to grips with," and "encounter." In some cases the word *Auseinandersetzung* has a more usual connotation; there we translated it with "debate" or "discussion." Each decision was implemented according to the context and based on the insight that these contexts merit slightly different renditions.

9. *Da* and Related Words

The difficulty of translating Heidegger's word *Da* has been recognized all along by Heidegger's translators, demonstrated by the fact that the German word *Dasein* has been almost universally retained in English translations. Untranslatability of the word *Dasein* extends also to the word *Da,* a central word of *Contributions,* and to the words derived from *Da,* namely *Daheit, Dagründung,* and *Dagründer.* Since there is no single word in

English that would reflect what goes on as *Da*—in this word "here" and "there" merge and become one—we decided to indicate this merging thus: *t/here* [*Da*]. Throughout *Contributions* the reader will find *t/here* followed by the word *Da* in square brackets. *Da* follows *t/here* in order to alert the reader that this word refers to the merging of "here" and "there" and that with this word Heidegger exposes a central being-historical theme.

We translated the two words *Daheit* and *Dagründung* with *t/hereness* and *grounding of the t/here*, each followed by the respective German word in square brackets. For *Dagründer* we chose to say: founder of t/here followed by *Dagründer* in square brackets.

10. *Zeit-Raum* and Related Words

In order to say what is being-historically ownmost to time and space, Heidegger uses the word *Zeit-Raum*. We translated *Zeit-Raum* with *time-space*. Note that this hyphenated word is quite different from *Zeitraum* (written without a hyphen), which we have translated as "a span of time."[21] The phenomenological context of *Zeit-Raum* includes the word *Zwischen* and its variants, such as *das Zwischenhafte, Zwischengrund, Zwischenfall, zwischendeutig, inzwischen,* and *die Inzwischenschaft.* Translating *das Zwischen* with "between," we have put the German word in square brackets throughout, in order to draw the reader's attention to the phenomenological context of this word.

11. *Gott* and Related Words

The clue for translating *Gott, Götter, Göttern, göttern,* and *Götterung,* as well as for the rendition of the title of section 279, *"Wie aber die Götter?"* is found in the word *Götterung.* In understanding, interpreting, *and* translating this word, we were guided by what might be considered to be *the* central being-historical insight into what is ownmost to gods, or to god, and differentiates god and gods from be-ing—as articulated in section 126 of *Contributions:*

> Be-ing is not and can never "be" more-being than a being, but also not less-being than gods, because gods "are" not at all.[22]

If gods, or god, "are" not at all, then how are we to grasp them? The response is that we must grasp them in terms of *Götterung.* In order to translate this word into English, we were guided by its orienting power which, as a being-historical word, refers neither to an already existing divine being nor to a being that is in the process of "becoming" god. In *Contributions* the word *Götterung* distinguishes "the passing of the last god" from *Gottwerdung,* which as "god's becoming" has been a preoccupation of German philosophy from Jakob Böhme to Max Scheler.

How to translate *Götterung*? We found "divine unfolding" and "godly unfolding" unacceptable, since the word divine in "divine unfolding" indicates a being, which is what Heidegger is keen to keep away from gods as well as from *"the last god."* The expression "godly unfolding" would be in danger of a similar misunderstanding. In both cases the word "unfolding" could be mistaken as referring to a being that unfolds. Finally, "divinization" proved not to be an option, because as a noun this word lacks the dynamism that is inherent in the "passing" of "the last god." Thus in order to translate *Götterung,* we opted for "godding," because this word comes closest to showing the "dynamism" that is "the last god," avoids the reference to an already existing and extant being, and recognizes and accepts the *cleavage* of be-ing wherein the passing of "the last god" takes place.

Our rendition of *Göttern* with *"gods' godding"* comes directly from the decision to render *Götterung* with *godding*. It is quite clear from various contexts in *Contributions* that *Göttern* indicates gods' manner of *godding.* Moreover, when seen from within the "dynamism" called *godding,* the plural *"gods"* no longer functions as a collective designation for the Greek or other peoples' gods. *Contributions* makes this point quite clear:

> But the talk of "gods" here does not indicate the decided assertion on the extantness of a plurality over against a singular but is rather meant as the allusion to the undecidedness of the being of gods, whether of one single god or of many gods. . . . The undecidability concerning which god and whether a god can . . . once again arise, from which way of being of man . . . is what is named with the name "gods."[23]

We faced one of the many challenges and hazards of this translation work when we had to render into English the title of section 279: *"Wie aber die Götter?"* Realizing that this title needs a careful interpretation and elucidation and accepting the fact that a translation cannot afford to do either of the two, we reluctantly decided to translate this title with "What about Gods?" However, the English reader should bear in mind that the word *"wie"*—rendered here as *"what about"*—does not refer to beings that already exist and are extant or to beings that existed and were extant and are called gods. Moreover, the reader should be aware that this title is not to be confused with a rhetorical question that as such would already contain the answer, namely, a knowledge about gods. The title of section 279 is intended to point *not* to a *"what"* but to a *"how,"* i.e., to how *"gods"* (which also includes God) come

> not from within "religion"; not as something extant, nor as an expedient of man; rather [they come] from out of be-ing, as its decision. . . .[24]

In short the phrase "what about gods?" is actually intended to ask *how* gods appear and shine forth from within the *cleavage* of be-ing.

12. *Leben* and Related Words

Not all the members of the family of words and phrases that gather around *leben/Leben*, namely *erleben, Erlebnis, nahe dem Leben,* and *lebensnah,* can be brought into English with *living/life* and its variants because the element of experience so crucial for an understanding of *erleben, Erlebnis, nahe dem Leben* and *lebensnah* is not present in the English word *life.*

How to translate *erleben* and *Erlebnis*? For *Erlebnis* we decided to use its standard English translation, namely *lived-experience,* which clearly preserves the element of experience. However, in order to render *erleben* into English, we opted for *live-experience* ("live" read as an adjective) as an experience that is on-going and is actually occurring. We found that the options "life-experience" and "life's experience" run the risk of being confused with the factual experience that is accumulated in the course of a given life. On the other hand, the English word *life* is perfectly suitable for the rendition of the German *nahe dem Leben* and *lebensnah.* We translated both these expressions with *"true to life,"* since in German these expressions point to a state of affairs which can be measured by nothing other than factual life.

II. The Group of Words with the Prefix "Er"

It is obvious that the prefix *er-* plays a very significant role in the thinking of *Contributions,* beginning of course with *Ereignis,* which often appears in hyphenated form: *Er-eignis.* The significant role of the prefix *er-* must be accounted for and the issue of translating a large number of words with the prefix *er-* must be addressed. English rendering of these words cannot proceed from translating one root word (as is the case in the preceding eight groups of words) but must seriously consider the impact of the prefix *er-* on the word that follows this prefix. In order to achieve a translation that shows the being-historical character of words that start with *er—erdenken, eröffnen, erfragen, erzittern, erwinken, erfügen, ersagen, Eröffnung, Erschweigung, Erwesung, Erzwingung, Erklüftung, Erzitterung,* to mention only a few—we must understand and interpret the function of the prefix *er-* within the context of being-history and then indicate how we brought this function into English.

Contemporary German philology recognizes three functions of the prefix "er":

> 1. *"Er"* indicates an achieving, whereby the infinitive states the means by which something is to be achieved. . . . Examples are *erjagen, erbitten, ersingen.*
> 2. *"Er"* indicates enhancing . . . and welling up of what is indicated by the infinitive. . . . Examples are *erklingen, erblühen, erröten.*
> 3. *"Er"* indicates that the activity indicated by the infinitive will be carried thoroughly through. . . . Examples are *ertragen, ersticken, erschlagen.*[25]

Accordingly, the prefix *er-* in each case fulfills only *one* of these functions.

Moreover, how this single function is fulfilled depends on the infinitive to which the prefix *er-* is attached. Thus it is *jagen* (hunting) that determines the function of the prefix *er-* in *erjagen* (hunting for), *klingen* (sounding) that determines the function of this prefix in *erklingen* (resounding), and *tragen* (carrying) that determines the function of this prefix in *ertragen* (bearing up). In these cases the prefix *er-* either *achieves* something indicated by the infinitive or *enhances* something indicated by the infinitive, or *carries* something *forth* that is indicated by the infinitive. In short, the infinitive enjoys a priority over the prefix *er-*.

However, in *Contributions*, this priority of the infinitive is no longer there. Also, in this work the three functions of the prefix *er-* are unified in one.[26] That is to say, here the prefix *er-* does not separate what is achieved by the infinitive from *enhancing* of what goes on there and these two from *carrying forth* what happens in the infinitive. Thus, when we come upon the word *erdenken,* for example, our translation must reflect this interpretation of the prefix *er-*. The first step in accomplishing this is to realize that the prefix *er-* in *Contributions* determines what goes on in the infinitive and *not the other way around*. Thus, translation must take seriously the impact of the prefix *er-* on the infinitive and must bring this impact into English. Like Heidegger, his translators too must be responsive to the prefix *er-* as it determines the infinitives to which this prefix is attached.

Heidegger himself assists us in understanding this point in that he briefly explains how a particular *er*-word, *ersehen,* is to be interpreted and translated. In the *Basic Questions of Philosophy: Selected "Problems" of "Logic,"* a university lecture text written at the same time as *Contributions,* we come upon an explanation as to how *sehen* (seeing) is to be grasped as *ersehen.* There Heidegger says: "We therefore call this seeing which *erbringt* into visibility and *ersieht* what is to be seen *Er-sehen.*"[27] How are we to interpret *erbringt* and *ersieht*? The clue for responding to this question lies in how we interpret and translate the prefix *er-*. How is this prefix to be interpreted and translated as a significant element of language?

The prefix *er-* in both words has an impact upon the infinitive that follows it in that this prefix indicates a direction that *bringen* (bringing) and *sehen* (seeing) have to take. In the case of *bringen* this direction gives a specificity to *bringen* by enhancing and putting forth what this *bringen* is all about in *bringen*. In these cases the prefix *er-* shows that *erbringen* is other than mere *bringen* (bringing) and *ersehen* is other than mere *sehen* (seeing). It is the impact of the prefix *er-* on these infinitives that gets this "other than" across. This means that translating words in *Contributions* such as *erdenken, eröffnen, erbringen, ersehen* depends on how this prefix is brought into English. Rather than defining this prefix each time it precedes an infinitive (something unmanageable and counter-productive), we opted for using the prefix *en-* in English. The English prefix *en-* works in the same way and as well as the German *er-*.

In our effort to come up with a word that approximates Heidegger's *Ereignis*, we have already seen the crucial role that the prefix *en-* plays. The same prefix *en-* that opened the possibility for an approximating rendition of *Ereignis* also opens the road to an interpretation and translation of other *er-*words in *Contributions*. When in the above-mentioned university lecture text Heidegger elucidates *seeing* as *ersehen* and *bringing* as *erbringen*, he intends to bring together the three moments—of achieving, enhancing, and carrying forth—in such a way as to shift the emphasis from the root infinitive to the prefix *er-*. Thus, by calling *Er-sehen* "a seeing which *erbringt* into visibility what is to be seen," Heidegger refers to a seeing which *enables* the coming into visibility of what is to be seen. If we keep in mind that the prefix *en-* in English conveys all three senses of "enabling something," "bringing it into a certain condition," and of "carrying thoroughly through," then we can say that "*ersehen* is an *en-seeing* which *en-brings* into visibility what is to be seen." By utilizing words like *enseeing* and *enbringing*, we allow translation to reflect the connection between the *en-* in *enowning* and the *en-* of *enseeing* as an *en-* that *enables* this word to become an *enabling seeing*. Thus rendition of *ersehen* with "enseeing" allows the translation to distinguish between *mere seeing* and an *enabling seeing*; translating shows the shift from mere *seeing* to an *enabling seeing*. Thus translation lets *en*owning echo in *enthinking, enseeing, enbringing, enopening*, etc. The last word, *enopening*, is of particular importance insofar as it directly renders the German *Eröffnung* and distinguishes this word from *das Offene* and its variants.

In general we have taken note of the unique orienting power of the *er-* in German by using the prefix *en-* in English: *enthinking* for *erdenken*, *enquivering* for *erzittern*, and sometimes *enopening* for *Eröffnung*, or *eröffnen*, etc. However, sometimes the prefix *er-* belongs to a German word in ordinary usage with an established meaning (*erfahren, ermessen,* and sometimes *eröffnen*) and thus is more appropriately translated into English with a word without the prefix *en-*.

III. Technical Aspects of the Translation

All additions to the text by the translators are placed within square brackets [ ]. These additions include (1) important and problematic German words within the text where we thought it necessary and/or useful to indicate that the translation tends to hide an important nuance, and (2) minor additions to the text that are intended to enhance readability. (The one instance of brackets in the German—to designate that portion of the text that was lost—is shown here with {}.)

Footnotes from the German edition are at the bottom of the page. All footnotes with an asterisk contain the references put forth by Heidegger in the hand-written version, either to sections within *Contributions to Philosophy* or to other writings and manuscripts of his. The editor of the original German text, F.-W. von Herrmann, has filled out all abbreviations in the references. To the extent that the other manuscripts to which Heidegger refers have already appeared in the *Gesamtausgabe* or have already been firmly assigned to volumes not yet published, the editor and translators noted this in parentheses or in brackets. The few numbered footnotes contain bibliographical data for quotations of other authors quoted by Heidegger, data added by the editor. There are no translators' footnotes.

References in the text itself to other published works by Heidegger are given here in an English version—except for the text *Das Wesen des Grundes*. Since both these words (*Wesen* and *Grund*) play a significant role in *Contributions to Philosophy (From Enowning)* and thus call for more appropriate words in English, we have left that title in German throughout.

References in the footnotes to volumes of the *Gesamtausgabe* that have been translated into English include the English translation of the title in brackets.

References—in both the text and in the footnotes—to texts by Heidegger that have not yet been published have been left in German. Here is a list of those texts, in the chronology of their composition and showing in each case the volume of the *Gesamtausgabe* in which each text will eventually appear:

GA 80 *Vom Wesen der Wahrheit,* Freiburg Lecture (1930)

GA 80 *Vom Ursprung des Kunstwerkes,* Freiburg Lecture (1935)

GA 82 *Anmerkungen zu "Vom Wesen des Grundes"* (1936)

GA 82 *Eine Auseinandersetzung mit "Sein und Zeit"* (1936)

GA 82 *Laufende Anmerkungen zu "Sein und Zeit"* (1936)

GA 88 *Die neuzeitliche Wissenschaft* (1937)

GA 73 *Die ἀλήθεια: Die Erinnerung in den ersten Anfang; Entmachtung der φύσις* (1937)

GA 87 *Übungen SS 1937. Nietzsches metaphysische Grundstellung. Sein und Schein* (1937)

GA 88 *Übungen WS 1937/38. Die metaphysischen Grundstellungen des abendländischen Denkens (Metaphysik)* (1937/38)

GA73 *Das Da-sein*

GA 84 *Leibniz-Übungen*

GA 83 *Marburger Übungen. Auslegungen der Aristotelischen "Physik"*

GA 94 *Überlegungen* II–VI

GA 95 *Überlegungen* VII–XI

GA 96 *Überlegungen* XII–XV

GA73 *Wahrheitsfrage als Vorfrage*

The following abbreviations have been used throughout the text:

GA refers to volumes of the *Gesamtausgabe*

SS stands for *Sommersemester*

WS stands for *Wintersemester*

*

In conclusion, the reader should be cautioned against forming an opinion about this work of translation, as well as about the work presented here in translation, on the basis of this Foreword alone. The purpose of this Foreword is to inform the reader that, in keeping with our interpretation and understanding of *Contributions,* we heeded the orienting power of being-historical words as we translated the keywords. The purpose of this Foreword is not to objectify that orienting power or to offer an "introduction" to being-historical thinking. This is another way of saying that this Foreword is not a substitute for unmitigated engagement with the work of thinking that *is* this present work in translation.

However, for this engagement to unfold, we must bear in mind that English translations of Heidegger cannot mirror exactly what goes on in the German original and cannot push the original aside or do away with it altogether. The undeniable fact is that English translations of Heidegger remain referentially dependent on the original. This present translation is no exception. For this reason the German pagination is given on each page in the running heads.

Considering the tension between the German original and the English translation of Heidegger's work, we should not lose sight of the fact that the German original *itself* is not readily accessible to German readers. Interpreting and understanding Heidegger's work is no less a challenge and a task for his German than it is for his English readers. This must not be taken as reflecting on Heidegger's person. To say that the original as well as the translation of Heidegger's work is difficult is to draw attention to a fact that can easily be overlooked: Heidegger the thinker is not in total command of the thinking of being. He is not in total command and control of the thinking of being because this thinking is not a thinking *about* being but rather is *enowned by* being. The key to an appropriate assessment of the difficulty of the thinking of being lies in this enownment.

If thinking of being is not a thinking *about* being but a thinking *enowned by* being, then it comes as no surprise that Heidegger is almost always dissatisfied with his *work* of thinking. It is in this *enownment* that we must look for the roots of the distinction between *work* and *pathways of thinking*—a distinction that Heidegger chose as a motto for the *Gesamtausgabe.* With good reasons this distinction also applies to his second major work, *Contributions to Philosophy (From Enowning).*

If we look at the entirety of the passage in *Besinnung* in which Heidegger addresses the syntax of *Contributions,* we find that the distinction between *work* and *pathway of thinking* is implied. Heidegger views *Contributions* as a pathway of thinking when he acknowledges *its* success in implementing a new approach to the question of being—an approach that advises him against a detailed unfolding that would narrow down the actual horizon and the thrust of questioning. But at the same time Heidegger looks at the *Contributions* from the standpoint of what a *publication* should be in order for it to be a *work*. In its entirety that passage reads:

> In its new approach this *Contributions to Philosophy* should render manifest the range of the question of being. A detailed unfolding here is not necessary because this all too easily narrows down the actual horizon and misses the thrust of questioning. But even here that form has not yet been attained which, precisely at this point, I demand for a publication as a "work."[28]

Here we must distinguish Heidegger's way of giving recognition to *Contributions* from his critical appraisal of it. As a *work* it initiates a new approach to the question of being, without needing further unfolding. This means that *Contributions* opens up a horizon hitherto inaccessible to thinking. But considering the form in which this work is shaped, it falls short of meeting the demands of a publication that is to be a "work." This means that, the new horizon notwithstanding, *Contributions* does not attain the status of a *work* in the usual sense and remains necessarily a *pathway of thinking*. To put it succinctly, we can say that in *Contributions* two strong currents merge: the current that flows into a new horizon of thinking and the current that hits rockbottom and recoils. It is this recoil which is crystallized in the fragmentations that are part and parcel of the *Contributions*.

Could Heidegger not have taken the time for reviewing, examining, and weighing his options in order to present *Contributions* in a "more perfect" shape? Surely he returned again and again to this text, in its completed form and with the full force of his intellectual acumen. It would seem that he must have *deliberately chosen* to leave *Contributions* as it now is, with its syntax intact. However, the question of why Heidegger did not improve the syntax originates from within the privileged standpoint of those who come *after* Heidegger. It is the question that ineluctably remains tied to the immeasurable advantage of having access to the *Gesamtausgabe*. But this access and that privileged standpoint must not misunderstand themselves. Since no one has the slightest idea how *Contributions* would have looked had Heidegger smoothed out its syntax, no one has any idea of the measure by which to "reproach" him for the present shape of this work.

It is easy to say that Heidegger *could have done this or that*; it is easy to reproach him for *having failed to do this or that*. But what is not easy to do is to realize the extent to which any reproach remains referred to the very existence of the body of work that we who come after Heidegger are referred to. Hans Kock succinctly and memorably points out how deeply the very possibility of reproaching Heidegger must take into account his body of work when he says:

> It is not a question of reproaching Heidegger or of demanding posthumously different ways of behaving. Rather, it is we who come after him who are put to the test because of our access to his *Nachlaß* and to all of his work.[29]

In the final analysis, then, what counts is how those who come after Heidegger respond to being put to the test. By offering this translation to the English reading public, we as translators actually show how we have stood the test of having to come to terms with another major work of Heidegger's from his *Nachlaß*. It is our conviction that contemporary philosophy fails the task that *Contributions* allocates to it as long as this philosophy remains stuck in merely "assessing" this work as "working notes" or as a "collection of aphorisms." For the message of *Contributions* to the unprejudiced and open-minded reader seems to be: Let us get on with the task of thinking at the end of philosophy.

Parvis Emad
Kenneth Maly

Notes

1. *Contributions*, p. 332.
2. Ibid., p. 333.
3. Cf. ibid., Editor's Epilogue, pp. 365f.
4. Martin Heidegger, *Besinnung*, GA 66, p. 427.
5. This happens in philosophical thinking both *within* languages and *between* languages. For example, *within the same language* the Greeks coined the word δικαιοσύνη in order to render the thought "righteousness," a concept that did not exist earlier in Greek thought. The same phenomenon transpires often in Heidegger's thinking: *Jemeinigkeit, Daheit, Dagründung,* etc. And *between languages,* for example, in order to translate the German *Einfühlung,* English coins "empathy." For the Greek rendition of "righteousness," see Werner Jaeger, *Paideia: The Ideals of Greek Culture,* vol. 1, *Archaic Greece. The Mind of Athens,* trans. Gilbert Highet (New York: Oxford University Press, 1973), pp. 105 and 443; for *empathy,* see Oxford English Dictionary, entry "empathy."
6. Martin Heidegger, *Identität und Differenz* (Pfullingen: Neske, 1957), p. 25; English translation, *Identity and Difference,* trans. Joan Stambaugh (New York: Harper and Row, 1969), p. 36.
7. *Contributions*, p. 307.
8. William J. Richardson, *Heidegger: Through Phenomenology to Thought* (The Hague: Nijhoff, 1967), pp. 554f.

9. *Contributions*, p. 366.

10. Ibid., p. 319.

11. According to F.-W. von Herrmann, one of the significant meanings of the word *Wesen* in Heidegger is *das Eigenste einer Sache*. For more on this point, see the Translators' Foreword to Heidegger, *Phenomenological Interpretation of Kant's Critique of Pure Reason* (Bloomington: Indiana University Press, 1997), pp. xv-xviii.

12. *Contributions*, p. 18.

13. See ibid., p. 4.

14. The present rendition of *entwerfen* and *Entwurf* owes a great deal to the etymological and philosophical analyses of F.-W. von Herrmann. See his *Hermeneutische Phänomenologie des Daseins: Eine Erläuterung von "Sein und Zeit,"* vol. 1, *Einleitung: Die Exposition der Frage nach dem Sein* (Frankfurt am Main: Klostermann, 1987), pp. 108-109. In this work von Herrmann shows that, in contrast to its usual everyday understanding as a projection, *entwerfen* and *Entwurf* in Heidegger should always be understood as *throwing-opening* (*entwerfend-aufschließend*).

15. *Contributions*, p. 314f.

16. See ibid., section 263.

17. Ibid., p. 222.

18. Ibid., p. 265.

19. Ibid.

20. Ibid., p. 47. Emphasis added.

21. See ibid., p. 264.

22. See ibid., p. 172.

23. Ibid., p. 308.

24. Ibid., p. 357.

25. Wolfgang Kayser, *Die Vortragsreise: Studien zur Literatur* (Bern: Francke Verlag, 1958), p. 18.

26. Regarding this prefix, see also Susanne Ziegler, *Heidegger, Hölderlin und die ἀλήϑεια: Martin Heideggers Geschichtsdenken in seinen Vorlesungen 1934/1944* (Berlin: Duncker & Humblot, 1991), p. 94.

27. Martin Heidegger, *Grundbegriffe der Philosophie: Ausgewählte "Probleme" der "Logik,"* GA 45, p. 85; for an English translation, see *Basic Questions of Philosophy: Selected "Problems" of "Logic,"* trans. Richard Rojcewicz and André Schuwer (Bloomington: Indiana University Press, 1994), p. 76.

28. Martin Heidegger, *Besinnung*, GA 66, p. 427.

29. Hans Kock, *Erinnerungen an Martin Heidegger,* Jahresgabe der Martin-Heidegger-Gesellschaft, 1996, p. 10; reprinted in *Die Frage nach der Wahrheit,* vol. 4 of the Martin-Heidegger-Gesellschaft Schriftenreihe (Frankfurt am Main: Klostermann, 1997), pp. 55–68.

Acknowledgments

We would like to express our gratitude to those who helped us in completing this translation project. In the first place our thanks are due to Herr Dr. Hermann Heidegger, Martin Heidegger's literary executor, for immediately realizing the peculiar needs that confront the translator of *Beiträge zur Philosophie (Vom Ereignis)* and for permission to write a "longer" and "more detailed" foreword to this translation because of "the special circumstances in the language of *Contributions*."* Our special thanks are due Professor Friedrich-Wilhelm von Herrmann for his response to our numerous queries—and especially for devoting three months during the fall of 1993 to an informal research seminar with Parvis Emad in which, among other things, the entire text of *Beiträge zur Philosophie (Vom Ereignis)* was read and interpreted and its syntax clarified. His assistance is present on virtually every page of this translation, even as we translators are fully responsible for our work here. Our thanks are due to Frau Dr. Veronica von Herrmann and Herr Vittorio E. Klostermann for their unwavering support of this translation. Finally, we would like to express our deepest gratitude to Gertrude Emad for the careful typing of the manuscript.

*Letter from Hermann Heidegger to Parvis Emad, dated 9 November 1993.

Contributions to Philosophy
(From Enowning)

What was held back in prolonged hesitation
Is here held fast, hinting,
As the "level" used for giving it shape.

I. Preview*

*Cf. *Überlegungen* II, IV and V, VI [GA 94].

The Public Title: *Contributions to Philosophy*
and
the Essential Heading: *From Enowning*

The public title must now necessarily sound bland, ordinary, and saying nothing and must give the impression that it is dealing with "scholarly contributions" aimed at some "progress" in philosophy.

Philosophy cannot appear in public in any other way, since all essential titles have become impossible, because all fundamental words have been used up and the genuine relation to the word has been destroyed.

However, the public title *does* correspond to the "matter," insofar as, in the age of crossing from metaphysics into be-ing-historical thinking, one can venture only an *attempt* to think according to a more originary basic stance within the question of the truth of be-ing. But even the attempt, when successful and when made in accordance with the fundamental enowning of what is to be en-thought, must avoid all false claim to be a "work" of the style heretofore. Future thinking is a thinking that is *underway*, through which the domain of be-ing's essential swaying — completely hidden up to now — is gone through, is thus first lit up, and is attained in its ownmost enowning-character.

It is no longer a case of talking "about" something and representing something objective, but rather of being owned over into enowning. This amounts to an essential transformation of the human from "rational animal" (*animal rationale*) to Da-sein. Thus the *proper* title says: *From Enowning*. And that is not saying that a report is being given on or about enowning. Rather, the proper title indicates a thinking-saying which is en-owned by enowning and belongs to be-ing and to be-ing's *word*.

1. *Contributions to Philosophy* Enact the
Questioning Along a Pathway . . .

Contributions to Philosophy enact a questioning along a pathway which is first traced out by the crossing to the other beginning, into which Western thinking is now entering. This pathway brings the crossing into the openness of history and establishes the crossing as perhaps a very long sojourn, in the enactment of which the other beginning of thinking always remains only an intimation, though already decisive.

Thus, even though the *Contributions to Philosophy* always and only say be-ing's essential sway as enowning, still they are not yet able to join the free jointure of the truth of be-ing out of be-ing *itself*. If this ever succeeds, then the enquivering of be-ing's essential sway will determine the jointure of the work of thinking. This enquivering then grows stronger, becoming the power of a gentle release into the *intimacy* to the *godding* of the god of gods, from out of which Dasein's *allotment* to be-ing comes into its own, as grounding truth for be-ing.

And yet here already, as in a preparatory exercise, we must attempt the thinking-saying of philosophy which comes from an other beginning. This saying does not describe or explain, does not proclaim or teach. This saying does not stand over against what is said. Rather, the saying itself *is* the "to be said," as the essential swaying of be-ing.

This saying gathers be-ing's essential sway unto a first sounding, while it itself [this saying] sounds only out of this essential sway.

What is said in the preparatory exercise is a questioning that belongs neither to the purposeful activity of an individual nor to the limited calculation of a community. Rather, it is above all the further hinting of a hint which comes from what is most question-worthy and remains referred to it.

Disengaging from all "personal" fabrication succeeds only in intimacy to the earliest belonging. No grounding will be granted to us that is not warranted by such a disengagement.

The time of "systems" is over. The time of re-building the essential shaping of beings according to the truth of be-ing has not yet arrived. In the meantime, in crossing to an other beginning, philosophy has to have achieved one crucial thing: projecting-open, i.e., the grounding enopening of the free-play of the time-space of the truth of be-ing. How is this one thing to be accomplished? In this we have neither precedent nor support. Mere modifications of what we now have do not get us underway, even if they happened with the help of the greatest possible mixture of historically known ways of thinking. And in the end every manner of scholastic worldview stands outside philosophy, because it can only persist on the basis of a denial of the question-worthiness of be-ing. In appreciating this question-worthiness, philosophy has its own non-deducible and incalculable dignity. All decisions about philosophy's activity are made by preserving this dignity and *as* preservations of this dignity. In the realm of what is most question-worthy, however, philosophy's activity can enact only one single question. If at any of philosophy's hidden times it has to have decided what is its ownmost in the light of its knowing, then certainly in the crossing to an other beginning.

The "other" beginning of thinking is named thus, not because it is simply shaped differently from any other arbitrarily chosen hitherto existing philosophies, but because it must be the only other beginning according to the relation *to* the one and only first beginning. The style of thoughtful mindfulness in the crossing from one beginning to the other is also already determined by the allotment of the one beginning to the other beginning. Thinking in the crossing accomplishes the grounding projecting-open of the truth of be-ing as *historical* mindfulness. Thus history is not the object or domain of an observation. Rather, it is that which first awakens and effects thinking-questioning as the site of thinking-questioning's decisions. Thinking in the crossing brings into dialogue what has first been of be-ing's truth and that which in the truth of be-ing is futural in the extreme — and in that dialogue brings to word the essential sway of be-ing, which has remained unquestioned until now. In the knowing awareness of thinking in the crossing, the first beginning remains decisively the *first* — and yet is overcome as beginning. For this thinking, reverence for the first beginning, which most clearly and initially discloses the uniqueness of this beginning, must coincide with the relentlessness of turning away from this beginning to an other questioning and saying.

The outline of these *Contributions* is designed to prepare for the crossing and is drawn from the still unmastered ground plan of the historicity of the crossing itself:

> echo
> playing-forth
> leap
> grounding
> the ones to come
> the last god.

This outline does not yield an arrangement of various observations about various objects. It is also not an introductory ascent from what is below to what is above. It breaks ahead into the free-play of time-space which the history of the crossing first opens up as its realm, in order, with its law, to decide about those who are without a future, i.e., those who are always only "eternal," and about those who are to come, i.e., those who are but once.

2. Saying from Enowning as the First Response
to the Question of Being

The question of being is the question of the truth of be-ing. When accomplished and grasped as it historically unfolds, it becomes the *grounding-question* — over against the hitherto "guiding-question" of philosophy, which has been the question about beings.

The question concerning the truth of be-ing, of course, pushes into what is deeply sheltered. For the truth of be-ing, which as thinking is inabiding knowing awareness of how be-ing holds sway, essentially, perhaps does not ever rest with the gods, but belongs solely to that destiny [*Fügung*] to which even gods are subordinate, and which holds to abground.

And yet: Whenever a *being is,* be-ing must sway. But how does be-ing sway? But *is* a being? From where else does thinking decide here if not according to the truth of be-ing? Thus be-ing can no longer be thought of in the perspective of beings; it must be enthought from within be-ing *itself.*

At times those founders of the abground must be consumed by the fire of what is deeply sheltered, so that Da-sein becomes possible for humans and thus steadfastness in the midst of beings is rescued—so that in the open of the strife between earth and world beings themselves undergo a restoration.

Accordingly, beings move into their steadfastness when the founders of the truth of be-ing *go under.* Be-ing itself requires this. It needs those who go under; and, wherever beings appear, it has already *en-owned* these founders who go under and allotted them to be-ing. That is the essential swaying of be-ing itself. We call it *enowning.* The riches of the turning relation of be-ing to Da-sein, which is en-owned by be-ing, are immeasurable. The fullness of the enowning is incalculable. And here this inceptual thinking can only say little "from enowning." What is said is inquired after and thought in the "playing-forth" unto each other of the first and the other beginning, according to the "echo" of be-ing in the distress of being's abandonment, for the "leap" into be-ing, in order to "ground" its truth, as a preparation for "the ones to come" and for "the last god."

This thinking-saying is a *directive.* It indicates the free sheltering of the truth of be-ing in beings as a necessity, without being a command. Such a thinking never lets itself become a doctrine and withdraws totally from the fortuitousness of common opinion. But such thinking-saying directs the few and their knowing awareness when the task is to retrieve man from the chaos of not-beings into the pliancy of a reserved creating of sites that are set up for the passing of the last god.

But if enowning is what makes up the essential swaying of be-ing, how close must the danger be that be-ing refuses and must refuse en-ownment because man has become feeble for Da-sein—because the unfettered hold of the frenzy of the gigantic has overwhelmed him under the guise of "magnitude."

But when enowning becomes refusal and not-granting, is that simply the withdrawal of be-ing and surrender of beings into not-beings, or can not-granting (the not-character of be-ing) become in the extreme the remotest en-ownment—given that man grasps this enowning and given that the shock of deep awe puts him back into the grounding-attunement of reservedness and thus already sets him out into Da-*sein*?

To know be-ing's essential sway as enowning means not only to know the danger of not-granting, but also to be ready for the overcoming. Because this is all so far ahead, the first thing here continues to be: to put be-ing into question.

No one understands what "I" *think* here: to let *Da-sein* emerge from within the *truth of be-ing* (and that means from within the essential swaying of truth), in order to ground beings in the whole and as such and to ground man in the midst of them.

No one grasps this, because everyone tries to explain "my" attempt merely historically [*historisch*] and appeals to the past, which he *thinks* he grasps because it seems already to lie behind him.

And he who will someday grasp it does not need "my" attempt. For he must have laid out his own path thereunto. He must be able to think what has been attempted *in such a way* that he thinks that it comes unto him from far away while still being what is ownmost to him, to which he has been owned-over as the one who is needed and thus does not have the inclination or opportunity to mean "himself."

Following a simple *shift* of essential thinking, the happening of the truth of be-ing must be transposed from the first beginning into the other, so that the wholly other song of be-ing sounds in the playing-forth.

And thus what is happening everywhere here is really *history* [*Geschichte*], which remains out of the reach of what is merely historical [*das Historische*], because this history is not a matter of allowing the past to come up but rather is in all respects the momentum over [*Überschwung*] to what is to come.

3. From Enowning

Echo

Playing-Forth

Leap

Grounding

The Ones to Come

The Last God

The *echo* of be-ing as not-granting.

The *playing-forth* of the question of be-ing: The playing-forth is initially the playing forth of the first beginning, so that the first beginning brings the other beginning into play, so that, according to this mutual playing forth, preparation for the leap grows.

The *leap* into be-ing: The leap enleaps the abground of the cleavage and thus first the necessity of grounding Da-sein, who is allotted from within be-ing.

The *grounding* of truth as the truth of be-ing [is] (Da-sein).

4. From Enowning

Here everything is geared toward the sole and single *question* of the truth of be-ing, i.e., toward *questioning*. So that this attempt turns into an impetus, the wonder of enactment of questioning must be experienced and made effective for awakening and strengthening the *force* of questioning.

Questioning immediately raises the suspicion that an empty rigidity settles upon what is uncertain, undecided, and undecidable. It looks as if "knowing" is drawn out into a stagnant reflection. It gives the appearance of being constrictive and inhibiting, and even negating.

And yet, in the driving onset of questioning, there is affirmation of what is not yet accomplished, and there is the widening of questioning into what is still not weighed out and needs to be considered. What reigns here is going beyond ourselves into what raises us above ourselves. Questioning is becoming free for what is compelling, though sheltered.

In what is seldom experienced as its ownmost, questioning is quite different from the semblance of what is precisely *not* its ownmost. This often robs the *dis*-encouraged of their last reserve of fortitude. But then neither do they belong to the invisible circle which encircles those who in questioning receive the hint of be-ing as a response.

The questioning which is concerned with the truth of be-ing cannot be reckoned from out of what has gone on up to now. And if this questioning is to prepare the beginning of another history, then the enactment of this questioning must be originary. As unavoidable as it is to come to terms with the first beginning of the history of thinking, just as certainly must questioning itself ponder its distress alone, forgetting all that surrounds it.

History emerges only in the immediate skip of what is "historical" [*das Historische*].

The question concerning the "meaning" [of being], i.e., in accordance with the elucidation in *Being and Time*, the question concerning grounding the domain of projecting-open—and then, the question of the *truth of be-ing*—is and remains *my* question, and is my *one and only* question; for this question concerns what is *most sole and unique*. In the age of *total lack of questioning anything*, it is sufficient as a start to inquire into the question of all questions.

In the age of infinite needing that originates according to the hidden distress of *no-distress-at-all*, this question necessarily has to appear as the most useless jabbering—beyond which one has already and duly gone.

Nevertheless the task remains: *to restore beings from within the truth of be-ing.*

The question of the "meaning of being" is the question of all questions. When the unfolding of this questioning is enacted, what is ownmost to what "meaning" names here is determined, along with that in which the question dwells as mindfulness and along with what the *question* as such opens up, namely the openness for self-sheltering, i.e., truth.

The question of being is *the* leap into be-ing which man as seeker of be-ing enacts, insofar as he is one who creates in *thinking.* The one who seeks be-ing, in the ownmost overflow of seeking power, is the poet who "founds" be-ing.

But we of today have only this one duty: to prepare for that thinker by means of a grounding that reaches far ahead, of a secure prepared-ness for what is most question-worthy.

5. For the Few and the Rare

For the few who from time to time again *ask the question,* i.e., who put up anew the essential sway of truth for decision.

For the rare who bring along the utmost courage for solitude, in order to think the nobility of be-ing and to speak of its uniqueness.

Thinking in the other beginning is in a unique way originarily histor-ical: the self-joining enjoining of be-ing's essential swaying.

We must risk a projecting-open of be-ing's essential swaying as *enowning,* precisely *because* we do *not* know the mandate of our history. May we be able to experience in a fundamental way the essential sway-ing of this unknown, in its self-sheltering.

May we indeed want to unfold this knowing, so that the unfamiliar which is assigned to us lets the will be in solitude and thus forces Da-sein to be steadfast by way of the utmost reservedness over against the self-sheltering.

The nearness to the last god is silence. This silence must be set into work and word in the style of reservedness.

To *be* in the nearness of the god—whether this nearness be the remotest remoteness of undecidability about the flight of gods or their arrival—this cannot be counted as "happiness" or "unhappiness." The steadfastness of be-ing carries its own measure within itself—if it still needs a measure at all.

But to whom among us today is this steadfastness allotted? We are hardly capable of being *prepared* for the necessity of being's steadfast-ness—or even of *hinting* at this preparedness as the beginning of another course of history.

The relapses into the hardened ways and claims of metaphysics will continue to disturb and to block the clarity of the way and the deter-minedness of the saying. Nevertheless, the historical moment of the crossing must be enacted out of knowing that all metaphysics (grounded upon the guiding question: What is a being?) remains incapable of shift-ing man into the basic relations to beings. And how should metaphysics be able to do that? Even the *will* to do that gets no hearing as long as the *truth* of being and its uniqueness has not yet become *distress.* But how should thinking succeed in achieving what earlier remained withheld from the poet (Hölderlin)? Or do we have simply to wrest his path and his work from its being buried—wrest it in the direction of the truth of be-ing? Are we prepared for this?

It is only through the ones who question that the truth of be-ing becomes a distress. They are the genuine *believers,* because, in opening themselves up to what is ownmost to truth, they maintain their bearing to the ground (cf. Grounding, 237: Faith and Truth).

Those who *question*—alone and without the help of any enchantment—establish the new and highest rank of inabiding in the midpoint of be-ing, in the essential swaying of be-ing (enowning) as the midpoint.

The ones who question have set aside all curiosity; their seeking yearns for the abground, wherein they know the oldest ground.

If a history is ever to be allotted to us again, i.e., if we are to be creatively exposed to beings out of belongingness to being, then we cannot turn away from *this* destiny, namely to *prepare* the time-space for the final decision concerning whether and how we experience and ground this belongingness. Therein lies [the task of] grounding, in thinking, the knowing of enowning, through grounding the essential sway of truth as Da-sein.

However the decision on historicity or the lack of history may be made, those who question and thus prepare for that decision in thinking must *be;* each is to bear the solitude in his highest hour.

What saying accomplishes the utmost reticence in thinking? What procedure best brings about the mindfulness of be-ing? The saying of the truth. For truth is the between [*das Zwischen*] for the essential swaying of be-ing and the beingness of beings. This between grounds the beingness of beings in be-ing.

But be-ing is not something "earlier"—subsisting for and in itself. Rather, enowning is the temporal-spatial simultaneity for be-ing and beings (cf. Leap, 112: The "Apriori").

In philosophy propositions never get firmed up into a proof. This is the case, not only because there are no *top* propositions from which others could be deduced, but because here what is "true" is not a "proposition" at all and also not simply that about which a proposition makes a statement. All "proof" presupposes that the one who understands—as he comes, via representation, before the content of a proposition— remains unchanged as he enacts the interconnection of representations for the sake of proof. And only the "result" of the deduced proof can demand a changed way of representing or rather a representing of what was unnoticed up until now.

By contrast, in philosophical knowing a transformation of the man who understands takes place with the very first step—not in a moral, "existentiell" sense but rather with Da-sein as measure. This means that the relation to be-ing and even before that the relation to the truth of be-ing is transformed by way of shifting into Da-sein itself. The thinking of philosophy remains strange because in philosophical knowing everything—humanness in its standing in the truth, truth itself, and thus the relation to be-ing—is always exposed to displacement and thus no immediate representation of anything extant is ever possible.

Especially in the other beginning—following upon the question of the truth of be-ing—the leap into the "between" must be immediately enacted. The "between" of Da-sein overcomes the χωρισμός, not, as it were, by building a bridge between be-ing (beingness) and beings—as if there were two riverbanks needing to be bridged—but by simultaneously transforming be-ing and beings in their simultaneity. Rather than possessing an already established standpoint, the leap into the between first of all lets Da-sein spring forth.

The grounding-attunement of thinking in the other beginning resonates in the attunings that can only be named in a distant way, as

startled dismay
reservedness (cf. Preview, 13: Reservedness) $\Big\}$ intimating

deep awe (cf. Preview, 6: The Grounding-Attunement.)

The inner relation among these will be experienced only by thinking through the individual joinings to which the grounding of the truth of be-ing and of the essential swaying of truth must be joined. There is no word for the onefold of these attunements, even as it might seem necessary to find a word, in order to avoid the easy misunderstanding that everything here amounts to a frightful weakness. Thus would the noisy "heroism" judge it.

Startled dismay: This can be most appropriately clarified by contrasting it with the grounding-attunement of the first beginning, with *wonder.* But clarifying an attunement never guarantees that attunement really occurs, instead of merely being represented.

Startled dismay means returning from the ease of comportment in what is familiar to the openness of the rush of the self-sheltering. In this opening what has been familiar for so long proves to be estranging and confining. What is most familiar and therefore the most unknown is the abandonment of being. Startled dismay lets man return to face *that* a being *is,* whereas before a being was for him just a being. Startled dismay lets man return to face that beings *are* and that this—be-ing—has abandoned all "beings" and all that appeared to be beings and has withdrawn from them.

But *this* startled dismay is not a simple evading, nor is it a helpless surrender of the "will." Rather, *because* it is precisely the self-sheltering of be-ing that opens up in this startled dismay and *because* beings themselves and the relation to them want to be preserved, the ownmost "will" of this startled dismay allies itself *to* startled dismay from within—and that is what we call here *reservedness.*

Reservedness (cf. Preview, 13: Reservedness) is the fore-attuning of preparedness for refusal as gifting. In reservedness—and without eliminating that [above mentioned] return—the turn into the hesitant self-refusal reigns as the essential swaying of be-ing. Reservedness is the *midpoint* (cf. below) for startled dismay and deep awe. These simply make more explicit what belongs *originarily* to reservedness. Reservedness determines the style of inceptual thinking in the other beginning.

But in accord with what has been said, *deep awe* should not be confused with bashfulness or understood only in this direction. Far from allowing this confusion, the deep awe that is meant here outgrows even the "will" of reservedness—and this out of the depth of the ground of the onefold grounding-attunement. This onefold, and deep awe in particular, gives rise to the necessity of reticence. And *that* is the letting-hold-sway of be-ing as enowning that through and through attunes every bearing in the midst of beings and every comportment to beings.

Deep awe is the way of getting nearer and remaining near to what is most remote as such (cf. The Last God), that in its hinting—when held in deep awe—still becomes the nearest and gathers in itself all relations of be-ing (cf. Leap, 115: The Guiding-Attunement of the Leap).

But who is capable of tuning *into* this grounding-attunement of awe-full, startled reservedness in the essential man? And how many will still assess that *this* attunement by be-ing does not justify evading of beings, but the opposite? For it constitutes the opening of the simplicity and greatness of beings and the originarily needed necessity of sheltering the truth of be-ing in beings, in order then once again to give historical man a goal: namely, *to become the founder and preserver of the truth of be-ing*, to *be* the "t/here" [*Da*] as the ground that is used by be-ing's essential sway: to be *care*, not as a minor concern with some arbitrary thing, nor as denial of exultation and power, but more originarily than all that, because this care is always a care *"for the sake of be-ing"* —not the be-ing of man, but the be-ing of beings in the whole.

The directive, already often repeated, to think "care" only in the inceptual realm of the question of being and not as some arbitrary, personal accidental, "ideological," or "anthropological" view regarding humans—this directive will continue to be without effect in the future, as long as those who only "write" a "critique" of the question of being do not experience—and do not *want* to experience—the distress of the abandonment of being. For in an age of "optimism"—poorly enough displayed—already the words *care* and *abandonment of being* sound "pessimistic." But that now precisely the attunings that are indicated by these names, along with their opposite, have from the ground up become *impossible* in the inceptual realm of questioning—because they presuppose value-thinking (ἀγαθόν) and the usual interpretations of beings and the familiar conception of man—who is willing to think mindfully, so far as to let this at least become a question?

In inceptual thinking one must especially traverse the realms of the truth of be-ing, even as these realms again retreat into hiddenness in the lighting up of beings. This going off to the side belongs inseparably to the mediacy of the "efficacy" of all philosophy.

In philosophy what is essential—after it, almost hidden, has gone to the fore—must retreat and become inaccessible (for the many), for this essential is insurpassable and *therefore* must withdraw into the enabling of the beginning. For when it comes to be-ing and its truth, one must begin again and again.

All beginnings are in themselves completed and insurpassable. They withdraw from mere history [*Historie*], not because they are super-temporal and eternal, but because they are greater than eternity: they are the *thrusts* of time which spatialize be-ing's opening of its self-sheltering. The ownmost grounding of this time-space is called Da-*sein*.

Reservedness, the tuning of the midpoint of startled dismay and deep awe—and the basic *thrust* of the grounding-attunement—in this reservedness Da-*sein* attunes itself to the *stillness* of the passing of the last god. Situated creatively in this grounding-attunement of Da-sein, man becomes the *guardian and caretaker* of this stillness.

In this way the inceptual mindfulness of thinking becomes necessarily genuine thinking, i.e., a thinking that sets *goals*. What gets set is not just any goal, and not *the* goal in general, but the one and only and thus singular goal of our history. This goal is the *seeking* itself, the seeking of be-ing. It takes place and is itself the deepest find when man becomes the preserver of the truth of be-ing, becomes guardian and caretaker of that stillness, and is resolute in that.

Seeker, preserver, guardian, and caretaker: this is what *care* means as the basic trait of Dasein. Man's determination is gathered in these names, insofar as he is grasped according to his ground, i.e., according to Da-sein, which in turning is enowned by *enowning* as by be-ing's essential sway. And it is only on the strength of this origin as the grounding of time-space ("temporality" [*Temporalität*]) that Da-sein can become an inabiding for transforming the distress of the abandonment of being into the necessity of creating as the restoring of beings.

And joined up in the joining of be-ing, we stand at the disposal of the *gods*.

Seeking itself is the goal. And that means that "goals" are still too much in the foreground and still take place ahead of be-ing—and thus bury what is needful.

If gods are the undecided, because at the beginning the opening for godding is still denied, what does it mean to say: *at the disposal of the gods*? That word means to stand ready for being used in opening the open. And those are used the hardest who must first tune to the openness of *this* opening and accomplish the attunement to this opening, by enthinking and making questionable the essential sway of truth. At the "disposal of the gods" means to stand far away and outside—outside the familiarity of "beings" and interpretations of them. It means to belong to those who are most remote, to belong to those for whom the flight of the gods in their furthest withdrawal remains most near.

We are already moving within an other truth, even as we are still in the crossing (within a more originary transformation of what is ownmost to "true" and "correct").

Of course, the grounding of this "ownmost" requires an exertion from thinking as had to have been accomplished only in the first beginning of Western thinking. For us, this exertion is strange because we do not have a clue as to what mastering the *simple onefold* requires. For people of today, who are hardly worth mentioning as one turns away from them, remain excluded from knowing the pathway of thinking. They flee into "new" contents, and, with the construction of the "political" and the "racial," construct for themselves a hitherto unknown facade for the old trimmings of "school-philosophy."

They appeal to the shallow pools of "lived-experiences," incapable of estimating the broad jointure of the arena of thinking, incapable of thinking the depth and height of be-ing in such an opening. And when they believe themselves superior to "lived-experience," they do so with an appeal to an empty cleverness.

But from where is the education to essential thinking to come? From thinking ahead to and going along the deciding pathways.

For example, who goes along the path of grounding the truth of be-ing? Who has any inkling of the *necessity* of thinking and inquiring—that necessity that does not need the crutches of Why or the props of What for?

The more necessary the thinking saying of be-ing is, the more unavoidable becomes the reticence of the truth of be-ing along the *passageway* of questioning.

More readily than others the poet veils the truth in image and thus bestows it to our view for keeping.

But how does the thinker shelter the truth of be-ing, if not in the pondering steadiness of the path of his questioning steps and their resulting consequences? Unpretentiously, as in a solitary field, under the big sky, the sower paces off the furrows with a heavy, faltering step, checking at every moment, and with the swing of the arm measures and molds the hidden space for all growth and ripening. Who is capable of still enacting this in thinking, as what is most inceptual to his power and as his highest future?

If a thinking question is not so simple and so outstanding as to determine the will and the style of thinking for centuries—by yielding to them what is the most profound issue to think—then it is best that it not be asked. For, if that question is simply recited, it only augments the incessant "carnival" of colorful and changing "problems," those "objections" which strike no one and by which no one is struck.

Given this comparison, how is it with the be-ing question, as the question of the truth of be-ing, a question which in and of itself, in turning, simultaneously asks the question of the be-ing of truth? But how long must be the way along which the question of truth even only begins to be encountered?

Whatever in the future and in truth dares to be called philosophy must as its first and foremost accomplish this: first to find the site for thinking questioning of the renewed inceptual question, i.e., to ground *Da-sein* (cf. Leap).

The thinking question of the truth of be-ing is the moment that carries the crossing. This moment can never be really fixed—and even less calculated. *It* first establishes the time of enowning. The unique simpleness of the onefold of this crossing can never be grasped in merely historical [*historisch*] fashion, because publicly historical "history" has long since passed this crossing by—granting that this crossing can ever be shown directly to history. Thus a long future is in store for this moment, assuming that the abandonment of beings by being is to be broken once again.

In and *as* Da-sein, be-ing en-owns the truth which it manifests as the not-granting, as that domain of hinting and withdrawal—of stillness—wherein the arrival and flight of the last god are first determined. *For that* man can do nothing—least of all when he has been given the task of preparing for the grounding of Da-sein—so much so that this task once again inceptually determines what is ownmost to humans.

6. The Grounding-Attunement

In the first beginning: deep wonder.
In another beginning: deep foreboding.

Everything would be misinterpreted and would fail if we wanted to prepare the grounding-attunement with the help of an analysis, or even a "definition," and to bring it into the free-space of its tuning power. It is only because for a long time now "psychology" has limited what the word *attunement* demonstrates, only because today's on-going mania for "lived-experience" would all the more confuse whatever is being said about the attunement, without any mindfulness of it—for this reason alone an orienting word must again and again be said "about" attunement.

All essential thinking requires that its thoughts and sentences be mined, like ore, every time anew out of the grounding-attunement. If

the grounding-attunement stays away, then everything is a forced rat-
tling of concepts and empty words.

Given that for a long time now a mis-concept of "thinking" has ruled
the opinion about "philosophy," the representation and judgment about
attunement can in the end only be an offshoot of misinterpretation of
thinking (attunement is a weakness, a stray, an unclarity, and a dull-
ness—over against the acumen and exactness and clarity and agility of
"thought"). At the very best, attunement might be tolerated as an orna-
mentation of thinking.

But grounding-attunement *attunes* Da-sein and thus attunes *thinking*
as projecting-open the truth of be-ing in word and concept.

Attunement is the spraying forth of the enquivering of be-ing as
enowning in Da-sein. Spraying forth: not a mere disappearing and
extinguishing, but the opposite—as preserving the sparks, in the sense
of the clearing of the "t/here" [*Da*] in accord with the full cleavage of
be-ing.

The grounding-attunement of another beginning can hardly ever be
known merely by one name—and especially in crossing to that beginning. And yet, the manifold names do not deny the onefoldness of this
grounding-attunement; they only point to the ungraspable of all that is
simple in the onefold. The grounding-attunement calls to us: startled
dismay, reservedness, deep awe, intimating, deep foreboding.

The intimating opens up the expanse of the concealing of what is
allotted and perhaps withheld.

Understood in terms of grounding-attunement, intimating does not
at all aim only at what is futural, what stands before—as does the intimating that is generally thought in a calculative way. Rather, it traverses
and thoroughly takes stock of the whole of temporality: the free-play of
the time-space of the "t/here" [*Da*].

Intimating in itself keeps the attuning power in store and grounds it
back into itself. Towering far above all uncertainty of common sense,
intimating is the hesitant *sheltering* of the unconcealing of the hidden as
such, of the refusal.

Intimating puts the inceptual inabiding in Da-sein. It is in itself both
the shock and the zeal—always assuming that here, as grounding-attunement, it tunes and be-tunes the enquivering of be-ing in
Da-sein as Da-*sein*.

Every naming of the grounding-attunement with a single word rests
on a false notion. Every word is in each case taken from tradition. The
fact that the grounding-attunement of another beginning has to have
many names does not argue against its onefoldness but rather confirms
its richness and strangeness.

Every mindfulness of this grounding-attunement is always only a gentle preparation for the attuning breaking-in [*Einfall*] of the grounding-

attunement, which must remain fundamentally an unintended happening [*Zu-fall*]. Of course, according to the sway of grounding-attunement, the preparation for such an unintended happening consists only in a thinking that deals with crossing. And this must grow out of a genuine *knowing awareness* of preservation of the truth of be-ing.

But if be-ing holds sway as not-granting, and if this not-granting itself should come forth into *its* clearing and be preserved as not-granting, then the preparedness for the not-granting can consist only in *renunciation*. However, here renunciation is not the mere "not-wanting-to have" or "leaving-on-the-side" but rather takes place as the highest form of possession whose highness gets decided [*Entschiedenheit findet*] in the carefree openness for the zeal for the gifting of the not-granting, a gifting that cannot be thought exhaustively.

The openness of the crossing is maintained and grounded in this decidedness [*Entschiedenheit*]; it is the midpoint of abground between the no-longer of the first beginning and its history *and* the not-yet of the fulfillment of the other beginning.

All guardianship of Da-sein must get its footing in this decidedness, insofar as man, founder of Da-sein, has to become guardian of the stillness of the passing of the last god (cf. Grounding).

As an intimating decidedness, however, this decidedness is only the dispassionate power to suffer [*Leidenskraft*] of the creative one, i.e., the thrower of the truth of be-ing—a truth that opens stillness up for the essentially coercive force of beings, a stillness from which be-ing (as enowning) can be heard.

7. From Enowning

How far removed from us is the god, the one who designates us founders and creators, because what is ownmost to god needs these [founders and creators]?

God is so far removed from us that we are incapable of deciding whether it is moving toward us or away from us.

And to enthink fully *this* remoteness in its essential swaying, as the time-space of the utmost decision, means to inquire into the truth of be-ing, into the enowning itself, from which every future history springs—granted that there will still be history.

This remoteness of the undecidability of the utmost and the foremost is what is cleared for self-sheltering; it is the essential swaying of truth itself as the truth of be-ing.

For the self-sheltering of this clearing, the remoteness of the undecidability is not a merely extant and indifferent emptiness, but the essential swaying of enowning itself as the sway of enowning—of the hesitant refusal that already enowns Dasein; the staying within the moment and within the abode of the foremost decision.

Everything true is decided upon and grounded, all beings become beings, and not-being slides into the appearance of be-ing—all of this simultaneously with the essential sway of the truth of enowning. This remoteness is also the furthest and our closest nearness to god, while at the same time it is the distress of the abandonment of being, sheltered by the lack-of-distress evidenced in the evading of mindfulness. The last god is sheltered within the essential swaying of the truth of be-ing, *in* and *as* enowning.

The prolonged Christianization of god and the growing publicizing of every attuned relation to beings have both stubbornly and covertly buried the preconditions by virtue of which something stays in the remoteness of undecidability of the flight or arrival of god, whose essential swaying will nevertheless be most intimately experienced in a knowing awareness, which stands in truth only as a creative knowing. In its broadest sense, creating means every sheltering of truth that is in beings.

When we speak of god and gods, we think—according to a long-standing habit of representation—in that form which still indicates primarily and above all the multi-faceted name of "transcendence." By this term one means that which transcends extant beings, including especially human beings. Even where particular ways of transcending and of transcendence are denied, still this way of thinking itself cannot be denied. With this way of thinking one can easily gain an overview of today's "worldviews":

1. The transcendent one (also imprecisely called "transcendence") is the God of Christianity.

2. This "transcendence" is denied and replaced by the "people" itself—however undetermined the latter is in its way of being—as goal and direction for all history. This counter-Christian "worldview" is only *apparently* unchristian; for it is *essentially* in agreement with that way of thinking that is called "liberalism."

3. The transcendent that is meant here is an "idea" or a "value" or a "meaning," something for which one does not put one's life on the line, but which is to be realized through "culture."

4. Any two of these meanings of the transcendent—peoples' ideas and Christianity or peoples' ideas and a culture-oriented politics or Christianity and culture—or all three of these couplings are mixed up in various degrees of definitiveness. And this mixed product is what is today the average and dominant "worldview," which intends everything but can no longer make a decision about anything.

As varied as these "worldviews" are and as vehemently as they openly or covertly attack one another—if one can still call spinning around in what is undecided an "attack"—these "worldviews," unbeknownst and without thinking, all agree that what is ownmost to man is already known—man as that being unto and from which every "transcendence" is determined and indeed as that which in the end primarily determines man. But this has become fundamentally impossible, because in his determinability man has already been established, instead of determining him as that which needs to be dis-placed from out of his hitherto accepted determination, in order first to be attuned to a determinability.

But how is man to be displaced from out of where he runs aground and where the domination of those "transcendences" and their mixtures above all belong? If he is to accomplish this by himself, is not then the presumption of the measure *even greater* than when he simply remains set up as the measure?

Or is it possible that this displacing comes over human beings? Indeed. And that is the distress of the abandonment by being. This distress does not first need help but must itself become first of all the helping one. But this distress must still be *experienced*. And what if man has become hardened against this distress and, as it seems, is as stubborn as ever? Then those must come who awaken, who in the end maintain that they have discovered distress because they know that they *suffer* distress.

The awakening of this distress is the first displacing of man into that *between* [*Zwischen*] where chaos drives forth at the same time as god remains in flight. This "between" is, however, not a "transcendence" with reference to man. Rather, it is the opposite: that open to which man belongs as the founder and preserver wherein as Da-sein he is en-owned by be-ing itself—be-ing that holds sway as nothing other than enowning.

If thanks to this displacing man comes to stand in enowning and has his abode in the truth of be-ing, then he is primarily still only ready for the leap into the deciding experience whether, within enowning, it is god's staying away or god's onset that decides for or against god.

Only when we estimate how singularly necessary being is and how it nevertheless does not hold sway as god itself, only when we have tuned what is our ownmost to these abgrounds between man and be-ing and be-ing and gods—only then do "presuppositions" for a "history" again begin to be real. Thus only mindfulness of "enowning" is appropriate for thinking.

Finally and above all "enowning" can only be en-thought (forced in front of inceptual thinking) if be-ing itself is grasped as the "between" for the passing of the last god and for Da-sein.

Enowning owns god over to man in that enowning owns man to god. This "owning-to" that "owns-over" is enowning, wherein the *truth* of be-ing as Da-sein is grounded (as transformed, man is shifted into the decision to be-there and to be-away [*Da-sein und Weg-sein*]) and wherein history takes its other beginning from be-ing. But the truth of be-ing as openness for the self-sheltering is simultaneously the removal unto the decision of remoteness and nearness of gods and thus the preparation for the passing of the last god.

Enowning is the between with regard to the passing of god and the history of man. But this between is not some indifferent intermediate field. Rather, the relation to the passing is the opening of the cleavage used by god (cf. Leap, 157–158: Cleavage and "Modalities"); and the relation to man is the enowning-letting-spring-forth of the grounding of Da-sein and thus the necessity of sheltering the truth of be-ing that is in beings as a *restoring* of beings.

Passing is not history and history is not enowning and enowning is not passing—and yet all three (if we are permitted to degrade them to a numerical order at all) are experienced and enthought only in their relations, i.e., in terms of enowning itself.

The remoteness of undecidability does not, of course, mean "what is otherworldly" but rather is what is *nearest* to the as yet not grounded *Da* [t/here] of Da-sein, which has taken up its abode in preparedness for the refusal, refusal as the essential swaying of be-ing.

What is thus the nearest is so near that every unavoidable pursuit of machination and of lived-experience must have already passed it [what is nearest] by and thus can also never immediately be called back to it. Enowning remains the most estranging.

8. From Enowning*

The flight of gods must be experienced and endured. This steadfast enduring grounds the most remote nearness to enowning. This enowning is the truth of be-ing.

The distress of the abandonment by being first opens up in this truth.

The grounding of the truth of be-ing, the grounding of Da-sein, becomes necessary from within this distress.

This necessity is accomplished in the ongoing decision which runs through everything that is historical in man: whether in the future man belongs to the truth of being—and thus, from within and for this belongingness, shelters the truth as what holds true in beings—or whether the beginning of the last man drives man into a deranged animality and refuses to grant the last god to historical man.

What happens when the struggle for measures dies out, when the same willing no longer wants greatness, i.e., no longer brings forth a will for the greatest difference of the ways?

If the other beginning is still being prepared, then this preparation is concealed as a great transformation; and the more hidden it is, the greater is the occurrence. The error, of course, consists in thinking that

---

* Cf. Preview, 16: Philosophy.

an essential overturn [*Umschlag*]—one that lays hold of everything in a fundamental way—should also be immediately and generally known and comprehended by all and displayed for the public eye. Only the few constantly stand in the brightness of this lightning.

The many have the "good fortune" of finding themselves in something extant and *thus* of pursuing what belongs to them by following what is useful for a whole.

In the other beginning that wholly other [dimension] that is called the domain of the decision is thought in advance. In that domain the genuinely historical be-ing of peoples is won or lost.

This being—historicity—is not the same in all ages. Right now it stands before an essential transformation insofar as it has been given the task of grounding *that* domain of the decision and the relational context of enowning by virtue of which historical human being first of all comes to itself. The grounding of this domain requires a privation that is the opposite of self-effacement. It can be accomplished only with the courage for the ab-ground. This domain—assuming that such a designation is at all sufficient—is *Da-sein,* that "between" which first grounds itself and sets humans and god apart and together, owning one to the other. What opens up in the grounding of Da-sein is enowning. With that is not meant an "over against," something intuitable, or an "idea." Rather, what is meant is the beckoning-inviting and a holding-over across into the open of the "t/here" [*Da*], which is the clearing-sheltering turning-point in this turning.

This turning obtains its truth only insofar as it is striven as the strife between earth and world and thus shelters what holds true in beings. Only history which is grounded in Da-sein has the guarantee of belonging to the truth of being.

9. A Glance

Be-ing as enowning is hesitant refusal as (not-granting). Ripeness is *fruit* and *gifting.* The nihilating in be-ing and its counter-resonance has *the character of strife* (be-ing or non-being).

Be-ing holds sway in *truth* and is clearing for self-sheltering.

Truth [holds sway] as the essential sway of *ground:* Ground is the *wherein* of the grounding (not the wherefrom as cause).

The ground grounds as *ab-ground: distress* as the open of self-sheltering (not "emptiness," but inexhaustability of the abground.)

Abground [holds sway] as *time-space.*

Time-space [is] the *site for the moment* of strife, (be-ing or non-being).

Strife [is] the strife of *earth and world,* because truth of be-ing [takes place] only in sheltering, sheltering as grounding the "between" in beings: the tug of earth and world.

The pathways and manners of sheltering are *beings.*

10. From Enowning

Be-ing holds sway as enowning.

The essential swaying has its center and breadth in the turning [where] strife and countering [are carried out].

The essential swaying is warranted and sheltered in truth.

Truth occurs as the clearing sheltering.

The grounding-jointure of this occurrence is the time-space that originates from within it.

Time-space is what towers up for fathoming the cleavage of be-ing.

As en-joining truth, time-space is originarily the site for the moment of enowning.

The site for the moment holds sway from out of enowning, as the strife of earth and world.

Strifing of this strife is Da-sein.

Da-sein occurs within the ways of sheltering truth from within the warranting of the lit-up and sheltered enowning.

The sheltering of truth lets the true as beings come into the open and into dissemblage.

Thus a being first of all stays in be-ing.

A being is. Be-ing holds sway.

Be-ing (as enowning) needs beings so that be-ing may hold sway. Beings do not need be-ing in the same way. Beings can still "be" in the abandonment of being, under whose dominance the *immediate* availability and usefulness and serviceability of every kind (e.g., everything must serve the people) obviously make up *what is a being* and what is not.

But this seeming independence of beings over against be-ing—as if be-ing were only an addendum of representational, "abstract" thinking—is not a priority but rather only the sign of a privilege for a blinding deterioration.

Understood from within the truth of be-ing, what is an "actual" being is a not-being under the domination of what is not ownmost to shine, a shining whose origin thereby remains hidden.

As the grounding that takes the strifing of the strife into what is opened up by strife, Da-*sein* is awaited by humans and is carried in the inabiding which sustains the "t/here" [*Da*] and belongs to enowning.

Thinking of be-ing as enowning is the inceptual thinking that prepares for an other beginning by putting the first beginning in proper perspective.

The *first* beginning thinks be-ing as presence from within a presencing which manifests the first flashing of *the one* essential swaying be-ing.

11. Enowning—Dasein—Man*

1. *Enowning:* the sure light of the essential swaying of be-ing in historical man's most extreme range of the deepest distress.

---

* Cf. Grounding.

2. *Dasein:* the "between" [*Zwischen*] which has the character of a mid-point that is open and thus sheltering, between the arrival and flight of gods and man, who is rooted in that "between."
3. The origin of Dasein is in enowning and its turning.
4. Thus Dasein has only to be *grounded* as and in the truth of be-ing.
5. From the *human* side, grounding—not creating—is letting the ground be (cf. For the Few and the Rare . . .), so that man once again comes to *himself* and recovers self-being.
6. The grounding ground is at the same time the abground for the cleavage of be-ing and the unground for beings' abandonment by being.
7. The grounding-attunement of grounding is *reservedness* (cf. there).
8. Reservedness is the outstanding moment of relation to enowning in having been called by the call of enowning.
9. Dasein is the fundamental occurrence of future history. This occurrence emerges from enowning and becomes the possible site for the moment of decision regarding man—his history or non-history, as its passage to going under.
10. In their essential sway, i.e., in their belonging together as the ground of history, enowning and Dasein are still fully hidden and will remain strange for a long time yet. For there are no bridges, and the leaps are not yet accomplished. Lacking is the depth of an experience of truth and mindfulness that is sufficient to both: the power of the peak *decision* (cf. there). On the other hand, the path is strewn with many opportunities and means for misinterpretation, because the knowing awareness of what takes place in the first beginning is also lacking.

12. Enowning and History

History here is not meant as one domain of beings among others, but solely with a view to the essential swaying of be-ing itself. Thus already in *Being and Time* the historicity of Dasein needs to be understood solely from within the fundamental-ontological intention and not as a contribution to the existing philosophy of history.

En-owning is originary history itself—which could be understood to mean that here be-ing's essential sway is grasped "historically" after all. Yes, of course, "historically," but not by picking up a "concept" of history, rather *historically* because now the essential sway of be-ing no longer bespeaks only presence, but the full essential swaying of the temporal-spatial ab-ground and thereby of truth. Thus a knowing awareness of the *uniqueness* of be-ing continually ensues. However, it is not as if "nature" is hereby set back; rather, nature, too, is originarily transformed. In this originary concept of history we first attain the domain where it becomes manifest why and how history is "more than" deed and will. "Fate," too, belongs to history without exhausting what is ownmost to it.

The way toward what is ownmost to history—grasped according to the essential swaying of be-ing itself—is prepared "fundamental-onto-logically" by means of grounding historicity on temporality. In the sense of the one guiding question of being in *Being and Time,* this means that, as *time-space,* time retrieves into itself what is ownmost to history. But insofar as time-space is the abground of the ground, i.e., of the truth of being, its interpretation of historicity contains the directive toward being's essential sway itself, inquiry into which is the sole task there—being neither theory of history nor philosophy of history.

13. Reservedness*

Reservedness is the style of inceptual thinking only because it must become the style of future humanness, one grounded in Da-sein, because it thoroughly attunes and carries this grounding.

Reservedness—as style—is the self-assuredness of the grounding measure and fierce steadfastness of Dasein. It attunes the style because it is the *grounding-attunement.*

Attunement (cf. the Hölderlin lectures**) is meant here in the sense of inabiding: the onefold of carrying out all charming-moving-onto, of all projecting-open, of carrying in all removal-unto and the *steadfastness and enactment of the truth of being.* Here every other external and "psy-chological" representation of "attunement" must be kept at a distance. Thus attunement is never merely the how that accompanies and lights up and shadows all human dealings that would already be set. Rather, it is primarily by attunement that the extent of Dasein's removal-unto is fathomed and the simpleness of charming-moving-unto is allotted to Dasein, insofar as we are dealing here with *reservedness* as the ground-ing-attunement.

Reservedness is the grounding-attunement because it tunes the engrounding of the ground of Da-sein, of enowning, and thus tunes the grounding of Da-sein.

Reservedness is the strongest and at the same time gentlest pre-paredness of Dasein for en-ownment, for being thrown into the owned standing within the truth of the *turning in enowning* (cf. The Last God). The mastery of the last god only comes upon reservedness; reserved-ness furnishes *the deep stillness* for the mastery and for the last god.

Reservedness attunes each grounding moment of a sheltering of truth in the future Dasein of man. This history, grounded in Da-sein, is the hidden history of deep stillness. In this stillness alone there can still *be* a people.

This reservedness alone enables all human being and gathering to be

---

*Cf. above, 5: For the Few and the Rare, 9ff.; cf. below, Grounding, 193: Da-sein and Man.
**WS 1934/35 *Hölderlins Hymnen "Germanien" und "Der Rhein"* (GA 39).

gathered unto itself, i.e., into the destination of its assignment: the steadfastness of the last god.

Are we still, in the future, *destined* to a history [*Geschichte*] — one that is totally other than what history now seems to be taken to be: the gloomy chasing after self-devouring events, which can only be fleetingly held by means of the loudest of noises?

If a history is still to be granted to us, i.e., a style of Da-sein, then this *can* only be the *sheltered history of deep stillness,* in and as which the mastery of the last god opens and shapes beings.

Thus the deep stillness must first come over the world for the earth. This stillness only springs forth from reticence. And this reticence only grows out of reservedness. As grounding-attunement, reservedness thoroughly tunes the intimacy of the strife between world and earth and thus the strifing of the onset of en-ownment.

As strifing of this strife, Dasein keeps what is its ownmost in the sheltering of the truth of be-ing, i.e., [sheltering] of the last god, unto a *being* (cf. Grounding).

Reservedness and Care

Reservedness is the ground of care. Reservedness of Da-*sein* first of all grounds care as the inabiding that sustains the "t/here" [*Da*]. But one has to say again and again that care does not mean gloom or a gripping fear or agonizing trouble about this or that. All of this is simply what is *not* ownmost to care, insofar as care is subject to yet another misunderstanding, namely that it is one "attunement" and "attitude" among others.

In the expression "he will provide for order" or "take care of," something of what is ownmost to care comes to the fore: reaching ahead into decidedness. But at the same time care is no mere attitude of will and cannot be accounted for as a capacity of the soul.

As steadfastness of Da-*sein,* care reaches ahead into decidedness for the truth of be-ing and especially sustains the allotment to being-captive to the "t/here" [*Da*]. The ground of this "especially" is the reservedness of Dasein. This attunes only as enowned belongingness to the truth of being.

Reservedness as origin of stillness and as law of the gathering. The gathering [gathers] in the stillness and [is] the sheltering of truth. Sheltering of truth and its unfolding [unfolds] into the caring-for and dealing with [things].

Reservedness as openness for the reticent nearness of the essential swaying of be-ing, tuning to the remotest enquivering of hints that enown from the distance of what is undecidable.

Reservedness and seeking; the highest find in seeking itself [is] the nearness to decision.

Reservedness: the self-restraining leaping forth into the turning of enowning (thus neither a romantic flight nor a bourgeois repose).

Reservedness, Silencing, and Language

The word fails, not as an occasional event—in which an accomplishable speech or expression does not take place, where only the assertion and the repetition of something already said and sayable does not get accomplished—but originarily. The word does not even come to word, even though it is precisely when the word escapes one that the word begins to take its first leap. The word's escaping one is enowning as the hint and onset of be-ing.

The word's escaping is the inceptual condition for the self-unfolding possibility of an originary-poetic-naming of be-ing.

When will the time of language and deep stillness come, the time of the simple nearness of the essential sway and the bright remoteness of beings—when the word would once again work? (cf. inceptual thinking as non-conceptual.)

Reservedness is the creative sustaining in ab-ground (cf. Grounding, 238–242: Time-Space).

14. Philosophy and Worldview

Philosophy is useless but at the same time masterful knowing.
Philosophy is fruitful but rare inquiry into the truth of be-ing.
Philosophy is the grounding of truth while being deprived of what is true.
Philosophy is wanting to go back to the beginning of history and thus wanting to go beyond oneself.

Thus, from an external point of view, philosophy is merely a decoration—perhaps a cultural discipline and show-piece, perhaps even a heritage whose ground is lost. *This* is how the many must take philosophy—and especially then and there when philosophy is a distress for the few.

The "worldview" arranges the experience in a certain direction and into its range—always only so far that the worldview is never put into question. Thus the worldview constricts and thwarts genuine experience. Seen from the standpoint of worldview, that is its strength.

Philosophy *opens up* experience, but because of that philosophy is precisely *not* capable of grounding history in an *immediate way*.

Worldview is always an end, mostly very drawn out and as such never known.

Philosophy is always a beginning and requires an overcoming of itself.

Worldview has to refuse any new possibility, in order to preserve itself.

Philosophy can cease for a long time and apparently disappear.

Both have their various times and, within history, hold onto wholly different stages of Da-sein. The differentiation of "scientific philosophy" and "philosophy of worldviews" is the last offshoot of the philosophical helplessness of the nineteenth century, in the course of which "science" achieved a particularly technical cultural significance, whereas, as a substitute for the foundations that disappeared, the "worldview" of individuals was in a weak sort of way to continue still to hold "values" and "ideals" together.

What lies within the thought of "scientific" philosophy as the last genuine remnant (cf. the deeper understanding in Fichte and Hegel) is this: grounding and establishing the knowable systematically (mathematically) in the manner of a unity, on the basis and following the idea of knowing as certainty (self-certainty). In this intention of "scientific" philosophy there still lives an urge in philosophy itself, namely still to rescue its *ownmost matter* from the arbitrariness of opinion in terms of worldview and from the necessarily limiting and dictatorial manner of worldview in general. For even in the "liberal" worldview there lies this self-righteousness, in the sense that it demands that each be allowed his opinion. But the arbitrariness is slave to what is "accidental."

But the ownmost matter of philosophy is forgotten and misconstrued in "epistemology." And where "ontology" is still understood (as in Lotze), it still remains *one* discipline among others. That and how the old guiding-question here (τί τὸ ὄν) is rescued throughout the whole of modern philosophy—and of course modified—this never reaches the clarity of knowing, because philosophy already lacks necessity and owes its "cultivation" to its character as "cultural commodity."

"Worldview," like domination of "world-pictures," is an outgrowth of modernity, a *consequence* of modern metaphysics. Herein is also the reason why "worldview" then tries to set itself *above* philosophy. For along with the emergence of "worldviews" the possibility of a will to philosophy disappears, to such a degree that in the end worldview had to ward off philosophy. Meanwhile, the more philosophy had to sink away and become mere erudition, the more worldview succeeds. This remarkable appearance of the dominance of *"worldviews"* attempted to bring into its service—and not accidentally—even the last great philosophy, that of Nietzsche. That was all the more easy in that Nietzsche himself rejected philosophy as "erudition" and thus *seemingly* took the side of "worldview" (as a "philosopher-poet"!).

"Worldview" is always "machination" over against what is handed down to us, for the sake of overcoming and subduing it, with the means that are proper to worldview and which it has itself prepared, though never brought to fruition—all of this slid over into "lived-experience."

As the grounding of the truth of be-ing, *philosophy* has its origin in itself; it must take itself back into what it grounds and only build itself up from that.

Philosophy and worldview are so incomparable that there is no model possible for demonstrating this differentiation visually. Every image would always still bring both of them too close to each other.

The hidden but used up "dominion" of the churches; the easiness and accessibility of "worldviews" for the masses (as substitute for "spirit," that has long been wanting, and for the relation to "ideas"); the continued and indifferent pursuit of philosophy as erudition and simultaneously, both mediately and immediately, as ecclesiastical scholasticism and the scholasticism of world views—all of this, from within the familiar and flexible omniscience of public opinion, will for a long time keep philosophy as creative cogrounding of Dasein at a distance. Of course, this is nothing to "regret" but rather only an indication that philosophy is heading toward a genuine destining of what is ownmost to it. And everything depends on not disturbing this destining and not disregarding it with an "apologetic" for philosophy, a machination that necessarily always remains below the rank of philosophy.

But distress is indeed mindfulness of the approaching of this destining of philosophy, the knowing awareness of that which disturbs and disfigures and would like to validate a semblance of the being of philosophy. But this very knowing would misconstrue itself, if it let itself be enticed to make that contrary being into an object of refutation and dispute. The knowing awareness of what is not ownmost [to philosophy] must persist in disregarding what is not ownmost.

What is ownmost to worldview in terms of machination and lived-experience forces the shaping of each worldview to vacillate in the broadest of opposites and therefore also always to solidify itself through adjustment. That "worldview" can be the ownmost matter for the individual and his respective life-experience and his very own formation of opinion, that in opposition to this "worldview" a "total worldview" can come forward in order to extinguish every individual opinion—even this belongs to what is ownmost to worldview as such. As boundless as the former is in its arbitrariness, so rigid is the latter in its finality. Indeed, what is opposite and the same here is easy to grasp: The ultimate validity is only the particularity that extends into the completeness of universal validity, and the arbitrariness is what is possible for each individual as finally valid only for him. The necessity of what has taken a long time to grow—and with that the abground character of what is creative—is lacking everywhere.

In each case the suspicion and mistrust against philosophy is equally great and equally different.

Every total posture that claims to determine and regulate every kind of action and thinking must unavoidably reckon as oppositional and even demeaning everything that might additionally still come up as necessity. How would a "total" worldview be able to cope with something like this being even possible, let alone essential—something which this worldview itself simultaneously undermines and raises and includes in other necessities—other necessities that cannot be brought to it from the outside at all but rather arise from its hidden ground (e.g., from the way of being of a people)?

Thus there arises here an unsurpassable difficulty, one that can never be removed either by adjustment or by excuse. *The total worldview must close itself off from the opening of its ground and from engrounding the domain of its "creating"; that is, its creating can never arrive at what is its own-most way of being and become creating-beyond-itself, because thereby the total worldview would have to put itself into question.* The consequence is that creating is replaced in advance by *endless operations.* The ways and risks that belong to what was once creating are arranged according to the machination's gigantic character, and the machinational gives the appearance of the liveliness of creating.

Only questioning and decidedness to question-worthiness can be set over against "worldview." Every attempt at mediation—regardless of the side from which it comes—weakens the positions and eliminates the domain's possibility of genuine struggle.

It should come as no surprise that, even though they are incompatible, total political belief as well as total Christian faith are nevertheless engaged in adjustment and tactics. For they share the same way of being. Because of their total posture, total political belief and total Christian faith are based upon renouncing essential decisions. Their struggle is not a creative one but rather "propaganda" and "apologetics."

But does philosophy not also and even above all and altogether lay claim to "the total," especially when we define philosophy as a knowing awareness of beings as such and *in the whole*? The answer is yes, as long as we think in the form of philosophy up to now (metaphysics), and as long as we take philosophy in its distinctively Christian cast (in the systematization of German Idealism). But it is precisely here that modern philosophy is already on the way to "worldview." (It is no accident that this word becomes more and more legitimate in the orbit of this "thinking.")

However, insofar and as soon as philosophy finds its way back into its inceptual way of being (in the other beginning) and the question of the truth of be-ing becomes the grounding midpoint, the abground character of philosophy reveals itself. As such, philosophy must return to the beginning, in order to bring into the free-space of its mindfulness the cleavage and the beyond-itself, the estranging and always unfamiliar.

15. Philosophy as "Philosophy of a People"

Who would deny that philosophy is philosophy "of a people"? As evidence that quashes any opposing view, can we not appeal to the greatness of the beginning of Western philosophy? Is it not philosophy of "the" *Greek* people? And the enormous end of Western philosophy—"German Idealism" and "Nietzsche"—is it not philosophy of "the" *German* people?

But what do we say when we make such self-evident statements? We do not say anything about what is ownmost to philosophy itself. On the contrary, such a characterization of philosophy levels it off and makes it into an indifferent "accomplishment," a "fulfillment," a manner of comportment similar to the one that can also exemplify the style of clothing and food preparation and the like. Such an obvious way of philosophy's belongingness to the "people" gives the false impression that, by indicating such belongingness, we say something essential about philosophy—or even about creating a future philosophy.

Thus, the phrase "philosophy of a people" immediately proves to be extremely ambiguous and obscure—not to mention that the vagueness of talking about "people" remains entirely undetermined.

In what way does a people become a people? Does a people become only what it *is*? If so, what then *is* a people and how do we come to know: 1. What is a people in general? 2. What is this or that people? 3. What kind of people are we ourselves?

Here all platonizing manner of thinking fails when it prescribes for the health of a people an idea, a meaning, and a value in accord with which that people is to "become." From where does such a prescription come and how does it happen?

Mindfulness of what belongs to "being a people" constitutes an essential passage-way. As little as we dare not misunderstand this, just as important is it to know that a very high order of be-ing has to be achieved if a "people principle" is to be mastered and brought into play as standard for historical Da-sein.

A nation first becomes a people when those who are its most unique ones [*Einzigsten*] arrive and begin to intimate. Thus a people first becomes free for its law, which it must struggle for, as the ultimate necessity of its most noble moment. Philosophy of a people is that which makes a people into a people of a philosophy, which historically founds the people in its Da-sein, and which prevails upon a people to become guardians of the truth of be-ing.

Philosophy of "a" people is what freely and uniquely comes *over* the people as much as what comes "from within" the people—over the people, insofar as it already decides for itself, Da-sein.

Therefore, philosophy of "a" people cannot be calculated and prescribed according to some kinds of dispositions and abilities. On the contrary, thinking about philosophy comes from "the people" only if it grasps that philosophy has to spring forth from its very ownmost origin and that this "leap" can succeed only if philosophy as such still belongs to its first, essential beginning. Only thus can philosophy move "people" into the truth of be-ing—instead of, vice versa, being assaulted by a so-called people, as an extant one, and thus being driven into what is not its ownmost.

16. Philosophy*

Philosophy is the immediate, useless, but at the same time masterful knowing from within mindfulness.

Mindfulness is inquiring into the *meaning* (cf. *Being and Time*), i.e., into the truth of be-ing.

Inquiring into the truth is leaping into its essential sway and thus into be-ing itself (cf. Grounding, 227: On the Essential Sway of Truth).

The question reads: whether and when and how we belong to being (as enowning).

This question has to be asked *for the sake of the essential sway of being, which needs us*—needs us, not as beings who happen to be extant, but insofar as we sustain and inabide—by persevering in—Da-*sein*, and ground Da-*sein* as the truth of being. Hence mindfulness—leap into the truth of being—is necessarily self-mindfulness. That does not mean (cf. Grounding) an observation turned back upon us as "given." Rather, it is grounding the truth of self-being according to Da-sein's ownhood.

According to what was just said, the question whether we belong to being is in itself also the question of the essential sway of be-ing. This question of belongingness is a question of deciding between the belongingness, which still has to be determined, and the abandonment of being as hardening unto non-beings in the shining of beings.

Because philosophy is such a mindfulness, it leaps ahead into the utmost possible decision and by its [own] opening dominates in advance all sheltering of the truth in and as beings. Therefore, philosophy is *masterful knowing* itself, even though not an "absolute" knowing in the style of the philosophy of German Idealism.

But because mindfulness is self-mindfulness and thus along with it we are moved into the question of who we are and because our being is historical—especially one that has come over us in its having-been—mindfulness becomes necessarily the question concerning the truth of the history of philosophy and mindfulness of philosophy's all-surpassing first beginning and its unfolding into the end.

A mindfulness of what transpires today is always too short-sighted. What is essential is mindfulness of the beginning as it anticipates its end and still includes "today" as the extension of the end—and this in such a manner that what is today becomes being-historically manifest only from the beginning (cf. Echo, 57: History of Be-ing and Abandonment of Being).

Even more shortsighted is the alignment of philosophy with the "sciences," which has become customary—and not accidentally—since the beginning of modernity. This direction of inquiry—and not just the *explicit* "philosophy of science"—must be given up completely.

---

*Cf. Preview, 7: From Enowning, pp. 17–20; *Überlegungen* IV, 85 ff. [GA 94].

Philosophy never builds immediately upon beings; it prepares the truth of being and stands ready with the viewpoints and perspectives that hereby open up.

Philosophy is a joining in beings as the conjoining of the truth of be-ing, a conjoining enjoined to be-ing.

17. The Necessity of Philosophy

All necessity is rooted in distress. As the first and utmost mindfulness of the truth of be-ing and of the be-ing of truth, the necessity of philosophy lies in the first and utmost distress.

This distress is that which drives man round among beings and brings him first of all in front of beings in the whole and into the midpoint of beings, thus bringing man to himself—and *thus* in each case letting history begin or founder.

What drives man round is his *thrownness* into beings, a thrownness that determines him as the thrower of being (of the truth of be-ing).

The thrown thrower enacts the first, grounding throw as *projecting-open* beings unto be-ing (cf. Grounding, 203: Projecting-Open and Da-sein). In the first beginning, where man first of all takes a stand *in front of* beings, the projecting-open itself and its manner and its necessity and distress are still obscure and covered over, and nevertheless powerful: φύσις – ἀλήθεια – ἕν – πᾶν – λόγος – νοῦς – πόλεμος – μὴ ὄν – δίκη – ἀδικία.

The necessity of philosophy consists in the fact that as mindfulness it does not have to eliminate that distress but rather must persevere in it and ground it, i.e., make it the ground of man's history.

To be sure, that distress varies in the essential beginnings and transitions of man's history. But this distress should never be taken superficially and reckoned with summarily as a lack or misery or something like that. This distress exists outside any "pessimistic" or "optimistic" valuation. The grounding-attunement that attunes unto necessity differs according to the inceptual experience of this distress.

The grounding-attunement of the first beginning is *deep wonder* that beings are, that man himself is extant, extant in that which *he* is *not*.

The grounding-attunement of the other beginning is *startled dismay:* startled dismay in the abandonment of being (cf. Echo) and the *reservedness* that is grounded in such startled dismay in its creative mode.

Distress is that driving round that first brings about the decision and severance of man *as* a being *from* beings—and in the midst of beings brings that decision back again to beings. This distress belongs to the truth of be-ing itself. Most originarily, it is distress in the *pressing need* for the necessity of the highest possibilities, on whose pathways man—creating and grounding—goes beyond himself and back into the ground of beings. Where this distress fully culminates, it brings about *Da-sein* and its grounding (cf. now WS 37/38, pp. 18ff.*).

Distress, that on-going driving round—how would it be if it were the truth of be-ing itself, how would it be if, with the more originary grounding of truth, at the same time *be-ing* would *sway more* as enowning? How would it be if distress thus would become more pressing and would drive round more, but this driving round in this intensity would be just that strife which had its self-refusing ground in the overflowing of the intimacy of beings and of be-ing?

18. The Powerlessness of Thinking

This powerlessness appears to be obvious, especially if power means: the force of immediate effect and prevailing. But how would it be if "power" means: grounding and consolidating into the essential sway from within the "capability" for transformation? Even then no decision has yet been made about the powerlessness and power of thinking.

What is understood normally by the powerlessness of thinking has several reasons:

1. that at this time no essential thinking at all is enacted and enactable.
2. that machination and lived-experience claim to be all that is effective and thus "powerful" and that they leave no room for genuine power.
3. that, assuming that essential thinking might succeed, we do not yet have any strength to open ourselves to its truth, because to that a proper rank of Dasein belongs.
4. that, with the growing deadening vis-à-vis the simplicity of an essential mindfulness and with the lack of perseverance in questioning, every turn on the path is disregarded if in its first stage it does not bring some "result"—a result with which something is "to be made" or by which something is to be "experienced" [*zu erleben*].

Therefore, "powerlessness" is not yet straightforwardly an objection against "thinking" but rather only against its despisers.

And on the other hand the genuine power of thinking (as en-thinking of the truth of be-ing) does not tolerate an immediate conclusion and evaluation, especially when thinking must shift into be-ing and bring into play the entire strangeness of be-ing—thus when thinking can never be based on a successful result in beings.

This is the most hidden ground for the solitariness of thinking-questioning. The often evoked solitariness of thinking is only a conse-

---

* Lecture course WS 1937/38, *Grundfragen der Philosophie. Ausgewählte "Probleme" der "Logik"* (GA 45, 67ff.) [trans. R. Rojcewicz and A. Schuwer, *Basic Questions of Philosophy: Selected "Problems" of "Logic"* (Bloomington: Indiana University Press, 1994)].

quence, that is, it does not result from withdrawing oneself or being away from . . . , but rather springs forth from the origin from within the domain of be-ing. Therefore, this solitariness will never be eliminated by "results" and "successes" that a thinker achieves. Rather, that solitariness will thereby only be increased, assuming that it makes any sense at all to speak here of increasing.

19. Philosophy
(On the Question: Who Are We?)

As mindfulness of be-ing, philosophy is necessarily self-mindfulness. The foregoing claim regarding this interconnection is essentially different from any way of securing the "self"-certainty of the "I" for the sake of "certainty" and not for the sake of the truth *of be-ing*. But this claim reaches deeper still, into a domain that is more originary than the one which the "fundamental ontological" approach to Da-sein in *Being and Time* had to set forth in *crossing*—an approach that even now is not yet sufficiently unfolded and brought to the knowing awareness of those who are engaged in questioning.

But now, insofar as "we" ourselves move into the domain of questioning, after grounding the way of being of mindfulness originarily as self-mindfulness, from that point on the philosophical question can be put in the form of the question: *Who are we?*

Apart from the who-question, *whom* do we mean with the "we"? (Cf. SS 34, Logik.*) Do we mean us ourselves, who right now are extant, here and now? Where will the encircling circle take its course? Or do we mean "man" as such? But man as such "is" unhistorical only in being *historical.* Do we mean ourselves as our own people? But even then we are not the only ones but a people among other peoples. And by what means is what is ownmost to a people determined? What becomes immediately clear is that the way in which what is questioned in the inquiry is set forth—the "we"—already contains a decision about the Who. That is to say, we cannot pass through the who-question untouched by taking up the "we" and "us" as if they were extant and only lacked the determination of the Who. Even in this question, the turning reverberates. This question can be neither asked nor responded to straightforwardly. But as long as what is philosophy's ownmost—mindfulness of the truth of be-ing—is not grasped and thus the necessity of a self-mindfulness that here springs forth has not become effective, this question is as question already exposed to weighty reservations.

---

*Lecture course SS 1934, *Über die Logik als Frage nach der Sprache* (GA 38).

1. In spite of the "we," the question is indeed directed *back* to us ourselves and thus "reflected"; it requires a posture that looks back and runs against the straightforward character of acting and being effective.

2. But it is not only because of this reflective posture that the question seems to deviate from the path. Rather, as a question it is altogether a deviation. Even when this question is not "reflective" and only "occupies itself" with "us," it would still be a "theoretical" brooding by man—a brooding that takes him away from acting and being effective and in any case weakens both of these. Both reservations join hands in the one demand: In acting and being effective, we must *be* ourselves and not question or undermine ourselves.

3. This also shows that it is not clear *for what purpose* this question is to be asked, and to what the difficulty connects; it is not clear how to figure out *from where* we are to get any answer at all.

Here, too, the most obvious solution seems to lie in the demand just mentioned: We should be ourselves in acting, and precisely this way of being answers the question of Who we are, even before it is ever asked.

The will to self-*being* renders the question futile.

This consideration is clear, but only because it tries—almost unintentionally—to stay on the surface.

For, what does self-being mean? Is *man, are* we, only on the basis of the fact that we let that which attaches itself to us and in which we are imprisoned take its course? It is not at all clear in what sense man is and how we *are*. And the reference to an acting and being effective is not sufficient. Every "operation," every manner of being concerned with things moves man—but the question still is whether he thereby already "is." Of course, it cannot be denied that by being in this way he is a being; but precisely therefore the question gains in intensity, whether man already "is," if he is and occurs in this way; whether a people "is" itself only when it increases and decreases its "existence" [*Bestand*]. Obviously there is "more" to a people's way of being; this "being" has in itself its own relationality of essential determinations whose "unity" initially remains pretty much in the dark. For, whence should come, for example, the effort "institutionally" and "organizationally" to shape up the extant body of the people? That man is made up of body-soul-spirit does not say much. For this overlooks the question of the *being* of this unified extant thing—not to mention that these "extant pieces" and their application, considered as man's determinations, still presuppose his specific historical experiences and his relation to beings. What do "soul"— *anima*—ψυχή mean? What do spirit—*animus, spiritus*—πνεῦμα mean?

If we take or want to take even the very next step in the direction of a *clarity* that goes beyond the mere, hollow use of words, then essential tasks of elucidation emerge, which in the end are not indifferent but actually quite crucial for taking up and enacting what it means to *be* human and to *be* a people.

But let us leave aside, for the moment, the question concerning man's "being" when we ask in this manner. Let us instead ask: What do we mean by *self* in the self-being which is called for?

Self—does that not mean that we put ourselves forth into the engagement of being—that is, already have ourselves in view and have the right feel for ourselves, are at home with ourselves? By what means and how is man certain that he is at home with himself and not merely with a semblance and a surface of what is his ownmost? Do we know ourselves—as selves? How are we to *be* ourselves, if we are not our *selves?* And how can we be *ourselves* without knowing *who* we are, so that we are certain of being *the ones* who we are?

The who-question is thus not an external and additional question, as if by means of responding to it we get additional information about man—information that from a "practical" point of view is superfluous. Rather the who-question asks the question concerning the *self*-being and thus the question concerning what is ownmost to selfhood.

In the question "who are we?" is lodged the question of *whether* we are. Both questions are inseparable; and this inseparability once again indicates the hidden, ownmost being of man, indeed of historical man.

Here the view opens up into totally different kinds of interrelations that are shaped differently from the ones that mere calculation and control of human beings as extant knows—as if what counts is reshaping him, just as the potter reshapes a lump of clay.

Man's selfhood—the historical man's selfhood as the selfhood of the people—is a domain of events wherein man will be owned unto himself only when he himself reaches into the open time-space in which an owning can take place.

Man's ownmost "being" is thus grounded in belonging to the truth of being as such; and this, in turn, because being's essential sway as such—and *not* what is ownmost to man—contains in itself the call to man, the call which attunes man to history (cf. Grounding, 197: Da-sein—Ownhood—Selfhood).

From this it becomes clear that the who-question, as the enactment of self-mindfulness, has nothing in common with a curious ego-addicted lostness in the full-fledged brooding over "one's own" lived-experiences. Rather the who-question is an essential path for the enactment of the question concerning what is most question-worthy, i.e., that question that alone opens up the worthiness of the question-worthy: the question of the truth of being.

Only the one who comprehends that man must historically ground what is ownmost to him by grounding Da-sein, only the one who comprehends that inabiding the sustaining of Da-sein is nothing other than residing in the time-space of that event that is enowned as the flight of gods, only the one who in creating takes the dismay and bliss of enowning back into reservedness as grounding-attunement—only this one is capable of having an inkling of the essential sway of being and, in such a mindfulness, is capable of preparing truth for what is coming as true.

Whoever sacrifices himself to this preparation stands in the crossing and has grasped far ahead and thus ought not to expect any understanding—as immediately urgent as that might be—from those of today. Rather he ought to *expect* resistance.

Mindfulness as self-mindfulness, as it becomes necessary here following the question of the essential sway of be-ing, is far removed from that *clara et distincta perceptio* in which the *ego* rises and becomes certain. Because selfhood—the site for the moment of the call and the belongingness—must first be set up for decision, the one who is in the crossing cannot know what comes unto him.

All "recourse" to what is past remains unproductive if it does not stem from the utmost decisions and instead only serves to avoid them by as much mixing as possible.

In and through mindfulness what necessarily happens is what is always-still-something-else, whose preparation is actually the issue but which would not find the site for enowning if there were no clearing for what is sheltered. Philosophy as self-mindfulness, in the way just indicated, is enactable only as inceptual thinking of the other beginning.

This self-mindfulness has left all "subjectivity" behind, including that which is most dangerously hidden in the cult of "personality." Wherever this has set in—and correspondingly the "genius" in art—everything moves, despite assurances to the contrary, in the track of modern thinking of "I" and consciousness. Whether one understands personality as the unity of "spirit-soul-body" or whether one turns this mix upside down and then, for example, puts the body first, this does not change anything in the dominating confusion of thinking that avoids every question. "Spirit" is thereby always taken to be "reason," as the faculty of being able to say "I." In this regard even Kant was further along than this biological liberalism. Kant saw that person is more than the "I"; it is grounded in self-legislation. Of course, this too remained Platonism.

And does one want to ground the ability to say I *biologically*? If not, then reversing this ability is just a game—what it is even without this reversal, because here unquestioningly the concealed metaphysics of "body," "sensibility," "soul," and "spirit" is presupposed.

Self-mindfulness as grounding selfhood occurs outside the doctrines just mentioned. Of course, this mindfulness is aware of the fact that something essential is decided, whether the question "who are we?" is asked or whether this question is not only held back but as such denied.

Not wanting to ask this question means either stepping aside from the truth about man in question here or disseminating the conviction that the question of who we are has been decided for all eternity.

If the latter is what happens, then all experiences and accomplishments are enacted only as *expression* of "life" that is "self" certain — and therefore can be believed to be organizable. In principle there are no experiences that ever set man beyond himself into an unentered domain from within which man as he is up to now could become questionable. That is — namely, that self-security — that innermost essence of "liberalism," which precisely for this reason has the appearance of being able to freely unfold and to subscribe to progress for all eternity. Thus "worldview," "personality," "genius," and "culture" are decorations and "values" to be realized, in whatever way.

At this point to ask the question "who are we?" is indeed *more dangerous* than any other opposition that we face on the same level of certainty about man (the final form of Marxism, which essentially has nothing to do with Judaism or with Russia; if anywhere a spiritualism still lies dormant and unevolved, then in the Russian people; Bolshevism is originally Western, a European possibility: the emergence of the masses, industry, technicity, the dying off of Christianity; but insofar as the dominance of reason as equalization of all people is merely the consequence of Christianity and Christianity is fundamentally of Jewish origins — cf. Nietzsche's thought on slave-rebellion in morality — Bolshevism is actually Jewish; but then Christianity is fundamentally Bolshevist! And then what decisions become necessary from this point on?).

But the dangerousness of the question "who are we?" — if danger is capable of en-forcing what is highest — is the one and only way to come to ourselves and thus to open the way for the originary saving, i.e., justifying the West through its history.

Dangerousness of this question is in itself so essential for us that it loses the semblance of being opposed to the new German will.

But as a philosophical question, it must be prepared for a long time to come and cannot — as it understands itself — lay claim to wanting immediately to replace, or even to determine, what at the moment is a necessary way of action.

Above all the question "who are we?" must remain purely and fully enjoined with the inquiry into the grounding question: How does be-ing hold sway?

20. The Beginning and Inceptual Thinking*

The beginning is what grounds itself as it reaches ahead: It grounds itself in the ground that is to be engrounded by the beginning; it

---

*On the "beginning," cf. lecture course SS 1932, *Der Anfang der abendländlischen Philosophie* (GA 35); rectoral address, *Die Selbstbehauptung der deutschen Universität* (GA 16); Freiburg lecture 1935, *Vom Ursprung des Kunstwerks* [GA 80].

reaches ahead as grounding and thus is unsurpassable. Because every beginning is unsurpassable, in being encountered it must be placed again and again into the uniqueness of its inceptuality and thus into its unsurpassable fore-grasping. When this encountering is inceptual, then it is originary—but this necessarily as *other* beginning.

Only what is unique is retrievable and repeatable. Only *it* carries within itself the ground of the necessity of going back to it and taking over its inceptuality. Repetition here does not mean the stupid superficiality and impossibility of what merely comes to pass as the *same* for a second and a third time. For beginning can never be comprehended as the *same,* because it reaches ahead and thus each time reaches beyond what is begun through it and determines accordingly its own retrieval.

What is inceptual is never that which is new, because this is merely the fleeting item of yesterday. Beginning is also never the "eternal," precisely because it is never removed or taken out of history.

But what is the beginning of thinking—in the sense of mindfulness of beings as such and of the truth of be-ing?

21. Inceptual Thinking*
(Projecting-Open)

En-thinking the truth of be-ing is essentially a projecting-open. What is ownmost to such a projecting-open is that, in enactment and unfolding, it must place itself back into what it opens up. Thus one might get the impression that, wherever a projecting-open prevails, things are arbitrary and ramble in what is ungrounded. But the projecting-open comes precisely to the ground and transforms itself first into a *necessity* to which it is related from the ground up—even though prior to its enactment the ground is still hidden.

The projecting-open of the essential sway of be-ing is merely a response to the call. When unfolded, the projecting-open loses every semblance of self-empowerment, without ever becoming self-effacement and surrender. What it opens up lasts only within the grounding that shapes history. What is opened up in the projecting-open overwhelms the projecting-open itself and rectifies it.

The projecting-open unfolds the thrower and at the same time seizes it within what opens up. This seizure that belongs to the essential projecting-open is the beginning of the grounding of the truth that has been achieved in the projecting-open.

What and who the thrower "is" is graspable only from within the truth of the projecting-open—while at the same time it is still sheltered. For this is what is most essential: that the opening as clearing brings the self-sheltering-concealing to pass and the sheltering of truth thus first

* Cf. Grounding.

of all receives its ground and spur (cf. Grounding, 244 and 245: Truth and Sheltering).

22. Inceptual Thinking

Inceptual thinking is enthinking of the truth of be-ing and thus engrounding of the ground. By resting on the ground, this thinking first of all manifests its grounding, gathering, and holding power.

But how is enthinking of be-ing a resting-on? By opening up what is most worthy of questioning, this thinking enacts the appreciation and thereby the highest transfiguration of that on which the question rests, i.e., does not *come to a stop.* For otherwise *it,* as an enopening questioning, could not rest on anything.

Resting-on means that questioning finds its way into the domain of the utmost resonance into belongingness as belonging to the utmost occurrence, which is the *turning in enowning* (cf. The Last God, 255: Turning in Enowning). This "finding-its way" happens in the leap, which unfolds as the grounding of Dasein.

23. Inceptual Thinking:
Why Thinking from within the Beginning?

Why a more originary retrieval of the first beginning?

Why the mindfulness of its history?

Why encountering its end?

Because the other beginning (from within the truth of being) has become necessary?

Why a beginning at all? (Cf. *Überlegungen* IV on the beginning and crossing.)

Because only the greatest occurrence, the innermost enowning, can still save us from being lost in the bustle of mere events and machinations. What must take place is enopening being for us and putting us back into this [being] and thus bringing us to ourselves and before the work and the sacrifice.

But now the greatest enowning is always the beginning—even if it is the beginning of the last god. For the beginning is what is *sheltered,* the origin that has not yet been misused and managed, the origin that is always withdrawing as it grasps far ahead and thus preserves within itself the highest reign. This unused-up power of the closure of the richest possibilities of courage (of the attuned-knowing will to enowning) is the only rescue and attestation.

For this reason *inceptual* thinking is necessary as an encounter between the first beginning, which still needs to be won back, and the other beginning, which is still to be unfolded. And within this necessity inceptual thinking yields the broadest, keenest, and steadiest mindfulness, blocking all evading of decisions and expedients.

Inceptual thinking appears to be standing completely off to the side as useless. And yet, if one wants to think usefulness, what is more useful than being saved unto being?

Accordingly, what is the *beginning,* that it can become what is most essential among all beings? It is the essential swaying of *being* itself. But *this* beginning first becomes enactable as the *other* beginning when the *first* beginning is put into proper perspective. Grasped inceptually, the beginning is be-ing itself. And in accordance with it *thinking* is also more originary than re-presenting and judging.

The *beginning* is *be-ing itself* as enowning, the hidden reign of the origin of the truth of beings as such. And be-ing as enowning is the beginning.

Inceptual thinking:

1. lets be-ing tower into beings, within the reticent saying of the grasping word—building on this mountain range.
2. prepares for this building by preparing for the other beginning.
3. commences the other beginning by putting the first beginning in proper perspective as it is more originarily retrieved.
4. is in itself *sigetic*—in the most enunciated mindfulness, precisely reticent.

The other beginning has to be realized totally from within be-ing as enowning and from the essential swaying of its truth and its [truth's] history (cf., e.g., the other beginning and its relationship to German Idealism).

Inceptual thinking locates its inquiry into the truth of be-ing *very far back* into the first beginning as the origin of philosophy. Thus it guarantees that in its other beginning it will come *from far away* and, by mastering the heritage, will find its utmost futural steadfastness—and thus will reach back to itself in a transformed necessity (over against the first beginning).

What is ownmost to inceptual thinking and what distinguishes it is its *masterful* sway, whereby the encounter with the highest and simplest is initially enforced and enacted. Inceptual thinking is masterful knowing. Whoever wants to go *very far back*—into the first beginning—must think ahead to and carry out a great future.

The claim of philosophical thinking can never be met by way of a prompt co-enactment that is common to all. It does not tolerate exploitations. Because such thinking thinks be-ing, i.e., what is most unique in its strangeness and most ordinary and familiar in the usual understanding of being, such thinking remains necessarily rare and foreign. But because it has this uselessness about it, it must immediately exact and affirm in advance those who can plow and hunt, who do manual labor and drive, who build and construct. This thinking itself must know that it can at any time count as unrewarded effort.

In the domain of the other beginning there is neither "ontology" nor anything at all like "metaphysics." No "ontology," because the guiding question no longer sets the standard or determines the range. No "metaphysics," because one does not proceed at all from beings as extant or from object as known (Idealism), in order then to *step over to* something else (cf. Playing-Forth). Both of these are merely transitional names for initiating an understanding at all.

What are the ways and directions for presenting and communicating the jointure of inceptual thinking? The first full shaping of the jointure (from Echo to The Last God) cannot avoid the danger of being read and acknowledged as a vast "system." Singling out individual questions (like the origin of the work of art) must renounce a uniform enopening and full shaping of the whole domain of jointure.

Enhancing both of these always remains a way taken in distress. But are there other ways in the epoch of distress? What good fortune here is preserved for the poet! Markings and images are what is most inner for him, and the overseeable shape of the "poem" is at any given time capable of putting into itself what is most essential to it.

But what about the case where the concept wants to measure the necessity and where the question wants to measure its direction?

24. The Wayward Claim on Inceptual Thinking

Such a claim is the demand that one should be able immediately to say where the decision lies (without putting up with distress); that one should indicate what is to be done without having grounded the historical place for future history from the ground up; that one should immediately accomplish a rescue, without its running into a will that reaches far out into a transformed setting of goals.

In taking a stand toward thinking, there are two *misestimations:*

1. an over-estimation, insofar as immediate answers are expected for a comportment that wants to spare itself a resolute openness to mindfulness and to staying in distress in the enactment of *questioning.*
2. an under-estimation, in that thinking is measured against ordinary re-presenting and thinking's power for grounding the time-space — the preparatory character — is misconstrued.

Whoever wants to be a teacher in the domain of inceptual thinking must possess the reservedness of being able to forego an "effect" and must not deceive himself with illusionary success of being famous and being talked about.

But inceptual thinking finds its most severe hindrance in the unexpressed self-understanding of humans today. Totally aside from individual interpretations and assignment of goals, a human being takes itself to be an extant "specimen" of the species "human." This is then transferred to historical being as an event within an unfolding belongingness. Wherever this interpretation of humanness (and along with it interpretation of being a people) prevails, there is lacking any point of engagement and any claim to an arrival of the god—not to mention the claim to the experience of the flight of gods. It is precisely this experience that presupposes that the historical human being knows itself to be removed unto the open midpoint of beings that are abandoned by the truth of their being.

Every waywardness of the claims stems from misconstruing the essential sway of truth as the clearing sheltering of the t/here [*Da*], which must be endured in the inabiding of questioning.

But every gathering unto a more originary belongingness *can* be prepared for the basic experience of Da-sein.

25. Historicity and Being

Historicity is understood here as *one* truth, the clearing sheltering of being as such. *Inceptual thinking* is enacted as historical; it co-grounds history through a self-joining injunction.

Mastery over the masses who have become free (i.e., rootless and self-seeking) has to be established and maintained with the fetters of "organization." Can what is organized in this way grow back into its originary soil—not only blocking what belongs to the masses but *transforming* it? Does this possibility still have any chance at all in the face of the growing "artificiality" of life, which renders easier and itself organizes that "freedom" of the masses, the arbitrary accessibility of all for all? No one should underestimate the importance of standing up to and resisting the unswerving uprooting. That is the first thing that must happen. But does that—and above all the means necessary to achieve it—guarantee the transformation of the uprootedness into a rootedness?

Here yet another mastery is needed, one which is sheltered and reserved, ongoingly sporadic and quiet. Here preparation is to be made for those who are to come, those who create new sites within being itself, from within which once again a stability in the strife of earth and world takes place.

Both forms of mastery—fundamentally different—must be wanted and *simultaneously* affirmed by those who know. Here is also a truth in which the essential sway of be-ing is intimated: the cleavage, swaying in be-ing, into the highest singularity and the most superficial generality.

26. Philosophy as Knowing Awareness

When *knowing as preserving* the truth of what holds true (preserving the essential sway of the truth in Da-sein) distinguishes future man (vis-à-vis the hitherto rational animal) and lifts him into the guardianship of be-ing, then the highest knowing is that which is strong enough to be the origin of a *renunciation*. We take renunciation, of course, as weakness and evasion, as suspension of the will; thus experienced, renunciation is giving-away and giving up.

But there is a renunciation that not only holds fast but also even gains by fighting and en-during, that renunciation that emerges as the pre-paredness for the *refusal,* for holding fast to this estranging that in such a shape sways as *be-ing itself*—that "in the midst of" of beings and of god-ding which makes room for the open between [*Zwischen*], in whose free-play of time-space the sheltering of the truth into beings and the flight and arrival of gods pulsate in each other. Knowing awareness of not-granting (Da-*sein* as renunciation) unfolds as the long preparation for the decision of truth, whether truth again becomes master of what holds true (i.e., holding true as "correct") or whether truth gets measured only according to what holds true and thus according to what is under truth— whether truth remains not only the goal of technical-practical knowing (a "value" and an "idea") but rather grounds the uproar of refusal.

This knowing awareness unfolds as enactment of a *questioning* that reaches far ahead into be-ing, whose question-worthiness forces all cre-ativity into distress, sets up a world for beings, and saves what of earth is reliable.

27. Inceptual Thinking
(Concept)

"Thinking" in the ordinary and long since customary determination is the re-presentation of something in its ἰδέα as the κοινόν, re-presenta-tion of something in general.

But, for one thing, this thinking relates to what is extant and already present (a definite interpretation of beings). But, for another, this thinking is always *supplementary* in that it provides what is already interpreted with only what is most general to it. This thinking rules in different ways in science. The grasp of the "general" is twofold, espe-cially since characterization of what is thought as κοινόν does not come originarily from the "general" but from the "many" and from "beings" (as μὴ ὄν). The *many* as starting point and the basic relation to the many are decisive and, initially—also within the standpoint of conscious-ness—*such* that it is an "*over-against*" without first properly being deter-mined and grounded in its truth. This is first to be achieved by means of the "general." How does this understanding of thinking, coupled with determining and obtaining "categories," become the criterion for the "form of thinking" called *assertion*?

This thinking was once—in the first beginning—still creative in Plato and Aristotle. But it *did* erect the realm in which from then on repre-sentation of beings as such was maintained and in which then the abandonment of being unfolded in ever more hidden fashion.

Inceptual thinking is the originary enactment of the onefold of echo, playing-forth, leap, and grounding. Enactment here wants to say that these—echo, playing-forth, leap, and grounding, in their onefold—are taken over and sustained in each case only in human terms, so that they themselves are always essentially an other and belong to the occurrence of Da-sein.

The keenness of saying in this thinking and the simpleness of the shaping word are measured by a conceptuality that rejects any mere acumen as empty obtrusiveness. What is grasped here—and what is only and always to be grasped—is be-ing in the joining of those join-tures. The masterful knowing of this thinking can never be said in a proposition. But what is to be known can just as little be entrusted to an indefinite and flickering representation.

Concept [*Begriff*] is here originally the "in-grasping" [*Inbegriff*], and this is first and always related to the accompanying co-grasping of the turning in enowning.

At first the ingrasping can be shown by the relation that each con-cept of being, *as concept*—i.e., in its truth—has to Da-sein, and thus to the inabiding of historical man. But insofar as Da-*sein* grounds itself first as belongingness to the call of the turning in enowning, the innermost in the *in*grasping lies in grasping the turning itself, i.e., in that knowing that sustains the distress of the abandonment of being and inheres in the preparedness for the call—in that knowing awareness that speaks by first keeping silent in Dasein's sustaining inabiding.

In-grasping here is never a comprehensive grasping in the sense of a species-oriented inclusiveness but rather the knowing awareness that comes out of *in*-abiding and brings the intimacy of the turning into the sheltering that lights up.

28. The Immeasurability of Inceptual Thinking as Finite Thinking

This thinking and the order it unfolds are outside the question of whether a system belongs to it or not. "System" is only possible as a consequence of the mastery of mathematical thinking (in its widest sense) (cf. WS 35/36*). A thinking that stands outside this domain and outside the corresponding determination of truth as certainty is there-fore essentially without system, un-systematic; but it is not therefore arbitrary and chaotic. Un-systematic would then merely mean some-thing like "chaotic" and disordered, if measured against system.

Inceptual thinking in the other beginning has a *rigor* of another kind: the freedom of joining its jointure. Here the one is joined to the other according to the mastery of the questioning-belonging to the call.

The rigor of reservedness is other than the "exactitude" of a "reason-ing" that is let loose, is indifferent, belongs to every man—a "reasoning"

---

* Lecture course WS 1935/36, *Die Frage nach dem Ding. Zu Kants Lehre von den transzen-dentalen Grundsätzen* (GA 41).

whose results are equally valid for every man and compelling for such certainty-claims. Here something is compelling only because the claim to truth is content with the *correctness* of derivation and of fitting into an established and calculable order. This contentment [is] the reason for the compelling.

29. Inceptual Thinking*
(The Question of What Is Ownmost)

In the domain of the guiding-question, comprehension of what is ownmost is determined from the point of view of beingness (οὐσία-κοινόν); and what is most ownmost lies in its greatest possible generality. Taken in the opposite direction, this says that the particular and the manifold, which come under and launch the concept of essence, are random. It is precisely the randomness of beings—a randomness that nevertheless and precisely indicates belonging to essence—that is essential.

On the other hand, when be-ing as enowning is grasped, what is ownmost is determined in terms of the originality and uniqueness of be-ing itself. What is ownmost is not what is general but rather precisely the essential swaying of the respective uniqueness and rank of a being.

The question of "what is ownmost" has in itself the character of decision [*Entscheidungshafte*], which now dominates the question of being from the ground up.

Projecting-open is setting rank and deciding.

The basic principle of inceptual thinking is thus twofold: Everything of the ownmost is essential swaying [*alles Wesen ist Wesung*].

All essential swaying is determined according to what is ownmost in the sense of what is originary and unique.

30. Inceptual Thinking
(As Mindfulness)

In enacting and preparing for echo and forth-play, inceptual thinking as mindfulness is essentially first of all crossing and as such a going-under.

In the crossing, mindfulness is enacted; and mindfulness is necessarily self-mindfulness. But this indicates that this thinking is still referentially dependent on us ourselves and thus on humans and requires a new determination of what is ownmost to humans. Insofar as this is launched in modernity as consciousness and self-consciousness, the mindfulness in crossing seems to have to become a new clarification of self-consciousness. Especially since we cannot simply take ourselves out of the present situation of self-consciousness, which is more like a

---

* Cf. in Leap: the be-ing of the essential sway.

calculation. Thus the basic experience of inceptual thinking is still a being in the sense of today's man and his situation and thus man's "reflection" on "self."

There is something correct in this deliberation, and yet it is not true. Insofar as history and historical mindfulness carry and rule humans, all mindfulness is *also* self-mindfulness. However, the mindfulness that is to be enacted in inceptual thinking does not assume that the *self*-being of today's humans can be immediately obtained by representing the "I" and the we and their situation. For the selfhood is precisely *not* obtained *thus* but rather definitively lost and distorted (cf. Grounding, 197: Da-sein—Ownhood—Selfhood).

The mindfulness of inceptual thinking is, on the other hand, so originary that it above all asks how the *self* is to be grounded, the self in whose domain "we," I and you, each come to *ourselves*. Thus it is questionable whether through reflection on "ourselves" we ever find our *self*, whether therefore Dasein's projecting-open ever has anything to do with the clarification of "self"-consciousness.

Now, it is not at all established that the "self" is ever determinable by way of representing the I. Rather it is important to recognize that selfhood first springs forth out of the grounding of Da-sein and that this grounding is enacted as enownment of belonging to the call. Thus the openness and grounding of the self springs forth from within and as the truth of be-ing (cf. Grounding, 197: Da-sein—Ownhood—Selfhood). It is neither the analysis of human beings in another direction nor the announcing of other ways of their being—all of which is, strictly speaking, improved anthropology—that brings about self-mindfulness; but rather it is the question of the truth of being that prepares the domain of selfhood in which man—we—historically effecting and acting and shaped as a people, first comes to his self.

Of course, the *ownness* of Da-sein as grounded in self-being can initially be indicated by crossing from the hitherto accepted I-oriented self-consciousness and only from that perspective; Da-sein is *always mine*. With that one must keep in mind that in Kant and German Idealism this I-oriented self-consciousness also already reached a totally new shape, in which a referential dependence on the "we," on the historical and the absolute, is co-established. Besides, with Da-sein the transference into the open is given at once. To want to find a "subjectivity" here, disregarding everything else, is always superficial.

The mindfulness of inceptual thinking has to do with us (ourselves) and then again not. *Not* with us, in order from here on to demarcate the decisive determinations, but *with us* as historical beings and indeed in the distress of the abandonment of being (initially the collapse [*Verfall*] of the understanding of being and forgottenness of being). With *us,* who are already exposed to beings, with us in this way, in order to find our way beyond ourselves to self-being.

The crossing character of inceptual thinking unavoidably brings this ambiguity with it, as if we are dealing with an anthropological, existentiell deliberation in the usual sense. But in truth every step is born up by the question of the truth of be-ing.

The look to *us* is enacted according to the *leap ahead into Da-sein.* But an initial *mindfulness* must, in the utmost ways of being human, try to distinguish the otherness of Dasein over against all "lived-experience" and "consciousness."

The temptation is still close at hand to take the entire deliberation in the first half of *Being and Time* as confined to the range of an anthropology, only with an other orientation.

31. The Style of Inceptual Thinking

Style is the self-certainty of Dasein in its grounding *legislation* and in its withstanding the fury.

The style of *reservedness* is the remembering awaiting of enowning, because reservedness thoroughly attunes the inabiding.

This reservedness also thoroughly attunes every strifing of the strife between world and earth.

Reservedness yields—in reticence—to the soft measure and carries out utter fury, both of which—belonging each to the other—meet up with each other in very different ways, from the earth as from world.

As grown certainty, *style* is the law of enactment of truth in the sense of sheltering in beings. Because art, for example, is setting-into-*work* of truth and because in the work the sheltering comes *in itself* to stand unto itself, therefore style is visible, although hardly understood—especially in the field of art. But the thinking about style is here *not* expanded further and transferred from art to Da-sein as such.

32. Enowning
A Decisive Glance *after* the Enactment
of Echo and Playing-Forth

The task is to see into and to follow in advance the relation of being and truth and the way in which from this point on *time and space,* in all strangeness, are grounded in their originary belonging-together.

Truth is sheltering that lights up, sheltering which occurs as removal-unto and charming-moving-unto. These, in their onefold as well as in their overflow, proffer the transposed open for the play of a being, which in the sheltering of its truth become a being as thing, tool, machination, work, deed, sacrifice.

But removal-unto and charming-moving-unto can also become solidified in an *indifference;* and then the open is held to be what is generally extant, what gives the appearance of being *a* being, because it is real. From the vantage point of this hidden indifference of the apparent lack of removal-unto and charming-moving-unto, the removal-unto and charming-moving-unto appear as exceptions and strange, whereas they indeed show the ground and essential sway of truth. That indifference is also the domain in which all re-presentation, meaning, all correctness, is played out (cf. Grounding: on *Space*).

That essential sway of truth, however, the removing-unto-charming-moving-unto clearing and sheltering as origin of the t/here [*Da*], sways in its ground, which we experience as en-ownment. The nearing and flight, arrival and departure, or the simple staying away of gods; for us in being master, i.e., as the beginning and being master over this happening, this inceptual mastery of the end will show itself as the last god. In its hinting, being itself, enowning as such, first lights up; and this lighting-up needs the grounding of the essential sway of truth as clearing and sheltering-concealing and [needs] their *final sheltering* in the altered shapes of beings.

What one otherwise and up to now has thoughrJ about space and time, which belong back into this origin of truth, is—as Aristotle for the first time worked out in the *Physics*—already a consequence of the previously established essence of beings as οὐσία and of truth as correctness and of all that which follows from that as "categories." When Kant calls space and time "intuitions," that is within this history only a weak attempt to rescue what is ownmost to space and time. But Kant had no access to the *essential sway* of space and time. In any case the orientation to "I" and "consciousness" and re-presentation mislays all the ins and outs.

Truth*

What was indicated about truth by means of the lectures on the work of art and what was seen as "arrangement" is already the *consequence* of the *sheltering* that actually preserves what is lit up and hidden. It is precisely this preserving that first of all lets beings *be*—and indeed *those* beings that they are and can be in the truth of the not-yet-differentiated being and the manner in which this truth is unfolded. (What counts as a being [*seiend*], something present, the "actual," [is] initially referred to only insofar as necessary and possible—the usual example from the history of the first beginning.)

The *sheltering* itself is enacted in and as Da-*sein*. And this occurs—gains and loses history—in the inabiding care [*Be-sorgung*] that belongs in advance to enowning but hardly knows it. This care is understood, not from everydayness but rather from the selfhood of Dasein; this care maintains itself in manifold ways, ways which require one another:

---

* Cf. Grounding.

tool-preparation, machination-arrangement (technicity), producing works, deeds that establish states, and thoughtful sacrifice. In all of them, though in different ways, there is a pre- and co-shaping of knowledge and essential knowing as the grounding of truth. "Science" [is] only a distant offshoot of a definite proliferation of tool-preparation, etc.; there is nothing independent [in science], and it is *never* to be brought into connection with the essential knowing of enthinking of being (philosophy).

But sheltering maintains itself not only in the ways of producing but also and originarily in the way of taking over the meeting of the lifeless with what lives: stone, plant, animal, human. Being-taken-back into the earth that is closed in upon itself—that is what happens here. But this happening of Da-sein is never for itself; rather it belongs with kindling the strife of earth and world, belongs in the inabiding in enowning.

Philosophy is finding the simple looks and secret shapes and letting them appear, in which appearance the essential swaying of be-ing is sheltered and lifted into the hearts.

Who can do *both:* the distant look into the most hidden essential sway of be-ing *and* the nearest prospering of the emerging shape of sheltering beings.

How do we, leaping in advance into the essential swaying of be-ing, create for this [be-ing] the rush of its beings, so that the truth of be-ing may preserve its historical staying power as thrust?

What remains for thinking is only the simplest saying of the simplest image in purest reticence. The future first thinker must be capable of this.

33. The Question of Be-ing

As long as we do not recognize that all calculating according to "purposes" and "values" stems from an entirely definite interpretation of beings (as ἰδέα), as long as we do not comprehend that hereby the *question* of be-ing is not even intimated, let alone asked, as long as in the end we do not testify by enactment that we know of the necessity of this unasked question and thus already ask it, as long as all of this remains *outside* the purview of that which still behaves like "philosophy"—just so long is all noisy talk of "be-ing," of "ontology," of "transcendence and paratranscendence," of "metaphysics," and of the assumed overcoming of Christianity without foundation and empty. Without knowing it, one *still* moves within the ruts of neo-Kantianism, which one gladly scolds. For nowhere is a work of thinking accomplished, and no steps of enopening questioning are taken.

Only the one who has grasped the question of being and has once really attempted to traverse its course can cease expecting anything from "antiquity" and its attendants—unless it be the terrible warning once again to relay questioning into the same ground of necessity—not that one-time necessity that *has* definitively *been* [*gewesen*] and only *thus* is swaying [*wesend*]. Rather *"retrieval"* here means to let the *same*, the uniqueness of be-ing, become a distress *again*—and that means *thus from a more originary truth.* "Again" here says precisely "totally other." But as of yet there is no hearing for that terrible warning and no will for sacrifice, for staying on the barely enopened next stretch of the way.

Instead of this, one deceives oneself and others about one's own perplexity by being *noisily* enthusiastic about the "antiquity" endured by Nietzsche.

To what extent, for example, does the figure and work of Hermann Lotze, the most genuine witness of the easily and much maligned nineteenth century, stand removed from such practices?

34. Enowning and the Question of Being

Enowning is that self-supplying and self-mediating midpoint into which all essential swaying of the truth of be-ing must be thought back in advance. This thinking thither and back in advance is the enthinking of be-ing. And all concepts of be-ing must be said from there.

Turned around: All that is initially thought about be-ing in distress and only in the *crossing* from the unfolded guiding-question to the grounding-question—and all that is inquired into as way to the truth of be-ing (the unfolding of Da-sein)—all this dare not be translated into the groundless desert of a traditional "ontology" and "doctrine of categories."

The unspoken intimating of enowning manifests itself in the foreground and simultaneously in historical remembering (οὐσία = παρουσία) as temporality [*Temporalität*]: the happening of the removal-unto which shelters what has been and anticipates what is to come, i.e., the enopening and grounding of the t/here [*Da*] and thus the essential sway of truth.

"Temporality" [*Temporalität*] is never meant as a correction of the concept of time, as the familiar substitution of the calculable time-concept with "experienced-time" (Bergson-Dilthey). All such [thinking] remains outside the acknowledged necessity of crossing from the guiding-question, conceived as such, to the grounding-question.

In *Being and Time* "time" is the *directive* to and *echo* of that which happens as the truth of the essential swaying of be-ing, in the uniqueness of en-ownment.

Only here, in this originary interpretation of time, does one reach the region where time along with space attain the most extreme differentness and thus precisely the most intimate essential swaying [*Wesungsinnigkeit*]. This relation [is] prepared for in the presentation of the spatiality of Da-sein, and not for example of the "subject" and of the "I" (cf. Grounding, Space).

In the confusion and lack of rigor in today's "thinking," one needs an almost scholastic grasping of thinking's ways in the shape of characterized "questions." Of course, the crucial will to thinking and its style never consist in a more *didactic* deliberation on these questions. But, in order to offer a clarification vis-à-vis the idle talk of "ontology" and of "being," one has to know the following:

A being is.

Be-ing holds sway.

"A being": This word names not only what is actual—and this only as extant and still only as object of knowledge—names not only what is actual of whatever kind, but rather also and at the same time names the possible, the necessary, and the accidental—everything that in any way whatsoever is in be-ing, including what is not and the nothing. Whoever, thinking himself quite clever, immediately discovers here a "contradiction"—because what is not cannot "be"—he always thinks way too short with his non-contradiction as the standard for what is ownmost to beings.

"Be-ing" means not only the actuality of the actual, and not only the possibility of the possible—and not at all only the being of a given being—but rather be-ing in its originary essential swaying in the full cleavage, where the essential swaying is not limited to "presence."

Of course the essential swaying of be-ing itself, and with that be-ing in its most unique uniqueness, cannot be experienced arbitrarily and just like beings but rather opens up only in the momentariness of Dasein's leap-ahead into enowning (cf. The Last God, 255: Turning in Enowning).

Also, there is no way that leads directly from the being of beings to *be-ing*, because the look to the being of beings already takes place outside the momentariness of Dasein.

Henceforth an essential differentiation and clarification can be brought into the question of being. Such clarification is never an answer to the question of being but rather only a thorough grounding of questioning, awakening and clarifying the *power* to question this question—which always arises out of Dasein's distress and upward swing.

If we inquire into beings as beings (ὄν ᾗ ὄν) and thus inquire into the being of beings in *this* starting point and direction, then whoever inquires stands in the realm of *the* question that guides the beginning of Western philosophy and its history up to its end in Nietzsche. Therefore we call *this* question concerning being (of beings) the guiding-question. Its most general form was formulated by Aristotle, as τί τὸ ὄν; What is a being, i.e., for Aristotle, what is οὐσία as the beingness of a being? Being here means *beingness*. This says at the same time that, despite rejection of the species-character, being (as beingness) is always and only meant as the κοινόν, i.e., what is common and thus common for every being.

On the other hand, if one inquires into be-ing, the approach here is not from beings, i.e., from this and that being respectively—and also not from beings as such in the whole—but rather the leap is enacted into the *truth* (clearing and sheltering) of be-ing itself. Here what is experienced and questioned is that which is hidden in the guiding-question and sways in advance: the *openness for essential swaying* as such, i.e., for *truth*. Along with what is asked here is the questioning that questions ahead into truth. And insofar as be-ing is experienced as the ground of beings, the question of the essential swaying of be-ing, when asked in this way, is the *grounding-question*. Going from the guiding-question to the grounding-question, there is never an immediate, equi-directional and continual process that once again applies the guiding-question (to be-ing); rather, there is only a leap, i.e., the necessity of an *other* beginning. Indeed and on the contrary, a *crossing* can and should be created in the unfolding overcoming of the posing of the guiding-question and its answers as such, a crossing that prepares the other beginning and makes it generally visible and intimatable. *Being and Time* is in service to this preparation, i.e., it actually stands already within the grounding-question, without unfolding this question purely out of itself, inceptually.

The *being* of beings, the determination of beingness (i.e., the declaration of "categories" for οὐσία), is the *answer* to the guiding-question. For the later, post-Greek history, various domains of beings become important in different ways; and the number and kind of categories and their "system" change. However, this point of departure remains essentially the same, whether it is rooted immediately in λόγος as assertion or as the result of definite transformations in consciousness and absolute spirit. From the Greeks to Nietzsche, the *guiding-question* defines the same manner of the question of "being." The clearest and best example of this unity in the tradition is Hegel's *Logic*.

For the grounding-question, on the other hand, being is neither the answer nor even the domain of the answer. Rather, being is what is most question-worthy. What fits being is an appreciation that leaps ahead and is unique, i.e., itself is opened up as *mastery* and thus is brought into the open as that which is not and can never be conquered. Be-ing as the ground in which all beings first of all and as such come to their truth (sheltering, arranging and objectivity); the ground in which beings sink (abground), the ground in which their *indifference* and *matter-of-factness* is also presumed (unground). That be-ing in its essential swaying sways in this way as ground shows its uniqueness and mastery. And this in turn is only the hint into enowning, wherein we have to seek the essential swaying of being in its supreme hiddenness. Be-ing as what is most question-worthy has in itself no question.

The guiding-question, when unfolded in its whole context, lets us always recognize a *grounding-stance* toward beings as such, i.e., a stance taken by the inquiring (man) on a ground that is not fully groundable as such out of the guiding-question and not knowable at all, but a ground that is brought into the open by the *grounding*-question.

Whereas a continuity from the guiding-question to the grounding-question is not possible, still, on the other hand, the unfolding of the grounding-question at the same time proffers the ground for taking the whole history of the guiding-question back into a more originary ownership—instead of perhaps discarding it as something merely in the past (cf. Playing-Forth, 92: Setting the First and the Other Beginning into Perspective).

35. Enowning

Mindfulness of the way [means asking]:
1. What inceptual thinking is.
2. How the other beginning is enacted as *reticence*.

"Enowning" would be the proper title for the "work" that here can only be prepared for; and therefore instead of that the title must be: *Contributions to Philosophy.*

The "work" is the self-unfolding structure in turning back into the towering ground.

36. Enthinking Be-ing and Language

The truth of be-ing cannot be said with the ordinary language that today is ever more widely misused and destroyed by incessant talking. Can this truth ever be said directly, if all language is still the language of beings? Or can a new language for be-ing be invented? No. And even if this could be accomplished—and even without artificial word-formation—such a language would not be a saying language. All saying has to let the ability to hear arise with it. Both must have the same origin. Thus only one thing counts: to say the most nobly formed language in its simplicity and essential force, to say the language of beings as the language of be-ing. This transformation of language pushes forth into domains that are still closed off to us, because we do not know the truth of be-ing. Thus speaking of "refusal of follow-through," "clearing of sheltering," "en-owning," "Da-sein," is not picking truths out of the words but rather opening up the truth of be-ing in such a transformed saying (cf. Preview, 38: Reticence in Silence).

37. Be-ing and Reticence in Silence*
(The Sigetic)

The grounding question is: *How does be-ing hold sway?*

Reticence in silence means mindful lawfulness of being reticent and silent (σιγᾶν). Reticence in silence is the "logic" of philosophy, insofar as philosophy asks the grounding-question from within the other begin-

---

* Cf. lecture course SS 1937, *Nietzsches metaphysische Grundstellung im abendländischen Denken. Die ewige Wiederkehr des Gleichen* (GA 44), the conclusion and *passim* on language.

ning. Philosophy looks for the *truth of the essential swaying* of be-ing, and this truth is the hinting-resonating hiddenness (mystery) of enowning (the hesitating refusal).

We can never say be-ing itself in any immediate way, precisely when it arises in the leap. For every saying comes from be-ing and speaks out of its truth. Every word and thus all logic stands under the power of be-ing. Hence what is ownmost to "logic" (cf. SS 34*) is the sigetic. What is ownmost to language is also grasped first of all in sigetic.

But "sigetic" is only a title for those who still think in "disciplines" and believe to have knowledge only when what is said is classified.

38. Reticence in Silence

The foreign word *sigetic* in its correspondence to "logic" (onto-*logy*) is meant here, retrospectively, only in the context of crossing and not at all as a mania for replacing "logic." Because the question of be-ing and the essential swaying of be-ing persist, this questioning is more originary and therefore less able to be locked into an academic discipline and to suffocate. We can never say be-ing (enowning) immediately — and thus also never say it mediately in the sense of an enhanced "logic" of dialectic. Every saying already speaks from within the truth of be-ing and can never immediately leap over to be-ing itself. Reticence in silence has a higher law than any logic.

In the end, however, reticence in silence is not an a-logic, which would like to be logic in a real sense but only cannot. On the contrary, the will and knowing of reticence in silence are oriented in a totally different direction. And just as little does it deal with the "irrational" and "symbols" and "ciphers," all of which presuppose traditional metaphysics. On the other hand, reticence in silence includes the logic of beingness, in the same way as the grounding-question transforms in itself the guiding-question.

Reticence in silence stems from the swaying origin of language itself.

The basic experience is not the assertion or the proposition, and consequently not the principle — be it "mathematical" or "dialectical" — but rather the reservedness that holds unto itself over against the hesitating self-refusal in the truth (clearing of sheltering) of *distress*, from which the necessity of *decision* arises (cf. Preview, 46: Decision).

Whenever this reservedness comes to word, what is said is always enowning. But to understand this saying means to enact the projecting-open and to execute knowing's leap into enowning. Saying grounds as reticence in silencing. Its word is not somehow only a sign for something totally other. What it names is what it means. But "meaning" is owned up to only as *Da-sein* and that means in thinking-questioning.

---

*Lecture course SS 1934, *Über Logik als Frage nach der Sprache* (GA 38).

Reticence in silence and enactment of questioning is putting the essential questioning up for deciding what is ownmost to truth.

The search for be-ing? The originary find is in originary seeking.

Seeking is already holding-oneself-in-the-truth, in the open of self-sheltering and self-withdrawing. Originary seeking is the grounding relation to hesitating *refusal*. Seeking as questioning and nevertheless reticence in silencing.

Whoever seeks has already found! And originary seeking is that engrasping of what has already been found, namely the self-sheltering as such.

Whereas ordinary seeking first finds and has found by ceasing to search.

Therefore the originary find in the originary sheltering is sheltered precisely as seeking as such. Acknowledging what is most question-worthy [means] staying in the questioning and inabiding.

39. Enowning

This is the essential title for the attempt at inceptual thinking. The *public* title, however, has to be: *Contributions to Philosophy.*

Projecting-open intends to be a *jointure* of inceptual thinking, i.e., that which can be willed solely in the attempt at this thinking and which knows little about itself.

That is to say:

1. In the structure nothing of *the rigor of jointure* is left out, as if what counts—and what always counts in philosophy—is the impossible: to grasp the truth of be-ing in the completely unfolded fullness of what is ownmost to it in its groundedness.

2. Here is allowed only the *access* to *one* way which an individual can open, foregoing a survey of the possibility of other perhaps more essential ways.

3. The attempt has to be clear that both, the jointure and the access, remain an *endowment* of be-ing itself, of the hint and withdrawal of its truth—something not forceable.

The jointure in this threefold sense must be attempted, so that something more essential and more successful—endowed to those who are to come— [can] be attempted, something from which a leap may be made— a leap joined and enjoined in anticipation, in order to be overcome.

If this being-overcome is genuine and necessary, then it has the greatest yield; it first of all allows a thinking attempt to stand historically in its futurality and to stand out into the future and inevitability.

The jointure is something essentially other than a "system" (cf. WS 35/36 and 36*). "Systems" are only possible—and toward the end

---

* Lecture course WS 1935/36, *Die Frage nach dem Ding. Zu Kants Lehre von den transzendentalen Grundsätzen* (GA 41) and lecture course 1936, *Schelling: Über das Wesen der menschlichen Freiheit* (GA 42).

become necessary—in the domain of the history of responses to the guiding-question.

Each of the six joinings of the jointure stands for itself, but only in order to make the essential onefold more pressing. In each of the six joinings the attempt is made always to say the same of the same, but in each case from within another essential domain of that which enowning names. Seen externally and fragmentarily, one easily finds "repetitions" everywhere. But what is most difficult is purely to enact in accord with the jointure, a persevering with the same, this witness of the genuine inabiding of inceptual thinking. On the other hand, it is easy to progress continuously in the sequence of "materials" that offer themselves in constantly differing ways because that progression comes "naturally."

Every joining stands for itself, and yet there is a hidden inter-resonating and an enopening grounding of the site of decision for the essential crossing into the still possible transformation of Western history.

Echo carries far into what has been and what is to come—hence in and through the playing-forth its striking power on the present.

Playing-forth receives its necessity primarily from the echo of the distress of the abandonment of being.

Echo and playing-forth are the soil and field for inceptual thinking's first leaping off for *leaping* into the essential swaying of be-ing.

The leap first of all opens up the ungone expanses and concealments of that into which the *grounding* of Da-sein, which belongs to the call of enowning, must press forth.

All of these joinings must be sustained in such a onefold, from within the inabiding in Da-sein, which distinguishes the being of *those who are to come.*

Those who are to come take over and preserve belongingness to enowning and its turning, a belongingness that has been awakened by the call. They come thus to stand before the hints of the *last god.*

The jointure is the conjoining that enjoins the call and thus grounds Da-sein.

40. The Work of Thinking in
the Epoch of the Crossing

The work of thinking in the epoch of the crossing (cf. *Überlegungen* IV, 90) can only be and must be a *passage* in both senses of the word: a going and a way at the same time—thus a way that itself goes.

Can one give shape to this in saying, so that the simplicity of this task comes to light? Does this correspond to the jointure "From Enowning"? Who wants to know this? But only for that reason is it to be wagered.

Will this attempt ever find its expounder? The one who can speak of the way that goes into and prepares for what is futural? But not the one who calculates out of it only what belongs to much of today and thus "explains" and destroys everything.

41. Every Saying of Be-ing Is Kept in
Words and Namings

Every saying of be-ing is kept in words and namings which are under-standable in the direction of everyday references to beings and are thought exclusively in this direction, but which are misconstruable as the utterance of be-ing. Therefore it is not as if what is needed first is the fail-ure of the question (within the domain of the thinking-interpretation of be-ing), but the word itself already discloses something (familiar) and thus hides that which has to be brought into the open through thinking-saying.

This difficulty cannot be eliminated at all; even the attempt to do so already means misunderstanding all saying of be-ing. This difficulty must be taken over and grasped in its essential belongingness (to the thinking of be-ing).

This conditions an approach that within certain limits must extend to ordinary understanding and must go a certain stretch of the way *with* it—in order then at the right moment to exact a turning in thinking, but only under the power of the same word. For example, "decision" can and should at first be meant as a human "act"—not of course in any moral sense but still in terms of enactment—until it suddenly means the essential sway of be-ing. This does not mean that be-ing is inter-preted "anthropologically" but the reverse: that man is put back into the essential sway of be-ing and cut off from the fetters of "anthropol-ogy." In the same way, "machination" means a way of human comport-ment—and suddenly and properly the reverse: what is ownmost (or precisely *not* ownmost) to be-ing, within which first of all the ground for the possibility of "operations" is rooted.

This "reverse," however, is not simply a "formal" trick to alter the meaning into mere words but rather *transformation of man himself.*

However, the proper comprehension of this transformation and above all of the scope of its happening—and that means: its grounding—is inti-mately bound to the knowing awareness of the truth of be-ing.

The transformation of man here means becoming other in what is ownmost to him, insofar as in the hitherto accepted interpretation (*ani-mal rationale*) the relation to beings is included, though psychologically hidden and misconstrued, but not grounded and unfolded as the ground of what is ownmost. For this includes asking the question of the truth of being and includes "metaphysics."

In being-historical thinking the essential power of the not-character and of turning around first comes free.

42. From "Being and Time" to "Enowning"

On this "way"—if stumbling and getting up again can be called that—the same question of the "meaning of be-ing" is always asked, and *only* this question. And therefore the locations of questioning are constantly different. Each time that it asks more originarily, every essential questioning must transform itself from the ground up. Here there is no gradual "development." Even less does that relationship exist between what comes later and what is earlier, according to which what is earlier already includes what comes later. Because in the thinking of be-ing everything steers toward what is unique, stumblings are, as it were, the rule! This also averts the historical [*historisch*] approach, which gives up what is earlier as "false" or proves what comes later as "already meant" in what is earlier. The "changes" are so essential that their full import can only be determined when each time the *one* question is thoroughly asked from its questioning location.

The "changes," however, are not conditioned from the outside, by means of objections. For up until now no objection has become possible, because the question has not yet been grasped at all. The "changes" stem from the growing abground character of the be-ing question itself, in which every historical [*historisch*] support is taken away from this question. Therefore, however, the *way* itself becomes more and more essential, not as "personal development," but as the exertion of man—understood totally nonbiographically—to bring be-ing itself within a being to its truth.

Here something is merely repeated that since the end of the first beginning of Western philosophy, i.e., since the end of metaphysics, must be always more decisively owned up to, namely that thinking of be-ing is not a "doctrine" and not a "system," but rather must become actual history and thus what is most hidden.

This happens for the first time as the thinking of Nietzsche; and what comes to us as "psychology" and as *self-analysis* and undoing and *"Ecce homo,"* with all the contemporaries of that desolate time—all of this has its actual truth as the history of thinking, a thinking that with Nietzsche still *seeks* what is to be thought and still finds it in the sphere of the *metaphysical* way of putting the question (will to power and eternal recurrence of the same).

In the attempts since *Being and Time* the question is indeed put forth *more originarily,* but everything is kept in more modest measure—if one can compare measures at all.

Enactment of the being-question allows for no imitation. Here the necessities of the way are each time historically first, because unique. Whether these necessities, seen "historically" [*historisch*], are "new" and "actual" is here not even a possible perspective for judging.

The historical mastery over the history of Western thinking becomes increasingly important, and dissemination of a "merely historical" or "systematic" erudite philosophy becomes increasingly impossible.

For what counts is not to voice new representations of beings but rather to ground human *being* in the truth of be-ing and to prepare for this grounding by enthinking be-ing and Da-sein.

This preparation does not consist in acquiring preliminary cognitions as the basis for the later disclosure of actual cognitions. Rather, here preparation is: opening the way, yielding to the way—essentially, *attuning*. But again, not as if what is thought and to be thought is merely an indifferent occasion for setting *thinking* in *motion*. Rather the truth of be-ing, the knowing awareness of mindfulness, is what counts.

But the pathway of this enthinking of be-ing does not yet have a firm line on the map. The territory first comes to be *through the pathway* and is unknown and unreckonable at every stage of the way.

The more genuinely the way of enthinking is the way to be-ing, the more unconditionally is it attuned to and determined by be-ing itself.

Enthinking is not thinking-out and haphazard invention but rather [is] that thinking that through questioning places itself before be-ing and demands of be-ing that it attune the questioning, all the way through.

But in enthinking of be-ing, beings in the whole must be put up for decision every time. In each case this succeeds only in *one* purview and turns out to be all the more needy, the more originarily the hinting of be-ing strikes this thinking.

The territory that comes to be through and as the way of enthinking of be-ing is the *between* [*Zwischen*] that *en-owns* Da-sein to god; and in this enownment man and god first become "recognizable" to each other, belonging to the guardianship and needfulness of be-ing.

43. Be-ing and Decision

Being used by gods, shattered by this heightening, in the direction of what is sheltered-concealed, we must inquire into the essential sway of be-ing *as such*. But we cannot then explain be-ing as a supposed addendum. Rather, we must grasp it as the origin that *de-cides* gods and men in the first place and *en-owns* one to the other.

This inquiring into be-ing opens up the free-play of the time-space of its essential swaying: the grounding of Da-sein.

When we speak here of de-cision, we think of an activity of man, of an enactment, of a process. But here neither the human character in an activity nor the process-dimension is essential.

Actually it is hardly possible to come close to what is ownmost to decision in its be-ing-historical sense without proceeding from men, from us, without thinking of "decision" as choice, as resolve, as preferring one thing and disregarding another, hardly possible in the end not to approach freedom as cause and faculty, hardly possible not to push the question of decision off into the "moral-anthropological" dimension; indeed it is hardly possible not to grasp this dimension anew in the "existentiell" sense.

The danger of misinterpreting *Being and Time* in this direction, i.e., "existentiell-anthropologically," and of seeing the interconnection of disclosedness, truth, and Dasein from the perspective of a moral resolve—instead of *the other way,* proceeding from the prevailing ground of Da-sein and grasping truth as openness and dis-closedness, as temporalizing-spatializing of the free play of the time-space of be-ing—such danger looms and gets stronger by many things that are unaccomplished in *Being and Time.* But this misinterpretation is basically excluded (although not in the overcoming that is worked out), if from the beginning we hold on to the grounding-question of the "meaning of be-ing" as the *only* question.

Thereupon what is called here de-cision shifts into the innermost swaying mid-point of be-ing itself and then has nothing in common with what we call making a choice and the like. Rather, it says: the very going apart, which divides and in parting lets the en-ownment of precisely this *open* in parting come into play as the clearing for the still un-decided self-sheltering-concealing, man's belongingness to be-ing as founder of be-ing's truth, and the allotment of be-ing unto the time of the last god.

In the thinking of modernity we set out from ourselves and, when we think away from ourselves, always only come upon objects. We hasten back and forth to and with this familiar way of re-presenting and explain everything in its context, never pondering whether, underway, this way might not allow a leap-off [*Absprung*] by which we first of all leap into the "space" of be-ing and give rise to de-cision.

Even if we leave behind the "existentiell" misunderstanding of "decision," still the danger of another misunderstanding looms before us, one which, of course, is today readily thrown together with the preceding one.

What lies in the dimension of decision as "will-oriented" and "power-driven" could be understood in contrast to "system" by referring to Nietzsche's word: "The will to system means a lack of uprightness" (VIII, 64).[1] However, to clarify this opposition is necessary, because decision does come into opposition to "system," but in a more essential sense than Nietzsche himself saw. For to Nietzsche "system" is still always the object of "system-building," of the subsequent putting together and ordering. But even if we grant Nietzsche a more appropriate comprehension of the essence of system, we must say that he did not and could not grasp this essence, because for his inquiry he himself had still to affirm *that* understanding of "being" (of beings) on whose basis and as whose unfolding "system" arises: the *representedness* of beings as anticipatory unifying, re-presenting of the objectivity of the object (the essential clarification in Kant's determination of the transcendental). "Ordering" and surveyability (not the *ordo* of the Middle Ages) first *follow* from the

---

[1] F. Nietzsche, *Götzen-Dämmerung*, in: *Nietzsche's Werke (Großoktavausgabe)* (Leipzig: Kröner, 1919), VIII, 64.

system-dimension; they are not its essence. And in the end even "system" belongs to *uprightness,* not only as its inner fulfillment but as its presupposition. However, by "uprightness" Nietzsche means something else, just as with "system" he does not penetrate into what is *ownmost* to modernity. It is not enough to grasp "system" merely as a peculiarity of modernity; that can be correct, and modernity may still be grasped superficially.

And so it came about that Nietzsche's words about "system" have been readily abused as threadbare justifications of feebleness for a thinking intent upon going far ahead and through dark passages. Or at least one has rejected "system" as a marginal figure in favor of a "systematic" which nevertheless presents only the form of "scientific" thinking that has been borrowed for philosophical thinking.

When "decision" comes to stand over against "system," then that is the crossing from modernity into the other beginning. Insofar as "system" contains the essential designation of beingness of beings (representedness) in modernity, while "decision" means being for beings and not only beingness in terms of beings, then de-cision is in a certain manner "more systematic" than any system, i.e., it indicates an originary determination of beings as such from within the essential sway of be-ing. In that case not only the "system-building" but also the "systematic" thinking is still easily founded on a secured interpretation of beings, over against the task of inquiring into the truth of be-ing, into the thinking of de-cision.

But initially we think "decision" as what comes to the fore within an either-or polarity.

And it is advisable to prepare the originary being-historical interpretation of *decision* by means of indicating "decisions" that arise as historical necessities out of that de-cision.

The prolonged and not only modern habituation in the whole of Western thinking to what is superficial about man (as *animal rationale*) makes it difficult to say words and concepts of a seemingly established anthropological-psychological content from out of a totally different truth and for the sake of grounding this other truth, without avoiding the anthropological misinterpretation, as well as the convenient rebuttal that *everything* is in the end "anthropological." The cheapness of this objection is so boundless that it has to be suspect. At its basis lies the fact that one never *wants* to put man into question, i.e., put oneself into question—perhaps because one is secretly not at all that fully certain of the anthropological glory of man.

44. The "Decisions"

whether man wants to remain a "subject," *or* whether he founds Da-sein—
    whether with subject the "*animal*" should continue to remain as

"substance" and the *"rational"* as "culture," *or* whether the truth of be-ing (see below) finds in Dasein an evolving site—

whether beings take being as what is "most general" to them and thus hand being over to "ontology" and bury it, *or* whether be-ing in its uniqueness comes to word and thoroughly attunes beings as happening but once—

whether truth as correctness degenerates into the certainty of representation and the security of calculating and lived-experience, *or* whether the inceptually ungrounded essential sway of ἀλήθεια as the clearing of self-sheltering-concealing comes to be grounded—

whether beings as what is most obvious consolidate everything mediocre, small, and average into what is rational, *or* whether what is most question-worthy makes up the purity of be-ing—

whether art is an exhibition for lived-experience *or* the setting-into-work of truth—

whether history is degraded to the arsenal of confirmations and pioneering *or* surges as the mountain train of the estranging and unclimbable mountains—

whether nature is degraded to the realm of exploitation by means of calculation and ordering, degraded to an occasion for "lived-experience," *or* whether as self-closing earth it bears the open of the imageless world—

whether de-deification of beings celebrates its triumphs in the Christianization of culture, *or* whether the distress of undecidability of the nearness and remoteness of gods prepares a "space" for decision—

whether man ventures be-ing and thus the going under, *or* whether he is satisfied with beings—

whether man still ventures decision *at all, or* whether he relinquishes himself into undecidedness, which the epoch construes as the state of the "utmost" activity.

All of these decisions, which seem to be many and varied, are gathered into one thing only: whether be-ing definitively withdraws, *or* whether this withdrawal as refusal becomes the first truth and the other beginning of history.

What is most difficult and magnificent about the decision *for* be-ing remains closed off by staying invisible; and should it ever exhibit itself, it is unhesitatingly misinterpreted and thus actually protected from every vulgar touch.

Why must decisions be made at all? If so, then they are necessities that belong to our epoch—not only as these specific decisions, but as decisions in general.

What is decision here [in our epoch]? What is ownmost to decision is determined by what is ownmost to crossing from modernity into what is other than modernity. Does decision thereby *determine* its ownmost, or is crossing only a hint of what is ownmost? Do the "decisions" arrive because there must be an other beginning? And must the other beginning be because the essential sway of be-ing is the very de-cision and, in this unfolding of what is its ownmost, gifts its truth for the first time to the history of man?

It is necessary here perhaps to say, even somewhat extensively, what is *not* meant with the words *truth of be-ing.*

The expression does not mean "truth" "about" be-ing, as if it were the conclusion of correct propositions about the concept of be-ing or were an irrefutable "doctrine" of be-ing. Even if such would be appropriate for be-ing (which is impossible), one would have to presuppose, not only *that* there is a "truth" about be-ing, but above all of what kind that truth really is, the truth in which be-ing comes to stand. But from where else should what is ownmost to *this* truth and thus to truth as such be determined, except from be-ing itself? And that not only in the sense of a "derivation" from be-ing, but in the sense of effecting this "ownmost" by be-ing—such an effecting in terms of which we cannot access be-ing through any "correct" notions but rather one that belongs solely to the sheltered moments of being-history.

But the expression also does not mean "true" be-ing, as in the unclear meaning of "true" beings in the sense of true or actual. For here once again a concept of "actuality" is presupposed and laid at the foundation of be-ing as a measure, whereas be-ing not only grants to beings what they are but also and primarily unfolds for itself that truth that is appropriate for what is ownmost to be-ing.

This truth of be-ing is in no way something different from be-ing, but rather its own essential sway. Hence it depends on the history of be-ing, whether be-ing gifts or refuses itself and this truth and thus first of all actually conveys into its history what is of abground. This indication that the current concepts of "truth" and the current failure to differentiate "being" and "beings" lead to a misinterpretation of the truth of be-ing and above all *always already presuppose* this truth—this very indication can still deteriorate into a mistake if it accepts the conclusion that what counts is to state the unstated "presuppositions," as if *pre*suppositions could be graspable without what is posited *as* such having already been grasped. Within beings and the interpretation of beings unto their beingness in the sense of representedness (and already of ἰδέα), it makes sense and is correct to go back to "presuppositions" and "conditions." Such a return, therefore, has become the basic form of "metaphysical" thinking in manifold modifications, to such a degree that even the overcoming of "metaphysics" toward an inceptual understanding cannot do without this way of thinking (cf. *Being and Time* and *Vom Wesen des Grundes, here* the attempt at a leap into be-ing).

As long as "be-ing" is grasped as beingness, as what is somehow "general" and thus as a condition for beings inserted behind beings, i.e., condition for their representedness and objectness, and finally for their being "in-themselves," be-ing itself is lowered to the truth of beings, to the correctness of re-presentation.

Because all of this is accomplished in its purest form in Kant, one *can* attempt to make manifest with his work something even more originary and thus not derivable from that work, something totally other, but at the risk that such an attempt will be read again in a Kantian way and be misinterpreted and made harmless as an arbitrary "Kantianism."

The Western history of Western metaphysics is both "proof" for the fact that the truth of be-ing could not become a question *and* the directive for grounding this impossibility. But the grossest misunderstanding of the truth of be-ing would reside in a "logic" of philosophy. For this "logic" is the deliberate or undeliberate relaying of "theory of knowledge" back unto itself. "Theory of knowledge" is, however, only the form of perplexity of modern metaphysics about itself. The confusion reaches its culmination when this "theory of knowledge" in turn is passed off as "metaphysics of knowledge" and when calculating on the slide-rule of "aporetic" and "aporetic" discussion of the very extant "directions" and "problem-areas" becomes rightfully *the* method of the most modern erudite philosophy. These things are simply the last off-shoots of the process by which philosophy loses what is its ownmost and deteriorates into the crudest ambiguity, because what philosophy seems to be *can no longer* be unequivocal for the one who knows. And therefore all attempts to say what the truth of be-ing is *not* must have come to terms with the fact that at most they give new nourishment to the ignorant willfulness in further misinterpretation—in case such elucidations believe that through *instruction* non-philosophy could become transformed into philosophy. But, to be sure, since mindfulness of what the truth of be-ing is *not* is essentially an *historical* mindfulness, it has as its task, insofar as it can, to make the basic movements in the basic metaphysical positions of Western thinking more transparent and the shelteredness of being-history more penetrating.

In all of this, of course, we are also saying that, in the genuine sense of the word, any rejection of philosophy as operational [*Betrieb*] has its necessity only when it has recognized that mindfulness of the truth of be-ing includes a transformation of the cogitating attitude into a thinking comportment—a transformation which, of course, cannot be brought about by moral instructions, but rather must be *pre*-transformed, and indeed in the openness [*Öffentlichkeit*] of what is unmanifest and free of noise.

Why is the *truth* of be-ing not an addendum or a frame for be-ing and also not a presupposition but rather the very essential sway of be-ing itself?

Because the essential sway of be-ing sways in the en-ownment of de-cision. But from where do we know this? We do not know it, but rather enquire it, and in so doing open up for be-ing the site—perhaps even a site exacted by be-ing—in case be-ing's essential sway should be refusal, to which questioning, even as it does not reach far enough, remains the only appropriate nearness.

And therefore for a long time to come every creating that grounds Da-sein (and *only* this creating, not the everyday rigid operation of arranging beings) must awaken the truth of be-ing as question and as distress, all the way through the most crucial pathways and in fluctuating and seemingly disconnected starts unknown to one another. Every creating that grounds Da-sein must also prepare *for* the stillness of be-ing but also decidedly *against* any attempt to confuse and weaken the relentless distressing into the distress of mindfulness by merely wanting to go backwards, even to the "most valuable" traditions.

To be aware of the persistent thoughtfulness of what is rare belongs to guardianship of be-ing, whose essential sway radiates as truth itself, in the darkness of its own glow.

The truth of be-ing is the be-ing of truth. Said in this way, it sounds like an artificial and forced reversal and—taken to the extreme—like a seduction to a dialectical game. However, this reversal is only a fleeting and external sign of the *turning* that sways in be-ing itself and throws light on what might be meant here with decision.

45. The "Decision"

The decision that has long ago broken out within hiddenness and disguise is the one of history or loss of history. But *history [Geschichte]* understood as the strifing of the strife of earth and world, taken over and enacted from belongingness to the call of enowning as the essential swaying of the truth of be-ing in the shape of the last god.

The decision is made when the necessity of the utmost *mandate* from within the innermost distress of abandonment of being is experienced and empowered unto endurable power.

But in the light and path of decision the *mandate* is: *sheltering the truth of enowning out of the reservedness of Dasein into the great stillness of be-ing.*

By what means is the decision made? By the *granting* or *staying away* of those outstanding ones marked as—or that we call—"the ones to come," distinguished from the many random and unending ones who come later but who have nothing more ahead of them and nothing more behind them.

These so marked include:

1. *Those few individuals* who, on the essential paths of grounding Dasein (poetry—thinking—deed—sacrifice), prepare in advance the sites and moments for the domains of beings. They thus create

the swaying possibility for the various shelterings of truth in which Da-sein becomes historical.

2. *Those many allied ones* to whom it is given to intimate and to make manifest, in enactment, the laws of recasting beings, of the preservation of earth and projecting-open of world in the strife of earth and world—by grasping the knowing-willing and the groundings of the individuals.

3. *Those many who are interrelated* by their common historical (earth- and world-bound) origins, through whom and for whom the recasting of beings and with that the grounding of the truth of enowning achieves durability.

4. *The single ones, the few, the many* (not taken in a quantitative sense but in respect to their being marked) still stand partly in the old and current and planned arrangements. These arrangements are either only the husk of a protection for their endangered existence or still the guiding forces of their willing.

The *consent* of the single ones, the few, and the many is hidden, is not produced, is sudden, and grows by itself.

It is dominated through and through by the always different reigning of enowning, in which an originary gathering is prepared—a gathering in and as which what dares to be called a *people* becomes historical.

5. In its origin and destiny this people is singular, corresponding to the singularity of be-ing itself, whose truth this people must ground but once, in a unique site, in a unique moment.

How can this decision be prepared? Do knowing and willing here have a place at their disposal, or would that be merely a blind grabbing into hidden necessities?

But necessities light up only in distress. And the preparing of preparation for decision indeed rests in the distress of finally only accelerating the growing lack of history and the distress of hardening its conditions, whereas this preparation wants something else.

Whoever does not know of *this* distress has no inkling at all of the decisions that are ahead of us.

The decision is made in stillness. But in this way the destruction of the possibility of decision follows all the more, through the threatening unrelenting uprooting.

The more the events of the "world-historical" upheavals need the noise, and the more exclusively all listening and hearkening appeals only to the gigantic and the loud and lets everything that is set over against that, even the great stillness, sink into nothingness, all the more difficult is it to perceive the decision and its necessity and even the preparation for it.

The "world-historical" events can take on proportions never before seen. This at first speaks only for the growing frenzy let loose in the domain of machinations and numbers. It never speaks immediately for the emergence of essential decisions. But when a gathering of the people, or its existence [*Bestand*], is established unto itself in these events — and partly according to their style — could not a way open up there, a way into the nearness of decision? Certainly, but with the utmost danger of completely missing the domain of decision.

The decision must create *that time-space*, the site for the essential moments, where the most serious mindfulness, along with the most joyful mission, grows into a will to found and build — a will which is not exempt from chaos. Only Da-sein — and never "doctrine" — can bring about the transforming of beings from the ground up. As ground for a people, such Da-sein needs a very long preparation in terms of inceptual *thinking*; but this always remains only *one* way of *recognizing* the distress — one way among many ways commencing simultaneously.

Does decision once again bring on the grounding of the site for the moment of grounding the truth of be-ing? Or does everything roll on simply as a "struggle" for the barest conditions for continuing life and surviving in gigantic proportions, so that "worldview" and "culture" are *themselves* only props and means for this "struggle"? What is being prepared for *then*? The *transition to a technicized animal*, which begins to replace the instincts, which have already grown weaker and less refined by the gigantism of technicity.

What is characteristic of this direction of decision is not the technicizing of "culture" and imposition of "worldview." Rather, characteristic of this direction is that "culture" and "worldview" become the means for the strategy of struggle for a will that no longer wants a goal; for, preservation of a people is never a possible goal but only the condition for setting goals. But if the condition becomes unconditioned, then what comes to power is not-wanting a goal and cutting off any mindfulness that reaches ahead. In the end, then, the possibility of knowing that "culture" and "worldview" are already offshoot of a world-order that supposedly should be overcome — this possibility disappears. By being utilized politically, "culture" and "worldview" do not lose their character — whether they are seen as values "in themselves" or as values *"for"* the people. Every time mindfulness — if it is that at all — is rigidly constrained in not-wanting originary goals, i.e., in not-wanting the truth of be-ing, through which the possibility and necessity of "culture" and "worldview" is first decided.

Only the utmost decision from within and about the truth of be-ing still brings about clarity; otherwise what remains is the continual dawning of renovations and disguises, or even a total collapse.

Presumably all of these possibilities still have their long pre-history, in which they still remain unrecognizable and misconstruable.

But from where does future philosophy receive its distress? Must it not itself awaken this distress—inceptually? This distress is other than misery and grief, which always haunts only some corner or other of solidified beings and their "truth." This distress, on the other hand, cannot be eliminated—and even be denied—by the cheerfulness of a supposed delight in the "wonders" of "beings."

As ground for the necessity of philosophy, this distress is experienced by startled dismay in the jubilation of belongingness to being, which as hinting moves abandonment of being into the open.

46. Decision
(Fore-Grasping)

Decision about what? About history or loss of history, i.e., about belongingness to be-ing or abandonment in non-beings.

Why decision, i.e., on account of what? Can that be decided?

What *is* decision at all? Not *choice*. Choosing always involves only what is pregiven and can be taken or rejected.

De-cision here means grounding and creating, disposing in advance and beyond oneself or giving up and losing.

But is that not here and everywhere a presumption and impossibility at the same time? Does not history [*Geschichte*] come and go, hidden as to how it goes? Yes and no.

Decision comes about in the stillest stillness and has the longest history.

Who decides? Everyone, even in not-deciding and not wanting to hear of it, in dodging the preparation.

What stands for decision? We ourselves? Who are we? In our belongingness and not belongingness to be-ing.

Decision [is] related to the truth of being, not only related but determined only from within it.

Thus decision is meant in an exceptional sense, thus also the talk of outermost decision that is simultaneously innermost.

But why this decision? Because a *saving* of beings [is possible] *only out of the deepest* ground of be-ing itself—saving as justifying preservation of the law and mission of the West. *Does that have to be?* To what extent at this point [is there] still a saving? Because the danger has grown to the extreme, since everywhere there is uprooting and—what is even more disastrous—because the uprooting is already engaged in hiding itself, the beginning of the lack of history is already here.

Decision comes about in stillness, not as resolve but as opening-resoluteness [*Entschlossenheit*] which already founds *truth* and that means recasts beings—and thus is a creative decision or a numbing.

But why and how [can one] prepare for this decision?

The struggle against destruction and uprooting is only the first step in preparation, the step into the nearness of the actual realm of decision.

47. What Is Ownmost to Decision: Being and Not-Being*

What is ownmost to decision can only be determined from within and out of its prevailing essential swaying. Decision is decision between either-or. But that already forestalls what has the character of decision. From where [comes] the either-or? Where does this come from, only *this* or only *that*? From where [comes] the unavoidability of thus or thus? Is there not a third, *indifference*? But that is *not at all* possible here.

What is the utmost here? Being or not-being and in fact not the being of any beings whatever, for example of man, but rather the essential swaying of being, or?

Why does it come down to either-or *here*?

The indifference would only be *being of non-beings,* only a *higher nothing.*

For "being" here does not mean being extant in itself; and "not-being" here does not mean total disappearance, but rather (a) not-being as a way of being: being and yet not; and (b) in the same way being: having the character of nothing and yet precisely being.

Taking this back into the essential swaying of being requires the insight into nothing's belonging to *being,* and only thus does the either-or receive its sharp focus and its origin.

Because being has the character of nothing [*nichthaft*], for the steadiness of its truth, being needs the *not* to last and that means also [it needs] the *opposition* of all that is nothing, the not-being.

That being demands and needs that which, seen from Da-sein, shows itself as either-or—the one or the other and only these—results from the prevailing nothingness of being (turning).

The prevailing essential swaying of decision is leaping unto decision or *indifference*—thus not *withdrawal* or *destroying.*

Indifference is not-deciding.

Decision deals originarily with deciding or not-deciding.

But decision means coming face to face with the either-or. Thus it means already *decidedness,* because here belongingness to enowning [reigns].

Decision about decision (turning) [is] not reflection but the opposite of that: [deciding] about *the* decision, i.e., already knowing enowning.

Decision and question: A more originary enactment of questioning means putting up the essential sway of truth for decision. But *truth* itself is already *the very thing to be decided.*

---

* Cf. Leap, 146: Be-ing and Not-be-ing.

48. In What Sense Decision Belongs
to Be-ing Itself

Decision and *distress* as it prods the thrownness of the thrower.
Decision and strife.
Decision and turning.

*

It appears as if the decision "being or not-being" is always already
decided in favor of being, since "life" means "wanting to be." So nothing at all is put up here for deciding.

But what does "life" mean and how far is "life" comprehended here?
As the drive to *self-preservation.*

Even the common and the lowly, the massive and the comfortable,
all have a drive to preserve themselves, and this above all. Consequently the question of decision can not be put in terms of such considerations.

49. Why Must Decisions Be Made?

Why must *decisions* be made? What is this, *decision*? [It is] the necessary
form of enactment of *freedom.* Indeed, this is how we think "causally"
and take freedom to be a *faculty.*

Is not "decision" also another very refined form of calculation? Or,
because of this illusion, is decision not simply the extreme opposite, but
also the *incomparable*?

Seen according to the course of a process, decision [involves] human
activity and is sequential.

What is necessary in *it* [is] what lies *before* the "activity" and reaches
beyond it.

The *time-space* character of decision [is] to be grasped being-historically
and not *morally-anthropologically,* i.e., as the bursting cleavage of be-ing
itself. Making room in preparation is, then, indeed not a supplementary
reflection but the other way around.

Overall [it is a question of] rethinking being-historically (but not
"ontologically") the whole of human being, as soon as it is grounded in
Da-sein.

II. Echo*

* Cf. lecture course SS 1935, *Einführung in die Metaphysik* (GA 40); then: lecture course WS 1937/38, *Grundfragen der Philosophie. Ausgewählte "Probleme" der "Logik"* (GA 45, pp. 151ff.) [trans. R. Rojcewicz and A. Schuwer, *Basic Questions of Philosophy: Selected "Problems" of "Logic"*]; cf. also *"Die Begründung des neuzeitlichen Weltbildes durch die Metaphysik"* (under the title *"Die Zeit des Weltbildes,"* in: *Holzwege* (GA 5)).

50. Echo

Echo of the essential swaying of be-ing
out of the abandonment of being
through the distressing distress
of the forgottenness of be-ing.

Bringing this forgottenness forth through a remembering *as* forgotten-ness in its hidden power—wherein the echo of be-ing resounds. *Recognizing* the distress.

The *guiding-attunement* of echo: shock and deep awe, but always rising out of the grounding-attunement of *reservedness*.

The utmost distress: the *distress of lack of distress*. First of all to let this reverberate, whereby much must necessarily remain incomprehensible and unquestionable; and nevertheless a faint hint becomes possible.

Which simple curve of saying is to be chosen here and to be drawn without any secondary consideration?

Echo must encompass the whole of the rift and above all be articulated as the mirroring of playing-forth.

Echo for whom? Whereunto? Echo of the essential swaying of be-ing in the abandonment of being.

How is this to be experienced? What is this abandonment? It is itself arisen from what is precisely not ownmost to be-ing, out of machination. From where does this come? *Not* from the not-character of be-ing! On the contrary!

What does machination mean? Machination and constant presence: ποίησις – τέχνη. Where does machination lead? To *lived-experience*. How does this happen (*ens creatum*—modern nature and history—technicity)? By disenchanting beings, as it makes room for the power of an enchantment that is enacted by the disenchanting itself. Enchantment and lived-experience.

The definitive consolidation of the abandonment of being in the forgottenness of being.

The epoch of total lack of questioning and of aversion to any setting of goals. Averageness as rank.

Echo of refusal—in which resonance?

51. Echo*

The echo of be-ing as refusal in the abandonment of beings by being—this already says that here something extant is not to be described or explained—or to be arranged. The burden of thinking in the other beginning of philosophy is different: It is enthinking that which is

---

* Cf. Echo, 72: Nihilism.

enowned as enowning itself; it is to bring be-ing into the truth of its essential swaying. However, because be-ing becomes enowning in the other beginning, the echo of be-ing must also be history, must pass through history by an essential shock, and must know and at the same time be able to say the moment of this history. (What is meant here is not a characterization and description according to a philosophy of history but rather a knowing awareness of history from within and *as* the moment of the faint echo of the truth of be-ing itself.)

And still it sounds as if what counts here is only a characterization of what belongs to the present time. One should speak of *the epoch of the total lack of questioning,* which extends its duration within time, beyond the present, far back and far ahead. In this epoch nothing essential—if this determination still has any meaning at all—is any longer impossible and inaccessible. Everything "is made" and "can be made" if one only musters the "will" for it. But that this "will" is precisely what has already placed and in advance reduced what might be possible and above all necessary—this is already mistaken ahead of time and left outside any questioning. For this will, which makes everything, has already subscribed to machination, that interpretation of beings as re-presentable and re-presented. In one respect re-presentable means "accessible to intention and calculation"; in another respect it means "advanceable through pro-duction and execution." But thought in a fundamental manner, all of this means that beings as such are re-presentable and that only the representable *is.* For machination, what apparently offers resistance and a limit to machination is only the material for further elaboration and the impulse for progress and an occasion for extension and enlargement. Within machination there is nothing question-worthy, nothing that could be esteemed through enactment of questioning as such, simply esteemed and thus lit up and elevated into truth.

By contrast, there *are* within machination, and even more so, "problems," the well-known "difficulties," which are there only to be overcome. In both re-presenting explanations as well as productive explanations, there are things that are not clear and not yet clarified, tasks that are not yet met. But all of this exists only because machination determines the beingness of beings—and not, for example, because machination itself could admit a limit.

But because in this way machination drives question-worthiness away and roots it out and brands it as the real deviltry and because, even in the epoch of total lack of questioning, this destruction of question-worthiness is perhaps and basically not fully possible, therefore this epoch still needs that which allows it—in this epoch's *own* way—to let the question-worthy *count* machinationally and at the same time to render it harmless. And this is *live-experience* [*Erleben*] which *decrees* that all of this should turn into a "lived-experience" [*Erlebnis*], always into a larger, more unprecedented, more screaming "lived-experience." "Lived-experience" is understood here as the basic kind of machinational representing and of residing therein; "lived-experience" means making what is mysterious, i.e., what is stimulating, provocative, stunning, and enchanting—which makes the machinational necessary—public and accessible to everyone.

The epoch of total lack of questioning does not tolerate anything worthy of questioning and destroys any and all solitude. Therefore, precisely this epoch must spread the word that "creative" men are "lonely," and that therefore everyone is apprised and is promptly informed in "picture" and "sound" of the loneliness of these lonesome men and their deeds. Here mindfulness touches upon what is uncanny in this epoch, knowing full well that mindfulness is far removed from any kind of popular "critique of the times" and "psychology." For what counts is the awareness that here, in all desolation and terror, something of the essential sway of be-ing resonates and the abandonment of beings by be-ing (as machination and lived-experience) dawns. This epoch of total lack of questioning can be withstood only through an *epoch of simple solitude*, in which preparedness for the truth of be-ing itself is being prepared.

52. Abandonment of Being

Abandonment of being is strongest at that place where it is most decidedly hidden. That happens where beings have—and had to—become most ordinary and familiar. That happened first in *Christianity* and its dogma, which explains all beings in their origin as *ens creatum*, where the creator is the most certain and all beings are the effect of this most extant cause. But cause-effect relationship is the most ordinary, most crude, and most immediate, what is employed by all human calculation and lostness to beings in order to explain something, i.e., to push it into the clarity of the ordinary and familiar. Here, where beings have necessarily to be the most familiar, be-ing is necessarily and *all the more* ordinary and most ordinary.

And since now be-ing "is" in truth what is most *non*-ordinary, be-ing here has withdrawn completely and has abandoned beings.

Abandonment of beings by being means that be-ing has withdrawn from beings and that beings have become initially (in terms of Christianity) only beings made by an other being. The highest being as cause of all beings took over what is ownmost to be-ing. These beings, once made by the creator god, then became of human making, insofar as now beings are taken and controlled only in their objectness. The beingness of beings fades into a "logical form," into what is thinkable by a thinking that is itself ungrounded.

Man is so fully blinded by what is objective and machinational that beings already withdraw from him; how much more still does be-ing and its truth withdraw, wherein all beings must originarily first arise and appear strange, so that creating might receive its mighty impetuses, namely for generating [*schöpfen*].

Abandonment of being means that be-ing abandons beings and leaves beings to themselves and thus lets beings become objects of machination. All of this is not simply "decline" but the earliest history of be-ing itself, the history of the first beginning and of what is derived from this beginning—and thus necessarily stayed behind. But even this staying behind is not merely something "negative." Rather, in its end it merely brings to light the abandonment of being, granted that the question of the truth of be-ing is asked from within the other beginning and so begins the move toward encountering the first beginning.

Then one sees that, when being abandons beings, be-ing *shelters and conceals itself* in the manifestness of beings and is itself essentially determined as this self-withdrawing sheltering-concealing.

Be-ing already abandons beings, while ἀλήθεια becomes the basic self-withholding character of beings and so prepares for the determination of beingness as ἰδέα. Now beings allow beingness to count only as an addendum, which, on the level of conforming to beings as such, must then of course become πρότερον and *a priori*.

The most rigorous proof for this sheltered-concealed essential sway of be-ing (for self-sheltering-concealing [of be-ing] in the openness of beings) is not only the lowering of be-ing to the most ordinary and the emptiest. The proof is carried out through the whole history of metaphysics, for which beingness must become the most familiar and even the most certain to absolute knowledge—becoming in the end a necessary illusion in Nietzsche.

Do we grasp this important teaching of the first beginning and its history: what is ownmost to be-ing as *refusal,* utmost refusal in the unprecedented openness of machinations and "live-experience"?

Do we who are to come have an ear for the resonance of the *echo,* which has to be made to resonate in the preparation for the other beginning?

Abandonment of being must be experienced as the basic event of our history and be elevated into a knowing awareness that shapes and guides.

And for this it is necessary:

1. to remember the abandonment of being in its long, hidden, and self-hiding history. It is not enough to point to what belongs to the present time.

2. to experience the abandonment of being equally as the distress that *towers over into the crossing* and animates this crossing as access to what is

to come. The *crossing* too must be experienced in its entire range and its many ruptures (cf. *Überlegungen* IV, 96).

53. Distress

Why is it that, when one uses the word *distress,* people immediately think of "lack" and of "evil"—something toward which we must be ill-disposed? Because one esteems lack of distress as "good"—and rightfully so wherever welfare and fortune count. These are sustained only from the unbroken supply of what is useful, enjoyable, and already extant, which can be accrued through progress. But progress has no future, because it only transports the heretofore "further"on its own track.

But when what counts is that to which we belong, to which in a concealed manner we are distressingly urged—how is it then with "distress"? This "distressing"—ungrasped and undiminishing—essentially surpasses any "progress" because it is the genuinely futural itself, so that it falls out of the difference between good and evil and withdraws from any and all calculation.

Can such a distressing befall us (whom?) again? Would it not have to aim at a total transformation of man? Would it dare to be less than what is inevitably most estranging?

54. Abandonment of Being

To this abandonment belongs *forgottenness of being* and at the same time the *disintegration of truth.*

Both are basically the same. And yet, in order to necessitate the abandonment of being as distress, we must be mindful of each, so that the utmost distress, *the lack of distress in this distress,* breaks open and lets the remotest nearness to the flight of the gods echo.

But is there a stronger proof for the abandonment of being than this, that the masses of humanity, letting their rage out in gigantism and in its institutions, no longer even is deemed worthy of finding the shortest way to annihilation? Who intimates the echo of a god in such a refusal?

What would happen if we wanted to be serious for once and withdrew from all areas of supposedly "cultural activity" by admitting that here *no* distress reigns any longer? Would a distress, the most distressing distress, then not have to come to light and assume power? It is difficult to say whither and for what. But it would still be a distress and a ground for necessity. Why do we no longer have the courage for this retreat, and why does it immediately seem to us to be something worthless? Because for a long time we have consoled ourselves by the appearance of "doing culture" and do not want to renounce it, because, as soon as this also is taken away, not only will all necessity for acting be missing but all action itself.

But whoever is now still a creator must *have* fully enacted this retreat and have encountered that distress in order to have taken up into the innermost experience [*Erfahrung*] the necessity of the *crossing*—to be a transition and a sacrifice—and in order to know that this is precisely not renouncing and giving up for lost but rather the strength for a clear decidedness as precursor of what is essential.

55. Echo

The *echo* of the truth of be-ing and its essential swaying itself comes from within the distress of the forgottenness of being. This distress commences from its depth as lack of distress. *Forgottenness of being* is not aware of itself; it presumes to be at home with "beings" and with what is "actual," "true" to "life," and certain of "lived-experience." For it only knows beings. But in this way of the presencing of beings, beings are abandoned by being. *Abandonment of being* is the ground of the forgottenness of being. But abandonment of beings by being sustains the illusion that beings are now ready to be handled and used, not needing anything else. But abandonment of be-ing is debarring and warding off of enowning.

With the unfolding of the forgottenness of be-ing—in which the other beginning and thus also be-ing resonates—the echo must resonate and commence from within the abandonment of be-ing.

Abandonment of Be-ing

What Nietzsche is the first to recognize—in his orientation to Platonism—as *nihilism* is in truth, and seen according to the grounding-question that is foreign to him, only the foreground of the far deeper happening of the forgottenness of being, which comes forth more and more directly in the course of finding the answer to the guiding-question. But even the forgottenness of being (depending on the definition) is not the most originary destining of the first beginning; rather, it is the abandonment of being that was perhaps *most* covered over and denied by Christianity and its secularized descendants.

That beings as such can still be manifest and that the truth of be-ing nevertheless has abandoned them—regarding this, see the *disempowering* of φύσις and of ὄν as ἰδέα.

Unto what are beings being misused in such a manifesting that is abandoned by being (object and "in itself")? Consider the obviousness, leveling off, and actual unrecognizability of be-ing in the dominant understanding of being.

Abandonment of Be-ing

What is abandoned by what? Beings are abandoned by be-ing, which belongs to them and them alone. In this way beings are manifest then as object and as extant, as if be-ing did not hold sway. Beings are what is indifferent and obtrusive at the same time, in the same undecided-ness and randomness.

Abandonment of be-ing is basically a dis-swaying [*Ver-wesung*] of be-ing. What is ownmost is disturbed and only as such does it come into truth as the correctness of representing—νοεῖν—διανοεῖν—ἰδέα. Beings continue to be what is present; and what actually is constantly present and *in this way* conditions everything, is the un-conditioned, the ab-solute, *ens entium, Deus,* etc.

But which happening of which history is this *abandonment?* Is there a history of be-ing? And how rarely and scarcely does this history come to light, though hidden?

The abandonment of be-ing happens to beings, indeed to beings in the whole, and thus also and precisely to that being which as man stands in the midst of beings and thereby forgets their be-ing.

The echo of be-ing wants to retrieve be-ing in its *full essential swaying* as enowning, by disclosing the abandonment of being. This happens only when beings are put back into be-ing through the grounding of Da-sein—be-ing that is opened up in the leap.

56. The Lingering of the Abandonment of Being in the Concealed Manner of Forgottenness of Being

The dominant understanding of being, however, corresponds to this forgottenness of being. That is, this forgottenness as such is first com-pleted and concealed to itself through this understanding of being. What in that understanding counts as the unassailable truth about be-ing are:

1. its *generality* (the most general, cf. ἰδέα—κοινόν—γένη);
2. its *familiarity* (without question, because it is the emptiest, contain-ing nothing questionable).

But in this way be-ing as such is never experienced but rather always grasped only in terms of beings within the purview of the guid-ing-question: ὂν ᾗ ὄν and *thus* in a certain manner grasped rightfully as what is *common* to all (namely, beings as what is "actual" and extant). The *manner* in which *be-ing* must be encountered and grasped in the purview of the guiding-question is at the same time imparted to be-ing as *what is its ownmost.* And yet this is still only one manner of a very questionable conception by an even more questionable con-cept.

The innermost ground of historical uprooting is one that is more essential, grounded upon what is ownmost to be-ing: that be-ing itself withdraws from beings and thereby still lets beings appear as "beings" and even as "more beings."

Because this fall of the truth of be-ing is accomplished above all in the most graspable form of communicating truth, through cognition and knowing, genuine knowing on the other hand, i.e., knowing awareness of be-ing itself, must come to power here, if the uprooting is to be overcome by way of a new rooting. And, thereby, once again the first thing to do is precisely to recognize from the ground up—and initially to inquire into—that essential sway of be-ing, namely abandonment of being.

That wherein the abandonment of being announces itself:

1. the *total insensitivity to what is ambiguous* in that which is held to be essential; ambiguity brings about asthenia and disinclination for an actual decision. For example, all of what the *"people"* means: the communal, the racial, the lower, the higher, the national, the lasting; for example, all of what is called *"divine."*

2. no longer knowing which is the condition, the conditioned, and the unconditionable. *Fully idolizing* as *unconditioned* the *conditions* of historical be-ing, for example, of all the ambiguity having to do with a people.

3. getting stuck in thinking of and beginning with "values" and "ideas"—in which the *interconnective form* of historical Dasein is seen, without any serious question, as in something unchangeable—to which thinking in terms of "worldviews" corresponds. (Cf. Playing-Forth, 110: ἰδέα, Platonism, and Idealism.)

4. consequently everything is built into a "cultural operation"; and the highest decisions, Christianity, are not laid out according to their roots, but rather evaded.

5. art is subjugated to cultural usage and essentially misconstrued; blindness to what is ownmost to art, the manner of grounding truth.

6. generally noteworthy is the misestimation of oneself in relation to what is repulsive and negating; it is simply shoved away as "evil"— misinterpreted and thereby belittled and thus in its danger all the more enlarged.

7. therein is manifest—completely from afar—the not-knowing that the *not* and the nihilating belong to be-ing itself and the lack of an inkling of the finitude and uniqueness of be-ing.

8. not-knowing what is ownmost to truth goes along with that; [not knowing] that truth and its grounding must be decided prior to whatever holds true; [not knowing] the blind mania for what holds true in what appears to be serious willing (cf. *Überlegungen* IV, 83).

9. hence rejection of genuine knowing and anxiety in the face of questioning; evading mindfulness; the flight into the events and machinations.

10. every stillness and reservedness appears as inactivity and letting go and renunciation—and is perhaps the broadest swing-over back into letting being be as enowning.

11. the self-certainty of no-longer-letting-oneself-be-called; hardening against all hints; the *asthenia* for awaiting; only calculating.

12. all of these are only emanations of an intricate and rigidified dissembling of what is ownmost to be-ing, especially its cleavage: that uniqueness, seldomness, momentariness, chance and onset, reservedness and freedom, preserving and necessity belong to be-ing; that be-ing is not the emptiest and most common, but rather the richest and highest and holds sway only in en-ownment, by virtue of which Da-sein grounds the truth of being in the sheltering by beings.

13. the specific elucidation of the abandonment of being as derangement of the West; the flight of gods; the death of the moral, Christian God; its reinterpretation (cf. Nietzsche's remarks). The masking of this uprooting by the groundless but supposedly newly beginning self-finding of man (modernity); this masking eclipsed and enhanced by progress: discoveries, inventions, industry, the machine; at the same time the loss of individuality, neglect, pauperization, everything as the disengagement from the ground and from arrangements, uprooting—which is the deepest masking of distress—asthenia for mindfulness, powerlessness of truth; pro- gress into non-beings as the growing abandonment by be-ing.

14. abandonment of being is the innermost ground of the distress of lack of distress. How can distress be effected *as* distress? Must one not let the truth of be-ing light up—but what for? Who among the distressless ones is capable of seeing ? Is there ever a way out of such a distress—a distress which constantly denies itself as distress? The will to get out is lacking. Can *remembering* those possibilities of Da-sein which have been lead to mindfulness here? Or must here something unusual and not-conceivable thrust [us] into this distress?

15. the abandonment of being [is] brought nearer by being mindful of the darkening of the world and the destruction of the earth in the sense of *acceleration, calculation,* the *claim of massiveness* (cf. Echo, 57: History of Be-ing and Abandonment of Being).

16. the simultaneous "domination" of the powerlessness of empty sentiment and of the violence of the establishment.

57. History of Be-ing
and Abandonment of Being

The abandonment of being is the ground and thus also the more originary and essential determination of that which Nietzsche recognized for the first time as nihilism. Still, how little he himself and his strength succeeded in forcing Western Dasein to a mindful thinking on nihilism. Because of that, the hope is smaller yet that this epoch will muster the will for knowing the ground of nihilism. Or should clarity about the "fact" of nihilism come from this knowing in the first place?

Abandonment of being determines a singular and unique epoch in the history of the truth of be-ing. It is be-ing's epoch for a long time, in which truth hesitates to let its ownmost be clear. The time of the danger of avoiding any essential decision, the time of renouncing the struggle for measures.

Undecidedness is the domain for the unboundedness of machinations, where magnitude spreads out in the non-form of the gigantic and clarity spreads out as transparency of the empty.

The long hesitation of truth and of decisions is a refusal of the shortest way and of the greatest moment. In this epoch "beings" — what one calls the "actual" and "life" and "values" — are dis-enowned by be-ing.

Abandonment of being conceals itself in the growing validity of *calculation, acceleration,* and the *claim of massiveness.* In this concealment is hidden what is obstinately *not* ownmost to the abandonment of being and what makes it unassailable.

58. What the Three Concealments of the Abandonment of Being Are and How They Show Themselves

1. *Calculation* — comes to power primarily by the machination of technicity, is grounded in terms of knowing in the mathematical; here the unclear foregrasping into guiding principles and rules and thus the certainty of steering and planning, the *experiment;* the lack of questioning in somehow managing [*Durchkommen*]; nothing is impossible, one is certain of "beings"; there is no longer need for the question concerning what is ownmost to truth. Everything must be adjusted to the existing state of calculation. From here on the priority of *organization,* renunciation from the ground up of a freely growing transformation. The incalculable is here only what has not yet been mastered by calculation, although at some point also recuperable in itself — therefore not at all *outside the realm of all calculation.* "Fate" and "providence" are dealt with in "sentimental" moments, which precisely in the "dominion" of calculation are not seldom, but never so that a formative force might come out of that which is invoked there — a force that would dare ever to push the mania for calculation to its limits.

   Calculation is meant here as the basic law of comportment, not as the mere consideration or even cleverness of an isolated action, which belongs to every human action.

2. *Acceleration* — of any kind; the mechanical increase of technical "speeds," and these only a consequence of this acceleration, which means not-being-able-to-bear the stillness of hidden growth and awaiting; the mania for what is surprising, for what immediately sweeps [us] away and impresses [us], again and again and in different ways; fleetingness as the basic law of "constancy." It is necessary

to forget rapidly and to lose oneself in what comes next. From this point of view, then, the false idea of what is high and "highest" in the dis-figuring [*Mißgestalt*] of maximum accomplishment; purely quantitative enhancement, blindness to what is truly momentary, which is not fleeting but opens up eternity. But from the point of view of acceleration the eternal is the mere lasting of the same, the empty "and-so-forth." The genuine restlessness of the struggle remains hidden. Its place is taken by the restlessness of the always inventive operation, which is driven by the anxiety of boredom.

3. *The outbreak of massiveness.* That does not only mean the "masses" in a "societal" sense. These masses mount up only because numbers and the calculable already count as what is equally accessible to everyone. What is common to the *many* and to *all* is what the "many" know as what towers over them. Hence responding to calculation and acceleration, just as on the other hand calculation and acceleration provide massiveness with its track and scope. Here is the sharpest opposition—because it is inconspicuous—to the rare and unique (the essential sway of being). Everywhere in these disguises of the abandonment of being, what is *not* ownmost to beings, the non-beings, spreads—and indeed in the semblance of an "important" event.

The spreading out of these disguises of the abandonment of being and thus precisely this abandonment itself is the strongest hindrance—because initially hardly noticeable—for appropriately estimating and grounding the grounding-attunement of reservedness, in which what is ownmost to truth first lights up, insofar as shifting into Da-sein happens.

But those ways of dwelling in beings and their "domination" are therefore so undermining, because they do not one day simply let themselves be removed as supposedly only external forms that encompass something inner. They occupy the place of the inner and in the end deny the difference between the inner and the outer, since they are foremost and everything. This corresponds to the way in which one attains knowledge [*Wissen*]—corresponds to the calculated, swift, massive distribution of ununderstood information [*Kenntnis*] to as many as possible in the shortest possible time. "Schooling" [becomes] a word that, in the meaning that it now has, turns upside down what is ownmost to *school* and to σχολή. But this too is only a new sign of the *collapse* which does not stop the growing uprootedness, because this collapse does not get at—or *want* to get at—the roots of beings, because there it would have to come up against its own lack of ground.

These three—calculation, acceleration, and massiveness—are accompanied by a fourth, one that is related to all three and takes over in an emphatic way the dissembling and disguising of the inner disintegration. That is:

4. *Divesting, publicizing, and vulgarizing of all attunement.* The desolation that is herewith created corresponds to the growing artificiality of every attitude and together with that the disempowering of the word. The word then is only the shell and magnified stimulation, in which there can no longer be a connection to a "meaning," because all gathering of a possible mindfulness is removed and mindfulness itself is scorned as something strange and weak.

All of this becomes all the more uncanny, the less obtrusively it is played out and the more automatically it takes possession of every-dayness and, as it were, is covered by the new forms of establishment.

The consequence of divesting attunement, which at the same time disguises the growing emptiness, shows itself finally in the incapacity to experience [*erfahren*] the very and actual happening, the abandonment of being, as attuning distress—granted that it could be shown within certain limits.

5. All of these signs of abandonment of being point to the beginning of the *epoch of total lack of questioning of all things and of all machinations.*

It is not only that basically nothing hidden will be admitted any more, but what is more decisive is that self-sheltering as such, as determining power, is no longer allowed entry.

In the epoch of total lack of questioning, however, "problems" *will* pile up and rush around, those types of "questions" which are not really questions, because their response dare not have anything binding about them, insofar as it immediately becomes a problem again. This says exactly and in advance that nothing is immune to dissolution and that deconstruction [*Auflösung*] is only a matter of numbers regarding time, space, and force.

6. But now, since beings are abandoned by be-ing, the opportunity arises for the most insipid "sentimentality." Now for the first time everything is "experienced live" [*erlebt*] and every undertaking and performance drips with "lived-experiences" [*Erlebnisse*]. And this "lived-experience" proves that now even *man* as *a being* has incurred the loss of be-ing and has fallen prey to his hunt for lived-experiences.

59. The Epoch of Total Lack of Questioning and Enchantment

One is accustomed to calling the epoch of "civilization" one of *dis*-enchantment, and this seems for its part exclusively to be the same as the total lack of questioning. However, it is exactly the opposite. One has only to know from where the enchantment comes. The answer: from the unrestrained domination of machination. When machination finally dominates and permeates everything, then there are no longer any conditions by which still actually to detect the enchantment and to protect oneself from it. The bewitchment by technicity and its constantly self-surpassing progress are only *one* sign of this enchantment, by virtue of which everything presses forth into calculation, usage, breeding, manageability, and regulation. Even "taste" now becomes a matter for this regulation, and everything depends on a "good ambiance." The average becomes better and better, and by virtue of this bettering it secures its dominion always more irresistibly and more inconspicuously.

It is of course a deceptive conclusion to believe that, the higher the average, the more unsurpassable the height of above-average efforts becomes. This conclusion itself betrays the calculating character of this attitude. The question remains: Is any room still needed at all for the above-average? Or does satisfaction with the average not become more and more soothing and legitimate, until it convinces itself that it has already achieved—and can immediately achieve at will—what the *above*-average claims to offer?

Constantly raising the level of the average and simultaneously broadening and widening the level up to the *platform* of every operation in general is the uncanniest indication of the disappearance of sites for decision—indicates the abandonment of being.

60. Whence the Lack of Distress as Utmost Distress?

The lack of distress is the greatest where self-certainty has become unsurpassable, where everything is held to be calculable and, above all, where it is decided, without a preceding question, who we are and what we are to do—where knowing awareness has been lost without its ever actually having been established that the actual self-being happens by way of a grounding-beyond-oneself, which requires the grounding of the grounding-space and its time. This, in turn, requires knowing what is ownmost to truth as what knowing cannot avoid.

But wherever "truth" is long since no longer a question and even the attempt at such a question is already rejected as a disturbance and an irrelevant brooding, there the distress of abandonment of being has no time-space at all.

Wherever possession of the true as the correct is beyond questioning and steers all dealings, what is then still the point of raising the question of what is ownmost to truth?

And wherever this possession of the true can even rely on deeds, who wants to wallow there in the uselessness of an essential questioning and to expose himself to ridicule?

The lack of distress comes from the collapse of what is ownmost to truth as the ground of Da-*sein* and of the grounding of history.

61. Machination*

In its ordinary meaning the word machination is the name for a "bad" type of human activity and plotting for such an activity.

In the context of the being-question, this word does not name a human comportment but a manner of the essential swaying of being. Even the disparaging tone should be kept at a distance, even though machination fosters what is *not* ownmost to being. And even what is *not* ownmost to being should never be depreciated, because it is essential to what is ownmost to being. Rather, the name should immediately point to *making* (ποίησις τέχνη), which we of course recognize as a human comportment. However, this comportment itself is only possible on the basis of an interpretation of beings which brings their makeability to the fore, so much so that beingness is determined precisely as constancy and presence. That *something makes itself by itself* and is thus also makeable for a corresponding procedure says that the *self-making by itself* is the interpretation of φύσις that is accomplished by τέχνη and its horizon of orientation, so that what counts now is the preponderance of the makeable and the self-making (cf. the relation of ἰδέα to τέχνη), in a word: machination. However, since at the time of the first beginning φύσις is disempowered, *machination* does not yet become fully manifest in its ownmost. It remains hidden in constant presence, whose determination culminates in ἐντελέχεια within inceptual Greek thinking. The medieval concept of *actus* already covers over what is ownmost to the inceptual Greek interpretation of beingness. It is in this connection that what belongs to machination now presses forward more clearly and that *ens* becomes *ens creatum in* the Judaeo-Christian notion of creation, when the corresponding idea of god enters into the picture. Even if one refuses crudely to interpret the idea of creator, what is still essential is beings' being-caused. The cause-effect connection becomes the all-dominating (god as *causa sui*). That is an essential distancing from φύσις and at the same time the crossing toward the emergence of machination as what is ownmost to beingness in modern thinking. The mechanistic *and* biological ways of thinking are always merely consequences of the hidden interpretation of beings in terms of machination.

Machination as the essential swaying of beingness yields a faint hint of the truth of be-ing itself. We know too little of it, even though it

---

* Cf. Echo, 70 and 71: The Gigantic.

dominates the history of being in Western philosophy up to now, from Plato to Nietzsche.

It seems to be a law of machination, whose ground is not yet established, that the more powerfully it unfolds—for example in the Middle Ages and in modernity—the more stubbornly and more machinatingly it hides itself *as such*, hiding behind *ordo* and the *analogia entis* in the Middle Ages and behind objectness and objectivity in modernity, as basic forms of actuality and thus of beingness.

And a second law is coupled with this first one, namely, that the more decidedly machination hides itself in this way, the more it insists on the pre-dominance of that which seems to be totally against what is ownmost to machination and nevertheless belongs to its ownmost: *lived-experience* (cf. everything referring to *lived-experience* in "Echo").

Then a third law joins these two: The more unconditionally lived-experience becomes the measure for correctness and truth (and thus for "actuality" and constancy), the less is the prospect of gaining, from this vantage point, a knowledge of machination as such.

The less the prospect for this unveiling is, the more unquestioned beings [are] and the more decidedly the aversion to any question-worthiness of be-ing [is].

Machination itself withdraws; and since it is the essential swaying of be-ing, be-ing itself withdraws.

But how would it be if all of what seems to be detrimental and failing would yield a totally other insight into the essential sway of be-ing and if be-ing itself would be disclosed as refusal and would nevertheless resonate?

If machination and lived-experience are named together, then this points to an essential belongingness of both to each other—a belongingness that is concealed but is also essentially *non-simultaneous* within the "time" of the history of be-ing. Machination is the early and still long hidden showing of what is precisely *not* ownmost to the beingness of beings. But even when in certain shapings it emerges into the openness of interpretation of beings—as in modernity—it is not recognized as such nor grasped at all. On the contrary, the spreading and rigidifying of what is not its ownmost is accomplished by actually retreating behind that which seems to be its utmost opposite, even as it remains totally and solely its own making. And this is lived-experience.

The belonging together of machination and lived-experience can be grasped only by returning to their broadest non-simultaneity and by dissolution of the illusion of their utmost oppositionality. When thinking-mindfulness (as questioning the truth of be-ing and only as this) attains the knowing awareness of this mutual belongingness, then the basic thrust of the history of the first beginning (history of Western metaphysics) is grasped along with that, in terms of the knowing awareness of the other beginning. Machination and lived-experience are formally [*formelhaft*] the more originary version of the formula for the guiding-question of Western thinking: beingness (being) and thinking (as re-presenting com-prehending).

62. Self-Dissembling of the Abandonment of Being by Machination and "Lived-Experience"

1. The belonging-together of machination and lived-experience.
2. The common root of both.
3. To what extent machination and lived-experience complete the dissembling of the abandonment of being.
4. Why Nietzsche's recognition of *nihilism* had to remain uncomprehended.
5. What—once recognized—does the abandonment of being reveal about be-ing itself? The origin of the abandonment of being.
6. On which paths must the abandonment of being be experienced as distress?
7. To what extent is the crossing into overcoming already necessary for this? (Da-sein)
8. Why does Hölderlin's poetry become above all futural—and thereby historical—for this crossing?

63. Live-Experience

To relate a being as what is represented unto *itself* as the relational midpoint and thus to draw it into "life."

Why man [is grasped] as "life" *(animal rationale)* (*ratio*—re-presenting!).

Only what is lived through live-experience and is *so* liveable, only what presses forth into the sphere of live-experience, only what man is able to bring to and before himself, [only that] can count as "a being."

64. Machination

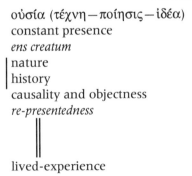

οὐσία (τέχνη — ποίησις — ἰδέα)
constant presence
ens creatum
| nature
| history
causality and objectness
re-presentedness

lived-experience

65. What Is *Not* Ownmost to Be-ing

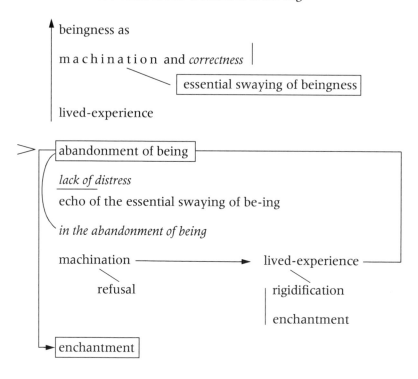

66. Machination and Lived-Experience

Knowing no limits, above all no embarrassment, and finally no deep awe—all this lies within what is ownmost to both [machination and lived-experience]. The strength for preserving and sheltering is farthest from them. The place of preserving and sheltering is taken by exaggeration and uproar and the blind and empty yelling, in which one yells at oneself and deludes oneself about the hollowing-out of beings. True to their lack of limits and embarrassment, everything is open to and nothing is impossible for machination and lived-experience. They must fancy themselves to be the whole and to be what endures, and therefore nothing is so familiar to them as the "eternal." Everything is "eternal." And the eternal—this eternal—how should it not also be the essential? But if it is the essential, what could possibly be named over against it? Can the nothingness of beings and the abandonment of being be better and more profoundly preserved in the mask of "true actuality" than by machination and lived-experience?

"Lived-Experience"

What is lived-experience?

To what extent [it lies] in the certainty of the I (already delineated in a particular interpretation of beingness and truth).

How the emergence of lived-experience demands and consolidates the anthropological way of thinking.

To what extent lived-experience is an end (because it unconditionally verifies "machination").

67. Machination and Lived-Experience

Machination is the domination of making and what is made. But in this regard one is not to think of human dealings and operating but rather the other way around; such [human activity] is only possible, in its unconditionality and exclusivity, on the basis of machination. This names a certain truth of beings (their beingness). Initially and for the most part this beingness is comprehensible for us as objectness (beings as object of representing). But machination grasps this beingness in a deeper way, more inceptually, because machination relates to τέχνη. At the same time machination contains the *Christian-biblical* interpretation of beings as *ens creatum*—regardless of whether this is taken in a religious or a secular way.

It is very difficult to grasp historically the emergence of what is machinationally ownmost to beings, because basically it has been effectively in operation since the first beginning of Western thinking (more precisely, since the collapse of ἀλήθεια).

The step taken by Descartes is already a first and decisive consequence, a "compliance" by which machination assumes power as transformed truth (correctness), namely as certainty.

What machinationally holds sway in the shape of *ens* as *ens certum* must first be shown. In the course of overcoming metaphysics, the *certum* must be laid out in terms of machination; and hence this must be decidedly determined.

Further consequences [are] the mathematical and the system and, together with that, "technicity."

"Lived-experience" corresponds to *machination* (ποίησις—τέχνη—κίνησις—νοῦς)—a correspondence which was long held back and only now finally emerges.

Both names name the *history* of truth and of beingness as the history of the first beginning.

What does *machination* mean? That which is let loose into its own shackles. Which shackles? The pattern of generally calculable explainability, by which everything draws nearer to everything else equally and becomes completely alien to itself—yes, totally other than just alien. The relation of non-relationality.

68. Machination and Lived-Experience

What kind of an extreme and oppositional matter is thus recognized in its belongingness [to be-ing], which above all points to that which we do *not yet* grasp, because the *truth* of this true is still not grounded?

But we can be mindful of this which belongs and, in doing so, remain always more aloof from every kind of self-gaping, "situational" analysis.

How machination and lived-experience (initially concealed as such for a long time, nay even concealed up to now) mutually drive each other into the extreme and thus, according to their utmost abandonment, unfold the *misshapings* of beingness and of man, in his relation to beings and to himself, and in these misshapings now mutually drive toward each other and form a onefold, which conceals all the more what enowns the onefold: the abandonment of beings by any truth of be-ing and ultimately even *by this* [be-ing] itself.

But this enowning of the abandonment of being would be misconstrued if one wanted to see therein only a process of decline, instead of considering that, by its own unique ways of uncovering beings and their "pure" objectification, it interpenetrates a definite appearing which is seemingly without background and fully groundless. [It is] the emergence of "what is natural" and the appearing of things themselves to which indeed belongs that illusoriness of the groundless. Of course "what is natural" no longer has any immediate relation to φύσις, but rather is fully set according to the machinational; it is, by contrast, prepared for by the former predominance of the supernatural. This uncovering of "what is natural" (finally of what is makeable, controllable, and experientially "liveable") must one day exhaust itself in its own riches and must harden into an increasingly dull mixture of prior possibilities, to such an extent that this mere-keeping-at-and-imitating it at the same time knows—and *can* know—less of itself and what it is and therefore appears to itself to be more creative, the more it pursues its end.

The coming together of machination and lived-experience encloses within itself a singular enowning within the sheltered and concealed history of be-ing. However, there is still no indication that the epoch has any awareness of it. Or must this awareness remain denied to this epoch, only becoming a truth—an echo of the truth of be-ing—for those already crossing?

69. Lived-Experience and "Anthropology"*

The fact that today one still puts "anthropology" at the center of the academic worldview indicates, more impressively than any historical [*historische*] demonstration of dependencies, that once again one is

---

* What lived-experience is! How its mastery leads to an anthropological way of thinking! How this is an end, because it unconditionally affirms machination.

preparing oneself to return totally to the Cartesian ground. What "hair-style" anthropology wears—whether enlightenment's moral one, a psychologically-natural-scientific one, a humanistic-personalistic one, a Christian one, or one which is politically oriented to the people—is totally insignificant for the crucial question, namely, the question whether modernity is grasped as an end and an other beginning is inquired into, or whether one sticks obstinately to the perpetuation of a decline that has lasted since Plato, which one can still ultimately manage only by persuading oneself that one's having no inkling is an overcoming of tradition.

And here it is perfectly all right if having no inkling (not to mention having no responsibility) goes so far that one poses as conquerer of Cartesian philosophy, while at the same time one's contemporaries have no inkling of having no inkling. But, just as at the time of neo-Kantianism the actual history of the time took no notice of the still considerable erudition and careful work, so will today's time of "lived-experience" make even less fuss about this boring and pedestrian stereo-typing of its own superficiality.

70. The Gigantic*

Initially we must characterize the gigantic in terms of what is nearest to us and itself still objectively extant in order to let resonate the abandonment of being and thus the domination of what is precisely *not* ownmost to φύσις (the domination of machination). But as soon as machination is in turn grasped being-historically, the gigantic reveals itself as "something" else. It is no longer the re-presentable objectness of an unlimited quantification but rather quantity as quality. Quality is meant here as the basic character of the *quale*, of the what, of the ownmost, of be-ing itself.

We know quantity-quality and ποσόν-ποιόν as "categories," i.e., in relation to "judgment."

But here it is not a matter of reversing one category for another or of a "dialectical" representational mediation of the forms of representation; rather, it is a matter of the history of being.

This "reversing" is prepared for in that beingness is determined in terms of τέχνη and of ἰδέα. Re-presenting and bringing-before-oneself include the "how far" and "to what extent," i.e., that which refers to *distance* in relation to beings as ob-ject—this without thinking of certain spatial things and relations.

As *systematic,* re-presentation turns this distance and its overcoming and securing into the basic law of determination of the object. Projecting-open of re-presentation in the sense of a *grasping* that reaches ahead,

* Cf. Machination.

plans and arranges everything before everything is already conceived as particular and singular—this re-presentation recognizes no limit in the given, and *wants* to find no limit. Rather the limitless is what is deciding, not as the mere flux and mere "and-so-forth," but as that which is bound to no limit of the *given*, bound to no *given* and to no giveable *as limit*. There is in principle no "impossible"; one "hates" this word; everything is humanly possible, if only everything is taken into account in advance, in every aspect, and if the conditions are furnished.

This already shows that here it is not a matter of reversing the "quantitative" into something qualitative, but rather of recognizing the originary essence of the quantitative and the essence of the possibility of its re-presentation (calculability) in what is ownmost to the domination of *re-presenting as such* and the *objectification* of beings.

Henceforth it becomes clear that, by virtue of *their* own self-consciousness, those who enact the unfolding of re-presentation (of the world as image) do not know anything of this essence of the quantitative—and thus know nothing of the history that prepares for and completes the dominion of the quantitative.

And they do not know *at all* that *abandonment* of beings by being is completed unto the gigantic as such, i.e., in the shine of that which lets all beings be most beings.

The "quantitative" is dealt with, i.e., calculated, quantitatively; but at the same time it is said that the quantitative is placed and bound into its limits by certain principles.

That is why still today—today more than ever—one cannot grasp space and time in any other way than quantitatively, at most as *forms* of these quantities. And even thinking time-space as something completely non-quantitative feels like a strange imposition. One gets out of this dilemma by pointing out that here the word "time" is transferred to something else.

The quantitative *(quantitas) is able* to emerge as a category because it is basically what is ownmost ([as] what is *not* ownmost) to be-ing itself; but this is initially sought only in the beingness of beings as what is present and constant.

To say that the quantitative becomes quality, therefore, means that what is precisely *not* ownmost to be-ing is not recognized in its essential belongingness to the essential sway of be-ing. However, this recognizability is prepared for by the being-historical knowing-awareness that the quantitative dominates all beings. The reason why it nevertheless does not appear as be-ing is that re-presentation, in which what is ownmost to the quantitative is grounded, holds itself to beings and closes itself off to be-ing or—what amounts to the same thing—lets be-ing "count" as mainly what is the most general (of representation) and as what is the emptiest.

But taken historically, the gigantic as such is above all unpredictable. But it *is* this from within the announcement of be-ing itself, ungraspable from an extremely near nearness—and shaped as the lack of distress in distress.

Why does the gigantic not know *what is overflowing*? Because it arises from the covering-up of a lack and puts *this* covering-up forth as the illusion of an unbounded openness, of a possession. Because the gigantic never knows what overflows—the inexhaustible unexhausted—therefore what is simple must be refused to it. For the essential simpleness arises out of fullness and its mastery. The "simpleness" of the gigantic is only an illusion that is meant to hide the emptiness. But by arranging all this illusoriness, the gigantic holds onto its own and is singular.

71. The Gigantic

According to the tradition (cf. Aristotle on ποσόν) the essence of the *quantum* lies in divisibility into parts of the same kind.

What then is *quantitas*? And the quantitative? And to what extent is the gigantic something quantitative as qualitative? Can that be made comprehensible in view of that determination of the *quantum*?

"Parts of the same kind" and *"dividing"* and "dividing and *distributing into parts"* (calculating—λόγος, differentiating—gathering).

Distributing into parts and *arranging*?

Arranging and re-presenting?

Quantum—according to Hegel, the sublimated quality that has become undifferentiated—includes the changeability of the what, without that being sublimated thereby.

Quantity and quantum (a *magnitude—such and such a magnitude?*)

↓

Magnitude—manner of having magnitude, a magnitude such as "much" and "little."

72. Nihilism

Nihilism in Nietzsche's sense means that all *goals* are gone. Nietzsche has those goals in mind that grow of themselves and transform humans (whereunto?). Thinking in terms of "goals" (the τέλος of the Greeks that has long been misinterpreted) presupposes the ἰδέα and "idealism." Therefore this "idealistic" and moralistic interpretation of nihilism remains provisional, in spite of its importance. Directed toward the other beginning, nihilism must be grasped more fundamentally as the essential consequence of the abandonment of being. But how can this become known and be decided upon when what Nietzsche first experienced and thought through as nihilism has remained uncomprehended up to now and above all did not come into mindfulness? Partially misled by the form of Nietzsche's manner of communication, one took cognizance of his "doctrine" of "nihilism" as an interesting cultural psychology. But already before doing so, one makes the sign of the cross in front of its truth, i.e., openly or surreptitiously keeping it at a distance as devilish. For, according to enlightening consideration, where would we come to if that were and would be true? And one has no inkling that *this very consideration,* as well as the attitude and comportment toward beings that sustains this consideration, is the actual nihilism: One refuses to admit the goal-lessness. For this reason one suddenly "has goals" again—even if it only means that what in any case can be a *means* for setting up and pursuing goals is itself raised to a goal: the *people,* for example. And therefore the greatest nihilism is precisely where one believes to have goals again, to be "happy," to attend to making equally available the "cultural values" (movies and seaside resort vacations) to all the "people"—in this drunken stupor of "lived-experience"—precisely there is the greatest nihilism: methodically disregarding human goallessness, being always ready to avoid every goal-setting decision, anxiety in the face of every domain of decision and its opening. Anxiety in the face of be-ing has never been greater than today. Proof for this is the gigantically organized event for shouting down this anxiety. The essential mark of "nihilism" is not whether churches and monasteries are destroyed and people are murdered, or whether this does *not* happen and "Christianity" can go its ways; rather, what is crucial is whether one knows and wants to know that precisely this tolerating of Christianity and Christianity itself—the general talk of "providence" and "the Lord God," however sincere individuals may be—are merely pretexts and perplexities in *that* domain which one does not want to acknowledge and to allow to count as *the* domain of decision about be-ing or not-be-ing. The most disastrous nihilism consists in passing oneself off as protector of Christianity and even claiming for oneself the most Christian Christianity on the basis of social accomplishments. The dangerousness in this nihilism consists in its being completely hidden and in distinguishing itself, sharply and rightfully, from what one could call crude nihilism (e.g., Bolshevism). However, what is ownmost to nihilism holds indeed so much to the abground (because it reaches deeply into the truth of be-ing and into the decision about that truth) that precisely these opposing forms can and must belong to nihilism. And therefore it also seems as if nihilism, thoroughly calculated in its entirety, is unsurmountable. When two extreme opposing forms of nihilism necessarily and most acutely do battle with each other, then this battle leads in one way or another to the *victory* of nihilism, i.e., to its renewed consolidation and presumably in *such* a form as to forbid one even to suggest that nihilism is still at work.

Be-ing has so thoroughly abandoned beings and submitted them to machination and "lived-experience" that those illusive attempts at rescuing Western culture and all "culture-oriented politics" must necessarily become the most insidious and thus the highest form of nihilism. And that is a process that is not connected to individual humans and their actions and doctrines but rather merely pushes forth what is ownmost to nihilism into the purest form granted to it. Of course to be mindful of this process already requires a standpoint which avoids attributing a deception, about what they achieve, to all "the good," "the progressive," and "the gigantic," *as well as* avoids a sheer desperation which simply cannot yet close its eyes to total meaninglessness. This standpoint, which grounds space and time anew for itself, is Da-sein, on whose ground be-ing itself as *refusal* and thus as en-owning attains knowing awareness for the first time. The preparation for the overcoming of nihilism begins with the fundamental experience that man as founder of Da-sein is *used* by the godhood of the other god. But what is most imperative and most difficult regarding this overcoming is the *awareness* of nihilism.

This awareness dare not get bogged down in either the word or in an initial elucidation of what is meant [by nihilism] in Nietzsche. Instead this awareness must recognize the abandonment of being *as* essential sway.

73. Abandonment of Being and "Science"*

In truth modern science as well as contemporary science never reach directly into the field of decision about the essential sway of be-ing. But why then does mindfulness of "science" belong to the preparation of the *echo*?

Abandonment of being is the inceptually preformed consequence of the interpretation of the beingness of beings that is led by *thinking* and by the early collapse of the hereby conditioned and not properly grounded ἀλήθεια.

But because, in and *as* modernity, truth stands fast in the shape of certainty and certainty in the form of a thinking of beings as re-presented ob-ject—a thinking that thinks itself in its immediacy—because the grounding of modernity consists in the establishing of this standing fast, and because this certainty of thinking unfolds as the institution and pursuit of modern "science," the abandonment of being (and that means at the same time repression of ἀλήθεια until it is pushed all the way into forgottenness) is essentially co-decided by modern science. And this [is so] always *only insofar as* modern science claims to be one or even *the* decisive knowing. *Therefore* the attempt to point to the abandonment of being as the echo of be-ing cannot avoid being mindful of modern science and its ownmost rootedness in machination.

---

* Cf. Echo, 76: Propositions about "Science."

Therein also lies this: The mindfulness of science that is thus formed is still the only philosophically possible one, granted that philosophy is already moving in the crossing to the other beginning. Any kind of the-oretical-scientific (transcendental) laying of the foundation [of science] has become as impossible as "endowing a meaning," which assigns to the existing—and thus in its essential content not alterable—science and its operation a national-political or some other anthropological purpose. Such "layings of the foundation" have become impossible because they necessarily presuppose "science" and then provide it with a "reason" (which is not one) and with a meaning (which does not come from mindfulness). In that way "science," and along with it con-solidation of the abandonment of being, attains more finality; and every questioning of the truth of be-ing (all philosophy) is excluded as unnecessary, dealt with without distress, and removed from the domain of acting. But exactly this withholding of the possibility of any (inner) mindfulness of thinking as thinking of being—since it does not know its own doings—is forced to stir up even more an "ideological" brew—by indiscriminately seizing forms and means and spheres of thinking from the existing metaphysics—forced to correct past philoso-phy and in all of this forced to conduct itself "subversively." In this "subversion" (which amounts to setting up all the platitudes) only the unsurpassable irreverence vis-à-vis the "great" thinkers deserves to be called "revolutionary." Reverence is indeed something other than praise and something other than approving [a thinker] in "his" time, if one should appeal to this sort of thing.

Mindfulness of "science" that is to be captured in a series of princi-ples must for once detach this name from the historical vagueness of randomly equating it with ἐπιστήμη, *scientia*, science, and must deter-mine it in terms of the modern essence of science. At the same time the variation in the appearance of knowing (as preservation of truth) which is consolidated in science must be made clear; and science must be pursued, all the way to the institutions and places of operation that necessarily belong to its machinational being (today's "universities"). A guide for characterizing the essence of this science, insofar as the rela-tion to beings is taken into account, is the now current differentiation into historical [*historische*] and experimental-exact sciences, although this distinction—as well as the distinction between "natural" and human sciences that arises from that distinction—is only superficial and actually only imperfectly covers the uniform essence of the seem-ingly very different sciences. What matters to this mindfulness throughout is not a description and elucidation of these sciences but rather the consolidation of the abandonment of being that sciences have enacted and which has been enacted in them—in short, of the lack of truth in all science.

74. "Total Mobilization" as Consequence of
Originary Abandonment of Being

[Total mobilization is] purely setting-into-motion and emptying all traditional contents of the still operative education [*Bildung*].

The priority of *method* [*Verfahren*] and of *institution* in overall readying the masses and putting them into service—for what?

What does this priority of mobilization mean? That thereby a new breed of man is necessarily forged is only the consequence that is *counter* to this event, but never the "goal."

But are there "goals" anymore? How does goal-setting arise? From within the beginning. And what is beginning?

75. On Being Mindful of Science

Today there are two and only two ways of being mindful of "science."

One way grasps science, not as the establishment that is now extant, but as *one* specific possibility of unfolding and building of a knowing whose essence is primarily rooted in a more originary grounding of the truth of be-ing. This grounding is enacted by coming to terms with the *beginning* of Western thinking for the first time and becomes at the same time the other beginning of Western history. Oriented in this way, mindfulness of science goes just as decidedly *back* into what has been as, wagering everything, it reaches out into what is futural. It never operates within a discussion of what belongs to the present and its immediate achievement. As a reckoning with what belongs to the present, this mindfulness of science gets lost in what is not actual, which is at the same time also what is impossible for all reckoning and calculation (cf. Self-Assertion of the German University*).

The *other* way, which will be delineated in the following guiding propositions, grasps science in its present and actual constitution. This mindfulness tries to grasp the essence of modern science in terms of strivings that belong to this essence. But as mindfulness, it is also not a simple description of an extant state. It is instead elaboration of a process, insofar as this process aims at a decision concerning the truth of science. This mindfulness remains led by the same standards as the first one and is only its reverse.

76. Propositions about "Science"**

1. "Science" must always be understood in the modern sense. The medieval "doctrine" and Greek "knowledge" are fundamentally different from it, although in a mediate and transformed way they

---

* Rectoral address 1933 (GA 16).
** Cf. *Die neuzeitliche Wissenschaft* [GA88].

co-determine what we now know as "science" and what we now can exclusively pursue, in accordance with our historical situation.

2. Accordingly, "science" itself is *not a knowing* in the sense of grounding and preserving an essential truth (n. 23). Science is a derived *mechanism* of a knowing, i.e., it is the machinational opening of a sphere of accuracies within an otherwise hidden — and for science in no way question-worthy — zone of a truth (truth about "nature," "history," "right," for example).

3. What is "scientifically" knowable is in each case *given in advance* by a "truth" which is never graspable by science, a truth about the recognized region of beings. Beings *as a region* lie in advance for science, they constitute a *positum,* and every science is in itself a *"positive" science* (including mathematics).

4. Thus there is never and nowhere anything like *the* science, as perhaps there is "art" and "philosophy," which are always in themselves essentially and fully what they are, if they *are* historical. "Science" is only a formal title whose essential understanding requires that the breakdown into disciplines, into *individual* and separate sciences, be thought along. Thus, to the extent that every science is a "positive" science, it must also be an "individual" scientific discipline.

5. "Specialization" is not somehow a manifestation of decline and degeneration of "the" science, and not somehow an unavoidable evil as a result of progress and vastness and division of labor, but rather a *necessary* and inherent consequence of its character as an individual scientific discipline and inalienable condition for its existence and that always means: its progress. Where is the actual ground for the division [of sciences]? In beingness as representedness.

6. Every science, even the so-called "descriptive" ones, *explains:* What is unknown in the region is led back, in various ways and ranges, to something known and understandable. Research provides the conditions for explanation.

7. Depending on how what is understandable here, and the claim to understandability, determines in advance the region of the individual scientific discipline, the context of *explanation* is shaped and circumscribed as in each case sufficient (e.g., explanation of a painting in its physico-chemical respect, explanation of its objectness in its physiologico-psychological respect, explanation of the "work" in its "historical" and its "artistic" respect).

8. Setting up a knowing (of an essential truth experienced in advance) (cf. n. 2) is accomplished by erecting and building an interconnection of explanations which requires for its possibility the *thorough binding* of research to the particular disciplinary field — and indeed within the connection into which research is shifted. *This* binding of

sciences as mechanisms of interconnections of accuracies is the *rigor* that belongs to them. Every science is rigorous inasmuch as it must be "positive" and individualized with respect to any given region.

9. The rigor of a science unfolds and is accomplished in the ways of proceeding (depending on the disciplinary field) and of operating (carrying out the investigation and the presentation), in the "method." This way of proceeding places the field of objects in each case in a definitive direction of explainability, which already basically guarantees that there will always be a "result." (Something always comes out.)

   The basic character of proceeding in every explaining is to follow and to lay out in advance individual series and sequences of consecutive cause-effect relations. Although not recognized *as such*, the machinational essence of beings not only justifies but also requires, in boundless intensification, this thinking in "causalities" that is assured of results—which strictly speaking are only "if-then" relationships in the form of when-then (to which the "statistics" of modern physics also belongs, which does not at all overcome "causality" but merely brings it to light in its machinational essence). To assume that one is able, with this apparently "free" causality, to grasp more easily what is "alive" merely betrays the secretly kept conviction that one will one day bring what is alive *also* under the jurisdiction of explanation. This step is all the closer because, on the side of history, i.e., that realm opposed to nature, the purely "historical" [*"historische"*], respectively "prehistorical" method dominates, which thinks totally in terms of causalities and makes "life" and what is "experienceable" available to causal verification and sees in it exclusively the form of historical "knowing." To admit that "accident" and "fate" co-determine historical events proves all the more the exclusive domination of thinking in terms of causality, insofar as "accident" and "fate" merely represent the imprecise and not unequivocally calculable cause-effect relations. That historical beings could have a totally different way of being (grounded on Da-sein) can never be made knowable to history [as a discipline], because history would then have to renounce itself (regarding what is ownmost to history, cf. *Überlegungen* VI, 33ff., 68f., 74f.). For, as part of the domain in which it runs its course, and which is established in advance, history *as science* has self-evidence, which unconditionally fits an average understandability—an understandability which is demanded by the essence of science as the order of accuracies within the domination and steering of all that is objective in service to *usage and education*.

10. Insofar as the task that is appropriate solely to "science" is the thorough investigation of its region, science carries within itself the

thrust toward *intensifying* the prioritization of the position of proceeding and operating over against the field of the subject matter
itself. The decisive question for science as such is *not* which essential
character a being itself has that lies at the basis of the field of the subject matter, but rather whether with this or that procedure a "knowledge," i.e., a *result* of the research, may be expected. What is key is
the view of the arrangement and readiness of "results." Results and,
in the end, their immediate appropriateness for use guarantee the
accuracy of the research—a scientific accuracy that counts as the
truth of a knowing. By appealing to the "results" and their usefulness, science must by itself seek verification of their necessity.
(Whether thereby "science" is justified as "cultural value" or as "service to the people" or as "political science" makes *essentially no difference.* For this reason all justifications and "endowings of meaning" of
this kind run pell-mell into one another and prove themselves more
and more to belong together in spite of [their] apparent enmity.)
Only a thoroughly modern (i.e., "liberal") science can be "a national
science." Only on the basis of prioritizing the position of procedure
over the subject-matter and of the accuracy of judgment over the
truth of beings does modern science permit an adjustable shifting to
various purposes, depending on need (implementing extreme mate-
rialism and technicism by Bolshevism; introducing four-year plan;
using political education). In all of this science is everywhere *the same*
and becomes, precisely with these various goal-settings, basically
and increasingly more uniform, i.e., more "international."

Because "science" is not a knowing, but rather a mechanism of
accuracies of a region of explanation, "sciences" also and at the
same time necessarily receive new "impetuses" in their respective
goal-settings, with the help of which they can evade every possible
threat (namely every essential one) and can continue to do research
with renewed "peace of mind." Thus it now took only a few years
for "science" to realize that its "liberal" essence and its "ideal of
objectivity" are not only compatible with the political-national "orientation" but also indispensable to it. And hence "science" as well as
"worldview" must now unanimously agree that the talk of a "crisis"
of science was actually only prattle. The "national" "organization" of
science moves along the same lines as the "American" [organization
of science]. The only question is which side has the greater means
and energies for a quicker and full disposal, in order to chase the
unchanged—and from itself unchangeable—essence of modern science unto its utmost end-stance. This is a task that can take centuries yet and in the end increasingly excludes every possibility of a
"crisis" of science, i.e., [excludes] an essential transformation of
knowing and of truth.

11. Every science is rigorous, but not every science is an *"exact science."*
    The concept of "exact" is ambiguous. Generally the word means:
    exact, measured, careful. In this sense every science is required to
    be "exact," namely in view of carefulness in *using* the method, by
    following the rigor that lies in the essence of science. But if "exact"
    means the same as determined, measured, and calculated accord-
    ing to numbers, then exactness is the character of a *method itself*
    (even already of the projected structure [*Vorbau*]), not merely how
    that method is used.

12. If "exactness" means the measuring and calculating procedure
    itself, then the sentence is valid: A science *can* be exact only
    because it must be rigorous.

13. But a science *must* be exact (in order to remain rigorous, i.e., sci-
    ence) if the field of its subject-matter is launched in advance as the
    realm that is accessible only to quantitative measuring and calcula-
    tion, only thus guaranteeing results (the modern concept of
    "nature").

14. The "human sciences" by contrast must remain *inexact* in order to
    be *rigorous*. That is not a lack, but an advantage of these sciences.
    Moreover, execution of rigor in the human sciences in terms of
    performance always remains much more difficult than carrying out
    the exactness of "exact" sciences.

15. As positive and individual in its rigor, every science is dependent
    upon cognizance of its field of subject-matter, dependent upon
    inquiry into the same, dependent upon ἐμπειρία and *experimentum*
    in the broadest sense. Even mathematics needs *experientia*, the sim-
    ple cognizance of its simplest objects and their determinations in
    axioms.

16. Every science is investigative inquiry, but not every science can be
    "experimental" in the sense of the modern concept of experiment.

17. Measuring (exact) science, by contrast, *must be experimental*. "Exper-
    iment" is a necessary, essential consequence of exactness; and a sci-
    ence is in no way exact simply because it experiments (regarding
    experiri, experimentum, and "experiment," as *ordering of experimenta-*
    tion in the modern sense, cf. Echo, 77).

18. The modern counter-form to experimental "science" is [the disci-
    pline of] "history," that draws from "sources," and its derivative
    mode, *"prehistory,"* on the basis of which what is ownmost to *every*
    history can perhaps be most sharply clarified, namely that it never
    reaches *history* [*Geschichte*].

    All of history [as discipline] is nurtured by comparison and
    serves the expansion of the possibilities of comparison. Although
    comparison has apparently focused on differences, yet *differences* for
    history [as a discipline] never become a decisive differentness and

that means never become the singularity of the unique and the simple, in the face of which history would have to recognize itself as insufficient—if it could ever come to face the unique and the simple. The not-known presentiment of history for negating its own essence—a negating that threatens history as it comes from the historical [*Geschichtliches*]—is the innermost reason why historical [*historische*] comparison grasps the differences only in order to place them into a wider and more entangled field of comparability. All comparison, however, is essentially an equalizing, a referral back to a same that as such never even enters knowing awareness but rather makes up what is self-evident in terms of which all explanation and relating receives its clarity. The less history itself is recorded, calculated, and presented and the more only the deeds, works, productions, and opinions as events are recorded, calculated, and presented in their succession and difference, the easier it is for history [as a discipline] to satisfy its own rigor. That it always operates in this field is proven most clearly by the kind of "progress" that historical sciences make. This consists in the respective and in each case variously caused exchanges of the key perspectives for comparison. The discovery of the so-called new "material" is always the consequence, not the ground, of the newly chosen view for explanation. Moreover, there can be times that— despite apparent exclusion of all "interpretations" and "presentations"—limit themselves to securing the "sources," which in turn are themselves designated as the genuine "finds." But even this securing of "finds" and the findable immediately and necessarily proceeds to an *explanation* and thus into the claim of a key perspective. (Explanation is the crudest arrangement and ordering of a find into that which has already been found.)

In the course of the development of history [as a discipline] the material not only grows, not only becomes more surveyable and more accessible more quickly and reliably through more refined institutions, but it also becomes above all more stable in itself, i.e., it remains the same within changes in the views to which it is subordinated. Thus historical work becomes increasingly more convenient, because it only requires the application of a new view for interpreting existing material. But history [as a discipline] never yields this view for interpretation; for it is always only the reflection of the present history in which the historian lives but which he cannot know historically—and in the end can only explain again in terms of history [as a discipline]. But the substitution of views for interpretation then guarantees for a longer time a profusion of new discoveries, which in turn strengthens history [as a discipline] in the self-certainty of its progressiveness and consolidates its own increased evasion of *history* [*Geschichte*]. But when a definitive view for interpretation becomes the only one that is standard, then history [as a discipline] finds in this unequivocation of the key perspective yet another means to raise itself above the heretofore history that is changing in its views, and to bring this stability of its "research" into the long desired correspondence with the "exact sciences" and actually to become "science." This announces itself when history [as a discipline] becomes capable of being operational and "institutionalized" (something like the institutions of the Kaiser Wilhelm Society). This completion of history [as a discipline] into a secured "science" is not at all contradicted by its major achievement that now takes place in the form of reporting that is suitable for the newspaper and historians' coveting such a presentation of world-history. For "newspaper science" is already underway, and not accidentally. One sees it as still another variety—if not a degeneration—of history [as a discipline]; but in truth it merely anticipates the final essence of history as a modern science. It is important to pay attention to the unavoidable coupling of this "newspaper science" in the broad sense with the publishing industry. In their unity both stem from the modern technicized way of being. (Hence, as soon as the "liberal arts faculty" is firmly expanded to that which it already now is, then newspaper science and geography will become its basic sciences. The clear and inherent stunted growth of this "faculty" everywhere is merely the consequence of a failing courage to discard resolutely its illusory character as philosophical and to give the operational character of future "human sciences" full opportunity for its establishment.)

Although theology continues to be determined differently, in terms of "worldview," it is far more advanced than the "human sciences"—being purely operational in its service to *its* determination *as science*. For this reason it is totally appropriate if the theology faculty is ranked after the medical and law faculty but *higher than* the philosophy faculty.

History [as a discipline], always understood in terms of the required character of modern science, is a continual evading of history [*Geschichte*]. But even while evading history, history [as a discipline] still retains a relation to history, and that makes history and the historian ambiguous.

If history is not explained in terms of [the discipline] of history and is not miscalculated by a definite image for definite purposes of forming opinions and convictions, if instead history itself is returned to the uniqueness of its unexplainability and if all the activity of history [as a discipline] and every opinion and belief that arises from it is put into question and given over to an ongoing decision of itself, then what can be called historical thinking is enacted. The historical thinker is as essentially different from the historian as from the philosopher. Least of all should he be brought together with that illusory "creation" that one is accustomed to calling "philosophy of history." The focus of the historical thinker's mindfulness and presentation is always on a definite domain of creating, of decisions, of the summits and precipices within history (whether it be poetry, plastic art, or grounding and leading a state). Insofar as the present and future epoch unfolds as historical, although each in a totally different way—the present-modern epoch, insofar as it suppresses history historically [*historisch*] without being able to avoid it; the future epoch, insofar as it must swing into the simpleness and keenness of historical being—the lines between the figures of historian and historical thinker, seen externally, are today necessarily blurred. This is true the more [the discipline of] history, corresponding to the growing formation of its character as newspaper-science, disseminates the insidious impression of being a super-scientific observation of history—and thus brings historically mindful deliberation into total confusion. But this confusion is increased once again by the Christian apologetics of history, which has come to power and been practiced since Augustine's *civitas dei* and in whose service all non-Christians have today already entered—those for whom everything depends on merely rescuing what has been up to now, i.e., on hindering essential decisions.

Genuine historical thinking will thus be recognizable by only a few. And from these few only the rare will rescue historical knowing all the way through the general hodgepodge of historical [*historischen*] opinion, *to* a future generation's being ready for decision.

Nature is even further removed than history; and blocking history from nature is all the more complete as the knowledge of nature develops into an "organic" observation, without knowing that "organism" simply presents the completion of "mechanism." Thus it happens that an epoch of unrestrained "technicism" can at the same time find its self-interpretation in an "organic worldview."

19. With the growing consolidation of the machinational-technical essence of all sciences, the objective and methodical difference between the natural and the human sciences will recede more and more. Natural sciences will become a part of machine technology and its operations; human sciences will unfold as a comprehensive and gigantic newspaper science, in which the present "lived-experience" will continually be interpreted historically [*historisch*] and in which its *publicness* will be conveyed to everyone by this interpretation, as quickly and as accessibly as possible.

20. "Universities" as "sites for scientific research and teaching" (in this way they are products of the nineteenth century) become merely operational institutions—always "closer and closer to actuality"—in which nothing comes to decision. They will retain the last remnant of a *cultural decoration* only as long as for the time being they must continue to be the instrument for "culture-oriented political" propaganda. Anything like what is ownmost to the "university" will no longer be able to unfold from them—on the one hand, because the political-national mobilization renders superfluous such an ownmost; but on the other hand because scientific operation maintains its course far more securely and conveniently *without* the will to mindfulness. Understood here as thinking-mindfulness of the truth, and that means question-worthiness of be-ing, and *not* as historical erudition that constructs "systems," philosophy has no place in the "university" and finally in the operational institution that it will eventually become. For philosophy "has" no such place at all, unless it be that place that philosophy itself grounds; but no way that proceeds from any established institution is capable of immediately leading to that place.

21. The preceding characterization of "science" does not arise from a hostility to it, because such is simply not possible. In all its present gigantic expansion and certainty of success and sturdiness, "science" does not at all meet the presuppositions of an *essential rank* on the basis of which it could ever move into opposition to the knowing of thinking. Philosophy is neither against nor for science but leaves it to its own mania for its own usefulness—for securing, always more easily and quickly, increasingly more useful results, and thus for making using and needing always more inextricably dependent upon the particular results and their surpassing.

22. If it comes, as it must, to recognizing the predetermined essence of modern science, of its pure and necessarily serviceable operational character and the organization necessary for that, then in the perspective of *this* recognition one must expect, nay even reckon with, a gigantic progress of sciences in the future. These advancements will bring exploitation and usage of the earth as well as rearing and training of humans into conditions that are still inconceivable today and whose onset can neither be hindered nor even held up in any way, by any romantic remembering of what was earlier and different. But these advancements will rarely be noted as something surprising and conspicuous, as cultural achievements, for example; rather, they will follow one after the other as trade secrets, as it were, and will be used up and then banished in their results. Only when science reaches this operational conspicuousness of unwinding is it at that place where it is driving itself to: then

it dissolves itself in and along with the dissolution of all beings themselves. In view of this end, which will be a very enduring final state that will always look like a beginning, science today stands in its best beginning. Only the blind and the foolish will talk today of the "end" of science.

23. In this way "science" pursues the goal of securing for knowing the state of total lack of need and therefore remains the "most modern" in the epoch of the total lack of questioning. All purposes and usefulness are firmly in place, all means are at hand, every usufruct is executable. The only thing that still counts is to overcome the differences in degree of refinement and possibly to bring about the greatest expanse for the easiest usage. The hidden goal toward which all of this and much more rushes, without having the slightest hint of it—and without being able in the slightest to have a hint—is the state of total boredom (cf. 1929/30 lecture course*) in the sphere of the best successes, which one day can no longer hide the character of boredom, in case a remnant of knowing power has then still remained, in order at least to shock in this condition and to disclose this condition and therein the gaping abandonment of beings by being.

24. However, the important *setting free* comes only from the essential *knowing* awareness that is already in the other beginning: it never comes from powerlessness and mere helplessness. But knowing awareness is inabiding in the question-worthiness of be-ing, which preserves its own dignity by gifting itself only too rarely in refusal, as the sheltered enowning of the passage of decision of the arrival and flight of gods in beings. Who is the one to come who grounds this moment of the passing toward the beginning of another "epoch," meaning: to an other history of be-ing?

Dissolution and Blending of the
Dominant Science Faculty

The historical [*historisch*] human sciences become *newspaper* science. The natural sciences become *machine* science.

"Newspaper" and "machine" are meant essentially as the dominant ways of ultimate objectification, which forges ahead (in modernity, the objectification that advances to completion) by sucking up all concreteness [*Sachhaltigkeit*] of beings and taking these [beings] only as an occasion for live-experience.

---

* WS 1929/30, *Die Grundbegriffe der Metaphysik. Welt—Endlichkeit—Einsamkeit* (GA 29/ 30) [trans. W. McNeill and N. Walker, *The Fundamental Concepts of Metaphysics: World, Finitude, Solitude* (Bloomington: Indiana University Press, 1995)].

Due to this priority of procedure in the activity of arranging and preparing, both groups of sciences agree with regard to what is essential, i.e., their *operational* character.

This "development" of modern science into its essence is today visible to only a few and will be rejected by many as non-existing. It can also not be proven by facts, as it can only be grasped by knowing something in terms of the history of being. Many "researchers" will still suppose themselves to belong to the tried and tested traditions of the nineteenth century. In relation to their objects, just as many will still find new concrete enrichment and satisfaction that they will perhaps still validate in teaching. However, all of this proves nothing against *that* process of which the whole institution of "science" is irrevocably a part. Science will not only never be able to detach itself from that process, but it will also and above all never want the detachment—and the more it progresses, the less it *can* want to detach itself.

But this process is above all also not just a phenomenon of the current German university. Rather it concerns everything that anywhere and anytime in the future will still want to be considered as "science."

If the heretofore and earlier forms of institution still hold out for a long time yet, one day they will all the more decidedly let it become clear what has transpired behind their apparent protection.

77. *Experiri—Experientia—Experimentum—*"Experiment"— ἐμπειρία—*Experience—*Probe

In order to be able to provide sufficient determination to the concept of scientific experiment in today's sense of modern science, a glance through the stages and manners of "experience" is necessary, to which connection "experiment" belongs. The long history of the word (and that means also the matter itself) that resonates with the word *experiment* dare not mislead us into wanting also to find knowledge of today's "experiment" or even only the immediate rudiments for it, there where *experimentum, experiri,* and *experientia* come up. The clearer the difference emerges in what the same word says, the more sharply will the essence of modern "experiment" be grasped—or at least the views will be determined according to which this essence becomes manifest. As a preparation for an essential delimitation of "experiment," we want here to sketch out a sequence of steps of "experiencing" and of the "empirical," in accord with the matter itself, without following the history of the word historically [*historisch*].

1. "experience": to come upon something and indeed such that comes upon one; having to take in what encounters one and does something to one, what "affects" one, what encounters one without one's having to *do* anything.

2. experience as *going up to something* that does not "concern" us immediately in the sense just mentioned, the looking around and looking after, explorations simply and only with respect to how it looks and whether it is extant at all and approachable.
3. the preceding going up to something, but in the manner of *testing* how it looks and how it is extant, if this or that is added or taken away.

What is experienced in 2 and 3 is always already somehow *sought*, by applying certain instruments. The mere looking around and looking at becomes an observing that *pursues* what is encountered and indeed under changing conditions of its encountering and coming forth.

Thereby these conditions and their very changing can be found again and expected. But they can also be altered, in this way or that, by an *intervention*. In the latter case we provide ourselves certain experiences by certain interventions and with the application of certain conditions of more exact seeing and determining.

Magnifying glass, microscope: sharpening the seeing and changing the conditions of observability.

The instruments and tools are themselves often prepared materials of the same kind, essentially, as what is being observed.

One can here already speak of an *experimentum* without revealing any trace of "experiment" and its conditions.

This [is] all the more so when observations are gathered, whereby again two cases are possible: an indiscriminate gathering up of observations solely on the basis of their unsurveyable manifoldness and conspicuousness; and a gathering with the intention toward an order, whose "principle" is not derived at all from the observed objects.

4. As testing going-up-to and observing, experiencing focuses in advance on working out a regularity. What is essential here is grasping ahead to what has the character of a rule and that means: to what constantly returns under the same conditions.

78. *Experiri (ἐμπειρία) – "Experiencing"*

1. *thrusting toward something* that thrusts toward one; something pushes up to one, touches one—and one must take it in; the thrusting-toward one. What thrusts itself to one, what concerns one, af-fection, and sense perception. Receptivity and sensibility and sense organs.
2. *going-up-to* something, looking around, looking after, exploring, measuring off.
3. going up-to as *testing*, asking questions, whether when-then, how-if.

In 2 and 3 what is *sought-after* is always *more or less something definite.*
In 2 it is not determined what thrusts itself upon me or what I meet
without my doing. In 3 it is an *intervention* or sharpening of the going-
up-to, laying apart, enlarging with certain aids: instrument, tool, itself
material-thingly. Magnifying glass, microscope, sharpening the vision,
conditions of observability, also a gathering up of many and varied
observations about "regularities" in a totally *indefinite* arrangement—
the conspicuous.

4. The equipmental going-up-to and testing focuses on *working out* a
   rule—grasping ahead to *regularity,* e.g. when so much, then so
   much. When-then as always again constant (ὄν). Testing, running
   a test; Aristotle, Metaphysics A 1: ἐμπειρία, ὑπόληψις, each time
   the when-then. *Probe,* not only "testing" but also bringing what is
   objective into "temptation," setting a trap, bringing into the trap—
   that, not that!

5. Going-up-to and testing, aiming at rules in such a way that generally the rule [*Regelhafte*] and *only* this determines in advance what is
   objective in its domain and that the domain is not graspable in any
   other way than by working out *rules,* and this only by demonstrating regularity (testing possibilities of regularity, probing "nature"
   itself)—and in such a way that the rule is the rule for the *regulation*
   of *measure* [*Maßordnung*] and for possible measurability (space,
   time). What does that say in principle for the tool as something
   material, something of nature?

   Only now [is manifest] the possibility as well as the *necessity* of
   modern experiment. Why necessary? The "exact" experiment (one
   that measures) [over against] the inexact experiment. Only where
   there is a grasping ahead to an essential and merely quantitatively and
   regulationally determined domain of the object is experiment possible; and grasping ahead determines it thus in its essence.

Experiri—Experientia—Intuitus (Argumentum ex re)

This stands *against componere scripta de aliqua re,* i.e., collecting earlier
opinions and authorities and discussing these opinions purely logically,
in order to identify the most insightful ones, above all those that agree
with religious doctrine, or at least do not contradict it *(argumentum ex
verbo).* Cf. medieval natural science, where *essentia* as the real is *the*
point of departure.

Experiri—in this way generally against *what is authoritatively proclaimed* and what is not demonstrable at all and cannot be brought to
light, inaccessible to *lumen naturale* (against *verbum divinum,* "revelation"). Cf. Descartes, *Regula* III.

Already before the Middle Ages this *experiri* [is] ἐμπειρία—[of] the
doctors, [as in] Aristotle! When-then! ἐμπειρία, τέχνη [as] already a

ὑπόληψις of the when-then (rule). But now [it assumes] an essential significance because of opposition, and especially when the transformation of humans [happens as] the certainty of salvation and certainty of the I.

But with that only the *general* presupposition for the possibility of "experiment" [is] initially [given]. The experiment itself is thereby not yet given as something that becomes a *necessary* and prime *component* of knowledge. For that a fundamentally new step has to be taken.

The specific and unique presupposition *for that* is — as remarkable as it sounds — that science become rational-mathematical, i.e., *not* experimental in the highest sense. Setting up nature as such.

Because modern "science" (physics) is mathematical (not empirical), therefore it is necessarily *experimental* in the sense of a *measuring experiment*.

It is sheer nonsense to say that experimental research is Nordic-Germanic and that rational [research] on the other hand comes from foreigners [*fremdartig*]. We would have then already to make up our mind to count Newton and Leibniz among the "Jews." It is precisely the projecting-open of nature in the *mathematical sense* that is the presupposition for the necessity and possibility of "experiment" as measuring [experiment].

Now experiment [is] *not only against* mere talk and dialectic *(sermones et scripta, argumentum ex verbo),* but also against random and merely curious exploration of a *vaguely represented domain (experiri).*

Now experiment [is a] *necessary* component of *exact* science — a science that is grounded in the quantitative projecting-open of nature that enlarges this projecting-open.

Now experiment [is] no longer only against mere *argumentum ex verbo* and against "speculation" but also against all mere *experiri*.

Thus [it is] a *fundamental error* and confusion of essential ideas to say (cf. Gerlach)[1] that modern science begins already in the Middle Ages, because, for example, Roger Bacon deals with *experiri* and *experimentum* and thereby also talks of *quantities*.

If so, then back to the source of this medieval "modernity": Aristotle, ἐμπειρία.

Now experiment over against experiri.

In the setting up of nature, as the interconnection of the "existence" of things according to laws, what co-determining but increasingly retreating role is played by the *harmonia mundi* and ideas of *ordo*, κόσμος.

Basic conditions for the possibility of modern experiment [are]:

1. the mathematical projecting-open of nature; objectness, re-presentedness;

---

[1]E.g. Walter Gerlach, *Theorie und Experiment in der exakten Wissenschaft,* in: M. Hartmann and W. Gerlach, *Naturwissenschaftliche Erkenntnis und ihre Methoden* (Berlin, 1937).

2. transformation of the essence of actuality from essentiality to individuality. Only with this presupposition can an *individual result* claim the force of justification and confirmation.

79. Exact Science and Experiment

1. To what extent does exact science require experiment?
2. Preliminary question: *What is an experiment?*
   experiri and experiment
3. To show that *within natural science* "experiment" and "experiment" are each different, each in its *character,* depending on objectness and the manner of *inquiring* into that character. The purely measuring experiment.
4. A "psychological" experiment.
5. A "biological" experiment.

A "Psychological" Experiment

[We consider a psychological experiment] not only in order to show what an experiment is (this, too), but also to show what other direction and stage of objectification [takes place].

What now to look to?	Facts
What not [to look at]?	and
What [is] the difference?	Laws

For what purpose and why this "experiment"?
In what context of questioning does it stand?

80. *Experiri — Experientia — Experimentum —* "Experiment"

[*Experiri* means] *experiencing, running into something, something thrust upon one;* I have had my experiences, my *"bad"* experiences.

In the Middle Ages and already earlier [*experiri* is] different from λόγος, different from *sermo (componere scripta de aliqua re),* different from what is merely said, or communicated, but in actuality not demonstrated, different from the *authoritatively* proclaimed and as such *not demonstrable at all.* By contrast: looking-*into* [something] and going-up-to [something], *making out,* thereby always *something sought* after depending on what is sought, a *testing.*

[*Experiri* occurs] *with the help of a directionality, arrangement, instrumentum,* or without these—for example, *testing* whether *water is warm or cold,* or from where the wind blows.

[*Experiri* is] a specific procedure, in order to render *something* given. But the question is "what" and "how," whether [it is] simply a such and such, *quale,* or whether [it is] the *existence of a relationship* if-then, "cause-effect," wherefrom, why? *(Use of the magnifying glass or microscope).* And again, whether *this relationship* [is] still determined quantitatively: if so many, then so many.

[*Experiri* is] grasping ahead to what is *sought* and that means *what is inquired about as such.* Correspondingly, [it is] the *arrangement* and *ordering of the procedure.* But all this *experiri* is not yet the modern "experiment."

The deciding factor in modern "experiment"—testing as *probing*—is not the "apparatus" as such, but the way of questioning, i.e., the *concept of nature.* "Experiment" in the modern sense is *experientia* in the sense of *exact science.* Because it is exact, therefore it is *experiment.*

Now the difference [in experiment is] no longer over against mere talking and collecting *opinions and "authorities" about a subject matter* but rather over against mere description, *taking in and identifying what offers itself,* without the definite preliminary concept that predelineates the procedure.

Even a *description* is already "interpretation," e.g., something *as* "color," *as* "sound," *as* "magnitude." Interpretation is different from interpretation. *Physical interpretation*!

Which is more certain: the immediate and naive description, or exact experiment? The first, because it presupposes "less theory"!

What does the demand for *repeatability* of the experiment mean?

1. Constancy of the circumstances and the instruments.
2. Communication of the theory and inquiry that belong to it.
3. Universally valid demonstrability (universal validity and "objectivity"); representedness and accuracy and truth—factuality.

III. Playing-Forth*

* Cf. in this regard SS 1937, *Übungen. Nietzsches metaphysische Grundstellung. Sein und Schein* [GA 87]; and WS 1937/38, *Übungen. Die metaphysischen Grundstellungen des abendländischen Denkens (Metaphysik)* [GA 88] and all historical [*geschichtliche*] lecture courses.

81. Playing-Forth

Coming to grips with the necessity of the *other* beginning from out of the originary positioning of the first beginning.

The *guiding-attunement:* delight in alternately surpassing the beginnings in questioning.

To this [belongs] everything involved in differentiating the guiding-question and the grounding-question; responding to the guiding-question and actually unfolding it; crossing to the grounding-question *(Being and Time).*

All lectures on the "history" of philosophy [belong here]. The decision of every "ontology" [is made here].

82. Playing-Forth

What is ownmost to playing-forth is historical. Playing-forth is a first foray into the crossing, a bridge that swings out to a shore that must first be decided.

But the playing-forth of the history of the first-ever-inceptual thinking is not an historical [*historische*] addendum to and a portending of a "new" "system" but rather is in itself essentially a transformation-initiating preparation for the other beginning. Therefore, in a manner more inconspicuous and more decisive, we must perhaps only direct the historically mindful deliberation toward the thinkers in the history of the first beginning and, by way of a questioning dialogue with their questioning posture, unexpectedly plant a questioning that one day finds itself expressly rooted in an other beginning. But because this historically mindful deliberation—as playing-forth of the beginnings which are self-grounding and belong, each in its own way, to the abground—originates in the crossing from within the other beginning and because understanding this already requires the leap, therefore this mindfulness is all too easily prone to the misinterpretation that finds only historical [*historische*] observations about works of thinking, whose selection is guided by some arbitrary preference. [This is] especially [the case] since the external form of these historically mindful deliberations (lectures on the "history of philosophy") does not distinguish itself at all from what a subsequent erudition presents with regard to a completed history of philosophy.

Historically mindful deliberations can be used—and even quite advantageously—merely as historical [*historisch*] observations that are immediately correctable and perhaps as discoveries, without there ever breaking forth from them the hint of *that* history that is of be-ing itself and that bears in itself *the* decisions of all decisions.

Historically mindful deliberations have the basis of their enactability in be-ing-historical *thinking.* But how is it if we have lost what is ownmost to thinking and if "logic" has been predestined to exercise control over "thinking," whereas "logic" itself is only a residue of the *powerlessness* of thinking, i.e., of the unsupported and unprotected questioning in the abground of the truth of being? And how would it be if "thinking" now only counts as error-free reasoning in correct representation of objects, as the *avoiding* of that questioning?

83. The View of All Metaphysics on Being

Metaphysics believes that being lets itself be found in beings—and in such a way that thinking goes beyond beings.

The more exclusively thinking turns to beings and seeks for itself a ground that exists *totally as a being* [*seiendste Grund*] (cf. Descartes and modernity), the more decisively philosophy distances itself from the truth of be-ing.

But how is the metaphysical renunciation of beings, i.e., renunciation of metaphysics, possible without falling prey to the "nothing"?

Da-sein is the grounding of the truth of be-ing.

The less a being [*unseiender*] man is and the less he insists upon the being which he finds himself to be, so much nearer does he come to being. (No Buddhism! The opposite.)

84. A Being

[A being] in its *emergence* unto itself (Classical Greece); [a being] *caused* by a supreme [being] of the same essence (Middle Ages); [a being as] the extant as *object* (modernity).

The truth of be-ing becomes increasingly more hidden, and the possibility becomes increasingly more rare that this truth as such will become the grounding power and will be known at all as such.

85. The Originary Coming-into-Its-Own of the First Beginning Means Gaining a Foothold in the Other Beginning

The first beginning's coming originarily into its own (and that means into its history) means gaining a foothold in the other beginning. This is accomplished in crossing from the *guiding-question* (what is a being? the question of beingness, being) to the *grounding-question:* What is the truth of be-ing? (Being and be-ing is the same and yet fundamentally different.)

Historically grasped, this crossing is the overcoming—and indeed the first and first possible overcoming—of *all* "metaphysics." "Metaphysics" now first becomes recognizable in what is its ownmost; and, in thinking in the crossing, all talk of "metaphysics" becomes ambiguous. Put into the domain of the crossing to the other beginning, the *question:* What is metaphysics? (cf. the lecture in connection with *Being and Time* and *Vom Wesen des Grundes*) already inquires into what is ownmost to "metaphysics" in the sense of gaining an initial footing in crossing to the other beginning. In other words, the question already asks from within this [other beginning]. What it makes manifest as determination of "metaphysics" is already no longer metaphysics but rather its overcoming. What this question wants to achieve is not the clarification and thus rigidifying of the hitherto necessarily confused ideas of "metaphysics" but rather the thrust into the *crossing* and thereby the knowing awareness that *any kind* of metaphysics has and must come to an end, if philosophy is to attain its other beginning.

If "metaphysics" is made to become manifest as a happening which belongs to Da-sein as such, then this does not mean a very cheap "anthropological" anchoring of the discipline of metaphysics in humans. Rather, with Da-sein that ground is obtained where the truth of be-ing is grounded, so that now be-ing itself originarily comes to mastery and the position of *surpassing* beings, i.e., proceeding from beings as extant and as objects, becomes impossible. And so is finally manifest what metaphysics was, namely this surpassing of beings to beingness (idea). But this determination of "metaphysics" unavoidably persists in being ambiguous insofar as it *looks* as if it is only a contemporary version [*Fassung*] of the prevailing concept that does not alter anything in the matter. That it is; but because grasping [*Fassung*] what is ownmost to "metaphysics" becomes in advance and thoroughly a grounding of *Da-sein,* this grasping blocks any access to a further possibility for "metaphysics." To understand [metaphysics] within the thinking of the crossing means to transpose what is understood into its impossibility. Is it still necessary specifically to protect this warding off of "metaphysics" from getting mixed up with the "anti-metaphysical" tendency of "positivism" (and its varieties)? Hardly, if we consider that "positivism" indeed presents the crudest of all "metaphysical" ways of thinking, insofar as it contains a completely definite decision about the beingness of a being (sensation), on the one hand, and, on the other hand, by fundamentally establishing a uniform "causality," continually *surpasses* even this being. But thinking in the crossing has nothing to do with an "opposition" to "metaphysics"—an "opposition" which would put metaphysics back into place anew—but with an overcoming of metaphysics from its ground up. Metaphysics is at an end, not because it inquired too much, too uncritically, and too misleadingly into the beingness of a being, but because, as a consequence of deviating from the first beginning, metaphysics with this inquiry could never inquire into be-ing as what is fundamentally sought after; and in the end, perplexed by this powerlessness, metaphysics lapsed into the "renewal" of "ontology."

Metaphysics as knowing the "being" of beings had to come to an end (consider Nietzsche) because it did not dare at all and ever yet to inquire into the truth of be-ing; and, therefore, even in its own history it always had to remain confused and uncertain about its guiding-thread (of thinking). But for this very reason, thinking in the crossing dare not succumb to the temptation of simply leaving behind that which it has grasped as the end and in the end but must *accomplish* this end, i.e., by grasping this end now for the first time in what is ownmost to it and by letting this be transformed and played into the truth of be-ing. The talk of the end of metaphysics should not mislead us into believing that philosophy is finished with "metaphysics." On the contrary: In its essential impossibility metaphysics must now first be played-forth into philosophy; and philosophy itself must be played over into its other beginning.

If we ponder *this task* of the other beginning (the question of the "meaning" of be-ing in the formulation of *Being and Time*), then it will also become clear that all attempts that *react against* metaphysics—which is everywhere idealistic, even as positivism—persist in being re-active and thus are in principle dependent upon metaphysics and thereby remain themselves metaphysics. All biologisms and naturalisms, which present "nature" and the non-rational as what sustains everything and from which everything arises as "all-life" wherein everything bubbles as night against day, etc.—all of this stays completely within the fundament [*Boden*] of metaphysics and needs it in order to brush up against it so that a spark of the knowable and sayable—and for these "thinkers" writeable—still springs up.

Many signs—e.g., the beginning predominance of the "metaphysics" of Richard Wagner and of [Houston Stewart] Chamberlain—indicate that the *end* of Western metaphysics, already creatively and singularly accomplished by Nietzsche, is once again covered over and that this "resurrection" of metaphysics once again uses the Christian churches for its own purposes.

86. What the History of Metaphysics Keeps Ready and Thus "Plays Forth" as Still Unyielded and Unrecognizable by This History

1. Beingness is *presence.*
2. Be-ing is *self-sheltering.*
3. Beings have *priority.*
4. Beingness is the *addendum* and *therefore* the *"a priori."*

We are not capable of grasping what is contained in all of this as long as the truth of be-ing has not become a necessary question for us, as long as we have not grounded the free play of time-space in whose stretches we can first estimate what has happened in the history of metaphysics: the prelude of en-owning itself as the essential swaying of be-ing. Only when we succeed in projecting-open the history of metaphysics into those stretches (1-4) do we grasp its unyielded ground. But as long as we obtain our perspectives from what could and had to become the actual knowledge of metaphysics (doctrine of ideas and its variation), we will be forced into what is historical [*historisch*] — unless we already grasp ἰδέα according to 1-4.

87. History of the First Beginning
(History of Metaphysics)

[History of the first beginning] is the history of metaphysics. It is not the individual attempts at metaphysics as doctrines that tell us anything now at the end of all metaphysics but rather "only" the history of metaphysics. However, this "only" is not a delimitation but the demand for something more originary. (Still less should we misconstrue the individual instances of "metaphysics" as mere games meant for being transcended.) Rather, now at the end metaphysics must be taken seriously in a way that essentially surpasses any inheriting and handing over of particular doctrines and any renewal of standpoints and any mixing and adjusting of many such doctrines.

In its history metaphysics becomes manifest only when its guiding-questions are grasped and when treatment of these questions is unfolded. To what extent does *history* teach? What is meant by that?

When the question of beings as such, the inquiry into beingness, occurs, there is in that occurrence a definite opening up of beings as such, so that man thereby receives his essential determination, which stems from this opening *(homo animal rationale).* But what opens up this opening of beings to beingness and thus to be-ing? There is a need for a history and that means for a beginning and its derivations and advancements, in order to allow for the experience (for the beginners who question) that refusal belongs to the essential sway of be-ing. Because this knowing awareness thinks nihilism still more originarily into the abandonment of being, this knowing is the actual overcoming of nihilism; and history of the first beginning thus completely loses the appearance of futility and mere errancy. Only now the great light shines on all the heretofore [accomplished] work of thinking.

88. The "Historical" Lectures Belong to
the Sphere of This Task

The "historical" lectures belong to the sphere of this task:

to make manifest *Leibniz's* unfathomable manifold shaping of the onset of the question but to think Da-sein instead of *monas;*

to re-enact *Kant's* main steps but to overcome the "transcendental" point of departure through Da-sein;

to question thoroughly *Schelling's* question of freedom and nevertheless to place the question of "modalities" on another ground;

to place *Hegel's* system in the commanding view and then to think in a totally opposite direction;

to dare to come to grips with *Nietzsche* as the one who is nearest but to recognize that he is farthest removed from the question of being.

Those are some of the ways, independent in themselves and yet interconnected, to coax into knowing awareness what is always only *sole and unique*, namely that the essential swaying of be-ing needs the grounding of the *truth* of be-ing and that this grounding must be enacted as *Da-sein*, by which all idealism, and along with that metaphysics *up to now* and metaphysics in general, is overcome as a necessary unfolding of the first beginning—which in this way moves anew into the dark, in order to be grasped as such only in terms of the other beginning.

89. Crossing to the Other Beginning

To grasp Nietzsche as the end of Western metaphysics is not a historical [*historisch*] statement about what lies behind us but the *historical* [*geschichtlich*] onset of the future of Western thinking. The question of beings must be placed on its own ground, on the question of the truth of be-ing. And what up to now made up the guiding clue and formed the horizon of all interpretation of beings—thinking ([as] re-present-ing)—will be taken back into *Da-sein* as the grounding of the truth of be-ing. "Logic" as doctrine of correct thinking will become mindfulness of what is ownmost to *language* as the instituting-naming of the truth of be-ing. However, be-ing, up to now the most general and most common in the shape of beingness, becomes—as enowning—the most unique and most estranging.

The *crossing* to the other beginning introduces a *caesura* that long since no longer runs along with directions of philosophy (idealism—realism, etc.) or even along with attitudes of "worldview." The crossing separates the emerging of be-ing and its truth-grounding in Dasein from any occurring and perceiving of beings.

What is separated is so decidedly separated that no common area of differentiation can prevail at all.

There is no adjustment and no agreement in this decidedness of the crossing but rather long lasting alonenesses and the stillest delights at the hearth of be-ing, although this be-ing is still completely shoved aside in the pallor of artificial shining of machinationally experienced "beings" (the "actuality that is "true to life").

The crossing to the other beginning is clear-cut; nevertheless we do not know *whither* we go nor *when* the truth of be-ing becomes the true nor whence history as the history of be-ing takes its steepest and short-est path.

As the ones who cross in this crossing, we must traverse an essential mindfulness of *philosophy* itself so that it obtains the beginning from within which it can once again be completely itself and not need any support (cf. Preview, 15: Philosophy as "Philosophy of a People").

90. From the First to the Other Beginning: Negation

How few understand—and how rarely those who understand grasp—"negation." One immediately sees in it only rejection, putting aside, degrading, and even destroying. Not only are these forms of negation often pretentious, they also most immediately encourage the common idea of "no." Thus the thought of the possibility that negation could perhaps have a still deeper being than "yes" is left out—especially since one quickly also takes "yes," in the sense of any kind of approval, as superficially as the "no."

But is approving and rejecting in the domain of representing and of representing "evaluation" the only form of yes and no? Is that domain after all the only and essential domain, or is it rather, like all correctness, derived from a more originary truth? And in the end is not the "yes and no" an essential possession of *being* itself—and the "no" even more originarily than the "yes"?

But how? Must not the "no" (and the "yes") have its essential form in the Da-sein that is used by be-ing? The "no" is the great leap-*off,* by which the t/here [*Da*] in Da-*sein* is leaped into: the leap-off that both "affirms" that from which it leaps off and has itself as leap no nothing [*nichts Nichtiges*]. The leap-off itself first undertakes to leap-open the leap, and in this way the "no" surpasses the "yes." Therefore, however, seen externally, this "no" sets the other beginning apart from the first beginning—never "negating" in the usual sense of rejecting or even degrading. Rather, this originary negating is like that not-granting that repels from itself a still-going-along-with out of knowing and recognizing the uniqueness of that which in its end calls for the other beginning.

Of course, such a negating is not satisfied with a leaping-off that simply leaves [the first beginning] behind. Rather, the negating unfolds by laying open the first beginning and its inceptual history and by putting what is opened up back into the possession of the beginning, where it, laid back, even now and in the future still towers over everything that once took place in its course and became an object of historical [*historisch*] reckoning. Such an erecting of the towering of the first beginning is the sense of "destruction" in the crossing to the other beginning.

91. From the First to the Other Beginning*

The first beginning experiences and posits the *truth of beings,* without inquiring into truth as such, because what is unhidden in it, a being as a being, necessarily overpowers everything and uses up the nothing, taking it in or destroying it completely as the "not" and the "against."

---

* Cf. Leap, 130: The "Essential Sway" of Being; 132: Be-ing and a Being.

The other beginning experiences the truth of be-ing and inquires into the be-ing of *truth* in order first to ground the essential swaying of be-ing and to let beings as the true of that originary truth spring forth.

Everything academic is always impossible — in very different ways — in the inceptuality of these beginnings, and what belongs to the crossing constitutes the actual struggle. But there is always the danger that, wherever the beginning turns into a start and a progression, these count as the standard according to which the inceptual is not only estimated but also interpreted.

From within the first beginning, thinking starts to consolidate itself, at first implicitly and then specifically grasped as the question: What is a being? (*the* guiding-question of Western "metaphysics," which begins with this question). But the belief that would want to come across this guiding question in the first beginning and as the beginning is erroneous. It is only as a crude and preliminary injunction that thinking the first beginning can be characterized with the help of the "guiding-question."

On the other hand the inceptual of the beginning gets lost, i.e., it withdraws into the ungrounded dimension of the beginning, as soon as the guiding-question sets standards for thinking.

If we actually look for the history of philosophy in the *occurrence* of thinking and its first beginning, and if we keep this thinking in its historicity open by *unfolding* the ununfolded guiding-question — which has been ununfolded throughout this whole history, up to Nietzsche — then the inner movement of this thinking can be delineated, even if only formally and by single steps and stages, as:

Following the guiding-thread and fore-grasping of "thinking" (receiving assertion), the experience, receiving [*Vernehmung*], and gathering of a being in its truth are consolidated into the question of the beingness of a being.

Beingness and Thinking

However, this priority and fore-grasping character of thinking (λόγος — *ratio — intellectus*) — not grounded any further — is consolidated in the conception of human-being as *animal rationale,* which arises from the inceptual experience of beings as such. The possibility is laid out in advance that *that* guiding character of thinking regarding the interpretation of beings would now more than ever presume to be the only site for decision about beings, especially when, beforehand and for a long time, *ratio* and *intellectus* were forced into a relationship of service (Christian faith), which did not give rise to a new interpretation of beings but to a strengthened importance of man as individual (salvation of the soul). Now came the possibility of a situation in which what was reasonable for faith had to be legitimate for *ratio,* insofar as everything was oriented toward this faith and all possibilities were exhausted in it.

Why should not *ratio* also—at first still in alliance with *fides*—claim the *same* for itself, secure itself for itself, and make this security the standard for all consolidation and "grounding" (*ratio* as ground)? Now the significance of thinking begins to transfer itself into the self-security of thinking (*veritas* becomes *certitudo*); and thus thinking must now be put into a formula—indeed into an altered claim for efficiency. Correspondingly, determination of the beingness of beings is transformed into objectness:

Thinking (Certainty) and Objectness (Beingness)

To show from this point on:

1. how modern thinking is determined up to Kant;
2. how the originality of Kant's thinking comes from this;
3. how, by means of a swing back into the Christian tradition, along with abandoning of Kant's position, the absolute thinking of German Idealism arises;
4. how the *asthenia* for metaphysical thinking, along with the effective forces of the nineteenth century (liberalism—industrialization—technicity), summons positivism;
5. but how at the same time the Kantian tradition and German Idealism is preserved and a resumption of Platonic thinking is sought (Lotze and his metaphysics of values);
6. how, going beyond all of this and yet carried by and wrapped in it and coming to grips with the most questionable mix (following from 3, 4, and 5) which is Schopenhauer, Nietzsche recognizes his task of overcoming Platonism without ever penetrating into *that* domain of questioning and *that* basic position from within which this task can be freed up and secured from what has gone on up to now.

In this history the attitude peculiar to the guiding-question remains increasingly self-evident and hence unthought in the sense of the formula: *thinking and objectness.*

Even where Nietzsche deploys becoming *against* "being" (beingness), it happens under the assumption that "logic" determines beingness. The flight into "becoming" ("life") is metaphysically only a way out, the *last* way out at the end of metaphysics, which everywhere carries the signs of what Nietzsche himself recognized early on as his task: the overturning of Platonism.

But every overturning is all the more a return to, and an entanglement in the opposite (sensible—supersensible), even though Nietzsche senses that this opposite too must lose its meaning.

For Nietzsche "beings" (the actual) remain becoming, and "being" remains solidification and inconstant constancy [*Verbeständigung*].

Nietzsche remains caught in *metaphysics:* from beings to being; and he exhausts all possibilities of this basic position, which in the meantime—

as he himself was the first to see most clearly—became in every possible form the common possession and "body of thought" for the worldviews of the masses.

The first step toward a creative overcoming of the end of metaphysics had to be taken in the direction by which thinking's posture is retained in one respect, but in another respect and at the same time is basically led beyond itself.

Retaining means: inquiring into the *being* of *beings*. But the overcoming means: inquiring first into the *truth* of be-ing—into that which in metaphysics *never* became a question— and never could.

This twofold character in the crossing, that grasps metaphysics more originarily and thus at the same time overcomes it, is through and through the mark of "fundamental ontology," i.e., the mark of *Being and Time*.

This title is chosen on the basis of a clear understanding of the task: no longer beings and beingness but rather being; no longer "thinking" but rather "time"; no longer *thinking* in advance but rather be-ing. "Time" as the name for the "truth" of being. And all of this as a task, as "being underway"—not as "doctrine" and dogmatics.

Now the guiding basic position of Western metaphysics is beingness and thinking; and "thinking"—*ratio*, reason—as guiding-thread for fore-grasping of the interpretation of beings is put into question, but by no means only so that thinking would be replaced by "time" and everything would be meant "more temporally" and more existentially—while all else would remain the same. Rather, now *that* has become a question which could not become a question in the first beginning: *truth* itself.

Now everything is and becomes different. Metaphysics has become impossible. For, what comes first is the truth of be-ing and the essential swaying of be-ing—not that *"to and from which"* [*wohinaus*] transcendence [*Überstieg*] is to ensue.

But now the issue is also not something like overturning the hitherto existing metaphysics. Rather, with the more originary essential swaying of the truth of be-ing as enowning, the relation to beings is a different relationship (no longer that of ὑπόθεσις and "condition of possibility"— of κοινόν and ὑποκείμενον).

Be-ing holds sway as *the enowning of the grounding of the t/here* [*Da*] and itself determines anew the truth of essential sway from within the essential swaying of truth.

The other beginning is the leaping into be-ing's more originary truth, which transforms *be-ing*.

Western thinking, in accordance with *its* beginning, gives priority in the guiding-question to beings over being; the *a priori* is only the veiling of the supplementarity of be-ing that must rule insofar as be-ing is opened up with the immediate, first receiving-gathering advance toward beings (cf. in "Leap": being and the *a priori*).

Thus it should not be surprising—but must be seen specifically as a consequence—how then, in certain interpretations, beings themselves become determinant [*maßstäblich*] for beingness. In spite of, or even on the basis of the priority of, φύσις and of φύσει ὄν, the θέσει ὄν and ποιούμενον become precisely that which now furnishes what is *understandable* for the receiving interpretation and determines the understandability of beingness itself (as ὕλη—μορφή, cf. Frankfurt lectures 1936*) (cf. Playing-Forth, 97: φύσις, τέχνη).

For that reason τέχνη as a basic characteristic of knowledge, i.e., as the basic relation to beings as such, is in the background and thereupon comes to the fore in a special way in Plato.

Does all of this not indicate that even φύσις, too, has to be interpreted in conformity with the ποιούμενον of ποίησις (cf. finally Aristotle) and that φύσις is not powerful enough to demand and sustain the unfolding of its truth over and above the παρουσία and ἀλήθεια?

But this is what the other beginning wants to and must achieve: leaping into the truth of be-ing so that be-ing itself grounds humanness—not even immediately but rather grounds humanness primarily as a consequence of, and as allotment to, *Da-sein*.

The first beginning is not mastered; and the truth of be-ing, in spite of its essential shining, is not expressly grounded. And this means that a *human fore-grasping* (of asserting, of τέχνη, of certainty) sets the standard for the interpretation of the beingness of be-ing.

But now the *great turning around* is necessary, which is beyond all "revaluation of all values," that turning around in which beings are not grounded in terms of human being, but rather human being is grounded in terms of be-ing. But this requires a higher strength for creating and questioning and at the same time a deeper preparedness for suffering and settling within the whole of a complete transformation of relations to beings and to be-ing.

Now the relation to be-ing can no longer be a corresponding retrieval of a relation to beings (διανοεῖν—νοεῖν—κατηγορεῖν).

But because that inceptual fore-grasping in terms of the receiving comportment (νοῦς—*ratio*) transfers humans into and out of beings, so that by virtue of that foregrasping a *highest* being as ἀρχή—αἰτία—*causa*—is thought as the unconditioned, it looks as if this is not a lowering of being into human being. That first-ever inceptual foregrasping of thinking as guiding-thread for interpreting beings can, of course, be understood in terms of the other beginning, as a kind of not yet having mastered the still unexperienceable *Da-sein* (cf. Grounding, 212: Truth as Certainty).

* *Der Ursprung des Kunstwerkes*, in: *Holzwege* (GA 5).

In the *first beginning* truth (as unconcealment) is a mark of beings as such; and, according to the transformation of truth to correctness of assertion, "truth" becomes a determination of beings as they are transformed to objectness. (Truth as correctness of judgment, "objectivity," *"actuality"* — "being" of beings.)

In the *other beginning* truth is recognized and grounded as the truth of be-ing and be-ing itself is recognized and grounded as be-ing of truth, i.e., as *enowning which is in itself turning [in sich kehriges Ereignis]*, to which belongs the inner issuance of the cleavage and thus the *ab-ground*.

Leaping into the other beginning is returning into the first beginning, and vice versa. But returning into the first beginning (the "retrieval") is not displacement into what has passed, as if this could be made "actual" again in the usual sense. Returning into the first beginning is rather and precisely distancing from it, is taking up that distant-positioning which is necessary in order to experience what began in and as that beginning. For *without* this distant-positioning — and only the positioning in the *other* beginning is a sufficient one — we always stay insidiously too close to that beginning, insofar as we are still covered over and pinned down by what issues from the beginning. Therefore our view remains totally constrained and transfixed by the sphere of the traditional question: What is a being? i.e., transfixed by metaphysics of every kind.

Only the distant-positioning to the first beginning allows the experience that the question of truth (ἀλήθεια) necessarily remained unasked in that beginning and that this *not* happening determined Western thinking in advance as "metaphysics."

And only this knowing awareness plays forth to us the necessity of preparing the other beginning and, by unfolding this preparedness, of experiencing the ownmost distress in its full light, the abandonment of being, which, deeply hidden, is the mirror-play to that not-happening and which therefore cannot be explained according to today's and yesterday's abuses and omissions.

If this distress did not have the greatness of its source in the first beginning, whence then would it obtain the power to urge on to preparedness for the other beginning? And hence the question of truth is the first step toward being prepared. In the future this question of truth — only *one* essential shape of the question of be-ing — holds this question outside the domains of "metaphysics."

92. Setting into Perspective the First and the Other Beginning

Not a *counter-movement,* because all counter-movements and counter-forces are to a large degree co-determined by *what* they are "against," even though in the form of reversing what they are against. And therefore a *counter*-movement never suffices for an *essential* transformation of history. Counter-movements become entangled in their own victory, and that means that they are clamped onto what they conquer. They do not free a creating ground but deny it as unnecessary.

Something entirely other must begin, beyond counter-forces and counter-drives and counter-establishments. For transforming and saving the history that is determined by the West, this means that future decisions do not fall in the hitherto existing domains—domains still occupied by counter-movements ("culture"—"worldview"). Rather, the place for decision has first to be grounded, by opening the truth of be-ing in be-ing's uniqueness, which precedes all oppositions in the hitherto existing "metaphysics."

The other beginning is not counter-directed to the first. Rather, *as the other* it stands outside the counter [*gegen*] and outside immediate comparability.

Thus setting [the beginnings] into perspective also does not mean opposition, neither in the sense of crude rejection nor in the manner of sublating [*Aufhebung*] the first in the other. From a new originariness the other beginning assists the first beginning unto the truth of its history—and thus unto its inalienable and ownmost otherness, which becomes fruitful solely in the historical dialogue of thinkers.

93. The Great Philosophies

[The great philosophies] are towering mountains, unclimbed and unclimbable. But they endow the land with what is highest and show its primeval bedrock. They stand as the aiming point and forever form the sphere of sight; they bear transparency and concealment. When are such mountains *really* what they are? Certainly not when we have supposedly climbed and conquered them. Rather, only when they truly *persevere* for us and for the land. But how few are capable of this, of letting the most lively soaring emerge in the stillness of the mountain range and of remaining in the sphere of this soaring-over? This alone is what thinking's genuine setting-into-perspective must strive for.

Setting the great philosophies into perspective—as basic metaphysical positions in the history of the guiding-question—must proceed in such a way that every essential philosophy comes to stand as one mountain among mountains—and thus to bring about what is its most essential.

To that end the guiding-question must each time be unfolded anew (out of the reticent grounding-question) according to its full structural texture, in the respective direction in which this question resonates (cf. Preview: Inceptual Thinking).

94. Setting Apart the Other Beginning

Setting apart the other beginning from the first beginning can never have the sense of proving that the history of the guiding-question and thus "metaphysics" heretofore are an "error." That way what is ownmost to truth would be as misunderstood as would be the essential swaying of be-ing, both of which are inexhaustible, because they are the most unique for every knowing awareness.

However, this setting-apart *does* show that the heretofore existing interpretation of beings is no longer necessary and that this interpretation can no longer experience and induce any distress for its "truth" and for the manner in which it leaves even the truth of itself unasked. For since Plato no inquiry has been made into the *truth* of the interpretation of "being." The correctness of representation and its demonstration by intuition was merely transferred back, from representing of beings to representing of the "essence"—most recently in pre-hermeneutical phenomenology.

95. The First Beginning

The shelteredness of the inceptual must be preserved above all. Every distortion by attempts at explaining is to be avoided, because every explaining necessarily never reaches the beginning but only draws the beginning down to itself.

[One needs to show] that in the first beginning "time" as presencing as well as constancy (in a double and entangled sense of "present") makes up the open, from which beings as beings (being) have their truth. Conforming to the greatness of the beginning is that "time" itself and time as the truth of be-ing are never deemed worthy of questioning and experiencing. And just as little did anyone ask why, for the truth of be-ing, time comes into play as the present and not as past and future. What is left unasked shelters and conceals itself as such and allows for inceptual thinking only the uncanniness of rising [*Aufgehen*]—of constant presencing in the openness (ἀλήθεια) of beings themselves—to make up the essential swaying. Without being grasped as such, essential swaying is presencing.

That for the retrieving mindfulness time first lights up *for us,* as the truth of be-ing, out of the first beginning—this does not mean that the originary, full truth of be-ing could be grounded only upon time. Indeed, one must first generally attempt to think what is ownmost to time so originarily (in time's "ecstasis") that time becomes graspable as the possible truth for be-ing as such. But already thinking time through in this way brings time, in its relatedness to the t/here [*Da*] of Da-sein, into an essential relationship with the spatiality of Da-sein and thus with space (cf. Grounding). But measured against their ordinary representations, time and space are here more originary; and ultimately, they are time-space, which is not a coupling of time and space but what is more originary in their belonging together. But what is more originary points to the essential sway of truth as the sheltering that lights up. The truth of *be-ing* is nothing less than the *essential sway of truth,* grasped and grounded as the sheltering that lights up, the happening of Da-sein, the happening of the turning point in the turning as the self-opening mid-point.

96. The Inceptual Interpretation of Beings as φύσις

How insufficient is the level of our ownership of genuine thinking capacity that we can no longer assess at all the uniqueness of this pro-jecting-open [of φύσις] but rather pass it off as the most natural thing, because of course human thinking does have "nature" immediately in front of it.

Not to mention that nowhere here are we dealing with "nature" (neither as object of natural science nor as scenery nor as sensibility), how do we rightly grasp the strangeness and uniqueness of this projecting-open?

Why, in the open of φύσις, did λόγος as well as νοῦς already have to be named early on as the grounding sites of "being" and why was all knowing arranged accordingly?

The oldest saying about beings that has been handed down is Anaximander's fragment (cf. SS 32*).

97. φύσις (τέχνη)

φύσις is so overpowering that νοεῖν and λόγος are experienced as belonging to it, even belonging to *beings* in their beingness (not yet grasped "generally" in terms of ideas). But as soon as experience, as originary knowing of beings themselves, unfolds *unto* inquiring *into* beings, questioning itself must retreat from beings, must be grasped as differentiated—and in a certain sense independently—from beings, must set itself up *before* [*vor*] them and put them *forth*. But at the same time, as inquiry it must master a direction for questioning. But this direction can be taken only from what is asked about. But how can this happen, if beings as such remain the first and the last and if constancy and presencing (as *rising*, ἀλήθεια) are experienced and held fast as rising out of and by itself, different from [*gegen*] and without questioning—and thus not, like questioning, a self-opening to beings and thereby a being well-versed in beings, in their beingness—as (the) τέχνη? Because φύσις is *not* τέχνη, indeed makes τέχνη first experienceable and manifest, therefore, the more questioning the question becomes and the more it brings itself before beings *as such* and thus inquires into beingness and is consolidated into the formula τί τὸ ὄν, the more τέχνη is in force as what determines the direction. φύσις is not τέχνη, i.e., what belongs to τέχνη; the well-versed look ahead into εἶδος and *re*-presenting and bringing before oneself of the outward look is precisely what

---

*Lecture course SS 1932, *Der Anfang der abendländischen Philosophie (Anaximander und Parmenides)* (GA 35).

happens *by itself* in φύσις, in ὄν ἡ ὄν. οὐσία is εἶδος, ἰδέα, as rising (φύσις), [as] coming forth (ἀλήθεια), and yet *offering a view.*

In order for Plato to be able to interpret beingness of beings as ἰδέα, not only is the experience of the ὄν as φύσις necessary but also the unfolding of the question under the guiding-thread of the counterhold of τέχνη, enforced *by* φύσις, which then indeed and especially in Aristotle offers the fore-grasping for the interpretation of beingness as σύνολον of μορφή and ὕλη, whereby that differentiation is established (*forma—materia,* form and content) which dominates the whole of metaphysical thinking—as point of departure and in the sense of a dominant guiding question—in its strongest and most secure, as well as most rigid form, in Hegel (cf. Frankfurt lectures, "On the Origin of the Work of Art," 1936˙).

98. Projecting Beingness Open unto Constant Presence˙˙

A being is what shows itself *thus,* in constancy and presence. With this stressing of its hidden domain of its projecting-open, beingness is referred to *time.* But it remains unclear how time is to be understood here and in what role "time," properly understood, is to be grasped.

But the answer to both of these questions reads: Time here is experienced in a concealed manner as temporalizing, as *removal-unto* and thus enopening; and it holds sway as such within what is ownmost to truth for beingness.

Time as what removes-unto and opens up is thus in itself simultaneously what *spatializes;* it provides "space." What is ownmost to space is not the same as what is ownmost to time, but space belongs to time— as time belongs to space.

But *space* here must also be grasped originarily as spacing (as can be *shown* in the spatiality of Da-sein, even if not fully and originarily grasped).

Constancy and presence in their onefold, therefore, are temporal-spatial [*zeiträumlich*]; and thus always to be determined in a double sense—if they are to be grasped in view of the truth of being.

Constancy is *endurance* of removal-unto "having-been" [*Gewesenheit*] and unto the future. And "duration" as mere continuity is only the consequence of endurance.

Presence is the *present* in the sense of the gatheredness of endurance in accord with its retreat from within removals-unto—removals-unto which are thus dissembled and thereby forgotten. Thus arises the illusion of *time-lessness* of what actually "is."

Grasped spatially, *constancy* is the fulfilling and en-filling of the space that is itself not actually experienced—thus a *spatializing.*

˙ *Der Ursprung des Kunstwerkes,* in: *Holzwege* (GA 5).
˙˙ Cf. Leap, 150: The Origin of Differentiation of the What and the That of a Being.

Presence is *spatializing* in the sense of providing space for beings that are deferred to it and thus are constant.

The onefold of temporalizing *and* spatializing—and indeed in the manner of presencing—makes up what is ownmost to beingness, makes up the intersecting.

But now whence comes this peculiarity, that a being [*das Seiende*] of such being [*Sein*] (eternity) is passed off as spaceless and timeless—even passed off as superior to space and time?

Because in their essential sway space and time remain hidden and, to the extent that they get determined, this determining happens on a path that leads to them, insofar as they themselves are taken as what in a certain sense is a being [*Seiendes*]—thus as "a certain present being."

But in this way space and time are referred to what is most graspably present, to σῶμα, the material and corporeal, and to the modes of reverting [*Umschlag*], μεταβολή, that occur here, which space and time follow or precede.

And as long as the dominion of the inceptual interpretation of being remains unbroken, this suppressing of space and time, within the domain of their nearest encounterability, still prevails; and an inquiry such as is indicated by the title *Being and Time* must necessarily remain ununderstood, since it demands a transformation of the questioning from the ground up.

99. "Being" and "Becoming" in Inceptual Thinking[*]

"Becoming" as *coming forth* and "passing away" as *disappearing*—this understood only in a Greek way and in itself related to φύσις.

Then *becoming* [is] as change of what is present, reverting, μεταβολή, the broadest concept of κίνησις, "movement."

Movement as Presencing of What Reverts as Such

In a Greek way Aristotle was the first to grasp what is ownmost to movement in terms of constancy and presence (οὐσία); and actually to do that, he had to proceed from the κινούμενον as such.

But that already presupposes the interpretation of beings as εἶδος—ἰδέα and thus μορφή—ὕλη, i.e., τέχνη, which is essentially related to φύσις.

Thus movement as *completeness* ensues, as what is ownmost to presencing, as holding-oneself in manufacturing and making.

Movement here should not be grasped in the modern sense of change of place in time; the Greek φορά, too, is something else.

For, because of this modern determination, the starting point of

---

[*] Cf. *Die Auslegungen der Aristotelischen "Physik" (Marburger Übungen)* [GA 83]; cf. lecture course SS 1935, *Einführung in die Metaphysik* (GA 40).

movement is what is moved, and what is moved is approached as a spatially-temporally accumulated matter [*Massenpunkt*]. Instead, at issue is to grasp *movement* as such as a mode of *being* (οὐσία). The essential difference between grasping movement metaphysically and grasping it physically becomes most clear with the concept of *rest* and what is own-most to *rest*.

Physically, rest is standing still, stopping, *absence of* movement; conceived in terms of numbers and this means calculatively, rest is a borderline movement, tending toward its decrease.

But *metaphysically*, rest in its proper sense is the utmost gathering of movedness [*Bewegtheit*], gathering as the *simultaneity* of possibilities in the most constant and fulfilled readiness.

Ens "actu" indicates precisely a being at "rest," not in "action," that which is *gathered unto itself* and is in this sense fully present.

Because we are accustomed to taking a being in terms of this "actual," actualized actualizing, we constantly overlook the basic character of *rest* in the essential sway of a being as "actual," in a thing, for example, as object. But who ever considered that this thing precisely *rests* and as a thing is an outstanding resting?

By overlooking the "metaphysical" rest in beings as such, beingness was not understood at all; and one was satisfied with "substance"—and later, dissatisfied with not having grasped substance, one was forced all the more into an inadequate "overcoming."

In this respect, what does the inceptual contrast of ὄν as "unmoved" over against "change" say? Seen from this point of view, what does interpretation of κινούμενον as μὴ ὄν in Plato say, even though, according to *The Sophist,* κίνησις belongs to the highest γένη of ὄν?

What does clarification of movement in terms of δύναμις and ἐνέργεια accomplish? And whither does their later, no-longer-Greek misinterpretation lead?

100. The First Beginning*

Ever-first-inceptually "what is" is experienced and named as φύσις. Beingness as constant presence is still hidden therein; φύσις is the reigning rising.

That beingness was grasped as constant presence *from long long ago* counts already as grounding to most people—if they even inquire into a grounding. But the inceptual and early character of this interpretation of beings does not immediately mean a grounding; rather, on the contrary, it makes this interpretation all the more questionable. Manifest to the appropriate questioning is that here the truth of beingness is not inquired into at all. For ever-first-inceptual thinking, this interpretation

---

* Cf. Playing-Forth, 110: ἰδέα, Platonism, and Idealism; cf. Disempowering of φύσις.

is not grounded and is ungroundable—and rightly so, if by grounding we understand an explanation that explains by going back to another being(!).

Nevertheless, this interpretation of ὄν as φύσις (and later ἰδέα) is not without a ground, even though with respect to the ground (i.e., of truth) it is hidden. One might believe that the experience of transitoriness, of coming into existence and of passing away, has suggested and demanded a point of departure in constancy and presence, as counterclaim. But why should what comes into existence and passes away count as non-being? Only when beingness is already established as constancy and presence. Therefore, beingness is not read off a being or a non-being, but rather a being is projected-open onto this beingness, in order to show itself first of all in the open of this projecting-open *as* a being or a non-being.

But whence and why is the opening up of beingness always a *projecting-open*? But whence and why does projecting-open open unto the ununderstood *time*? Are these both interconnected? (Ecstatic time and projecting-open [are] grounded as Dasein.)

That the truth of be-ing remains hidden, even though beingness is set into it ("time"), must be grounded in the essential sway of the first beginning. Does this concealing of the ground of the truth of being not mean simultaneously that the history of Greek Dasein that is determined by this truth takes the shortest path and that the present is completed in a great and unique moment of creating? That by contrast what follows the first beginning is subjected to hesitation and must put up with a refusal of being, all the way to the abandonment of being?

Crossing to the other beginning has to prepare a knowledge of this historical determination. Coming to grips with the first beginning and its history belongs to this context. This history is dominated by Platonism. And the specific way of unfolding the guiding question can be indicated by the title: *Being and Thinking* (cf. lecture SS 35*).

But in order to understand this title properly, we must heed the following:

1. *Being* here [in the first beginning] means beingness and not—as in *Being and Time*—being that is originarily questioned as to its truth; beingness as what is "general" to beings.

2. Thinking [in the first beginning] in the sense of re-presenting something in general and this as *making-present* and thus as proffering the sphere in which a being is grasped in terms of constant presence, without ever recognizing the time-character of this interpretation. That happens so little that, even after *Being and Time* for the first time interprets οὐσία as constant presence—and grasps this presence in its

---

*Lecture course SS 1935, *Einführung in die Metaphysik* (GA 40).

temporal character—the talk of *timelessness* of "presence" [*Präsenz*] and "eternity" continues. This happens because one holds on to the ordinary concept of time, which counts merely as a framework for the mutable and thus does not threaten what is constantly present!

Thinking here as νοεῖν, λόγος, ἰδεῖν, is reason [*Vernunft*], as the not at all grounded comportment from which and in whose sphere beingness is determined. This is to be distinguished from "thinking" in the wider and still-to-be-determined sense of enactment of philosophizing (cf. inceptual thinking). In this respect all grasping and determining (concept) of beingness and of be-ing is a thinking. Nevertheless, the crucial question still remains: In what realm of truth does the disclosing of the essential sway of being go on? Basically, even where beingness is grasped from within νοεῖν—as in the history of the guiding question— the *truth* of this thinking is not what is *thought* as such but rather is the time-space as essential swaying of truth, wherein all re-presenting must reside.

Inceptually a being is always also determined as ἕν; and in Aristotle ἕν and ὄν, a being and *one*, are then interchangeable. Oneness makes up beingness. And oneness here means: unifying, originary gathering unto sameness of what presences together-along-with and of what is constant. Correspondingly, then, the distinguishing determination for thinking of beingness (unity) becomes the *oneness* of the "I-think," the *unity of transcendental apperception,* the sameness of the I; in a deeper and richer sense both [are] combined in the monad of Leibniz.

101. From Early on Must, Clearly, and in a Secure Light . . .

The great simpleness of the *first* beginning of thinking the truth of be-ing must stand, from early on clearly and in a secure light. (What does it mean and what is founded, that εἶναι moves unto the ἀλήθεια of λόγος and of νοεῖν as φύσις?)

Bringing this beginning to light must already renounce bringing into play, as means for interpretation, what arises only when the beginning is not mastered and ἀλήθεια collapses: νοεῖν as νοῦς of ἰδεῖν of ἰδέα, κοινόν and λόγος as ἀπόφανσις of κατεγορίαι.

But in coming to grips with the first beginning, the heritage first *becomes* heritage; and those who belong to the future first *become* heirs. One is never an heir merely by the accident of being *one who comes later.*

102. Thinking: The Guiding-Thread of the
Guiding-Question of Western Philosophy

Inceptually, *thinking* is a receiving and gathering that fore-grasps the unconcealment of what arises and is constantly present as such.

But because ἀλήθεια continues to be ungrounded and thus *sinks into* correctness, thinking too as a faculty moves into the "psychological," i.e., ontic, interpretation. But seen from the viewpoint of the beginning, sinking into correctness means above all that, without being recognized as what it is, the free-playing space of correctness remains ungrounded and thus constantly disturbed. The relation between ψυχή and ἀλήθεια (ὄν) as ζυγόν, already *prepared* by Plato, turns with Descartes, in heightened intensity, into the connection of subject-object. Thinking becomes *I*-think; the *I*-think becomes: I unite originarily, I think unity (in advance).

Thinking is the in-advance proffering of presence as such.

But this connection is only the track of thinking on which, fore-grasping and unifying, thinking posits the unity of what it encounters and thus lets what it encounters be encountered as a being. A being becomes an object.

All effort aims implicitly at making this connection itself—thinking as the thinking of I-think-something—plainly the ground of the being-ness of beings and indeed by assimilating the inceptual determination of a being as ἕν.

In this way *identity* becomes the essential determination of a being as such. It comes from the ἀλήθεια of φύσις, from presence as the uncon-cealed gatheredness unto unconcealment.

And in modernity it obtains its distinction in the *I*, which soon there-after is grasped as the outstanding identity, namely that identity which *specifically* belongs to *itself*, that identity which knowing *itself* precisely is in this knowing.

This is the context from which first to grasp why *knowing* is itself the ground of beingness and thus is the actual being, why according to Hegel absolute knowing is absolute actuality.

In this history the dominion of thinking as the guiding-thread for determining beingness is expressed most sharply and absolutely.

By virtue of the guiding-thread that already dominates, *knowing as self-knowing* is the utmost *identity*, i.e., what is an *actual being;* and as such a being it is at the same time in the possibility for conditioning every other *objectness* in *its* manner as knowing—and indeed not only in a relatively transcendental sense but rather (as in Schelling) such that what is other to the I is itself determined as *manifest* spirit, whereby once again and ultimately identity is lifted up into the absoluteness of indifference, which of course is not meant as mere emptiness.

An equally essential evidence of this absolute position of thinking as the guide is the conception of philosophy as *"science of knowledge,"* as "system of science." This concept of "science" is to be kept completely at a distance from the later one that is derived from it (namely, the "posi-tive science" of the nineteenth century).

Philosophy as "science" does not mean that it should compete with the otherwise existing "sciences" (instead of being a "worldview," or an "art of living" and "wisdom"). Rather it means that thinking in its highest form is the unconditioned guiding-thread for the only task of philosophy, i.e., for interpreting beings as such. Thus for Fichte "science of knowledge" = metaphysics just as for Hegel metaphysics = "science of logic."

But insofar as the *pure relationship* of the *I-think-unity* (basically a tautology) becomes the unconditioned relationship, the *present that is present to itself* becomes the measure for all beingness.

And although everything in the deeper relations continues to be hidden, the *one* decisive thing thus manifests itself: Because thinking becomes unconditionally the guide—and the more it actually does so—the more decisively the *presentness* as such, i.e., "time," becomes in an originary sense that which, completely hidden and unquestioned, grants truth to beingness.

Absolute knowing, unconditioned thinking, is now the authoritative being that at the same time plainly and simply grounds everything.

Now for the first time it becomes clear that the guiding-thread does not help the process of enactment of thinking, but instead forms the underlying and as such hidden horizon for interpreting beingness. Coming from the not grounded ἀλήθεια, this formation of the horizon can unfold itself in the beginning only by forming out of itself and for itself the premises of correctness (the subject-object-relationship) with its own possibilities (self-knowing—reflection) —all the way to the unconditionality of identity as such.

Thus it becomes simultaneously manifest how in absolute knowing "correctness" is raised to the utmost, so that, as the present of present, correctness must in a certain way and on another level return to ἀλήθεια—of course in such a manner that now every explicit relation to correctness comes still more definitely into knowing and even into questioning.

How little this can succeed is shown by Nietzsche's conception of truth, for whom truth degenerates into a necessary illusion, into an unavoidable consolidation, entangled in beings themselves, determined as "will to power."

Thus Western metaphysics at its end is at its furthest distance from the question of the *truth* of be-ing, *as well as* closest to this truth—in that this metaphysics prepares the crossing to this truth as end.

Truth as correctness is not capable of recognizing and grounding its own full scope. It helps itself by raising itself to the unconditioned and by dominating everything in order that it does not need the ground (so it seems).

In order to work out the history of the "guiding-thread," i.e., the history of the fixing of the horizon in absolute knowing, the following steps are important:

From the *ego cogito sum* as the primary certainty—as the decisive *certum = verum = ens*—to *connaissance des verités necessaires* as condition for the possibility of *reflection,* as comprehending the I as "I." The most necessary truth is the essence of the true as *identitas,* and this is *the entitas entis,* as providing the horizon—known in advance as the principle—for comprehending *perceptio* and its *perceptum,* for *apperceptio,* the explicit comprehending of the *monas as monas.*

From here the way is opened to the original-synthetic unity of transcendental apperception.

From here [the way is open] to the "I" as the original identity that belongs to self-knowing and is therefore an "existing" identity. (A = A *grounded* in I = I, and not I = I as an exceptional instance of A = A.)

But insofar as the "I" is grasped transcendentally as I-think-unity, this original identity is simultaneously the unconditioned identity that conditions everything, even though it is still not *absolute* identity— because according to Fichte what is posited is posited only as the *not-I.* The way to absolute identity [is opened] only with Schelling.

103. On the Notion of German Idealism

1. *Idealism:*

a) is determined by the interpretation of ὄν as ἰδέα, being-seen, re-presentedness—and of course re-presented[ness of] κοινόν and ἀεί; among other things it anticipates the interpretation of beings as ob-jects for representation.

b) *representation* is *ego percipio,* the representedness as such for the *I* think, which is itself an *I think myself,* I represent myself to myself and am thus certain of myself.

   Origin of the priority of the *ego* lies in the will to certainty, [which is] being *certain of itself,* being dependent upon itself.

c) The "I"-represent as *self-representation* thus continues to be the particularity of precisely each particular I. What is thus *represented as the ground of representation* of ἰδέα does not yet correspond to this ground, is not yet κοινόν and ἀεί. Therefore self-representation must become *self*-knowing in the absolute sense—that knowing that knows the necessity of the relation of the object to the I *and* of the I to the object, as one.

   This self-knowing of this necessity is detached from onesidedness and is thus absolute. This absolute knowing—as arisen from the "I represent the representation and what it represents"—is *as absolute* equated with divine knowing of the Christian God. This equation becomes easier in that what is represented in the representation of this god are "ideas." Cf. Augustine, at a time when "idealism" had not yet evolved—for idealism exists only since Descartes.

2. *German Idealism,* delineated in advance in Leibniz, attempts to think the *ego cogito* of transcendental apperception in an absolute sense, on the basis of Kant's transcendental step beyond Descartes, and at the same time grasps the absolute in the direction of Christian dogma, such that this dogma reaches its own truth in this philosophy—a truth that has come to itself, and that means, speaking with Descartes, reaches the utmost self-certainty. The confusion of German Idealism—*if* it can be so judged in these domains—does not lie in its being excessively not "true to life" but rather, conversely, in its moving completely and totally in the track of modern Dasein and Christianity instead of going beyond "beings" and raising the question of being. German Idealism *was too "true"-to-life* and in a certain sense itself produced the non-philosophy of positivism, which took its place and now celebrates its biologistic triumphs.

104. German Idealism

Here truth becomes the *certainty* that unfolds into an unconditioned trust in spirit and thus unfolds first as spirit in its absoluteness. Beings are completely misplaced into objectness, which is by no means overcome in being "sublated"; on the contrary, objectness broadens itself to include the representing I and the relation of representing the object and representing the representation. Machination as the basic character of beingness now takes the shape of the subject-object-dialectic, which, as absolute, plays out and arranges together all possibilities of all familiar domains of beings. Here once again the continuous securing against all uncertainty is attempted, the definitive foothold in the *correctness* of absolute certainty, which avoids the truth of be-ing without knowing it. There is no bridge from here to the other beginning. But we must *know* this thinking of German Idealism, because it leads the machinational power of beingness to the utmost, unconditioned unfolding (raises the conditionedness of the *ego cogito* to the unconditioned) and prepares the end.

Instead of being placed in the triviality of an immediate evidence, being's "self-evidence" is now systematically extended to the richness of the historicity of spirit and its shapes.

And here and there individual thrusts are interspersed, like Schelling's treatise on freedom, which, as the transition to "Positive Philosophy" shows, nevertheless does not lead to any decision.

105. Hölderlin—Kierkegaard—Nietzsche

Let no one today be so presumptuous as to take it as mere coincidence that these three, who, each in his own way, in the end suffered profoundly the uprooting to which Western history is being driven and who at the same time intimated their gods most intimately—that these three had to depart from the brightness of their days prematurely.

What is being prepared for?

What does it mean that the *first* of these three, Hölderlin, became at the same time the one who *poeticized the furthest ahead,* in an epoch when thinking once again aspired to know all history up to that point absolutely? (Cf. *Überlegungen* IV, 115ff.)

What hidden history of the much invoked nineteenth century happened here? What motivating principle of those who belong to the future is being readied here?

Must we not turn in our thinking to totally different domains and standards and ways of being, in order to become ones who still belong to the necessities that are breaking open here? Or does this history as the ground of Dasein continue to be inaccessible to us, not because it is past, but because it is still too futural for us?

106. The Decision about All Ontology in Enactment: Contention between the First and the Other Beginning

Mindfulness of "ontology" is necessary in the crossing from one beginning to the other, so much so that the thought of "fundamental ontology" must be thought through. For in fundamental ontology the guiding-question is first grasped as question, unfolded and made manifest unto its ground and in its jointure. Merely rejecting "ontology" without overcoming it from within its origin accomplishes nothing at all; at most it endangers every will to thinking. For that rejection (e.g., in Jaspers) takes a very questionable notion of thinking as its measure and then finds that this thinking does not encounter "being"—meant, in great confusion, is *a being* as such—but rather is only forced into the frame and the confines of the concept. Behind this remarkably shallow "critique" of "ontology" (which talks aimlessly in a massive confusion of being and beings) nothing else is at work but the distinction between matter and form—the origin of which is not questioned at all—still "critically" applied to "consciousness" and the subject and its "irrational" "lived-experiences," i.e., the Kantianism of Rickert and Lask, which Jaspers never discarded, in spite of everything.

In contrast to such a "critique" as a simple rejection of "ontology," one must show why this critique became necessary within the history of the guiding-question (dominion of Platonism). Conversely, an overcoming of ontology requires above all and precisely the unfolding of ontology from within its beginning, to be distinguished from superficially accepting its doctrinal content and calculating its accuracies and mistakes (Nicolai Hartmann)—all of which continues to be irrelevant and thus does not intimate at all the thinking willing that in *Being and Time* seeks a way to cross from the guiding-question to the grounding-question.

Because *all ontologies*—whether developed as such or only prepared for development, like the history of the first beginning—inquire into beings *as* beings and in *this* respect and only in this respect also inquire into being, they move unto the domain of the *grounding-question:* How does being hold sway? What is the truth of being?—without intimating this grounding-question as such and without ever being able to admit be-ing in its utmost questionability, uniqueness, finitude, and strangeness.

[One needs] to show how, in and through *development* of *ontology into onto-theology* (cf. Hegel lectures 1930/31* and elsewhere), the grounding-question and its necessity are pushed aside and how in this history Nietzsche completes the creative end.

107. Responding to the Guiding-Question and the Form of Traditional Metaphysics

In accordance with the Platonic interpretation of beings as such as εἶδος-ἰδέα and this as κοινόν, the being of beings in general becomes κοινόν. To be the "most general" becomes *the* essential determination of being itself. The question of τί ἐστιν is always a question of κοινόν; and thus are given the parameters for the whole thinking through of beings as such, parameters of highest species, highest generality, and *individuality*. The major domains of *beings* are only *specialia* of the generality of beings, i.e., of being. And so, the distinction between *metaphysica generalis* and *metaphysica specialis* mirrors the character of the guiding-question. Here there is no longer any question of a possible coupling of *metaphysica generalis* and *metaphysica specialis,* for they are already coupled in the manner just mentioned, which is quite superficial to beings and above all to being. As long as the unrecognized basis of the guiding-question and the differences between disciplines are held to at the outset as something self-evident, what arise here are nothing but baseless and illusory questions.

Finally, confusion increases whenever one tries to find a solution to the question with the help of the "ontological" difference that emerges from fundamental ontology. For this "difference" sets off not in the direction of the guiding-question but rather as a leap into the grounding-question—not in order now to play in unclear fashion with the rigid designations (beings and being) but in order to go back to the question of the truth of the essential swaying of be-ing and thus to grasp the relation of be-ing and beings in another way—especially since *beings* as such also undergo a transformed interpretation (sheltering the truth of enowning) and since there is no possibility of still smuggling

---

*Lecture course WS 1930/31, *Hegels Phänomenologie des Geistes* (GA 32) [trans. P. Emad and K. Maly, *Hegel's Phenomenology of Spirit* (Bloomington: Indiana University Press, 1988)].

"beings" in inadvertently as "represented objects" or "extant in themselves," etc.

108. The Basic Metaphysical Positions within the History of the Guiding-Question and the Interpretation of Time-Space That Belongs to Each of Them*

1. How are space and time experienced, grasped, and named in the first beginning? What does "mythical" interpretation mean here?
2. How both space and time move into the domain of beings as what is constantly present and how both are in part a μὴ ὄν.
3. That here the domain of truth is closed off for being and remains unknown.
4. To what extent thinking space and time (place and now) back into their origin (belonging to ἀλήθεια) is neither possible nor necessary.
5. By what, then, space and time become the parameter for representations on the way of their interpretation in view of μέγεθος.
6. How this approach is then taken up by modern "mathematical" thinking.
7. How in Leibniz and finally in Kant the disjointedness of the essence of space and time and the relation to the "I" and to "consciousness" counts as established and conceptually confirmed, just as earlier the interpretation of beings as οὐσία. (How in this connection Nietzsche too does *not* inquire from the ground up.)

109. ἰδέα

ἰδέα is that interpretation of ἀλήθεια by which the later determination of beingness as objectness is prepared and the question of ἀλήθεια as such is necessarily cut off from the whole history of Western philosophy.

Only from within an *other* inceptual questioning into being and its relation to Da-sein can the question arise of what thinking in the first beginning named ἀλήθεια.

110. ἰδέα, Platonism, and Idealism**

1. The notion of ἰδέα (εἶδος) means the look of something, that as which something offers and makes itself, that, returned to which, something is the being that it is. Although ἰδέα is related to ἰδεῖν (νοεῖν), the word does *not* mean what is represented in representation, but the opposite: the *shining forth* of the *look* itself, which offers the *view for* a looking-to. The word does *not* want to indicate the

---

* Cf. Grounding.
** Cf. Leap, 119: The Leap into Preparation by Asking the Grounding-Question; cf. lecture course WS 1937/38, *Grundfragen der Philosophie. Ausgewählte "Probleme" der "Logik"* (GA 45, pp. 60ff.) [trans. R. Rojcewicz and A. Schuwer, *Basic Questions of Philosophy: Selected "Problems" of "Logic"*].

relation to the "subject"—if we would think in terms of modernity—but rather the *presencing*, the shining forth of the view in the look and exactly as that which *at the same time* provides *stability in presencing*. Here is the *origin of the differentiation* between τί ἐστιν *(essentiá, quidditas)* and ὅτι [ἔστιν] *(existentia)* in the temporality of the ἰδέα (cf. Leap). A being is in constant presence, ἰδέα, the seen *in its seenness* (ἀλήθεια).

2. ἰδέα is that *toward which* what still changes and is many is put back, the *unifying one* and therefore ὄν, *being* = unifying; and consequently ἰδέα is the κοινόν in relation to the many (ἔκαστα). And, strangely, this subsequent determination of ἰδέα as beingness, the κοινόν, then becomes the first and last determination of beingness (of being); this [being] is the "most general"! But that is not remarkable but necessary, because from the very beginning being as beingness is experienced and thought *only* in terms of "beings"—from beings, so to speak, from *and* back to the manifold.

3. When ἰδέα is once set up as beingness of beings and when it is grasped as κοινόν, then it must—again be thought from beings, as it were (the individual ones)—be among these the *most being*, the ὄντως ὄν. ἰδέα suffices at first and alone for the essence of beingness and can therefore claim to be the most-being [*Seiendste*] and actually a being. The individual and changeable becomes μὴ ὄν, i.e., what does not suffice and never suffices for beingness.

4. When being (always as beingness, κοινόν) is grasped thus—ἕν, the most-being and the *one* as the most unifying—and when the ἰδέαι themselves are many, then this *many* as the most being can be only in the manner of κοινόν, i.e., in the κοινωνία within itself. The presencing and constancy in beingness, i.e., unity, is gathered in this [κοινωνία]; the γένη as unities [are] self-unifying and thus sources or "species."

5. Interpretation of ὄν as οὐσία and the latter as ἰδέα (κοινόν, γένη) grasps the beingness of beings and thus the εἶναι of the ὄν (being, but not be-ing). In beingness (οὐσία) εἶναι, being, is intimated as what is somehow other, which is not fully fulfilled in οὐσία. Thus, in going further on the same way, i.e., by grasping presencing, one tries to go beyond beingness: ἐπέκεινα τῆς οὐσίας (cf. *Die metaphysischen Grundstellungen des abendländischen Denkens (Metaphysik): Übungen, WS 1937/38* [GA 88]). But since the only question concerns beings and their beingness, it can never encounter be-ing itself or come from it. The ἐπέκεινα can thus be determined only as something that henceforth designates beingness as such in its relation to man (εὐδαιμονία), as the ἀγαθόν, *befitting* [*das Taugliche*] that founds all *befittedness*—thus as condition for "life," for ψυχή, and thus its essence itself. With that the step is taken toward

"value," "meaning," and "ideal." The guiding-question about beings as such is already at its limit and simultaneously at the juncture where it falls behind and no longer grasps *beingness* in more originary fashion, but instead values it—and in such a way that valuation itself is passed off as the highest.

6. Together with that the relations of ἰδέα itself to ψυχή also become clear and decisive:
   a) as εἶδος to ἰδεῖν and νοεῖν—νοῦς
   b) as κοινόν and κοινωνία to διαλέγεσθαι and λόγος
   c) as ἀγαθόν—καλόν to ἔρως

7. Because the essence of a being is gathered in the ψυχή in this way, the ψυχή itself is the ἀρχή ζωῆς—and ζωή is the basic shape of a being.

    Here as well as in Aristotle ψυχή is not *subject*. Accordingly something essential is set up with this relation of the ὄν as οὐσία:
   a) a being as such is always the over-against, the *ob-ject*,
   b) that over against which is itself the constantly present and extant and the most being and unneedful of the being-question.

8. As ἀρχή τοῦ ὄντος, the ἐπέκεινα τῆς οὐσίας has the character of θεῖον and θεός in proportion to εὐδαιμονία (cf. Aristotle).

    The question of beings as such (in the sense of the guiding-question), ontology, is thus necessarily *theo-logy*.

9. With this unfolding of the *first* end of the first beginning (with Platonic-Aristotelian philosophy) the possibility is given that *this philosophy* then—and henceforth Greek philosophy in *its* form in general—sets the framework and domain for grounding for Judaeo (Philo) Christian (Augustine) faith; indeed, seen from that point of view, Greek philosophy can even be passed off as a precursor of Christianity, respectively as "paganism," and can be considered overcome.

10. But not only did Christianity and its interpretation of "world" find here its framework and primary indication of constitution, but also all post-Christian, anti-Christian, and non-Christian Western interpretation of beings and of man found their framework and constitution within the same. The ἐπέκεινα τῆς οὐσίας as ἀγαθόν (that means: the *fundamental denial* of any further and originary questioning of beings as such, i.e., questioning of being) is the primeval image for all interpretation of beings and their determination and shaping in the context of a "culture"; is assessment of cultural values; is interpretation of the "actual" with respect to its "meaning"; is the imaging of an ἰδέα, according to "ideas" and measuring *ideals;* is viewing beings in the whole, viewing "world," i.e., worldview. Wherever "worldview" dominates and determines beings, Platonism is at work, unweakened and unrecognized—and all the

more stubbornly where Platonism passed through the modern reinterpretation of ἰδέα.

11. The primary later version and the more appropriate version of Platonism (the doctrine of ideas as of the beingness of beings) is not "idealism" but "realism"; *res:* the matter, the thing; *realitas* as reality [*Sachheit*], *essentia,* the genuinely medieval "realism": *Universale* makes up *ens qua ens.*

12. But because of nominalism the reality of the individual is addressed as actual *realitas,* the *this;* and correspondingly *realitas* is used for designating the individual, [i.e.,] what is the nearest extant, here and now, *existentia.* What is remarkable is that "reality" now becomes the title for "existence," "actuality," "Dasein."

13. Correspondingly, on the basis of various motivations, the individual, the individual soul and individual human, the "I," are experienced as what is *most being* and most real; and *thus* the *ego cogito— ergo sum* first becomes possible. Here "being" is granted to the *individuum,* whereby one must pay heed to what this formulation really means: the certainty of the mathematical relation of *cogitare* and *esse,* the *primeval proposition of mathesis.*

14. ἰδέα no longer means *universale* as such in the Greek sense of the εἶδος of presencing but rather the *perceptum* as grasped in the *percipere* of the *ego,* "*perceptio*" in the ambiguity of the word "re-presentation" [*"Vor-stellung"*]; taken in this broad sense, even the individual and changeable is a *perceptum,* ἰδέα as *perceptum:* the idea in *reflecting-back;* ἰδέα as εἶδος: *idea in the shining forth of presencing.* And only by interpreting ἰδέα as *perceptio* does Platonism become "idealism," i.e., being-ness of beings now becomes represented*ness (esse = verum esse = certum esse = ego percipio, cogito me cogitare);* a being is thought "idealistically" — and as a consequence "ideas" are rescued in Kant, but as representations and principles of "reason" as human reason.

   This leads to absolute idealism. The concept of "ideas" in Hegel (see below), the absolute self-shining-to-itself of the absolute as absolute knowing. Thus the possibility of grasping Plato anew and of setting up Greek philosophy as the stage of immediacy. (Re "idealism," cf. *Übungen SS 1937: "Nietzsches metaphysische Grundstellung: Sein und Schein"* [GA 87]; re nominalism: *Übungen WS 1937/38: "Die metaphysischen Grundstellungen des abendländischen Denkens (Metaphysik)"* [GA 88]).

   [The following paragraphs, entitled "Hegel's Conception of Idea and the First Possibility of a *Philosophical* History of Philosophy from Its First End" and "What Belongs to the Concept of Idealism," constitute an interlude between nos. 14 and 15 of Section 110. Section 110 continues on p. 150.]

*

Hegel's Conception of Idea and the First Possibility of a
Philosophical History of Philosophy from Its First End

In this concept all essential determinations of the history of "idea" are originarily contained as completed:

1. Idea as appearance
2. Idea as *the* determination of the knowable as such (the actual)
3. Idea as the generality of the "concept"
4. Idea as re-presented in re-presentation, as thinking the "absolute" (Philo, Augustine)
5. Idea as what is known in the *cogito me cogitare* (self-consciousness) (Descartes)
6. Idea as *perceptio,* i.e., the representation that is unfolded step by step, in unity with the will, *perceptio* and *appetitus* (Leibniz)
7. Idea as the unconditioned and "principle" of reason (Kant)
8. All of these determinations are originarily united in the essence of self-mediating absolute knowing, which knows itself as completion not only of every form of consciousness but also even of philosophy itself up to now.
9. *Philosophically* seen, what comes *after* Hegel is overall relapse and falling off into positivism and philosophy of life or scholastic ontology; scientifically seen, it is dissemination and rectifying of much knowledge of the idea and its history; but Hegelian viewpoints are still key in this scholarly observation — even if often hardly recognizable — without being capable of unfolding their metaphysically sustaining power. Today's "philosophy" obtains its "notions" of "idea" from these muddy sources (cf. Grounding, 193: Da-sein and Man, especially pp. 220f.).
10. Because, with *this* founding of the "idea" as actuality of the actual, Hegel gathered the whole of the history of philosophy up to now — including the pre-Platonic — into a knowing as a belonging-together and because he grasped this knowing as absolute self-knowing-itself in its stages and their series, he gained possession of a necessity that stemmed from what is ownmost to beingness (idea), in proportion to which necessity the stages of the history of ideas had to be arranged.

In other words, seen from the viewpoint of Hegel's inquiry, his history of philosophy was the *first philosophical* history of philosophy, the first appropriate inquiry into history — but also at the same time the last and last possible inquiry of this kind.

What follows this inquiry as a whole is a significant work of erudition, but basically, i.e., philosophically, a helpless and disoriented stuttering which draws its unity only from the succession of philosophers and their writings or "problems."

What Belongs to the Concept of "Idealism"[*]

[To the concept of idealism belongs]

1. ἰδέα as *presencing* of the what and the constancy of that presencing (but this is ungrasped and falls into forgetfulness and is misconstrued as *ens entium* as *aeternum!*);
2. νοεῖν (λόγος), but not yet solidified in the "I," but rather ψυχή, ζωή;
3. nevertheless thereby anticipated: *perceptum*, the re-presented, what is bringable before itself, what presences, of a *percipere*, that is, *ego percipio* as *cogito me cogitare;* representing the *self* along with [representing] as that *along which* is re-presented, in *whose* view [*Sicht*] and countenance [*Angesicht*] the look appears;
4. representedness as ob-jectness and "self"-(I) certainty as the ground of objectness, i.e., of beingness (being and thinking).

*

15. In the sense of a strictly historical concept of "idealism," Plato was never an "idealist," but a "realist"; which does not mean that he did not deny the external world in itself, but taught ἰδέα as the *essence* of the ὄν, as *realitas* of the *res*. But, precisely as modern idealism, "idealism" is *Platonism,* insofar as for it also beingness has to be grasped in terms of "representation" (νοεῖν), i.e., in conjunction with the Aristotelian initiatives in terms of λόγος as διανοεῖσθαι, i.e., in terms of *thinking* that, according to Kant, is re-presentation of something in general (categories and table of judgments; categories and self-knowing-itself of reason in Hegel). In general: What furnishes the standard for the whole history of Western philosophy, including Nietzsche, is *being and thinking.* Although Nietzsche experiences beings as becoming, *by* this interpretation he remains, within the traditional framework, an *opponent:* Beings are merely interpreted differently, but the being-question as such is never raised.
16. If we remember that domination of Platonism, in various directions and shapings, now also guides the understanding of *pre*-Platonic philosophy (and indeed especially in Nietzsche), then it becomes clear how significant the crucial interpretation of ὄν as ἰδέα is and how important the question of what actually transpired here is.

---

[*] Cf. *Übungen SS 1937, Nietzsches metaphysische Grundstellung. Sein und Schein: Erscheinung—Schein* [GA 87].

17. What these considerations are about is not a history of Platonism in the sense of a series of doctrines as derivations of the Platonic teaching but solely the history of the treatment of the guiding-question within the essential domination of Platonism. [Thus these considerations have] the task of playing-forth from the first into the other beginning. Platonism is hereafter the concept of that question concerning being that inquires into the beingness of beings and places the being that is thus grasped into relation to re-presentation (thinking). *Being and thinking* is the title for the history of thinking within the first and the other beginning.

18. This history is essentially complemented by working out the history of ἀλήθεια, its premature collapse, its re-building as ὁμοίωσις and *adaequatio* and then as *certainty*. This history then leads to a corresponding misunderstanding of the question of truth; in the end in Nietzsche there is only the question of the *value* of truth, a genuinely *Platonizing* (!) question. Everything is far removed from the task of putting into question what is ownmost to truth as such in its intimate relation to the truth of be-ing and thus to be-ing itself.

19. The Platonic interpretation of beings gives rise to a way of representing which, in the future and in various shapings, dominates from the ground up the history of the guiding-question and thus Western philosophy as a whole. By setting up ἰδέα as κοινόν, the χωρισμός is set up as a being, as it were; and this is the origin of "transcendence" in its various shapings, especially when ἐπέκεινα, too, is grasped as the consequence of setting up ἰδέα as οὐσία. Here is also the root for representing the *a priori*.

20. Different things are understood by "transcendence," which then also intermingle:

    a) the "ontic" [transcendence]: the other being that still goes beyond beings; put in Christian terms: the creator that is already beyond created beings; in the completely confusing usage of the word *transcendence,* "transcendence" (like "His Magnificence!") = God himself, *the* being *above* the rest of beings; the encompassing and thus the general. Superfluously and in order to heighten the confusion, "being" is mentioned at the same time!

    b) "ontological" transcendence: What is meant here is the surpassing that lies in κοινόν as such, beingness as the general (γένη — categories — "above" and "prior to" beings, *a priori*). Here the relation and the manner of difference remains completely unclear; one is content to state the κοινόν and its consequences.

    c) the "fundamental-ontological" transcendence in *Being and Time*. Here the word's originary meaning is returned to it: surpassing as such; and it is grasped as the distinctive mark of Da-sein, in order thus to indicate that Dasein always already stands within the openness of beings. This joins and, at the same time, determines more precisely "ontological" "transcendence," insofar as transcendence is grasped here in accord with Dasein, i.e., originarily as *understanding of being.* *But* because now understanding is also grasped as thrown project-ing-open, transcendence means: standing in the truth of be-ing, indeed without initially knowing this or questioning it.

But now since Da-sein as Da-*sein* originarily sustains the open-ness of the sheltering-concealing, strictly speaking one cannot speak of a transcendence of Da-sein; in the context of this approach representation of transcendence in *every* sense must *disappear.*

d) This representation [of transcendence] is still frequently used in "epistemological" observation which, beginning with Descartes, pri-marily hinders the "subject" from going out and going over to the "object" or makes this relation doubtful. Even this kind of "tran-scendence" is overcome with the onset of Da-sein in that this tran-scendence is left behind in advance.

e) "Transcendence" overall includes the departure from "beings," what is known and familiar, to going somehow beyond beings. Seen from the grounding-question of the truth of be-ing, this means getting stuck in the mode of inquiry of the guiding-ques-tion, i.e., in *metaphysics.*

But with crossing to the grounding-question all meta-physics is overcome.

But this crossing must therefore be even more clearly mindful of the unavoidable forms of Platonism that still surround it, even if these forms still determine the crossing only in warding off.

21. The last offshoots and consequences of Platonism in the present are:
    a) everything that calls itself "ontology" and wants or does not want ontology; for example, even the opposition based on Kant-ianism continues to be in the same domain of conditions for "ontologies";
    b) every Christian as well as non-Christian metaphysics;
    c) all doctrines which focus on "values," "meaning," "ideas" and ideals; correspondingly, the doctrines that deny such, like positiv-ism and biologism;
    d) every type of philosophy of "life," for which the question of being continues to be strange, even in the genuine shape of the guiding-question up to now (Dilthey);
    e) in the end those directions that mix up the aforementioned, that teach ideas and values and at the same time stress "existence" in accord with a "life" philosophy. Here utmost confusion is made into a principle, and all genuine thinking and inquiring is abandoned;
    f) finally Nietzsche's philosophy, which, precisely because it sees itself

as the overturning of Platonism, falls back—through the back door, as it were—into Platonism. Even when Nietzsche— as the thinker who "goes over to"—is finally twisted out of Platonism *and* its over-turning, no inquiry into the truth of be-ing and into what is own-most to truth is made—no inquiry that is originary and overcoming.

22. On the other hand, Nietzsche is the first one to recognize the key position of Plato and the bearing of Platonism for the history of the West (emergence of nihilism). More precisely: He surmised the key position of Plato; for Plato's place between pre-Platonic and post-Platonic philosophy first becomes manifest when the pre-Pla-tonic philosophy is grasped inceptually in terms of itself—and not, as in Nietzsche, interpreted Platonically. Nietzsche was stuck in this interpretation because he did not recognize the guiding-question as such and did not enact the crossing to the grounding-question. But Nietzsche did detect Platonism in its most covert shapes—and this initially counts for more: Christianity and its secularizations are generally "Platonism for the people."

23. In its overt and covert dominion and as it was observed and shaped in the course of Western history, Platonism deflected beings in the whole into a definite constitution and turned certain directions in representation into self-evident pathways of "inquiring" (cf. above, "Transcendence"). And this is what really obstructs experiencing Dasein and leaping into it, so much so that Da-sein continues at first to be ununderstood, especially because no insight is gained into the necessity for its grounding, since distress for such a neces-sity is lacking. But this lack is grounded upon the abandonment of being as the most profound mystery of the current history of West-ern humanity.

24. Therefore, in order to bring about a preparedness for leaping into Da-sein, an unavoidable task is to initiate the overcoming of Pla-tonism by means of a more originary knowing awareness of what is its ownmost.

25. Accordingly, we must ask:

a) Upon which experience and interpretation is the installation of beings as ἰδέα founded?

b) In what truth (which essential sway) does the determination of beingness (οὐσία) of beings, ὄν, as ἰδέα reside?

c) When this truth was left undetermined—and it was so left—why was no inquiry made into it?

d) When no necessity for such inquiry asserted itself, wherein lay the reason for this? The reason can only rest in the complete ade-quacy of interpreting beings as ἰδέα for the question concerning beings—an adequacy which swallowed up in advance all other questioning. And this too must be founded upon the uniqueness of the interpretation of beings.

e) This interpretation projects beings open onto constant presence. ἰδέα holds sway as this constant presence and makes any step beyond that impossible; to this end being submits itself to essential swaying, in such a way that a being is entirely fulfilled as a being. The essential swaying as presencing and constancy leaves no room for an inadequacy and thus also no motive for the question of the truth of this interpretation; it confirms itself as that which confirms all beings as such. Beingness as ἰδέα is thus by itself *truly* (ἀληθῶς) a being, ὄν.

f) By this interpretation of beings man is henceforth allotted an unambiguous place, an allotment in accord with being: as constantly present, what is truly a being is always the over against, is always the prospect [*Aussicht*] that is in sight [*Angesicht*]; man is the one who appears as related to this over-against and is himself taken into it; to himself man can still *be* the over-against in reflection; the subsequent unfolding of consciousness, object, and "self"-consciousness are prepared for.

g) Nevertheless it is still the case that ἀλήθεια was experienced and seen in the inceptual interpretation of ὄν as φύσις. Accordingly, there is more to the first beginning than the Platonic interpretation. And therefore, in setting the first beginning into proper perspective, this beginning must be returned to its unfalsified greatness and uniqueness; setting this beginning into proper perspective does not cancel it but above all grounds its necessity for the other beginning.

26. Overcoming of Platonism in this direction and manner is a historical decision with the widest dimension. This overcoming simultaneously founds a philosophical history of philosophy that is different from Hegel's. (What unfolds as "destruction" in *Being and Time* does not mean dismantling as demolishing but as *purifying* in the direction of freeing basic metaphysical positions. But considering the enactment of echo and playing-forth, all of this is a prelude.)

27. The continued hiddenness of the truth of being and of the ground of this truth in the first beginning and in its history demands from the originary re-asking of the question of being a crossing over to the grounding-question: How does be-ing hold sway? Only in terms of this question can the question be asked anew: What is a being?

The utmost and at the same time most insidious offshoot of "idealism" is manifest at that place where idealism is seemingly abandoned, nay even opposed (e.g., when one denies that German Idealism is "true" to life). This idealism takes the shape of *biologism,* which is and wants to be essentially and necessarily ambiguous. For by setting up "life" as basic actuality ("life" as all-life and simultaneously as human "life"), a twofold is immediately established:

Life as dealing and acting is going-forth and going-further and thus going beyond itself, toward "meaning" and "value," thus to "idealism"; but—so can one immediately counter—not of the "life-form" of representing and of "consciousness" but rather of live-experience [*Erleben*] and of effecting, *life* and *live-experience;* all that sounds "realistic" and, when necessary, can indeed always afford to count also and precisely as the highest idealism.

These ambiguities give the impression of breadth and depth, but they are only the consequence of a total lack of depth of this "thinking," by which thinking is entirely superficially and intentionally blind to its historical origin and falsifies what is tangible as what is highest—with the doubtful advantage of immediately finding approval.

111. The *"A priori"* and φύσις

[The *a priori* and φύσις mean] τὸ πρότερον τῇ φύσει. φύσις is the measure and is "earlier than," source, origin.

The earliest, what comes to presence first, presencing is φύσις itself, although immediately covered over, along with ἀλήθεια, by ἰδέα.

How does one get to such a question as the πρότερον? On the basis of ἰδέα as ὄντως ὄν.

What is earliest in essential swaying is essential swaying itself, as essential swaying of be-ing.

A priori—from what is prior; *a priori* is where the guiding-question [dominates]: metaphysics.

But in the crossing the "a priori" is only *seemingly* still a "problem"; grasped in terms of enowning, the relation between be-ing and beings is totally different.

112. The *"A priori"*

The *a priori* is really only there where ἰδέα [is]—and that is to say that beingness (κοινόν) as ὄντως ὄν is more-being and thus *above all* a being.

Corresponding to its beginning with Plato, the *a priori* always—in the future in metaphysics—means the priority of beingness over beings.

With ἰδέα the *a priori* is transformed into *perceptio*, i.e., the *a priori* is attributed to the *ego percipio* and thus to the "subject"; it leads to the priority *of re-presentation.*

What in *Being and Time* gets started as "understanding of being" seemed to be merely the extension of this prior representation—but it is something entirely different (understanding as projecting-open—Da-sein); but as *crossing* it points back to metaphysics. The truth of be-ing and the essential swaying of be-ing is neither what is earlier nor what is later.

Da-sein is the simultaneity of time-space with what is true as a being; Dasein sways as the *grounding* ground, as the "between" and "the mid-point" in beings themselves.

113. ἰδέα and οὐσία

It needs to be shown how all essential determinations of a being are obtained from within the fundamental determination of a being, i.e., from beingness as *constant presence*, better: from it as the determining background.

In accord with that fundamental determination, a being is what is "conjoint with," what can accomplish the possibility of "conjointliness." Following-one-another, preceding and following (later cause and effect) are determined out of conjointliness; notice the Kantian interpretation of being-a-cause.

It is characteristic of the subsequent period of metaphysics that indeed the temporal designation is used for differentiating beings in each case, but that already here time is used as the *number* of what is changeable or countable, i.e., the form of arranging the same, thus time [is used] as a parameter. In other words, the more originary sway of time is never experienced, just as little as that of space is. οὐσία as "substance" is, as it were, put forth as "time-free," in order then to be determined as either "eternal" (unending) or "temporal," finite. Metaphysics never moves beyond this parameter. *Being and Time* therefore seems to be something self-evident!

114. On Nietzsche's Basic Metaphysical Position[*]

To this context [belongs] the question of "the order of ranks"—not the question of "values" in general and in themselves but the question of *humanness:* master and slave.

How is this question related to *metaphysics* and to the basic metaphysical position? In this regard, cf. the unfolding of the guiding-question: Man and humanness as inquirer, as founder of truth.

When and *how* is the actual "truth"—and that means at the same time its overcoming and its transformation—possible and transformed to the "noble one"?

Truth as consolidating and, because equalizing, is always necessary for those who look from below to above but not for those with the opposite view.

---

[*] On will to power, cf. lecture course WS 1936/37, *Nietzsche: Der Wille zur Macht als Kunst* (GA 43); on eternal recurrence, cf. lecture course SS 1937, *Nietzsches metaphysische Grundstellung im abendländischen Denken. Die ewige Wiederkehr des Gleichen* (GA 44); on both, cf. *Übungen* SS 1937, *Nietzsches metaphysische Grundstellung. Sein und Schein* [GA 87].

The question of the order of ranks is in this sense a question in the *crossing* [and implies] the necessity of distinction and uniqueness in order to enact the enopening of being.

But those questions about time-space, i.e., the *question of truth* as inceptual question of what is ownmost to the true (cf. 37/38*), must become more originary than this question.

* Lecture course WS 1937/38, *Grundfragen der Philosophie. Ausgewählte "Probleme" der "Logik"* (GA 45) [trans. R. Rojcewicz and A. Schuwer, *Basic Questions of Philosophy: Selected "Problems" of "Logic"*].

IV. Leap*

115. The Guiding-Attunement of the Leap

The leap, the most daring move in proceeding from inceptual thinking, abandons and throws aside everything familiar, expecting nothing from beings immediately. Rather, above all else it releases belongingness to be-ing in its full essential swaying as enowning. Thus the leap gives the impression of being most reckless—and yet it is precisely attuned by that *deep awe* (cf. Preview, 5: For the Few and the Rare, pp. 9ff.), in which the will of reservedness exceeds itself into inabiding and sustaining the most distant nearness to the hesitating refusal.

The leap is to dare an initial foray into the domain of *being-history.*

116. Being-History

In commencing a preparedness for crossing from the end of the first beginning into the other beginning, it is not as if man simply enters a "period" that has not yet been, but it is rather that man enters a totally different domain of history. The end of the first beginning will for a long time still encroach upon the crossing, nay even upon the other beginning.

As surely as the end-history continues to go on, and—measured by events—continues to be "more alive" and "swifter" and more confused than ever, the crossing itself will continue to be the most question-worthy and above all the most unrecognized. The few humans, who do not know of one another, will prepare themselves unto the free-play of time-space of Da-sein and will be gathered into a nearness to be-ing that must remain strange to everything that is "true to life." In long periods of time, which to be-ing-history are merely moments, be-ing-history recognizes exceptional enownings. Enownings such as: allotment of truth to be-ing, the collapse of truth, consolidation of what is not its ownmost (correctness), abandonment of beings by being, the return of be-ing into its truth, the enkindling of the hearth-fire (of the truth of be-ing) as the solitary site for the passing of the last god, the flashing of the once and only uniqueness of be-ing. While destruction of the hitherto existing world, as self-destruction, screams out its triumphs into the void, the essential sway of be-ing gathers into its highest calling: as en-ownment, to *own* the domain of decision of the godhood of gods *to* the ground and the free-play of time-space, i.e., Da-sein, in the onetimeness of its history.

Be-ing as en-owning is the triumph of what is indispensable in the confirmation of god. But will beings join the jointure of be-ing? Will uniqueness of going-under be granted to humans, instead of the desolation of a continuing progress? Going-under is the gathering of everything great in the moment of preparedness for the truth of the uniqueness and one-time-ness of be-ing. Going-under is the innermost nearness to refusal, in which enowning gifts itself to man.

Entry of man into being-history is unpredictable and independent of all progress or decline of "culture," as long as "culture" itself means consolidating the abandonment of beings by being, as long as it carries on the increasing entanglement of human-being in its "anthropologism," or even squashes man once again into the Christian mistaking of all truth of be-ing.

117. Leap

"Fundamental-ontological" mindfulness (laying the foundation of ontology as its overcoming) is *crossing* from the end of the first beginning to the other beginning. But this crossing is at the same time the take-off for the leap, by which alone a beginning and specifically the other beginning—as constantly overtaken by the first—can begin.

Here, in crossing, the most originary and therefore the most historical decision is being prepared, that either-or for which no hiding and evading places remain: *either* continuing to be held captive by the end and its flow, and that means renewed variations of "metaphysics," which become increasingly more crude, more without ground and aim (the new "biologism" and the like), *or* beginning the other beginning, i.e., being resolved for its long preparation.

But now, because the beginning happens only in the leap, even this preparation must already be a leaping and, as preparing, must simultaneously originate and arise from contention with the first beginning and its history (playing-forth).

What is entirely other in the other beginning, in comparison to the first beginning, can be clarified by a saying that seems only to play with a *turning around* whereas in truth everything is transformed.

In the first beginning being (beingness) is enthought (through νοεῖν and λέγειν), enseen, and placed into the open of its reign, so that a being shows itself. As a consequence of this beginning, then, being (beingness) becomes ὑπόθεσις, more precisely: ἀνυπόθετον, in whose light all beings and non-beings are present. And so, be-ing holds sway for the sake of beings. This basic relation, however, now undergoes two interpretations, which then tie together and mix: "being" as *summum ens* becomes the *causa prima* of beings as *ens creatum*; being as *essentia*, idea, becomes the *a priori* of the objectness of objects.

Being becomes the most common and the most empty and the most familiar and at the same time the most-being [*Seiendste*] as that cause, becomes "the absolute."

In all variations and secularizations of Western metaphysics, one again recognizes that being is at the service of beings, even when being appears to be dominating as cause.

But in the other beginning beings are such that they also carry the clearing into which they are placed, which clearing holds sway as clearing for self-sheltering and concealing, i.e., for be-ing as enowning.

In the other beginning all beings are sacrificed to be-ing, from which beings as such first receive their truth.

But be-ing holds sway as enowning, as the site for the moment of decision about the nearness and remoteness of the last god.

Here, in the unavoidable ordinariness of beings, be-ing is the most non-ordinary; and this estranging of be-ing is not a *manner* of its appearing but rather is be-ing itself.

In the domain of grounding its truth, i.e., in Da-sein, the uniqueness of death corresponds to the nonordinariness of be-ing.

The most terrifying rejoicing has to be the dying of a god. Only man "has" the distinction of standing before death, because man inabides in be-ing: Death is the utmost testimonial for be-ing.

In the other beginning the truth of be-ing must be ventured as grounding, as enthinking of Da-sein.

Only in Da-sein is *that* truth founded for be-ing in which all beings *are* only for the sake of be-ing—be-ing that lights up as the trace of the way of the last god. By way of grounding Da-sein, *man* is transformed (seeker, preserver, guardian).

This *transformation* opens up the space for other necessities of deciding the nearness and remoteness of gods.

118. Leap

[The leap] is projecting-open the essential sway of be-ing to the utmost, such that we place ourselves into what is thus opened up, become inabiding, and through enownment first become ourselves. But for determining what is ownmost to be-ing, must not a being continue to be the *guide*? But what does "guide" mean here? That we distinguish being as what is most general about a pre-given being—that would only be an addendum to comprehension. The question would continue to be: Why and in what sense a being is "a being" for us? There is always beforehand a projecting-open. And the question is only whether or not, as thrower, the one who projects-open itself leaps into the enopening trajectory of the throw (cf. Playing-Forth: The First Beginning); whether projecting-open is itself experienced and sustained as occurring from within enowning, or whether what shines forth in projecting-open as what rises (φύσις-ἰδέα) merely recoils unto itself as the rendering present that is released unto itself.

But from where comes the ground for deciding the direction and scope of projecting-open? Is determining what is ownmost to be-ing subject to random caprice or to utmost necessity and thus to a *distress*? But distress is always different, depending on the epoch of being and its history; shelteredness of the history of being (cf. Echo, 57: History of Be-ing and Abandonment of Being).

What counts in the *other beginning* is the leap into the encleaving mid-point of the turning of enowning in order thus to prepare—in knowing, inquiring, and setting the style—the t/here [*Da*] regarding its grounding.

We can never understand a being through explanation and deduction from other beings. A being can only be known in terms of its grounding in the truth of be-ing.

But how seldom man shifts into this truth; how easily and quickly he is content with a being and thus continues to be dis-enowned of being. How compelling the dispensability with the truth of being seems to be.

119. The Leap into Preparation by Asking the Grounding-Question*

For preparation it is necessary to know the guiding-question and the crossing. The guiding-question itself is knowable only in its hitherto hidden history (cf. Playing-Forth, 110: ἰδέα, Platonism, and Idealism).

1. The first beginning and its end encompasses the entire history of the guiding-question, from Anaximander to Nietzsche.

2. At the beginning the guiding-question is not asked in its explicit question-form, but for this reason it is all the more originarily engrasped and decisively answered: the rising of a being, presencing of a being as such in its truth, which is grounded in λόγος (gathering) and νοεῖν (receiving).

3. From here to the first and subsequently guiding formulation of the question, the path leads to Aristotle: the essential preparation in Plato and [then] Aristotle's coming to terms with the first beginning, which thus receives an abiding interpretation for posterity.

4. The effect of the version of the question that now recedes again but nevertheless dominates everything in terms of outcome and methods (doctrine of categories, theo-logy); reconstruction of the whole by Christian theology; in *this* form the first beginning continues to be solely historical—even yet in Nietzsche, in spite of his discovery of inceptual thinkers as men of rank.

5. From Descartes to Hegel [there occurs] a renewed re-forming, but no essential recasting; taking back into consciousness and absolute certainty. Hegel enacts for the first time a *philosophical* attempt at a history of the question concerning beings from within the fundamental position of absolute knowledge that had been won.

6. What lies between Hegel and Nietzsche has many shapes but is nowhere within the metaphysical in any *originary* sense—not even Kierkegaard.

---

* Cf. Playing-Forth.

*

In contrast to the guiding-question, the grounding-question commences with the question-form as a question *framed*, in order to leap out of it back into the originary and fundamental experience of thinking the truth of be-ing.

But the grounding-question, even as a *framed* question, has a totally different character. It is not the continuation of the version of the guiding-question in Aristotle. For it arises directly from the necessity of the distress of the *abandonment of being*, that occurrence that is essentially co-conditioned by the history of the guiding-question and its misconstrual.

Being dislodged into the essential sway of be-ing and thus asking the preliminary question (what is ownmost to truth) is different from all objectification of beings and all direct access to them; hereby either man is totally forgotten or beings as certain are referred to the "I" and consciousness. By contrast, the *truth* of be-ing and thus what is ownmost to truth holds sway only in the inabiding in Da-sein, in the experience of thrownness into the t/here [*Da*] from within belongingness to the call of enowning.

*

However, in order for this entirely different questioning, as Da-sein-steadfastness [*Da-seinsbeständnis*], to move at all to a decidable possibility, one must first attempt to bring about a crossing from the guiding-question to the leap into the grounding-question—through the complete unfolding of the guiding-question, never a direct transition to the grounding question. It has to be made manifest that and why the question of truth (meaning) of be-ing remains unasked in the guiding-question. This unasked question is the grounding-question, *seen* within the perspective of the path of the guiding-question, but only indicatively seen; time as the truth of be-ing; this initially experienced inceptually as presencing, in various forms.

Being and Time is the crossing to the leap (asking the grounding-question). As long as one accounts for this attempt as "philosophy of existence," everything remains uncomprehended.

"Time" as temporality, meaning the originary onefold of the removal-unto that lights up and conceals itself, provides the nearest ground for grounding Da-sein. With this starting point, it is not as if the hitherto form of responding should be retained, or even replaced; thus instead of "ideas" (or their misconstruction in the nineteenth century) and instead of "values," other "values" or even no values at all would any longer be posited. Rather "time" here—and correspondingly, everything that is grasped by the word "existence" [*Existenz*]—has a totally

different meaning, namely that of grounding the open site of momentariness for a historical being of man. Because so far all decisions in the
domain of "ideas" and "ideals" ("worldviews," cultural ideas, etc.) are no
longer decisions, because they no longer question at all their *space* of
decision and even less truth itself as truth of be-ing, therefore we must
above all become mindful of the grounding of a space for decision. And
that means that we must above all experience the distress of lack of distress, abandonment of being. But when everything stays put in the
domain of "culture" and "idea" and "value" and "meaning"—although
superficially imitating "philosophy of existence"—then, seen *being-historically* and from the viewpoint of inceptual thinking, abandonment of
being is consolidated anew and lack of distress is, as it were, raised to a
principle.

Here there is no inkling of the *incomparability* of taking a fundamental position in the other beginning. [Here there is no inkling] that the
leap—here as question concerning what is ownmost to truth itself—
above all puts man into the free-play of the onset and staying away of
the arrival and flight of gods. It is only this that the other beginning can
want. Reckoned from the vantage-point of the heretofore, this means
renouncing success and applicability in terms of a "worldview" and "doctrine" and proclamation.

It is not a matter of *proclaiming* new doctrines to a human operation
that has run aground, but of *displacing* man out of the lack of distress
into the distress of lack of distress, as the utmost distress.

120. Leap

If we knew the law of the arrival and the flight of gods, then we would
get a first glimpse of the onset and staying away of truth and thus of the
essential swaying of be-ing.

Be-ing is *not* the most general property and thus emptiest determination of beings—as a protracted and familiar representation suggests,
one that resides in the domain of decline of the first beginning—as if we
knew "beings" and all that counted would be to abstract that which is
"general."

Be-ing is also not a superior being which causes all other presumably
known "beings" and which encompasses them in this way or that.

Be-ing holds sway as the truth of beings. However roughly and indirectly grasped, the essential swaying of be-ing has always already
decided on these beings. Therefore the decision of truth in every respect
is made by leaping into the essential swaying of be-ing.

What do we mean with this word *leap*—here, like every other word,
easily misunderstandable?

The leap gives rise to preparedness for belongingness to enowning.
Onset and staying away of the arrival and the flight of gods, enowning,

cannot be forced by thinking with thinking as measure [*denkmäßig*], whereas, on the other hand, the open can be held ready by means of thinking [*denkerisch*]—the open that as time-space (the site for the moment) makes the cleavage of be-ing accessible and lasting in Da-sein. Enowning is only seemingly enacted by man; in truth humanness occurs as historical in and through en-ownment that fosters Da-sein in this way or that. The onset of be-ing, which is allotted to historical man, never makes itself known to man directly but is hidden in the ways of sheltering of truth. But the onset of be-ing, in itself seldom and sparing, always comes from be-ing's *staying* away, whose momentum and durability is no less than that of the onset.

Be-ing as the essential swaying of enowning is thus not an empty and indefinite ocean of determinables into which we, already "existing" [*seiend*], leap from somewhere; but rather the leap lets the t/here [*Da*]—belonging to and enowned by the call—first emerge as the site for the moment for a "somewhere" and a "when."

The whole cleavage of be-ing is thus already co-decided in the direction of the cleavage's inceptual manifestness and hiddenness. And it may be that the other beginning, too, is again capable of holding unto and of sheltering enowning in a singular lighting and as clearing—just as in the first beginning only φύσις was gathered (λόγος), even if barely and only for an instant.

Only a few come to the leap, and these on various paths. They are always those who ground Dasein in creating-sacrificing—Dasein, in whose time-space beings are preserved as beings and with that the truth of be-ing is sheltered. But be-ing is always at its utmost sheltering-concealing, is the removal-unto the incalculable and unique, unto the sharpest and highest ridge, which makes up the "alongside" for the abground of the nothing and itself grounds the abground.

Clearing and sheltering-concealing, which make up the essential swaying of truth, dare not ever be taken as an empty course and as object of "knowledge" or as object of representation. As removing-unto and charming-moving-unto, clearing and sheltering-concealing are enowning itself.

And wherever and as long as the illusion persists that there might be an empty—and by itself enactable—enopening for direct accessibility to beings, there man is then poised only in the no longer and not yet grasped initial zone of the abandonment that is left over and thus is still held as a remnant of a flight of gods.

The most actual and broadest leap is that of *thinking*. Not as if the essential sway of be-ing were determinable by *thinking* (assertion), but because here, in the *knowing awareness* of enowning, the cleavage of being can be climbed through the furthest and the possibility of sheltering of truth in beings can be measured the furthest.

As inceptual, thinking grounds the time-space in its jointure of removal-unto and charming-moving-unto and climbs through the cleavage of be-ing in the uniqueness, freedom, fortuitousness, necessity, possibility, and actuality of its essential swaying.

However, grounding time-space does not design an empty table of categories. Rather, as *inceptual,* thinking is historical in its very core; i.e., determined by the distress of the lack of distress, it reaches out into the necessities of essential shelterings of truth and into the necessities of a guiding knowing awareness of that truth.

When the distress of lack of distress breaks out, it strikes against the staying away of the arrival and flight of gods. This staying away is all the more uncanny the longer and seemingly persistently churches and forms of worship of a god are still maintained, without having the strength to ground an originary truth.

The leap is knowing leaping-into the momentariness of the site for the onset; the leap is that which comes first and ensprings the sheltering of en-ownment in the directing word (cf. the essential swaying of be-ing).

121. Be-ing and Beings

Place all things and what is extant on one side of the scale, including the machinations into which their frozenness is consolidated; and put on the other side of the scale the projecting-open of be-ing, including the weight of thrownness of the projecting-open—to which side will the scale tilt? To the side of the extant, in order to let the powerlessness of projecting-open fly up into ineffectiveness.

But who is the one who weighs on this scale? And what is the extant? And what raves in machinations? None of this ever reaches the truth of be-ing, but takes on only the appearance of ground and of what is unavoidable by withdrawing from truth and by wanting to deny as a nothing what is its foremost, namely extantness.

Who ordered the scale of the market? And who demands that everything be weighed on it alone?

Who surpasses this weighing and ventures the unweighable and defers beings to be-ing?

Moreover, where is the arena in which to accomplish this? Must not the weighable *be,* in order that the truth of be-ing hold sway? Must not the unweighable alone be ventured on the scale?

In what is the nearest and the ordinary and the continual, beings will always outdo and chase away be-ing. And this occurs, not when a being itself gathers unto itself and unfolds, but when a being has turned into the object and state of dissembling machinations and is dissolved into non-being. Here, in the most ordinary publicness of beings that have become all the same, the utmost *squandering* of be-ing occurs.

Do we understand from this point of view the untruth into which

be-ing has to fall? Do we esteem its truth enough, which, in the countering of squandering, holds sway as pure refusal and is itself uniqueness and full estrangeness?

The quietest and steepest paths and walkways must be found, in
order to lead out of the already protracted enduring ordinariness and
abusing of be-ing and in order to ground the site for be-ing's essential
swaying in what be-ing itself as enowning en-owns, namely in Da-sein.

122. Leap
(The Thrown Projecting-Open)

[The leap] is the enactment of projecting-open the truth of be-ing in
the sense of shifting into the open, such that the thrower of the projecting-open experiences itself as thrown—i.e., as en-owned by be-ing. The
enopening in and through projecting-open is such only when it occurs
as the experience of thrownness and thus of belongingness to be-ing.
That is the essential difference from every merely *transcendental* way of
knowing with regard to the conditions of possibility (cf. Leap, 134: The
Relation of Da-sein and Be-ing).

But thrownness is attested to only in the basic occurrences of the
hidden history of be-ing and indeed for us especially in the distress of
the abandonment of being and in the necessity of decision.

In that the thrower projects-open and speaks thinkingly "from
enowning," it becomes manifest that, the more the thrower projects-
open, the more the thrower as thrower is the thrown one.

In opening up the essential swaying of be-ing it becomes manifest
that Da-sein does not accomplish anything, unless it be to get hold of
the counter-resonance of en-ownment, i.e., to shift into this counter-
resonance and thus first of all to become itself: the preserver of the
thrown projecting-open, *the grounded founder of the ground.*

123. Be-ing

Let us venture the unmediated word:
Be-ing is the enquivering of gods' godding (of echoing ahead the gods'
decision about their god).

This enquivering widens the free-play of time-space in which it itself
comes into the open as refusal. Thus be-ing "is" the en-owning of en-
ownment of the t/here [*Da*], that open within which it itself enquivers.

Be-ing must be thought all the way out to this extreme matter. But
in this way it lights up as the most finite and the richest, as *most of all
holding to abground* its ownmost intimacy to itself. For be-ing is never a
determination of god itself. Rather be-ing is that which the godding of
gods needs, in order nonetheless to remain totally differentiated from
be-ing. Being (as in the beingness of metaphysics) is neither the highest
and purest determination of ϑεῖον and *Deus* and the "absolute," nor is

being—what belongs to this interpretation—the commonest and emptiest cover for everything that "is" *not* not.

But as refusal be-ing is not sheer retreat and withdrawal but the opposite: refusal is the intimacy of an allotting. In the enquivering the clearing of the t/here [*Da*] in its abground-dimension gets allotted. The t/here [*Da*] is allotted as what is to be grounded, as Da-sein.

Thus man is originarily and differently claimed by the truth of be-ing (for that is the allotted clearing). By this claim of be-ing itself man is named as the guardian of the truth of be-ing (humanness as "care," founded in Da-sein).

Refusal is the most intimate distressing of the most originary and again inceptual distress into the necessity of warding off distress.

The essential warding off of distress should not ward off in order to eliminate distress, but rather, by averting distress, warding off *preserves* distress and draws it out in accord with the broadening of enquivering.

Thus be-ing as the allotting refusal is the en-ownment of Da-sein.

This en-ownment, however, is drawn into its own as en-quivering of gods' godding, which needs the free-play of time-space for its own decision.

But the guardianship of man is the ground for an other history. For it is not enacted as a sheer focus on what is extant. Rather this guarding is a grounding one. It has to establish and shelter the truth of be-ing in "a being" itself, which then in turn—entering unto be-ing and its strangeness—unfolds the charming simpleness of its swaying, and passes over all machination, and withdraws from live-experience into erecting another mastery, i.e., the domain of that mastery, which the last god en-owns to itself.

Only after enormous ruinings and downfalls of beings do those beings which are already pressured into machination and live-experience and rigidified into non-beings yield to be-ing and thus to its truth.

Every feeble mediating and rescue-attempt entangles beings even more in the abandonment of being and makes the forgottenness of be-ing the sole form of truth, namely of the untruth of be-ing.

How can there be even the smallest room for intimating *that refusal is the foremost and utmost gifting of be-ing, nay even its inceptual essential swaying* itself? It enowns itself as withdrawal, which draws into stillness, in which truth—according to what is its ownmost—comes anew to decision of whether it can be grounded as the clearing for self-sheltering. This self-sheltering is the unconcealing of refusal, is letting-belong to the strangeness of an other beginning.

124. Leap

Raising the essential swaying of be-ing into the grasping word—what venture lies in such a projecting-open?

This knowing, such unpretentious boldness, can be born only in the grounding-attunement of reservedness. But then it also knows that every attempt to justify and to explain the venture from the outside — and thus not from within what it ventures — lags behind what is ventured and undermines it. But does that not continue to be arbitrary? Certainly. The only question is whether this arbitrariness is not the utmost necessity of a distressing distress — that distress that forces the thinking saying of being into word.

125. Be-ing and Time

"Time" was to become experienceable as the "ecstatic" free-play of the truth of be-ing. The re-moval-unto what is lit up was to ground the clearing itself as the open in which be-ing is gathered into its essential sway. Such essential sway cannot be demonstrated as something extant; its essential swaying must be awaited as a thrust. What comes first and lasts the longest is being able to wait in this clearing until the hints arrive. For thinking no longer enjoys the favor of the "system"; it is historical in the singular sense that be-ing itself as en-owning above all sustains all history and thus can never be calculated. Historical preparedness for the truth of be-ing replaces the systematization and deduction.

And this requires above all that this truth itself already might create the basic traits of its abode (Da-sein) out of its barely resonating essential sway, and that the subject in man must transform itself into the founder and guardian of this abode.

In the question of being we are dealing solely with the enactment of this preparation for our history. All specific "contents" and "opinions" and "pathways" of the first attempt in *Being and Time* are incidental and can disappear.

But reaching out into the free-play of time-space of be-ing must continue. This reaching out gets hold of anyone who has become strong enough to think through the initial decisions, in whose domain a knowing seriousness fits together with the epoch unto which we continue to be owned. This seriousness is no longer jarred by good and bad, by decline and rescue of the tradition, by good naturedness and violence, but only sees and grasps what *is*, in order to help this being — in which what is precisely *not* ownmost reigns as essential — out into be-ing and to bring history into its indigenous ground.

Being and Time is therefore not an "ideal" or a "program" but rather the self-preparing beginning of the essential swaying of be-ing itself — not what *we* think up but — granted that we are ripe for it — what compels *us* into a thinking that neither offers a doctrine nor brings about a "moral" action nor secures "existence"; instead "only" grounds truth as the free-play of time-space, in which a being can again become "a being," i.e., come to preserve be-ing.

Because many a distinguished one needs these preservations in order to let a being in itself arise at all, there must be art, which sets truth into its *work*.

126. Be-ing and a Being and Gods

Once, beingness became the most "being" (ὄντως ὄν); and, following this notion, be-ing became the essence of god itself, whereby god was grasped as the manufacturing cause of all beings (the source of "being" and therefore necessarily *itself* the highest "being," the most-being).

This gives rise to the impression that be-ing is thus prized the most (because transferred into this most "being") and hence is also encountered in what is ownmost to it. And yet, this misconstrues be-ing and evades inquiry into it.

Be-ing attains its greatness only when it is recognized as that which the god of gods and all godding *need*. The greatness that is "needed" thwarts all usage. For it is the en-owning of en-ownment of Da-sein, as the essential swaying of truth, wherein is founded the quiet abode, the free-play of time-space for the passing, and the unprotected in-the-midst-of, which unleashes the storm of en-ownment.

Be-ing is not and can never "be" more-being than a being, but also not less-being than gods, because gods "are" not at all. Be-ing "is" the between [Zwischen] in the midst of beings and gods—completely and in every respect incomparable, "needed" by the gods and withdrawn from a being.

Therefore be-ing is reachable only by the leap into the abandonment by being, as godding (refusal).

127. Cleavage

The cleavage is the unfolding unto itself of the intimacy of be-ing itself, insofar as we "experience" it as refusal and turning-in-refusal. Nevertheless if one wanted to attempt the impossible and to grasp the essential sway of be-ing with the help of "metaphysical" "modalities," then one could say: Refusal (the essential swaying of be-ing) is the highest actuality of the highest possible as possible and thus is the first necessity—discounting, of course, the origin of "modalities" in οὐσία. This "elucidation" of be-ing moves it out of its truth (clearing of Da-sein) and degrades it to something simply extant in itself, the most desolate of desolations that can happen to a being—let alone when this is transferred to be-ing itself. Instead we must try to think the cleavage according to that basic sway of be-ing by virtue of which it is the region of decision for the contention of the gods. This contention hinges on their arrival and flight, a contention in which gods first god [göttern] and put their god to decision.

Be-ing is the enquivering of gods' godding [*Göttern*], enquivering as the widening of the free-play of time-space in which enquivering itself, as refusal, enowns its clearing (the t/here [*Da*]).

The intimacy of this enquivering needs a cleavage that is held utmost to abground [*abgründigste Zerklüftung*]; and it is in this cleavage that the inexhaustibility of be-ing can be intimated and enthought.

128. Be-ing and Man

From where does intimation and representation of be-ing come for man? From the experience of beings, one happily responds. But how is this meant? Does the experience of a being continue to be only an occasion, *the* occasion, for that representing of be-ing; or is be-ing as being-ness immediately taken up "on" and "in" a being? Moreover, we immediately face the often asked question: How is one capable of experiencing a being as a being without knowing of be-ing?

Or does man's intimation of be-ing come precisely *not* from a being but rather from that alone which has equal rank with be-ing—because it continues to belong to be-ing—from the nothing? But how do we understand the nothing here? (Cf. Leap, 129: The Nothing.) *As the overflow of pure refusal. The richer the "nothing," the simpler the be-ing.*

But what counts above all is grounding the *truth* of be-ing. Only then do we take the nihilating from the insidious word *nothing* and give it the power of pointing to the *ab*-ground-dimension of be-ing.

Does intimation of be-ing come only to man? From where do we know this exclusivity? And is this intimating of be-ing the first and essential answer to the question: What is man? For the first answer to this question lies in recasting this question into the form: *Who* is man?

Man intimates be-ing—is the intimater of be-ing—because be-ing en-owns man to itself—and indeed in such a way that en-ownment first needs something that is its own [*ein Sich-eigenes*], a *self* whose self-hood man has to sustain in the *inabiding*, which lets man, standing in Da-sein, become *that* being which is encountered only in the who-question.

129. The Nothing

Seen from the perspective of beings, be-ing "is" *not* a being: It is the not-being and thus, following the ordinary concept, the nothing. No reservation can be entertained regarding this explanation, especially since a being is taken as what is objective and extant and the nothing is taken as the total negating of a being so intended, whereby negating itself has the character of objective assertion.

Considering the most general and emptiest concept of "being" as an object, this "negative" determination of the "nothing" is, however, the "most nihilating" to which everyone is at once and readily ill-disposed. If our inquiry were concerned merely with this pertinent (but nevertheless not yet grasped) nothingness, then this inquiry should not claim to put metaphysics into question and to determine more originarily how be-ing and the nothing belong together.

But how would it be if be-ing itself were the self-withdrawing and would hold sway as refusal? Is this something insignificant or the highest gifting? And is it even above all by virtue of *this* not-character of be-ing itself that the "nothing" is full of that allotting "power" whose steadfastness gives rise to all "creating" (a being becoming more-being)?

When now abandonment of being belongs to the "beings" of machination and live-experience, should we be surprised if the "nothing" is misconstrued as what is simply nihilating?

When affirmation of "making" and of "live-experience" so exclusively determines the actuality of the actual, how unwelcome then must all "no" and "not" appear! For decision about the not and the no always depends on the manner in which one directly and without hesitation enhances the usual yes to *that* yes as such which lends every no its measure.

But the essential, "creating" affirmation [*Jasagen*] is more difficult and rarer than the usual approving of what is current and conceivable and satisfying would have it. Therefore those who are anxious and despise the no must initially always be asked about their yes. And then it often becomes clear that they themselves are not so sure about their yes. Would this be the reason why they become the supposedly courageous adversaries of the "nothing"?

And finally, the yes and the no—of what origin are both, including their difference and opposition? Another question: Who founded the difference between affirmability and negatability, the *and* of the affirmable and the negatable? Here every "logic" and, even more so, every metaphysics fails, since it grasps beingness only from within *thinking.*

The counter-turning [*Gegenwendige*] must lie in the essential swaying of be-ing itself, and the ground is en-ownment as refusal, which is an allottment. Then the not and the no would be what is more originary in be-ing.

130. The "Essential Sway" of Be-ing

If one were to put this essential sway in a few words, then perhaps the following phrase would work:
Be-ing holds sway as *enowning the grounding of the t/here* [*Da*], put briefly: as *enowning.* But everything here is beset with misinterpretations; and even when these are rejected, one must always bear in mind that no formula says what is essential, because we are used to think and say

every formula on *one* level and in *one* respect. Nevertheless, an initial elucidation can offer some help in overcoming the formula-character.

The "of" in enowning *of the* grounding of the t/here [*Da*] is intended as a *genitivus objectivus;* the t/here/ [*Da*], the essential swaying of truth in its grounding (what is more originary of Da-*sein*), is enowned; and the grounding itself *lights up* the self-sheltering, the enowning. [This is] the *turning* and belongingness of truth (clearing of self-sheltering) to the essential sway of be-ing.

It is from within the originary essential sway of truth that what is true and thus is a being is above all determined, and in such a way that now a being no longer *is* but *be-ing* arises unto "a being." Therefore in the other beginning of thinking, be-ing is experienced as enowning, such that this experience, as arising, transforms all relations to "what is." From now on a human being—i.e., essential human being—and the few of its kind must build its history from within Da-sein and that means must effect a being in advance, from out of *be-ing* unto a being. Not merely like heretofore, where be-ing is something forgotten and unavoidably only meant in advance, but so that be-ing, its *truth,* expressly bears every relation to a being.

This requires reservedness as grounding-attunement, which thoroughly attunes that guardianship in the time-space for the passing of the last god.

Whether this re-casting of the hitherto existing human and, prior to that, the grounding of the more originary truth in a being of a new history is successful, cannot be calculated, but rather is the gift or withdrawal of enownment itself—even then when, in and through the present mindfulness, the basic traits of the essential swaying of be-ing are already thought ahead and known.

En-ownment of grounding of the t/here [*Da*] requires, of course, that man for his part comes to meet that grounding; but that means something essential and, perhaps for the man of today, something already impossible. For he must get out of the present basic state of affairs, which involves nothing less than the denial of all history.

Man's *coming to meet* requires above all the deepest preparedness for *truth,* for inquiring into what is ownmost to the true, by renouncing all support in correctness and whatever is made ready by machination.

In the other beginning a being can no longer supply the measure for be-ing—neither a specific domain and region nor a being as such. Here one must think so far ahead—or better: so far into—the t/here [*Da*] that the truth of be-ing lights up originarily.

Be-ing becomes what is strange—and indeed in such a way that the grounding of its truth increases this strangeness and thus holds all beings of *this* be-ing steady in the strangeness of be-ing. Only then is fulfilled the full uniqueness of en-owning and of all momentariness of

Da-sein that is allotted to uniqueness. Only then is the deepest joy freed from its ground—as the *creating* which by the most reticent reservedness is protected from degenerating into a sheer and insatiable driving around in blind urges.

131. The Overflow in the Essential Sway of Be-ing
(Self-Sheltering)

The overflow is not a mere abundance of too much quantity but self-withdrawing of all estimation and measuring. But in this self-withdrawing *(self-sheltering)* be-ing has its nearest nearness in the clearing of the t/here [*Da*], in that it [be-ing] enowns Da-sein.

Overflow of enownment belongs to enownment itself, not as an attribute, as if en-ownment could be enownment without overflowing.

Overflow is, of course, also not what is beyond as super-sensible, but as en-ownment is the en-forcing of a being.

Overflow is the self-withdrawing of a *survey*, because it lets emerge and holds open the strife and thus the arena of strife and whatever desists [*Abständige*].

The strife of be-ing against a being, however, is this *self-sheltering* of reservedness of an originary belongingness.

Thus in this gifting of self-withdrawing, enownment overall has the essential sway of *self-sheltering*, which, in order to hold sway, needs the widest clearing.

132. Be-ing and a Being

This distinction [between be-ing and a being] is grasped since *Being and Time* as "ontological difference"—with the intention of safeguarding the question of the truth of be-ing from all confusion. But this distinction is immediately pushed in the direction from which it comes. For here beingness is claimed as οὐσία, ἰδέα; and following these, the objectness is claimed as *condition for the possibility* of the object. Therefore, in attempting to overcome the first effort at the question of being in *Being and Time* and its emanations (*Vom Wesen des Grundes* and the Kantbook*), varying attempts were needed to master the "ontological difference," to grasp its very origin and that means its genuine *onefold*. Therefore, the effort was needed to come free of the "condition for the possibility" as going back into the merely "mathematical" and to grasp the truth of be-ing from within its *own* essential sway (enowning). Hence the tormenting and discording character of this distinction. For as necessary as this distinction is (to think in traditional terms), in order to provide at all a preliminary perspective for the question of be-ing, just as disastrous

---

* *Kant und das Problem der Metaphysik* (GA 3) [trans. R. Taft, *Kant and the Problem of Metaphysics* (Bloomington: Indiana University Press, 1990; 4th enlarged edition, 1997)].

does this distinction continue to be. For this distinction indeed *does* arise from a questioning of beings as such (of beingness). But in this way one never arrives directly at the question of be-ing. In other words, this distinction *itself* becomes the real barrier which misplaces the inquiry into the question of be-ing, insofar as, by presupposing this distinction, one attempts to go further than this distinction and to inquire into its one-fold. This onefold can never be anything but the mirroring of the distinction and can never lead to the origin, in view of which this distinction can no longer be seen as originary.

Therefore the task is not to surpass beings (transcendence) but rather to leap over this distinction and thus over *transcendence* and to inquire inceptually into be-ing and truth.

But in thinking in the crossing, we must sustain this ambiguity: *on the one hand* to begin an initial clarification with this distinction and *then* to leap over this very distinction. But this leaping-over occurs along with the *leap* as the en-grounding of the ground of the truth of be-ing, by leaping into the enowning of Da-sein.

133. The Essential Sway of Be-ing*

Be-ing needs man in order to hold sway; and man belongs to be-ing so that he can accomplish his utmost destiny as Da-sein.

But will be-ing not be *dependent* on another, if this needing even makes up what is ownmost to be-ing and is not merely an essential consequence?

But how do we dare to speak here of dependency, when this needing actually recasts the needed from the ground up and in the first place masters it unto its self ?

And how can man, on the other hand, bring be-ing under his domination, if indeed he must surrender his lostness to beings, in order to become the en-owned and to belong to be-ing?

This *counter-resonance* of *needing and belonging* makes up be-ing as enowning; and the first thing that is incumbent upon thinking is to raise the resonance of this counter-resonance into the onefoldness of knowing awareness and to ground the counter-resonance in its truth.

At the same time we must give up the habit of wanting to secure this essential swaying of be-ing as representable for everyone at any time one chooses.

Rather, we always achieve the uniqueness of the resonance in its pure self-sheltering only in the leap-into, knowing that here we do not attain the "ultimate" but the essential swaying of stillness, the most finite and most unique, as the site for the moment of the great decision

---

* Cf. Leap, 166: Essential Swaying and Essential Sway.

about the staying away and arrival of gods—and *therein* above all the stillness of the watch for the passing of the last god.

The *uniqueness* of be-ing (as enowning), the *unrepresentability* (no object), the utmost *strangeness,* and the essential *self-sheltering*—those are directives which we must follow to make ourselves initially ready for intimating what is most rare—in contrast to be-ing as self-evident—and staying in its openness, even if our humanness is mostly preoccupied with being-away.

Those directives speak to us only if we *withstand* the distress of the abandonment of being while *at the same time* we *expose ourselves* to the decision about the staying away and arrival of gods.

To what extent do those directives effect the grounding-attunement of reservedness and to what extent does reservedness attune to pliancy toward those directives?

134. The Relation of Da-sein and Be-ing

In *Being and Time* [this relation is] first grasped as "understanding of being," whereby understanding is grasped as projecting-open—and the opening-throwing as *thrown,* and that means: belonging to en-ownment by be-ing itself.

But if we fail to recognize in advance the strangeness and uniqueness (incomparability) of be-ing—and together with it what is own-most to Da-sein—then we succumb all too easily to the opinion that this "relation" corresponds to or is even commensurate with the relation between subject and object. But Da-sein has overcome all subjectivity; and be-ing is never an object, re-presentable. It is in every case only a being that is capable of becoming an object—and even here not every being.

But what if "subjectivity," and thus the relation to the *objectness* of the object, is grasped transcendentally (as in Kant); and what if, beyond this, the object "nature" counts as the solely experienceable being—and thus objectness coincides with beingness—is there not here an opportunity, even a historically unique basic position in which—in *spite of all essential differences*—for the first time to render accessible to those of today that relation of Da-sein and be-ing out of what has gone before? Of course. And that is attempted in the Kantbook; but that was only possible by using force against Kant, in the direction of a more originary grasping of precisely the *transcendental* projecting-open in its onefoldness, *by working out the transcendental power of imagination.* Certainly, this Kant-interpretation is "historically" [in history as a discipline] incorrect; but it is *historically* [*geschichtlich*] essential; i.e., considered as preparatory for future thinking—and only as that—it is a historical [*geschichtlich*] referral to something totally different.

But just as surely as Kant's work is "historically" [*historisch*] miscon-strued by such interpretation, so too is that which is to be brought nearer—as the other, as the futural—now misinterpreted: It seems to be nothing other than an "existentiell" or some other modernized "Kantianism." But, if one contends—and rightfully so—that historically [in history as a discipline] Kant here is distorted, then one must also avoid presenting as Kantianism the basic position from which and into which the distortion took place. In other words, such historically com-parative reckoning misses what is essential. Historical encounter (cf. Playing-Forth) is precisely a process that not only returns the earlier history into its hidden greatness but also and at the same time—and only so—contrasts it with the *other questioning* which it enacts, not for comparison but as pliancy vis-à-vis that greatness and its necessities.

And so the Kantbook is necessarily ambiguous, through and through—and is nevertheless not an accidental *communiqué*—because Kant continues to be the only one since the Greeks who brings the interpretation of beingness (οὐσία) into a certain relation to "time" and thus becomes a witness to the hidden reign of the connection between beingness and time.

Nevertheless, for him as for the Greeks, thinking (as λόγος—forms of judgment—categories—reason) gets the upper hand in establishing the perspective for interpreting beings as such. Additionally, following Des-cartes's procedure, thinking as "thinking" comes to dominate; and beings themselves become *perceptum* (represented) or *object*, in accor-dance with the same historical reason. Therefore thinking cannot get to a grounding of Da-sein; i.e., the question of the truth of be-ing is unaskable here.

135. The Essential Swaying of Be-ing as Enowning
(The Relation of Da-sein and Be-ing)

[This relation] includes the en-ownment of Da-sein. Accordingly, and strictly speaking, talk of a relation of Da-sein *to* be-ing is misleading, insofar as this suggests that be-ing holds sway "for itself" and that Da-sein takes up the relating to be-ing.

The relation of Da-sein *to* be-ing belongs in the essential swaying of be-ing itself. This can also be said as follows: Be-ing needs Da-sein and does not hold sway at all without this enownment.

En-owning is so strange that it seems to be complemented primarily *by* this relation to the other, whereas from the ground up en-owning does not hold sway in any other way.

Talk of relation of Da-sein to be-ing obscures be-ing and turns be-ing into something over-against [*ein Gegenüber*]—which be-ing is not, since be-ing itself always en-owns primarily *that to which* it is to hold sway as over-against. For this reason also this relation is entirely incomparable to the subject-object-relation.

136. Be-ing*

Be-ing—the remarkable heresy is that be-ing always has to "be" and that the more constantly and enduringly be-ing is, the more-being it is.

But first of all, be-ing "is" nothing at all but rather holds sway.

And then, be-ing is the rarest, because it is the most unique; and no one fully prizes the few moments in which it holds sway and grounds an abode for itself.

How is it that man misjudges so much when it comes to be-ing? Because he must be exposed to a being in order to experience the truth of be-ing. In this exposure a being is the true, the open—and it is this because be-ing holds sway as what shelters itself.

So man holds himself onto beings, makes himself of service to beings, and falls prey to forgottenness of be-ing—all of this with the illusion of accomplishing what is genuine and of staying close to be-ing.

Only when be-ing holds itself back as self-sheltering can beings appear and seemingly dominate everything and present the sole barrier against the nothing. And nevertheless all of this is grounded in the truth of be-ing. But then the immediate and only consequence is to leave be-ing in concealment and even to forget it. But: Leaving be-ing in concealment and experiencing be-ing as self-sheltering are two different things. The experience of be-ing and sustaining its truth *do* put beings back into their limit and take from them the seeming uniqueness of their priority. However, in this way beings do not become any less "beings"; on the contrary, they become more being, i.e., more holding sway in the essential swaying of be-ing.

How many (all) now talk of "being" and always only mean a being—and perhaps that being that offers them the opportunity of avoidance and calmness.

When we speak of man's relation to be-ing and vice versa of be-ing's relation to man, then this easily sounds as if be-ing holds sway for man like an over-against and an object.

But man as Da-sein is en-owned by be-ing as enowning and thus belongs to enowning itself.

Be-ing "is" neither roundabout man nor does it swing through him as a being. Rather, being enowns Dasein and only in this way holds sway *as enowning*.

Finally, however, enowning cannot be *re*-presented as an "event" and a "novelty." Its truth, i.e., *the* truth itself, holds sway only as *sheltered* in art, thinking, poetizing, deed—and therefore requires the ina-

---

* Cf. *Überlegungen* V, 17f., 34, 51f. [GA94].

biding of Da-*sein*, which rejects all illusion of immediacy of mere re-presenting.

Be-ing holds sway as enowning. This is the ground and abground for god's disposing on man and, in turn, for man's disposing unto god. But this disposal is born up only in Da-sein.

(If be-ing can never be determined as the "most general" and "emptiest" and "most abstract," because it remains inaccessible to all re-presenting, then for the same reason it does not let itself be considered as the "most concrete," and even less as the coupling of both of these inherently insufficient interpretations.)

With Dasein as measure, the turning disposal [*die kehrige Verfügung*] is attuned by the grounding-attunement of reservedness; and what attunes is enowning. But if we interpret attuning according to our representation of "feeling," then one might easily say here: Being is now related to "feeling" rather than to "thinking." But how sentimentally and superficially we are thinking here about "feelings" as "capacities" and "appearances" of a "soul"; how far removed we are from what is ownmost to attuning, let us say: from *Da-sein*.

In case it is still admissible, for purposes of an immediate understanding, to characterize be-ing in terms of beings, then we will appeal to the actual as what genuinely is. We know the actual as what is present, as the constant.

In the other beginning, however, a being is never actual in the sense of this "being-present." Even where this being-present is encountered in constancy, it is the most fleeting thing for the originary projecting-open of the truth of be-ing.

Actual, i.e., what is, is only the remembered and the still accessible. Remembering and access open the free-play of the time-space of be-ing, with regard to which thinking must disavow "presentness" as the heretofore only and unique determination. (Because here is the nearest region of decision about the truth of be-ing, leaping up [*Ansprung*] into the other beginning had to be attempted as *Being and Time*.) But considering the ordinary understanding of time (since Aristotle and Plato), one might leave the νῦν in its priority and derive past and future from the modification of this priority—especially since remembering can only remember from out of and by appealing to something present and something that has been present, especially since something futural is fated only to become something present.

Although what is present [*das Gegenwärtige*] is never the nothing and takes part in the grounding of remembering and access, all of this is so only if the presenting of what is always present is already carried and attuned by remembering and access, from whose intimacy the present [*Gegenwart*] flashes up. Originarily experienced, the present cannot be reckoned according to its fleetingness but according to its *uniqueness*.

This is the new and essential thrust of constancy and presencing, to be determined in terms of remembering and access.

137. Be-ing

In the other beginning, the essential swaying of be-ing itself in its full estrangement over against a being must be attained as what is inceptual. This is no longer the familiar, from which be-ing could be differentiated merely as a faded remainder, as if be-ing were the not-yet-grasped, most general determination of otherwise common beings.

In the other beginning the utmost removal from "a being"—as what supposedly *sets the standard*—is accomplished, even if it still very much dominates all thinking (cf. abandonment of being).

Be-ing here is not a subsequent species, not a cause that is added, not an encompassing that stands behind and above beings. Conceived in this way, be-ing continues to be debased as a supplement whose supplementarity is not canceled out by elevating it to "transcendence."

Be-ing—rather, the essential swaying—is that out of and back to which a being as a being is above all unconcealed and sheltered and comes to be (cf. Grounding, on truth).

The question concerning the difference between being and beings has here a character that is totally different from the one in the questioning domain of the guiding-question (ontology). The notion of "ontological difference" is only preparatory, as crossing from the guiding-question to the grounding-question.

The truth of be-ing, in and as which its essential swaying is sheltered in enopening, is enowning. And this is at the same time the essential swaying of truth as such. In the turning of enowning, the essential swaying of truth is at the same time the truth of the essential swaying. And this counter-turning itself belongs to be-ing as such.

The question, Why is there truth at all as clearing sheltering-concealing? presupposes the truth of the why. But both, truth and the why (the call for grounding), are the same.

Essential swaying is the truth that belongs to be-ing and springs from be-ing.

Only where the essential swaying emerges merely as presencing—as it does in the first beginning—does it *promptly* come to the *parting* of a being from its "essence," i.e., what is merely the essential swaying of be-ing as presence. Here the question of be-ing as such—and that means of its truth—remains necessarily unexperienceable and unasked.

138. Truth of Be-ing and Understanding of Being

Prefatory Remark: If one takes understanding as a kind of ascertaining recognition of inner "lived-experiences" of a "subject"—and correspondingly the one who understands as an I-subject—without first giving a hearing to what is said about understanding of being in *Being and Time,* then any comprehension of what is meant by the understanding of being is hopeless. Then the roughest misinterpretations will unavoidably follow—for example, that, through understanding of being, be-ing (and here beings are meant nonetheless) becomes "dependent" on the subject and everything amounts to an "idealism" whose concept still remains in the dark.

In response one has to refer to the basic determination of *understanding* as projecting-open, which consists in an opening-up and a throwing and putting oneself out into the open, *wherein* the one who understands first comes to himself as a self.

Besides, understanding as projecting-open is a thrown projecting-open, is coming into the open (truth) that occurs already in the midst of beings that are opened up—as rooted in the earth and rising in a world. Thus understanding of being as grounding of its truth is the opposite of "subjectification," because it overcomes all subjectivity and modes of thinking determined by subjectivity.

In accordance with the origin of Dasein, the turning [*die Kehre*] necessarily lies in understanding as thrown projecting-open; the thrower of the projecting-open is a thrown-thrower—but only in and through the throw.

Understanding is enacting and taking over the sustaining inabiding, Da-*sein,* taking over as under-going [*Er-leiden*], wherein what is closed off opens itself up as what sustains and binds.

139. The Essential Swaying of Be-ing: Truth and Time-Space[*]

Be-ing holds sway; a being is.

Be-ing holds sway as enowning. To enowning belongs the uniqueness and strangeness which inhere in the momentariness of the unexpectedly befalling and thus initially widening site.

The preliminary indication of the domain for the sheltering of the truth of the arriving and fleeing god shows in which shape the onset of be-ing is posed and preserved for the first time.

To what extent what has long become ungrounded and nevertheless continues to be a common thing, to what extent this can still be made susceptible to onset [*Anfallbereitschaft*]—this co-decides the possible domain for the breakthrough of the truth of be-ing.

Being holds sway as enowning. That is not a proposition but the nonconceptual reticence of the essential sway, which opens itself up only to the full historical [*geschichtlich*] enactment of inceptual thinking. Historically, a being first emerges out of the truth of be-ing, and the truth of be-ing is sheltered in the inabiding of Da-*sein.* Therefore "being" can never be made *common,* as much as the word sounds common to everything. And

---

[*] Cf. Leap and Grounding.

yet, wherever and whenever it holds sway, it holds sway nearer and deeper than any beings. Here, in terms of Da-sein, a totally different relation to be-ing is thought and enacted; and {*} that occurs in the time-space that emerges from removal-unto and charming-moving-unto truth itself. Time-space itself is a strifing domain of strife. From this strifing domain—following the immediate assault on beings as such (φύσις, ἰδέα, οὐσία)—in the first beginning only the *presencing* became graspable and seizable as the standard for all interpretation of beings. Along with that, time [was thought] as present and space, i.e., *place* as *here* and *there*, within presence and belonging to it. But in truth space has as little presence as it has absence.

Timing spacing—spacing timing (cf. the strifing of the strife) as the nearest region of joining for the truth of be-ing—but not as what falls into the common formal space- and time-concepts (!), rather as taking [time and space] back into the *strife,* world and earth—enowning.

140. The Essential Swaying of Be-ing

If one does not seek refuge in an explanation of being (of beingness) by setting up the first cause of all beings—which causes itself—if one does not disperse beings as such into objectness and then explain beingness in terms of re-presenting the object and its a priori, if be-ing itself should come to swaying and indeed every kind of beings in themselves be kept away from it, then this will be successfully carried out only as a necessary mindfulness (that outlasts the abandonment of being as distress), which gains insight into the following:

The truth of be-ing and thus be-ing itself holds sway only where and when there is Da-sein.

Da-sein "is" only where and when there is the being of truth.

[That is] a turning or rather *the* turning, which points out precisely the essential sway of being itself as the counter-resonating enowning.

Enowning grounds Da-sein in itself (I).

Da-sein grounds enowning (II).

Here grounding belongs to turning [*kehrig*]: I. sustaining soaring through, II. instituting projecting-open (cf. Leap, 144: Be-ing and the Originary Strife, p. 186).

141. The Essential Sway of Be-ing**

En-ownment of Da-sein by be-ing and grounding the truth of being in Da-sein—the turning in enowning—is contained neither solely in the call (staying-away) nor solely in belongingness (abandonment of being), or in both together. For this "together" and both of them deeply

{* See Epilogue, p. 366.}
** Cf. Grounding: the essential sway of truth.

resonate first in enowning. In enowning, enowning itself resonates in counter-resonance.

The enquivering of this deep resonance in the turning [*Kehre*] of enowning is the most sheltered and concealed essential sway of be-ing. This sheltering-concealing lights up as sheltering only in the deepest clearing of the site for the moment. In order to hold sway in that seldomness and uniqueness, be-ing "needs" Da-sein; and Da-sein grounds human-being and is its ground, insofar as, in sustaining and inabiding, man founds it.

142. The Essential Sway of Be-ing

The enquivering of deep resonance in the turning [*Kehre*], Dasein's owning to the hint—Dasein that belongs, grounds, and shelters—this essential swaying of be-ing itself is not the last god. Rather, essential swaying of being grounds the sheltering and thus the creating-preserving of god, who only *divinizes* [*durchgottet*] be-ing in work, in sacrifice, in deed and in thinking.

Thus, as inceptual thinking of the other beginning, thinking is also capable of coming into the remote nearness of the last god.

Thinking comes into that remote nearness in and through that god's history as self-grounding, but never in the form of a result, a producing kind of re-presenting that shelters god. All such claims—seemingly very high claims—are low and a degradation of be-ing! (Cf. Grounding, 230: Truth and Correctness.) En-owning and its enjoining in the abgroundness of time-space is the net in which the last god suspends itself, in order to rend it and to let itself come to its end in its uniqueness, godly and rare and the strangest among all beings.

The sudden extinction of the great fire that leaves behind what is neither day nor night, what no one grasps, and wherein man—reaching the end—still spins around, in order only still to numb himself with the products of his machinations, pretending that they are made for eternity, perhaps for that etcetera that is neither day nor night.

143. Be-ing

Be-ing as en-owning. En-ownment determines man as owned by be-ing.

Thus is be-ing then after all the other, over against enowning? No, for ownhood is belongingness into en-ownment, and this itself is be-ing.

Of course, enowning dare not ever be represented immediately objectively. Enownment is the counter resonance between man and gods—and it is precisely this *between* and its essential swaying which is founded by and in Da-sein.

God is neither "a being" nor a "not-being"—and also not commensurate with be-ing. Rather be-ing holds sway, temporally-spatially, as that "between" [*Zwischen*] that can never be grounded in god but also not in man as extant and living—but in *Da-sein.*

Be-ing and the essential swaying of its truth belongs to man insofar as he becomes inabiding as Da-sein. But this also immediately means that be-ing does not hold sway by the graces of man, by the fact that man only happens to be.

Be-ing "belongs" to man, so much so that man is needed by be-ing itself as the preserver of the site for the moment of the fleeing and arrival of gods.

Wanting to set off *be-ing,* from some snatched up being, is impossible, especially since "any being whatsoever," if it is only experienced as the true, is always already the other to itself—not like *some other* as the opposite that belongs to it. Rather *the other* means that which as sheltering the truth of be-ing lets a being be a being.

144. Be-ing and the Originary Strife*
(Be-ing or Not-Be-ing in the Essential Sway of Be-ing Itself)

The origin of the strife from within the intimacy of *the not in be-ing!* Enowning.

The intimacy of the not in be-ing: belonging above all to its essential swaying. Why? Can one still ask a question in this manner? If not, why not?

The intimacy of the not and what is strifing in being—is that not Hegel's negativity? No, but he nevertheless did—as did already Plato's *The Sophist* and before that Heraclitus, only more essentially but yet differently—experience what is essential but sublated it in absolute knowing: negativity only in order to let it disappear and to keep the movement of sublating going.

[That is] precisely not the essential swaying. Why not? Because [for Hegel] being as beingness (actuality) [is determined] in terms of thinking (absolute knowledge). What is important is not above all and exclusively that there "is" also an anti-thesis [*Gegen-teil*] and that both [*anti* and *thesis*] belong together, but that, if the anti [*Gegen*] [is] already, then as the counter of counter resonance, and as enowning. Before, there is always only sublating and gathering (λόγος), but now freeing and abground and the full *essential swaying* in the time-space of originary truth.

[What is important] now [is] not the νοεῖν, but the *sheltering inabiding*—and *strife* as the essential swaying of the "between" [*Zwischen*], not as letting the contrary also count.

Whereas one of the greatest insights of Western philosophy lies in

---

* Cf. being and not-being—the decision.

Heraclitus's πόλεμος-fragment, it was nevertheless as little unfolded for the question of truth as for the question of being (WS 1933/34).[*]

But from where [comes] the *intimacy* of the not in be-ing? Whence such essential swaying of be-ing? Again and again questioning runs against this; it is the question concerning the ground of the truth of be-ing.

But truth itself [is] the ground, and this [truth]? [It] arises from within the self-holding-in-the-truth! But how is this origin? Holding oneself in the truth [is] our breaking out and our will out of our distress, because we [are] delivered over and allotted to ourselves—us? Who are we *ourselves*?

But of course not *ours,* rather that we open up and sustain the self and that the "unto-itself" and thus be-ing as enowning opens up in the self (cf. Grounding) in a sheltering-concealing way.

And, nevertheless, "we" [are] not the starting point, rather "we" [are] as exposed and misplaced, but in the forgottenness of this misplacement.

When enowning shines thus into selfhood, therein lies the directive for *intimacy.*

The more originarily we are ourselves, the further we are already removed into the essential swaying of be-ing, and vice versa (cf. the essential swaying of be-ing—the turning [*die kehrige*] grounding of being and Da-sein).

Only when questioning arises from this deep point is the "ground" of intimacy open. This deep point has a deciding character. Be-ing is nothing "human" and no human product; and nevertheless the essential swaying of be-ing needs Da-sein and thus the inabiding of man.

145. Be-ing and Nothing

In the entire history of metaphysics, i.e., in all of thinking up to now, "being" is always grasped as beingness of beings and thus as these beings themselves. As the result of philosophy's asthenia in differentiation, still today all "thinkers" begin, as it were, by equating being with beings.

Correspondingly, the nothing is always grasped as a non-being and thus as something negative. If, moreover, one sets the "nothing" in this sense as the goal, then "pessimistic nihilism" is complete; and the contempt for all sickly "philosophy of the nothing" is legitimized. Above all one is relieved from any questioning, and the pursuit of such a relief is what distinguishes "heroic thinkers."

My questioning of the nothing, which arises from the question concerning the truth of be-ing, has nothing at all in common with all of that. The nothing is neither something negative nor is it a "goal"; rather

[*]Lecture course WS 1933/34, *Vom Wesen der Wahrheit* (GA 36/37).

it is the essential enquivering of be-ing itself and therefore *is more-being* than any beings.

When the sentence from Hegel's Logic is quoted in "*What Is Metaphysics?*" — "Being and nothing are the same" — that means, and can only mean, an analogue for bringing together being and nothing as such. However, for Hegel "be-ing" is exactly not only a certain first stage of what in the future is to be thought as be-ing, but this first stage is, as the *un*-determined, *un*-mediated stage precisely already pure negativity of objectness and of thinking (beingness and thinking).

As difficult as it will become for the future to shake off the thinking of "metaphysics," just as inaccessibly will the "nothing" initially continue to be for the future — the nothing that is higher than all "positivity" and "negativity" of beings taken together.

The thinking questioning must above all have attained an originariness in affirming power which essentially goes beyond all optimistic manipulation of power and all programmatic heroism in order to be strong enough to experience the nihilating [*das Nichtende*] in be-ing itself, which for the first time actually *sets* us *free* into be-ing and its truth as the most sheltered gift. However, it is then recognized that the nothing never reckons up and settles itself *against* be-ing — for example, as what one is to flee from or to deny — because be-ing (and that means the nothing) is the in-between [*Inzwischen*] for beings and for godding and can never become a "goal."

146. Be-ing and Not-Be-ing*

Because the not belongs to the essential sway of be-ing (fullness as the turning in enowning; cf. The Last God), be-ing belongs to the not; that is, the actually nihilating [*Nichtige*] has the character of the not [*Nichthafte*] and is not at all the mere "nothing," as when it is only represented by the representing negating of something, on the basis of which one says that the nothing "is" not. But the *not-be-ing* holds sway and be-ing holds sway; *the not-being holds sway in what is not ownmost, be-ing holds sway as what has the character of a not.*

Only because be-ing holds sway in terms of the not [*nichthaft*] does it have the not-being as its other. For this other is the other of itself.

Holding sway in terms of the not, it [be-ing] makes possible and enforces otherness [Andersheit] at the same time.

But whence comes the utmost confinement to the one and the other and thus to the either-or?

The uniqueness of the not that belongs to be-ing and thereby the uniqueness of the other follows from the uniqueness of be-ing.

---

* Cf. Leap, 144: Be-ing and the Originary Strife; cf. Preview, 47: What Is Ownmost to Decision.

The one *and* the other enforce for themselves the either-or as primary.

But regarding this seemingly most general and emptiest distinction, one has to know that it is such [a distinction] only for the interpretation of beingness as ἰδέα (being and thinking!): something (random and in general) and *not*-something (the nothing); the not is equally representable as without reason and empty.

But this seemingly most general and emptiest distinction is the most unique and fullest decision. Therefore, for this distinction we cannot presuppose, without self-deception, an indistinct representation of "be-ing," however such exists. Instead: be-ing as enowning.

Enowning as the *hesitating refusal* and therein the fullness of "time," the mightiness of the fruit and the greatness of the gifting—but in the *truth* as *clearing* for the *self-sheltering*.

Fullness is pregnant with the originary "not"; making full is not *yet* and *no longer* gifting, both in *counter-resonance*, refused in the very hesitating, and thus the *charming-moving-unto* in the removal-unto. Here [is] above all the swaying not-character of be-ing as enowning.

147. The Essential Swaying of Be-ing
(Its Finitude)

What does it mean to say: Be-ing "is" infinite? The question cannot be answered at all, if along with this question, the essential sway of be-ing is not put to question.

And the same is true for the proposition: Being is finite, if in-finity and finitude are taken as extant notions of magnitude. Or is a *quality* meant with that? And which quality?

In the end the question of the essential swaying of be-ing lies beyond the dispute between those propositions; and the proposition "Be-ing is finite" is only meant to ward off, in crossing, any kind of "idealism."

But if one operates within the dispute of those propositions, then we would have to say that, when be-ing is taken as infinite, then it is precisely *determined*. If be-ing is set as finite, then its ab-groundness is affirmed. For what is in-finite cannot be meant as what is endlessly in flux, and only endlessly goes astray, but as the closed *circle*! By contrast, enowning consists in its "turning"! ([is] strifing).

148. A Being Is

This "proposition" says nothing directly. For it only repeats what is already said with the word "*a* being." The proposition says nothing as long as it is understood directly, to the extent that that is possible at all, i.e., as long as it is thought unthinkingly.

If on the other hand this proposition moves over at once to the domain of truth—being holds sway—then it says that a *being belongs to the essential swaying of be-ing.* And now this proposition has crossed over from being unthinkingly self-evident to being question-worthy.

It becomes manifest that this proposition is not the final word in assertability, but instead the most temporary in questionability.

What does "belonging to the essential swaying of being" say? And immediately the question also arises: a being, which one? What is a being for us? The over-against? What is put aside, what we let be set [*hingestellt-sein lassen*] as object? A being from the encounter as "a being," and why *encounter*? *When* encountering, and how? For re-presenting?

Or is "a being" the *issuance* [*der Ausfall*] *of the essential swaying of be-ing*?

Or can nothing be said here about a being, as long as "a being" continues to be so taken up *into* representation in general, since, from within and in the manner of a *sheltering* "a being" always belongs to be-ing? Especially since this be-ing is itself historical and in due course enowning itself?

Are we not always and again stuck too deeply in the usual tracks of representing, especially with that mania for a being at all and in general, so that we still grasp too little and insufficiently that which the uniqueness of be-ing, once understood, contains in itself for the question of being?

149. Beingness of Beings Differentiated According to τί ἐστιν and ὅτι ἔστιν

This differentiation within the first beginning, emerging thus within the history of the guiding question, must in this beginning be related to the guiding interpretation of beings as such.

We call τί ἐστιν, in a certain way arbitrarily, the *constitution* (whatness, *essentia*) and the ὅτι ἔστιν the *manner* (that it is and how it is, *existentia*). More important than the names is the matter itself and thus the question of how this differentiation arises from the beingness of beings and so belongs to the essential swaying of be-ing.

The immediate representing of this difference and of what is differentiated leads to a dead end, the dead end of what is for us today long since the most familiar. "The door" has its what-ness, likewise the "clock" and the "bird"; and they each have their that-being and how-being.

If only "actuality" or even possibility and necessity are understood by these, are these "modalities" modalities of *actuality*? This actuality [is] itself always one [modality] among others, thus whence *modalities*?

In the sense and within the perspective of the guiding-question, is it initially enough to refer to differences of presence and absence—for example, regarding the extant and the ready-to-hand?

In any case immediate "thinking" of this difference does not yield anything by which to determine it as perspective and truth, as long as we persist in this thinking as last and first.

A merely formal discussion, which takes this difference as simply given and fallen from heaven—as a dialectical discussion of the relationship of *essentia* and *existentia*—remains empty scholasticism, distinguished by its remaining without perspective and without being mindful of truth with regard to the concepts of beingness in the broadest sense. A way out then, is to explain "being" in terms of the highest being as made and thought by this highest being.

However, the historical fact remains that the treatment of the guiding-question already very early on comes upon this differentiation in beingness itself! When? At the time when beings were interpreted in the light of ἰδέα and οὐσία. Why at this juncture and at that time? (Cf. Playing-Forth, 110: ἰδέα, Platonism, and Idealism.) Formalistically, one can say that every "constitution" has its mode and that every mode is that of a constitution. Thus both belong together. This then indicates a hidden and to some extent richer swaying of beingness.

Essentia and *existentia* are not what is richer or the consequence of something simple but the other way around: they are a definite impoverishment of a richer essential sway of be-ing, and of its truth (this truth's temporality-spatiality as the abground).

The next step that must be taken in the debate is to open up unto its perspective and ground the *thinking* of οὐσία as representing, as νοεῖν, and to bring to light the characterization of οὐσία as constant presence. Nowadays one acts as if that has always been known. That is correct and not correct. Correct, insofar as constancy and presence are implicitly meant and re-presented; and nevertheless incorrect, insofar as these two *as such* are not raised to knowing awareness and not understood as "time"-characteristics of a more originary time (of time-space) and—what is even more essential—are not first made into a question from that point on.

150. The Origin of Differentiation of the What and the That of a Being*

A being is thus already determined in its beingness and indeed as ἰδέα, the *look*, which in turn is determined as *constant presence*. To what extent are both temporal and spatial determinations in ἰδέα?

Presencing (temporal)	[understood] as *gathering* of what shines forth, of the look—*what*.
Constancy (temporal)	[understood] as *enduring* and lasting—*that* the look is not absent.
Constancy (spatial)	[is] what *fills out* and makes up stability.

* Cf. Playing-Forth, 98: Projecting Beingness Open unto Constant Presence; Playing-Forth, 110: ἰδέα, Platonism, and Idealism; cf. lecture course SS 1927, *Die Grundprobleme der Phänomenologie* (GA 24) [trans. A. Hofstadter, *The Basic Problems of Phenomenology* (Bloomington: Indiana University Press, 1982)].

Presencing (spatial)   [is] making room, the whither of deferring,
                                that it is stable.

In each determination—presence and constancy—*that* differentiation that is all too familiar to us and taken for granted as the what and
the that of a being is especially temporal and spatial, and each time in
terms of temporalizing as well as spatializing.

But whence comes the doubling in temporalizing and spatializing?
From their grounding sway as removal-unto *and* charming-moving-
unto—their grounding sway rooted in what is ownmost to truth (cf.
Grounding, 242: Time-Space as Ab-ground).

If the what and the that are not inquired into as determinations of
beingness—along with beingness with respect to their truth (time-space)—
then all discussions of *essentia* and *existentia* remain an empty pushing
around of uprooted concepts, as the Middle Ages already proves.

But beingness is already grounded on the hidden "differentiation" of
be-ing and beings—a "differentiation" that cannot be overcome.

151. Being and a Being*

This differentiation comes initially from the guiding-question of beingness and has remained stuck there (cf. Playing-Forth, 110: ἰδέα, Platonism, and Idealism). But this differentiation also has its truth in the
other beginning—nay, only now does it receive its truth. For now,
where "thinking" no longer inquires into beingness (not beingness and
thinking, but "being and time," understood in terms of crossing), this
"differentiation" names that domain of enowning of the essential
enswaying of being in truth, in its shelteredness, by which a being as
such first moves into the t/here [*Da*] (cf. Grounding, 227: On the Essential Sway of Truth, p. 247).

The t/here [*Da*] is the occurring, *en-owned and inabiding* site for the
moment of the turning [*Wendungsaugenblicksstätte*] for the clearing of
beings in enownment. The differentiation no longer has anything to do
with what is meant and needed merely logically-categorically-tran-
scendentally—and is without fundament. The mere representation of
being and a being as differentiated now says nothing and is misleading,
insofar as it holds unto mere representation.

What opens up for thinking in this differentiation can be thought
inclusively only in the full jointure of Dasein's projecting-open.

152. The Stages of Be-ing**

From where this series of steps? No doubt based on ἰδέα and nearness
to it, for example, in Plato's *Republic*, where they are stages of
"beings"—or of not-beings—to beings, all the way to ὄντως ὄν.

---

* Cf. Leap, 152: The Stages of Be-ing.
** Cf. Leap, 132: Be-ing and a Being; 154: "Life."

Then above all the *neo-Platonic* staging!

Christian theology [takes stages as] *ens creatum* and *analogia entis*.

[Staging is] everywhere where [there is] a *summum ens*. [In] *Leibniz:* sleeping monads ↔ central monads. Everything [reappears] in a new neo-Platonic systematic form in German Idealism. To what extent does all of this go back to Plato and be Platonism, always only stages of beings as different fulfillings of the highest beingness?

When inquired into from the perspective of the truth of being as enowning, are there even stages of this kind—and even stages of be-ing?

If we consider the differentiation of be-ing and a being as enownment of Da-sein and sheltering of a being and if we take into account that here everything is historical through and through and that a Platonic-idealistic systematization has become impossible—because it is insufficient—then the question remains: how to rank what is alive— "nature"—and what is not alive in nature, like a tool, machination, work, deed, sacrifice and their power of truth (originariness and sheltering of truth and thereby the essential enswaying of enowning). All ranking in terms of representation and calculation is superficial here; the one thing that is essential is the historical necessity in the *history* of the truth of be-ing, whose epoch is commencing.

How is it with "machination" (technicity) and how is all sheltering gathered in it? Above all how does the intrusion of the abandonment of being consolidate in it?

What is essential is the historical, Dasein-grounding power of sheltering and the decisiveness unto it and its bearing for the steadfastness of enowning.

But does there nevertheless not remain a way, at least provisionally, for furnishing—similar to the kind of "ontologies" of different "domains" (nature, history)—a purview for that projecting-open which accords with being and thus to make the domains experienceable anew? Something like that can become necessary as *crossing;* but this remains risky, insofar as in that perspective one can easily lapse into a systematization of the earlier style.

But when the "order" is a joining and is subordinate to forming history and carrying out its mystery, then this joining itself can—nay, must—have a domain and a pathway; no random way of sheltering (for example, technicity) can be subjected to mindfulness.

Here one must remember that sheltering is always the strifing of the strife of world and earth and that these two, each in its turn, heighten and suffuse the other and that sheltering of truth takes place above all and foremost in their counter-current.

World is "earthy" (of the earth). Earth is worldly. In one respect earth is *more originary* than nature, because it is related to history. World is higher than what is merely "created" because world is *history-forming* and thus closest to enowning.

Does be-ing then have stages? Actually not; but neither do beings. But whence and of what meaning is the manifold of *sheltering*? That cannot be explained and derived by taking stock of a providential plan. But a receiving that merely accords with representation counts just as little. Rather what counts is the *decision* in the historical necessities of the epoch of being-history.

What should technicity be? Not in the sense of an *ideal*. But how does technicity stand within the necessity of overcoming the abandonment of being, respectively, of putting up being's abandonment to decision, from the ground up. Is technicity the historical pathway to the *end, to the last man's falling back into a technicized animal, which thus loses even the originary animality of the enjoined animal—or can technicity be above all taken up as sheltering and then enjoined into the grounding of Da-sein?*

And so decision of every kind of sheltering is for a moment saved up for us, respectively, that is saved up for us which we pass by and passing by we simply wear away.

153. Life

Since all living beings are organismic, and that means bodily, one *can* view this bodily being as corporal—and then view the body mechanically. There are even certain tasks that demand such a view: Measuring sizes and weights (which of course are directly situated within the purview of an interpretation with respect to what is alive).

But the question remains whether what one *can* do here in such a manner (mechanically) ever *leads to* that which one first and foremost *must* do, granted that a fundamental relationship to what is alive is necessary. To what extent does this turn out to be true? What is a plant and an animal to us anymore, when we take away use, embellishment, and entertainment?

If what is alive *is* effortlessly alive, then that is the most difficult to see, if everything is set off toward effort and its overcoming and moves within machination!

Can there be "biology" as long as the fundamental relation to what is alive is lacking, as long as what is alive has not become the other resonance of Da-sein?

But then *is* it "biology" when it derives its legitimacy and its necessity from the domination of science within modern machination? Does not every biology destroy what is "alive" and neutralize the fundamental relation to it? Must the relation to what is "alive" not be sought totally outside "science"? And in what sphere should this relation be situated?

What is "alive" will offer endless possibilities to scientific progress—as does everything capable of becoming an object—while at the same time it will increasingly withdraw, the more science itself loses its ground.

154. "Life"*

["Life"] is a "mode" of beingness (be-ing) of beings. A being begins to open up to life in the preservation of the self. In the preservation of the self the first darkening grounds the numbness of what is alive, in which all excitement and excitability is enacted, as well as various stages of the dark and its unfolding.

The *darkening* and what is ownmost to *instinct:* preservation of the self and the *priority of the "species,"* which does not know any "individual" as self-related [*selbstisches*].

The darkening and *worldlessness:* (Earlier as *world-poorness*! Misunderstandable. The rock is not even worldless, because it is indeed without darkening.)

The numbing and life's falling-back [stem] from within the incipient enopening. Correspondingly there is also no closure [*Verschließung*], insofar as what is alive is not taken along with—"earth" (rock, plant, animal). Rock and river are not without plant and animal. How does the decision about "life" rise and fall? Being mindful of what is "biological."

155. Nature and Earth

What happens to nature in technicity, when nature is separated out from beings by the natural sciences? The growing—or better, the simple rolling unto its end—destruction of "nature." What was it once? The site for the moment of the arrival and dwelling of gods, when the site— still φύσις—rested in the essential swaying of be-ing.

Since then φύσις quickly became a *being* and then even the counterpart to "grace"—and, after this demoting, was ultimately reduced to the full force of calculating machination and economy.

And finally what was left was only "scenery"and recreational opportunity and even this still calculated into the gigantic and arranged for the masses. And then? Is this the end?

Why does earth keep silent in this destruction? Because earth is not allowed the strife with a world, because earth is not allowed the truth of be-ing. Why not? Because, the more gigantic that giant-thing called man becomes, the smaller he also becomes?

Must nature be surrendered and abandoned to machination? Are we still capable of seeking earth anew? Who enkindles that strife in which the earth finds its open, in which the earth encloses itself and is earth?

* Cf. Leap, 152: The Stages of Be-ing; cf. biologism, in: Playing-Forth, 110: ἰδέα, Platonism, and Idealism, pp. 154f.

156. Cleavage

In order to know the cleavage in its structural texture, we must experience the abground (cf. truth) as belonging to enowning.

The essential swaying of be-ing will always remain closed off to philosophy as long as it believes that one could know being somehow through puzzling out the various concepts of modality and with these concepts could, as it were, put being together. Aside from the questionable origin of modalities, one thing is decisive here: the leap into be-ing as enowning; and *only* from *this* does the cleavage open up. But this very leap needs the most extended preparation, and this includes the *complete disengagement* from being as beingness and as the "most general" determination.

Whether someday a better equipped thinker ventures the leap? In a creative sense he must have *forgotten* the way of *hitherto* inquiring into being, i.e., into beingness. *This* forgetting is not losing something nevertheless to be possessed but transformation into a more originary stance of questioning.

But here one must be equipped for the inexhaustibility of the simple, so that it no longer withdraw from him because of misconstruing it as something empty. The simple, in which all essential swaying has gathered, must be found again in each being—no, each being must be found in essential swaying. But we attain the simple only by preserving each thing, each being—in the free-play of its mystery and do not believe that we can seize be-ing by analyzing our already firm knowledge of a thing's properties.

This analysis and holding onto *an* experience as *the* experience was *once* necessary, so that Kant could initially point to that which the "transcendental" kind of knowledge was to grasp. And even this directive and its formation as a work in Kant's works needed the services of centuries of preparation.

What should we now expect from our initial groping, when something completely different is at stake, for which Kant can be only a distant prelude—and only if this prelude is already grasped from within the more originary task?

What does it mean that at the end of the analytic of principles the "modalities" are dealt with, thus pre-determining everything that has gone before?

157. Cleavage and "Modalities"

The "modalities" belong to beings (to beingness) and say nothing at all about the cleavage of be-ing itself. This cleavage can become a question only when the truth of be-ing as enowning is lit up, namely as that which god needs, while man belongs to it (cf. The Last God, 256: The Last God). Thus modalities lag behind the cleavage, just as beingness lags behind the truth of be-ing; and the question of modalities necessarily remains entangled in the framework of the guiding-question, whereas inquiring into the cleavage belongs to the grounding-question alone.

In one direction the cleavage has its primary and broadest bearing in god's needing; and in the other direction, in man's belongingness (to be-ing). Here hold sway god's precipitant descendings [*Abstürze*] and man's ascending [*Anstieg*] as the one who is grounded in Dasein.

The cleavage is the inner, incalculable settledness [*Ausfälligkeit*] of *en-ownment;* of the essential swaying of be-ing as the midpoint that is used and that grants belonging—the midpoint that continues to be related to the passing of god and the history of man at the same time.

En-owning owns god over to man in that it owns man to god (cf. Preview, 7: From Enowning, pp. 17ff.).

When Da-sein and thus man succeeds in leaping-into creating grounding, Da-sein and thus man, holding to abground, is grounded in enowning.

Here not-granting and staying-away are enowned, as are onset and accident, reservedness and transfiguration, and freedom and compulsion. Such are enowned, i.e., belong to the essential swaying of enowning itself. Every kind of arranging, canceling, and mixing of "categories" fails here, because categories speak *from* a being *unto* a being and never name or know be-ing itself.

In the same vein passing and enowning and history can never be thought as kinds of "movements," because *movement* (even when thought as μεταβολή) always relates to the ὄν as οὐσία—to which relationship δύναμις and ἐνέργεια and their later progeny also belong.

But above all what makes up the inner settledness of enowning and either remains hidden or emerges—according to enownment—can never be enumerated and presented in a "table" or any other type of compartmentalization of a system. Rather, every saying of the cleavage is a thinking word unto god and to man and thus into Da-sein—and so into the strife of world and earth.

Here there is no investigative analysis of "structures," and even less a stuttering in "signs" and acting, as if something were being addressed.

Escaping into "ciphers" is only the final consequence of "ontology" and "logic"—which have not been overcome but precisely presupposed.

The saying of inceptual thinking stands outside the difference between concept and cipher.

158. Cleavage and "Modalities"*

The source and domination of "modalities" is *even more* questionable than interpretation of beings unto ἰδέα, which has established itself in

---

* Cf. lecture course WS 1935/36, *Die Frage nach dem Ding. Zu Kants Lehre von den transzendentalen Grundsätzen* (GA 41).

the course of the history of philosophy, in order to become, as it were, an extant "set of problems."

Important for the source of modalities is the priority of "actuality" (cf. also *existentia* as *the* difference from *essentia*), actuality as ἐνέργεια, with possibility and necessity, so to speak, as its antennae.

But ἐνέργεια is here genuinely grasped in terms of the ununfolded φύσις, which is analyzed in the light of μεταβολή as beingness. Why μεταβολή? Because for the fore-grasping holding to what is constant and present, μεταβολή, especially as φορά, is *the* counter-appearance itself and thus allows coming back from it as an other, pointing to οὐσία. Here is the kernel of Aristotle's "ontology."

159. Cleavage

One essential cleft is *being in bending back* (capability, but not according to *possibility*, which up to now has always been thought in terms of beings as extant.)

Splitting this cleft and thus parting it in togetherness as *mastery*, that is the origin that leaps forth. Mastery *is*—or better: holds sway—as legacy and is not itself bequeathed but rather bequeaths the continuing originariness. Everywhere where beings are transformed *according to be-ing*, i.e., are to be grounded, mastery is necessary.

Mastery is the necessity of the free to be free. It holds mastery and sway as unconditionality in the domain of freedom. Its greatness consists in its not needing power and thus needing no coercion and still remaining more effective than power and coercion, although in the ur-own [*ureigene*] way of *its* steadfastness [*Beständigkeit*] (of the apparently long-drawn interrupted constancy [*Stetigkeit*] of moments drawn to themselves.)

Power—the capability of safeguarding a possession from possibilities of coercion. As *safeguarding*, power always faces an opposing power and is therefore never an origin.

Coercion—power-less capability for change which breaks unto beings, without leaping forth and without the prospect of possibilities. Everywhere where beings are to be changed by beings (not from out of be-ing), coercion is necessary. Every act is a coercive act, such that here coercion is mastered with power as its measure.

160. Being-toward-Death and Being

In its most hidden shapes being-toward-death is the spur for the utmost historicity and the veiled ground for decidedness of the shortest path.

But being-toward-death, unfolded as essential determination of the truth of Da-sein, shelters within itself two fundamental determinations of the cleavage and is their, mostly unrecognized, mirroring in the t/here [*Da*]:

On the one hand what is sheltered here is the essential belongingness of the not to being as such—*which here,* in Da-sein distinguished as grounding the truth of being, comes to light with a singular keenness.

On the other hand being-toward-death shelters the unfathomable and essential richness of *"necessity,"* again as the one cleft of being itself—again being-toward-death with Da-sein as its measure.

In being-toward-death is the collision of necessity and possibility. Only in such spheres can one intimate what in truth belongs to that which "ontology" deals with as the pale and empty *hodgepodge* of "modalities."

161. Being-toward-Death

No one has yet surmised or dared to ponder what was thought *ahead* regarding being-toward-death in the context of *Being and Time* and *only* there, i.e., what was thought "fundamental-ontologically" and never anthropologically and in terms of "worldview."

The uniqueness of death in human Da-sein belongs to the most originary determination of Da-sein, namely to be en-owned by be-ing itself in order to ground its truth (openness of self-sheltering). What is most non-ordinary in all of beings is opened up within death's non-ordinariness and uniqueness, namely be-ing itself, which holds sway as estranging. But in order to be able to intimate anything at all of this most originary connection in terms of the ordinary and used-up standpoint of common opinion and calculating, the relation of Da-sein to death itself, the interconnection of resolute disclosedness [*Entschlossenheit*] (enopening) and death, and running ahead [toward death] had to be made manifest in advance, with full keenness and singularity. But this running ahead toward death is not for the sake of reaching sheer "nothing" but on the contrary: so that openness for be-ing opens up, completely and from within the utmost.

But it is totally in order that, when thinking here is not done "fundamental-ontologically" with the intention of grounding the truth of be-ing, the worst and most absurd misinterpretations creep in and spread—and, naturally, a "philosophy of death" is made up.

The misinterpretations of precisely this section in *Being and Time* are the clearest indications of the incapacity—which is still in full bloom—for re-enacting the questioning that is prepared there, and that means always at the same time thinking more originarily and creatively explicating further.

That death is projected-open—in what is fundamental-ontologically ownmost to Dasein, within the essential context of the originary *futurality* of Dasein—means initially, in the confines of the task of *Being and Time,* that death is connected to "time," which is established as the domain of projecting-open the truth of be-ing itself. This is already an indication — clear enough for those who want to stay with the questioning — that here the question of death stands in an essential relationship to the *truth of be-ing,* and *only* in that relationship, that therefore death here is never taken as the negation of be-ing or that as "nothing" death is even taken for the essential sway of be-ing but exactly the opposite: death as the highest and utmost corroboration of be-ing. But this is knowable only to one who is capable of experiencing and co-grounding Da-sein in the ownedness [*Eigentlichkeit*] of self-being — which is meant, not moralistically and personalistically but again and again and solely "fundamental-ontologically."

162. Be-ing-toward-Death

Be-ing-toward-death is to be grasped as determination of Da-sein and *only* as such. Here the utmost appraisal of *temporality* is enacted, and thus along with it the occupying of the *space* of the truth of be-ing, *the announcing of time-space.* Thus *not* in order to negate "be-ing" but in order to install the ground of its full and essential affirmability.

How despicable and cheap it is, however, to yank the word *being-toward-death* out, then to put on it a crude "worldview," and finally to lay this back into *Being and Time.* It would seem that this calculation works particularly well, since this "book" also talks of the "nothing." Thus there follows the easy conclusion: being-toward-death, i.e., being-toward-nothing and this as the "essence" of Dasein! And that should not be nihilism?

But what is at stake is not to dissolve humanness into death and to declare it for sheer nothingness but the opposite: to draw death into Dasein, in order to master Dasein in its breadth as abground and thus fully to appraise the ground of the possibility of the truth of be-ing.

But not everyone needs to enact this be-ing-toward-death and to take over the self of Da-sein in this ownedness. Rather, this enactment is necessary only within the sphere of the task of laying the foundation for the question of be-ing — a task, however, that is not limited to philosophy.

The enactment of being-toward-death is a duty only for the thinkers of the other beginning. However, every essential human being among those creating in the future can know of it.

Being-toward-death would not have been encountered in its essentiality if the opportunity for insipid mockery were not given to scholars in philosophy and if the right to know better were not given to journalists.

163. Being-toward-Death and Being

[Being-toward-death and being] must always be grasped as determination of *Da-sein.* This means that Da-sein itself is not absorbed in it but, on the contrary, that Da-sein includes being-toward-death within itself; and only this inclusion holds Da-*sein* completely to ab-ground, i.e., makes it that "between" [*Zwischen*] that offers moment and site to "enowning" and can thus belong to being.

Considering being-toward-death as a matter of "worldview," it remains inaccessible; and if it is misconstrued in this fashion—as if being-toward-death teaches the meaning of being in general and thus its "nothingness" in the ordinary sense—then everything is ripped out of the essential context. The essential is *not* enacted, namely the inclusive thinking of Da-sein, in whose clearing the fullness of the essential swaying of be-ing is sheltered and revealed.

Death here enters the domain of foundational mindfulness, not in order to teach a "philosophy of death" as a matter of "worldview" but in order to put the *question of being* above all onto its ground and to open up Da-sein as the ground that is held to ab-ground, to shift Dasein into projecting-open, that means *under-standing* in the sense of *Being and Time* (not for example to make death "understandable" to journalists and philistines).

164. The Essential Swaying of Be-ing*

When a being "is" within be-ing [*das Seyende*], *being* cannot also be. Being would then have to be posed as a being and thus as a property of and addition to a being. And inquiry into this would thus have fallen behind the first beginning. Thus be-ing would have still not been inquired into in any shape or form but would have been denied—but in that way "a being," too, would have been covered over.

Being *is not*, and yet we cannot equate it with the nothing. But on the other hand we must decide to set being as the nothing, where "nothing" bespeaks what is "not-a-being." But beyond such a "nothing," be-ing "is" then not "something," such whereby we could relax, by representing it as something encounterable. Saying "Be-ing holds sway," we again avail ourselves of, and use a naming that in language belongs to, a being (consider *"what has been—presencing"* [*Gewesen— An-wesen*]).

But here, considering the extremeness of this matter, the word needs vigor; and *essential swaying* should not name something that yet again lies *beyond* be-ing but rather what brings its innermost to word: en-owning, that counter-resonance of be-ing and Da-sein in which both are not extant poles but pure and deep resonance itself.

The *uniqueness* of this counter-resonance and [its] *non-representability* in the sense of what is merely *present* is the keenest protection against determinations of beingness as ἰδέα and γένος, determinations that are necessary inceptually, when the breakthrough to be-ing from "beings" as φύσις occurs for the first time.

---

* Cf. Leap: the essential sway of be-ing.

165. Essential Sway as Essential Swaying*

"Essential sway" is no longer the κοινόν and γένος of οὐσία and of τόδε τι (ἕκαστον) but rather essential swaying as the happening of the truth of be-ing and indeed in its full history, which always includes the sheltering of the truth in a being.

But since truth must be grounded in Da-*sein*, the essential swaying of be-ing can only be achieved in the steadfastness which the t/here [*Da*] sustains in the knowing awareness that is so determined.

Essential-sway as essential swaying is never merely re-presentable but will be grasped only in the knowing-awareness of temporal-spatiality of truth and its respective sheltering.

Knowing-awareness of essential sway requires, and is itself the leap-into, Da-sein. Therefore, it can never be obtained by a merely *general* observation of what is given and its already established interpretation.

Essential swaying does not lie "above" and separated from a being. Rather, a being stands in be-ing and, standing therein and lifted away, has its truth as the *true* only *in be-ing*.

Along with this notion of essential swaying, "differentiation" of be-ing and a being, along with everything that is founded on differentiation, must now also be put forth and grasped, insofar as whatever belongs to "categories" and "ontologies" falls on the side of beingness.

166. Essential Swaying and Essential Sway**

Essential swaying and essential sway are grasped as the occurrence of the truth of be-ing. Be-ing does not let itself be translated back to *essential swaying*, since this would itself become a being. The question concerning the being of the essential sway is possible and necessary only when we approach essential sway as κοινόν (cf. later the question of universals). Regardless of how the question is answered, "essential sway" itself will always be degraded.

The notion of "essential sway" depends on the manner of questioning beings as such, or on inquiring into be-ing—and simultaneously on how the question of the *truth* of philosophical thinking is asked. Even in the question of truth the turning [*die Kehre*] intrudes: essential sway of truth and truth of the essential sway.

When, following the familiar direction of inquiry, we inquire into "essence," then the question is: What makes a being what it *is*? And thus: *What* makes up its *what*ness, i.e., the beingness of a being? Essence here is only the other word for being (understood as beingness). And accordingly *essential swaying* means enowning, insofar as it enowns what belongs to it, namely truth. Occurrence of the truth of be-ing—that is

---

* Cf. Differentiation.
** Cf. Preview: inceptual thinking.

essential swaying. Thus essential swaying is never a way of being that is added on to be-ing or even one which persists in itself above be-ing.

By what means must this manner of seemingly genuine continuation of questioning (a being—*its* being—and then being of being, etc.) be cut off and redirected into genuine questioning? As long as everything stays with οὐσία, a ground for no-longer-continuing-the-questioning-in-the-same-manner is not to be found. The only thing left is to deviate into ἐπέκεινα.

As soon as "being" is no longer what is re-presentable (ἰδέα) and, accordingly, as soon as it is no longer thought as away and separate from a being (out of the mania to grasp being as purely and unmixed as possible), as soon as be-ing is simultaneous (in the originary sense of time-space) with a being and is experienced and thought as the ground (not cause and *ratio*) of a being, there is no longer an occasion for inquiring anymore into be-ing's own "be-ing," in order to represent it in this way and to set it aside.

Oriented by this mindfulness, we can initially discuss the historical consequence of the concepts of essence, as they appear within the history of the guiding-question, as guiding-threads for the question of beingness:

1. οὐσία as ἰδέα
2. οὐσία in the Aristotelian discussion in Metaphysics Ζ Η Θ
3. the *essentia* of the Middle Ages
4. *possibilitas* in Leibniz (cf. Leibniz-Seminars)
5. the "condition of possibility" in Kant, the transcendental concept of essence
6. the dialectical-absolute idealistic concept of essence in Hegel.

167. Advancing into Essential Swaying

Essence is only re-presented, is ἰδέα. But essential swaying not only couples whatness *and* howness and is thus a richer representation but rather essential swaying is the more originary onefold of both of those.

Essential swaying does not belong to *all* beings but basically only to being and what belongs to being itself: truth.

Proceeding from the essential swaying of being and corresponding to the guiding-question's being drawn into the grounding-question, the earlier "essence" is also transformed.

Essential swaying is that *into* which we must advance. That means here: "experience" in the sense of advancing-into and abiding in and sustaining the essential swaying—and this happens as Da-sein and its grounding.

.

V. Grounding[*]

Grounding

Da-sein
Truth
Time-Space

---

[*] Cf. *Die Wahrheitsfrage als Vorfrage* [GA 73].

a) Da-sein and Projecting Being Open

168. Da-sein and Be-ing*

Da-sein means en-ownment in enowning as in the essential sway of be-ing. But be-ing comes to truth only on the ground of Da-sein.

But wherever plant, animal, rock and sea and sky become beings, without falling into objectness, there *withdrawal* (refusal/not-granting) of be-ing reigns — be-ing as withdrawal. But withdrawal belongs to Da-sein.

The abandonment of being is the first dawning of be-ing as self-sheltering-concealing from out of the night of metaphysics, in and through which beings pushed ahead into appearing and thus into objectness and be-ing became an addendum in the form of the *a priori*.

But how much in the light that belongs to abground must the clearing for self-sheltering-concealing be lit up, so that the withdrawal does not appear superficially as a mere nothing but rather reigns as gifting.

169. Da-sein**

It belongs to the most unbending rigor of the inner resonance of Da-sein that it does not count gods and also does not count on them and does not even reckon with an individual god.

Belonging to everyone, tuned to the unexpected, this not-counting on the gods is far from the randomness of letting everything count. For this not-counting is already the consequence of a more originary Da-sein — of its gatheredness unto the reversing-refusal [*Umweigerung*], the essential swaying of be-ing. Spoken in the language of metaphysics which has survived, this means that, as essential swaying of be-ing, refusal is the highest actuality of the highest possible *as* possible and is thus what is primary necessity. Da-*sein* is grounding the truth of this most simple cleavage.

170. Da-sein

[Da-sein is] not something that could be simply found in extant man but rather the ground of the *truth* of be-ing made necessary by the fundamental experience of be-ing as enowning, through which ground (and its grounding) man is transformed from the ground up.

* Cf. *Besinnung* [GA 66], 448ff.
** Cf. Leap, 121: Be-ing and Beings.

Only now comes the collapse of *animal rationale,* back into which we are again in the process of falling headlong, everywhere where neither the first beginning and its end nor the necessity of the other beginning is known.

The collapse of the heretofore "man" is possible only from within an originary truth of be-ing.

171. Da-sein*

Da-sein is the ground of the future humanness that holds sway in the grounding.

Da-*sein* [is] care.

On the basis of *this* ground of Da-sein man [is]:

1. the seeker of be-ing (enowning)
2. the preserver of the truth of be-ing
3. the guardian of the stillness of the passing of the last god.

Stillness and origin of the word.

But for its part, grounding of Da-sein is initially seeking-in-crossing, *care,* temporality; temporality unto temporality [*Zeitlichkeit auf Temporalität*]: as *truth* of be-ing. *Da*-sein is related to truth as openness of self-sheltering-concealing, launched by *understanding of being. In throwing-open* [Dasein is] the openness for being. Da-*sein* as *projecting-open* of the truth of be-ing ("t/here" [*Da*]).

172. Da-sein and the Question of Being

In *Being and Time* Da-sein still stands in the shadow of the "anthropological," the "subjectivistic," and the "individualist," etc.—and yet the opposite of all of this is what we have in view—of course, not as what was initially and solely intended, but rather this opposite, everywhere only the *necessary consequence* of the deciding transformation of the "question of being" from guiding-question into the grounding-question.

[In *Being and Time*] "understanding of being" and *projecting-open* [are thought] —*and indeed as thrown!* The *being-in-the-world* of Dasein. But "world" [is] not the *Christian saeculum* and the denial of god or atheism! *World* [is experienced] from within the essential sway of truth and of the t/here [*Da*]! World and earth (cf. lecture on the work of art**).

173. Da-sein

Da-sein is the *crisis* between the first and the other beginning. That is to say: According to the name and the matter itself, Da-sein means something in the history of the first beginning (i.e., in the whole history of metaphysics) that is essentially other than in the other beginning.

---

* Cf. *Überlegungen* V, 82f.: "Plato" [GA 94].
** *Vom Ursprung des Kunstwerkes,* Freiburg lecture 1935 [GA 80].

In metaphysics "Da-sein" is the name for the manner and way in which beings are *actually* beings and means the same as being-extant—interpreted one definite step more originarily: as presence. This designation of beings can even be thought back to the first-ever-inceptual naming, to φύσις and then to ἀλήθεια that determines it. Thus the name *Dasein* finally receives the genuine, first-ever-inceptual content: *rising out of itself, swaying (t/here [Da]) as unhidden.* But running throughout the whole history of metaphysics is the not accidental custom of transferring the name for the mode of actuality of beings to beings themselves and of meaning, with "Dasein," "the Dasein" [existence], i.e., a completely actual and extant being itself. Thus Dasein is only the good German translation of *existentia,* as a being's coming forth and standing out by itself, presencing by itself (in a growing forgetting of ἀλήθεια).

Throughout [metaphysics] "Dasein" means nothing else. And accordingly one could then speak of thingly, animal, human, temporal Dasein [as mere existence].

The meaning and matter of the word *Da-sein* in the thinking of the other beginning is completely different, so different that there is no mediating transition from that first usage to this other one.

Da-sein is not the mode of actuality for every type of being, but is itself the being of the t/here [*Da*]. The t/here [*Da*], however, is the openness of a being as such in the whole, the ground of the more originarily thought ἀλήθεια. Da-sein is a way of being which, in that it "is" the t/here [*Da*] (actively and transitively, as it were), is a unique being in accordance with and as *this* outstanding being (what is in sway in the essential swaying of be-ing).

Da-sein is the very own self-grounding ground of ἀλήθεια of φύσις, is the essential swaying of that openness which first enopens the self-sheltering-concealing (the essential sway of be-ing) and which is thus the truth of be-ing itself.

In the sense of the other beginning, which inquires into the truth of be-ing, Da-sein can never be encountered as the character of a being that is encountered and is extant, but also not as the character of a being which lets such a being become an object and which stands in relations to an object; Da-sein is also not the character of man, as if now the name that up to then was extended to all beings would become limited to the role of characterizing man's extantness.

Nevertheless, Da-sein and man are essentially related, insofar as Da-sein means the ground of the possibility of future humanness and insofar as man *is* futural, in that he takes over being the t/here [*Da*], granted that he grasps himself as the guardian of the truth of be-ing, which guardianship is designated as "care." "Ground of the possibility" is still *spoken* metaphysically, but *thought* from within the *belongingness* that inabides in abground.

In the sense of the other beginning, Da-sein is still completely strange to us; it is what we never find lying before us, what we leap into solely in leaping-into the grounding of the openness of self-sheltering-concealing, that clearing of be-ing in which future man must place himself in order to hold it open.

It is from Da-sein in this sense that Dasein as the presence of what is extant first becomes "understandable," i.e., *presence* proves to be *one* specific appropriation of the truth of be-ing, whereby the presentness [*Gegenwärtigkeit*], compared to what has been [*Gewesenheit*] and what will be [*Künftigkeit*], receives certain interpreted preference (consolidated in objectness, in objectivity for the subject).

As essential swaying of the clearing of self-sheltering-concealing, *Da-sein* belongs to this very self-sheltering, which holds sway as en-owning.

All domains and perspectives of metaphysics fail—and must fail—here, if Da-sein is to be grasped thinkingly. For "metaphysics" inquires into beingness in terms of beings (in the inceptual—and that means definite—interpretation of φύσις) and leaves the truth of this beingness—and that means the truth of be-ing—necessarily unasked. ἀλήθεια itself is the *primary* beingness of a being, and even this remains ungrasped.

In the hitherto and still customary usage Dasein means the same as being extant here and there, *occurring* in a where and a when.

In the other and future meaning "being" [*sein*] does not mean occurring [*vorkommen*] but inabiding *carriability* [*Ertragsamkeit*] as grounding the t/here [*Da*]. The t/here [*Da*] does not mean a here and yonder that is somehow each time determinable but rather means the *clearing* of be-ing itself, whose openness first of all opens up the space for every possible here and yonder and for arranging beings in historical work and deed and sacrifice.

Da-sein [is] the inabiding carriability of the clearing, i.e., of the free, unprotected, belonging of the t/here [*Da*], in which be-ing is sheltered and concealed.

The inabiding carriability of the clearing of self-sheltering-concealing will be taken over in the seeking, preserving, and guardianship of *that* man who knows himself to be enowned to being and to belong to enowning as the essential swaying of be-ing.

174. Da-sein and Inabiding

The inabiding is the domain of man grounded in Da-sein.

Belonging to inabiding:

1. *strength:* not at all a mere concentration of power but rather having the character of Da-sein [*da-seinshaft*]: mastery of the free granting of the broadest latitude of creative self-outgrowing;

2. *decidedness:* not at all consolidation of willfulness, but the sureness of belonging unto en-owning, getting into what is unprotected;

3. *mildness:* not at all the weakness of compassion, but the generous awakening of what is concealed and undiminished, what binds all creating into what is essential, in an always estranging manner;

4. *simpleness:* not at all what is "easy" in the sense of what is practicable, and not the "primitive" in the sense of what is not mastered and is without a future, but the passion for the necessity of the one thing: to shelter the inexhaustibility of be-ing in the protection of a being and not to abandon the strangeness of be-ing.

175. Da-sein and Beings in the Whole

The first allusion to Da-sein as grounding the truth of be-ing is accomplished *(Being and Time)* in pursuing the question of man insofar as he is grasped as the thrower of being and thus is removed from any "anthropology." This allusion could give rise to and strengthen the mistaken view that, if Da-sein is to be essentially and fully grasped, it is to be grasped only in this relation to man.

However, mindful deliberation on the t/here [*Da*] as *clearing* for self-sheltering-concealing (be-ing) must already intimate how decisive the relation of Da-sein to beings in the whole is, because the t/here [*Da*] sustains the truth of being. Thought in this direction, Da-sein—itself nowhere placeable—moves away from the relation to man and reveals itself as the "between" [*Zwischen*] that is unfolded by be-ing itself as the domain where beings tower up, where above all a being returns to itself. The t/here [*Da*] is enowned by be-ing itself; and, consequently, man, as guardian of the truth of be-ing and thus belonging to Da-sein, is enowned in an outstanding and unique way. Thus as soon as a first allusion to Da-sein succeeds, the essential dimension which is announced in this allusion must be granted: that Da-sein is enowned by be-ing and that be-ing as enowning itself builds the midpoint of all thinking.

Only thus does be-ing as enowning come fully into play—and yet it is not, as in metaphysics, the "highest" to which one only returns directly.

Accordingly, the t/here [*Da*] in its enjoined power of clearing must now be unfolded in terms of a being also, granted that a being already begins to be more-being. As en-*owned,* Da-*sein* itself becomes *more its own* and the self-opening ground of the self; and this self first gives the guardianship of man its keenness, decidedness, and intimacy.

Only now does the question of who man is break open a trail, which still runs its course in what is unprotected and thus lets the storm of be-ing come over it.

176. Da-sein: Elucidating the Word

In *that* meaning which is for the first time and essentially introduced in *Being and Time,* this word [Da-sein] cannot be translated, i.e., it resists the perspectives of the hitherto existing ways of thinking and saying in Western history: *Da sein.*

In the ordinary meaning it of course means, e.g., the chair "is there"; the uncle "is here," has arrived and is present: thus *présence*.

Da-sein itself means a "being," not the manner of being in the above sense; and nevertheless [it means] the manner of being in that unique distinction that *it* first determines the constitution, what-being as who-being, selfhood.

But this *"being"* is not *"man"* and Da-sein is not its how to be (still easily misunderstandable in *Being and Time*), but the being is *Da-sein* as ground of a definite, i.e., future humanness, not "of human in itself"; here, too, there is not enough clarity in *Being and Time*.

The talk of "human Dasein" (in *Being and Time*) is misleading to the extent that it implies that there is also an animal "Dasein" and a plant "Dasein."

"Human Dasein"—here "human" does not mean the qualification according to species and in view of specificity of "Dasein" in general (as being-extant), but the uniqueness of *that* being, human, to whom alone Da-*sein fits* [*eignet*]. But how?

Da-sein—the being that distinguishes a human *in its possibility; thus Da-sein then no longer needs the addition "human."* In what possibility? In its utmost [possibility], namely of being the founder and preserver of the truth itself.

Da-sein—what *undergirds* and *simultaneously elevates* man. Hence, the talk of Da-sein *in* humans as the occurrence of that grounding.

But one could also say "humans in Da-sein" or the Da-sein "of" humans.

All talk is here misunderstandable and unprotected if it does not receive the *favor* of those who enact the *questioning along* an essential stretch of the way and *from there*, and only from there, understand what is said and sacrifice the representations they brought along (cf. *Laufende Anmerkungen zu "Sein und Zeit"* [GA 82]).

177. Being-Away

Being-away thus [means] *being-away-from* [*Fort-sein*]; in this meaning it is simply commensurate with ἀπουσία over against παρουσία, Dasein = being-extant (cf. taking-away = taking away from [*Wegnehmen = Fort-nehmen*]).

On the other hand, as soon as Da-sein is grasped in an essentially different manner, then *being-away* is also grasped accordingly.

Da-*sein:* sustaining the openness of self-sheltering-concealing. Being-*away:* pursuing the closedness of mystery and of being, forgottenness of being. And this occurs in *being-away,* in the sense of *being infatuated by and smitten with something, lost in it.*

Being-away in this sense is only where *Da-sein* is. *Away: dispensing with or pushing be-ing aside,* seemingly only a "being" for itself. Herein the essentially counter-turning relation of Da-sein to be-ing is expressed. Mostly and generally we persist in being-away, especially when we are "true to life."

This "elucidation" could easily be presented as a prime example of how here one "philosophizes" merely with "words." But it is the opposite. Being-away names an essential manner in which humans relate, and must relate, to Da-sein—necessarily so—and Da-sein itself then undergoes a necessary determination.

[This is all] insufficiently indicated in disownedness [*Uneigentlichkeit*], insofar as indeed ownedness [*Eigentlichkeit*] is not to be understood in a *moral*-existentiell sense, but fundamental-ontologically as an indicator of *that* Da-sein in which the t/here [*Da*] is sustained by one or the other manner of sheltering the truth (in thinking, poetizing, building, leading, sacrificing, suffering, celebrating).

178. "Da-sein Exists for the Sake of Itself"

To what extent? What is Da-sein and what does "exist" mean? Da-sein is standing fast the truth of be-ing; and, as ex-isting, Da-sein "is" this and only this inabiding, sustaining the exposedness, being-a-*self*.

"For the sake of itself," i.e., purely as preserving and guardianship of being, if indeed understanding of being is what is still fundamental.

179. "Existence"
(*Being and Time*, GA 2, pp. 56–57)

Initially, in conjunction with the age-old *existentia* [existence], is *not* the what but the that-being and the how-being. But this [is] παρουσία, presence, extantness (the present).

Here on the other hand: Existence = the full temporality and indeed as ecstatic. *Ex-sistere—being exposed to beings.* For some time now [existence is] *no longer used, because* [it is] *misconstrueable—"Philosophy of Existence."*

Da-*sein* as ex-sistere means having been shifted into and standing out in the openness of be-ing. From this perspective the what, i.e., the *who*, and the selfhood of Da-sein are determined.

Existence—for the sake of Da-sein, i.e., grounding the truth of be-ing.

Metaphysically, *existence* [means] presencing, appearing. Being-historically, *existence* [means] inabiding removal-unto the t/here [*Da*].

180. Be-ing and Understanding of Being

Understanding of being, maintaining oneself in it, means, however, *staying within the openness,* because understanding [is] projecting-open what is open.

[Understanding of being means] being related to that which is enopened in the openness (the self-sheltering-concealing).

Understanding of being does not make be-ing either "subjective" or "objective." Indeed it overcomes all "subjectivity" and shifts man into the openness of being, poses him as the one who is exposed to beings (and before that, to the truth of be-ing).

But, contrary to common opinion, be-ing is the most estranging and self-sheltering-concealing; and nevertheless it holds sway *before* all beings that stand within it—something that of course can never be grasped according to the hitherto *"a priori."*

"Be-ing" is not the making of the "subject." Rather Da-sein as overcoming of all subjectivity arises from the essential swaying of be-ing.

181. Leap

The leap is the enopening *self*-throwing "into" Da-sein. This is grounded in the leap. That unto which the leap leaps in enopening is first grounded by the leap.

The self-throwing; the self only becomes its own in the leap; and yet this is not an absolute creating, but the opposite: The thrownness of self-throwing and of the thrower enopens in its *belonging to abground.* This is totally other than [creating] in all finitude of the so-called extant created and producing of the *demiurgos.*

182. Projecting Be-ing Open:
Projecting-Open as Thrown

What is meant is always merely the projecting-open of the truth of be-ing. The thrower itself, Da-sein, is thrown, en-owned by be-ing.

Thrownness occurs and is attested expressly by the *distress of the abandonment of being* and in the *necessity of decision.*

In that the thrower projects-open and enopens openness, the enopening reveals that the thrower itself is the thrown and does not accomplish anything other than getting hold of the counter-resonance in be-ing, i.e., shifting into this counter-resonance and thus into enowning and thus first becoming itself, namely the preserver of the thrown projecting-open.

183. Projecting-Open unto Be-ing

The projecting-open unto be-ing is unique, so much so that the thrower of the projecting-open essentially casts *itself* into the open of the enopening that is thrown-projected open, in order for the first time to become *itself* in this open as ground and abground.

Shifting into openness sounds misleading in a way, as if this openness stood ready, whereas openness occurs first of all and only along with the displacing.

Prior to this is being-away, and indeed constantly so. Being-away as denial of having been exposed to the truth of be-ing.

184. The Question of Being as Question
Concerning the Truth of Be-ing

Here the essential sway of be-ing can be read off neither a definite being nor all known beings together. Nay, a reading off is not possible at all. At stake is an originary projecting-open and leap that can draw its necessity only from the deepest history of man, insofar as man is experienced and his way of being is sustained as that being who is exposed to beings (and before that to the truth of be-ing); this exposure (preserver, guardian, seeker) makes up the ground of his way of being. Even the beginning made with ἰδέα is not a reading-off! To know this is to overcome ἰδέα.

Is the *truth* of be-ing to be determined *prior to* be-ing and without regard for it, or afterward, only with regard to be-ing, or neither, but rather together with be-ing, because [truth] belongs to its essential swaying?

[This is] only provisionally the *transcendental* pathway (but a different "transcendence"), in order to prepare the reversing-momentum [*Umschwung*] and leaping-into.

185. What Is Called Da-sein?

1. The task of "be-ing and time" [is to raise] the question of being as the [question] of the "meaning of be-ing"; see the prefatory note in *Being and Time*.

    Fundamental ontology [as] what is in the crossing. It founds and overcomes all ontologies but must necessarily proceed from what is familiar and current, and therefore it always stands in *ambi*guity.
2. *The question of being and the question of man:* fundamental ontology and anthropology.
3. Humanness as *Da-sein* (cf. *Laufende Anmerkungen zu "Sein und Zeit"* [GA 82]).
4. The question of being as overcoming the guiding-question, i.e., *unfolding the guiding-question;* cf. its jointure. What does *un-folding* mean? Deferral unto the ground that is to be enopened.

186. Da-sein

The necessity of the originary grounding question of Da-sein can be unfolded historically:
1. proceeding from ἀλήθεια as grounding-character of φύσις;
2. proceeding from the question of *the doubled repraesentatio*, enforced by the *ego cogito* and touched upon by Leibniz and German Idealism:
    1. I put something forth [*stelle vor*] — *have-there*;
    2. I put something forth [*stelle vor*] — am something; "*Da-sein*."
    In each case the "t/here" [*"Da"*] as well as ἀλήθεια is inceptually *unasked*.

And this "t/here" ["*Da*"] is always only the *open* that is derived, which the correctness of re-presenting must claim *for itself* and for its own possibility.

b) Da-sein*

187. Grounding

Grounding is two-fold in meaning:
1. *Ground grounds,* sways as ground (cf. essential sway of truth and time-space).
2. This grounding ground is gotten hold of and taken over as such.
   En-grounding:
   a. to let the ground hold *sway* as grounding;
   b. to *build* on it as ground, to bring something to ground.

The originary grounding of the ground (1) is the essential swaying of the truth of be-ing; the truth is *ground* in the originary sense.

The essential sway of ground originarily from within the essential sway of truth, truth and time-space (ab-ground).

See *Vom Wesen des Grundes* and the related notes from 1936.

Following its connection with "Leap," the title "Grounding" initially indicates meaning 2.a) and b), but therefore not only related to 1 but determined by it.

188. Grounding**

To enground the ground of the truth of be-ing and thus to enground be-ing itself means to let this ground (enowning) *be* the ground through Da-*sein's* steadfastness. Accordingly engrounding becomes grounding of Da-*sein* as engrounding the ground, i.e., the truth of be-ing.

$$
\begin{array}{ccccc}
\text{Ground} & - \text{ inaugurating } & - & \text{bearing } & - \text{ covering} \\
& ab\text{-}ground & \text{and} & & unground
\end{array}
$$

$$
\left(\begin{array}{c}\text{sheltering-concealing}\\ \text{of being}\\ \text{nihilating}\end{array}\right) \quad \left(\begin{array}{c}\text{dissembling}\\ \\ \text{disswaying}\end{array}\right)
$$

There exists an originary essential relation between ground and truth, but *truth* grasped as *sheltering that lights up.* The relationship of *ratio* and *veritas iudicii,* which becomes manifest in the history of the treatment of the guiding-question (especially in Leibniz) is only a very superficial semblance of the originary relation.

---

* Cf. *Laufende Anmerkungen zu "Sein und Zeit"* [GA 82]; WS 1937/38, *Übungen. Die metaphysischen Grundstellungen des abendländischen Denkens (Metaphysik)* [GA 88].
** Cf. Preview, 13: Reservedness: reservedness as grounding-attunement, reservedness and care.

Truth and with that the essential sway of ground become dis-jointed temporally-spatially. Thereby, however, time and space are grasped originarily from truth and are essentially related to the grounding.

This relation is seen in *Being and Time,* but in the background and not mastered.

Only in the engrounding of enowning does the inabiding of Da-sein succeed in the modes and on the pathways of sheltering truth unto beings.

The context within which *time and space* arrive at their essential concept is here in the sphere of *grounding* and its mastery by thinking.

What is ownmost to Da-sein and thus to the history which is grounded on it is the sheltering of the truth of being and of the last god unto beings.

This juncture determines the shape and kind of those who are to come.

189. Da-sein

When Da-sein holds sway simply as belonging to enowning, then, already with the first mentioning, *that* directive must be enacted by virtue of which Da-sein is essentially different from a merely formal determination of the ground of humanness—a determination that does not concern us.

Addressed from the perspective of the "formal," Da-sein must be experienced as *fulfilled,* i.e., as the primary preparation for the crossing into an other history of man.

Da-sein is experienced—not re-presented as object, but rather as Da-*sein,* enacted and sustained by a displacing shifting-into.

This requires: sustaining the distress of abandonment of being *along with* putting oneself in the decision about the staying away and arrival of gods: taking up for the first time the position for guardianship of the stillness of the last god's passing *in* that decision (cf. Leap, 133: The Essential Sway of Be-ing, p. 178).

Da-sein's projecting-open is possible only as shifting into Da-*sein.* But the shifting projecting-open arises only from within the *pliancy [Fügsamkeit]* vis-à-vis the most hidden conferment *[Fügung]* of our history in the grounding-attunement of reservedness. Immeasurable in its breadth and depth, the essential moment has begun, especially when the distress of abandonment of being dawns and *decision* is sought.

However, this basic "fact" of our history cannot be demonstrated by any "analysis" of the "spiritual" or "political" "situation" of the time, because even the "spiritual" as well as the "political" perspectives proceed from what is superficial and belongs to the heretofore and has already refused to experience the actual history—the struggle of enownment of man by be-ing—refused to inquire and to think along the tracks of the disposal of this history, i.e., to become historical from the ground of history.

190. On Da-sein*

One can speak of Da-sein only as grounding, only in enacting in thinking "Echo," "Playing-Forth," and "Leap."

But grounding always means grounding historically in and for our future history, enjoining its innermost distress (abandonment of being) and the necessity that springs forth out of it (grounding-question).

This joining, as the self-joining preparing the site for the moment of utmost decision, is the law of proceeding in thinking in the other beginning, as distinguished from the *system* in the historical end of the first beginning.

Nevertheless, it must be possible to attempt an initial naming which points to, and thus unto, Da-sein. Obviously it is never a direct "describing," as if Dasein could be found extant somewhere. Just as little can it be a "dialectic," which is the same thing on a higher level. Rather [this pointing to Da-sein is possible] in a properly understood projecting-open, which brings today's man perhaps only into his abandonment by being and prepares the echo according to which man is that being *who* is *broken out* into the open, but who initially and for a long time does not recognize this *break-out* and in the end completely assesses this breaking out above all *from within the abandonment by being.*

Breaking-out and abandonment, hint and returning all belong together as the occurrences of owning, in which *enowning* is enopened—apparently seen only from man's perspective (cf. *ownhood*):

$$\text{man} \quad \begin{pmatrix} & \text{world} & \\ & \uparrow & \\ \leftarrow & \text{E} & \rightarrow \\ & \downarrow & \\ & \text{earth} & \end{pmatrix} \quad \text{gods} \quad (\text{t/there } [Da])$$

From this perspective one can already see which unifying and enjoined power of projecting-open is needed in order to enact the enopening leap as the enspringing of Da-sein and to prepare sufficiently the grounding in questioning-knowing.

Da-sein is the occurrence of encleavage [Erklüftung] of the turning-midpoint of the turning in enowning. Encleavage is en-ownment, above all and especially encleavage from which [occur] *historical man and the essential swaying of being, nearing and distancing of gods.*

Here there is no longer any "encounter," no appearing for man, who already beforehand stands firm and henceforth only holds on to what has appeared.

---

* For an introductory elucidation of the notion, cf. *Eine Auseinandersetzung mit "Sein und Zeit,"* 1936 [GA 82]; cf. WS 1937/38, *Übungen. Die metaphysischen Grundstellungen des abendländischen Denkens (Metaphysik)* [GA 88].

What is ownmost to history in the deepest sense rests in the encleaving (truth-grounding) enownment, which above all lets those emerge who, needing one another, mutually turn to and away from one another only in enowning of turning.

This encleavage of nearing and distancing, deciding between abandonment and en-hinting or going from here to hide itself in undecidedness, is the origin of time-space and the kingdom of the strife.

Da-sein is: enduring the essential swaying of the truth of be-ing.

Unfolding the t/hereness [*Daheit*] of the t/here [*Da*] [occurs] as grounding of Da-*sein*.

The t/here [*Da*] holds sway; and while swaying, it must be taken over in the being of Da-*sein;* the "between" [*das "Zwischen"*].

191. Da-sein

Da-sein is the turning point in the turning of enowning, the self-opening midpoint of the mirroring of call and belongingness, the ownhood or *"own-dom"* [*Eigentum*], understood as king-dom, the mastering midpoint of en-ownment as owning the belonging-together to enowning, at the same time owning the belonging-together to *Da-sein:* becoming-self.

In this way Da-sein is the *between* [*das Zwischen*] between man (as history-grounding) and gods (in their history).

The between [*Zwischen*] [is] not one that first ensues from the relation of gods to humans, but rather that between [*Zwischen*] which above all grounds the time-space for the relation, in that it itself leaps forth into the essential swaying of be-ing as enowning and, as self-opening midpoint, makes gods and humans decidable for one another.

192. Da-sein

As grounding the openness of self-sheltering, Da-sein appears to the view accustomed to a "being" to be not-being and simply imagined. Indeed: *As thrown projecting-open grounding, Da-sein is the highest actuality in the domain of imagination,* granted that by this term we understand not only a faculty of the soul and not only something transcendental (cf. Kantbook) but rather *enowning* itself, wherein all *transfiguration* reverberates.

"Imagination" as occurrence of the *clearing* itself. Only, "imagination," *imaginatio,* is the name that names from within the perspective of the direct receiving of ὄν, a being. Reckoned from this perspective, all be-ing and its enopening is a *product* added to what is supposedly stable. But everything here is the other way around: What is "imagined" in the usual sense is always the so-called "actually" extant—imagined-into, brought into the clearing to shine, brought into the t/here [*Da*].

193. Da-sein and Man

What is ownmost to man has been determined for a long time out of an orientation to parts: body, soul, spirit. And the kind of layering and permeation and the manner in which each time one part has priority over the other are different. In the same vein the role changes which one of these "parts" assumes as the guiding-thread and aiming point for determining other beings (e.g., consciousness in the *ego cogito* or reason or spirit or, in Nietzsche, body or soul, depending on his *intention*).

See the λόγος (but not as subject and soul) and νοῦς in pre-Platonic philosophy, as well as the ψυχή in Plato and Aristotle (ἡ ψυχὴ τὰ ὄντα πώς ἔστιν); all of this points to something that man himself is and that nevertheless exceeds and surpasses him and always comes into play for determining beings as such in the whole.

And because, first-ever-inceptually, the question of beings had to be asked straight on and, as guiding-question, continued to be so asked into the future, *in spite of* Descartes, Kant, etc., such things as soul, reason, spirit, thinking, representing had to provide a guiding-thread, although in such a way that, given the unclarity in asking the guiding-question, the guiding-thread itself also continued to be undetermined in its character as guiding-thread—and in the end the question was *not* asked why such a guiding-thread is necessary or whether this necessity does not lie in the essential sway and in the truth of being itself, and to what extent.

As can easily be gleaned from this remark, the question of the truth of be-ing—in its essential difference from the guiding-question—must be raised beforehand as the grounding-question. But then what is unasked and unaccomplished truly emerges, namely that somehow man and then again not man—and indeed always through an extending and a displacing—is in play in grounding the truth of be-ing. And it is *this* question-worthy matter that I call Da-sein.

And this also indicates the origin of this question-worthy matter: It does not arise from just any approach, be it philosophical or biological, be it generally any anthropological observation and determination of man, but solely and exclusively from the question of the truth of being.

And if be-ing itself is the most unique and the highest, we thus arrive at one and the same time at a unique and very deep inquiry concerning man.

On the other hand, by coming to grips with the heretofore history of the guiding question, there is now the necessity of being mindful, and of asking:

1. Why and how precisely, in interpreting man in the connection with the question of beings, things like ψυχή, νοῦς, *animus, spiritus, cogitatio,* consciousness, subject, I, spirit, person come to prevail?

2. Whether and how hereby *that* necessarily comes into play—though at the same time necessarily hidden—which we call Da-sein?

In answering the first question, it is to be noted that stressing and interpreting ψυχή, νοῦς, etc., is guided by the interpretation of a being as φύσις and later as ἰδέα and ἐνέργεια, οὐσία; finally in Aristotle, by the interpretation of ψυχή as οὐσία and ἐντελέχεια ἡ πρώτη. This approach continues in various derivations until Hegel and Nietzsche, the turn into "subject" not changing anything essential. Correspondingly, "body" is an appendage or support and is always determined only by differentiating it from soul or spirit or both.

The issue never becomes one of determining and inquiring into the being of man thus interpreted—and indeed in his role as guiding-thread for the truth of a being from within this truth—and thus to focus on the possibility that here, in view of being, humanness in the end takes over a task that moves humanness away and displaces it into that question-worthy matter, Da-sein.

Da-sein does not lead out of a being and does not vaporize a being into a spirituality. On the contrary: In accordance with the uniqueness of be-ing Dasein opens up above all the unsettledness of a being, whose "truth" is sustained only in a renewed inceptual struggle with its sheltering-into what is created by historical man.

Only that which we, inabiding in Da-sein, ground and create and in creating let face us as an onrushing [Ansturm], *only that can be what is true and manifest and accordingly be recognized and known. Our knowing awareness reaches only as far as the inabiding in Da-sein extends, and that means as far as the power of sheltering truth in a being that is shaped.*

Kant's *Critique of Pure Reason,* in which after the Greeks another essential step is taken, has to presuppose this context without being able to grasp it as such and to ground it fully (the turning relation of Dasein and being). And because this ground was not grounded, the *Critique* remained without a ground and had to lead to its being overtaken—and in part with its own means (the means of transcendental inquiry)—by absolute knowing (German Idealism). Because spirit here became absolute, it had to hold covertly the destruction of beings and the complete forcing-away of the uniqueness and strangeness of be-ing and to hasten the lapse into "positivism" and "biologism" (Nietzsche), increasingly rigidifying this lapse and continuing until today.

For the present "debate" with German Idealism—if it deserves to be called this at all—is merely "reactive." It *absolutizes* "life" in all the indeterminateness and confusion that can hide in this name. The absolutization is not only an indication of being determined by the opposition; it shows above all that this absolutization even less than the opposition is mindful of the guiding-question of metaphysics (cf. Playing-Forth, 110: ἰδέα, Platonism, and Idealism, especially pp. 149f., Hegel).

Herein also lies the reason why the question of truth that Nietzsche raises—seemingly out of an originary power of questioning and deciding—is precisely *not* asked by him but is explained completely in terms of the basic positioning in "life"—explained biologically as securing life as extant, based upon the traditional interpretation of beings (as constancy and presence).

But in response to the second question (see above), the following needs to be said: Whenever Da-sein comes into play—and it must come into play wherever a being as such and thus the truth of be-ing, though hidden, is inquired—then we must examine what becomes manifest through and through and in general as the guiding-thread according to the inceptual interpretation of a being (as constant presence). This is "thinking" as re-presentation of something in general, and here *as most general,* and accordingly the utmost representation.

Re-presenting shows the trace of Da-sein, namely with regard to its *removal-unto* something. With Da-sein as measure, re-presenting, though hidden to itself, is standing out into what is open, whereby this open itself is as little inquired into as the openness, with regard to its essential sway and ground.

Moreover, re-presenting is a standing out which at the same time also stays behind in the *soul* as a process and act of this soul, which itself finally as "I" forms the over-against to the object.

Correctness as interpretation of what is open becomes the basis for the subject-object-relation.

But insofar as the one who re-presents re-presents itself to itself, this standing out is merely repeated and taken back unto this self—and *that* remains dissembled which distinguishes *Da*-sein, namely to *be* the t/here [*Da*], the clearing for the sheltering-concealing, in the inabiding of selfhood as grounding the truth into beings.

If now, finally, representing is drawn into "life," then the complete obfuscation of the originary character of being-t/here [*Da*] that inheres in re-presenting has been accomplished. Now re-presenting itself is assessed only in terms of its use and value; and such an assessing provides representing with that interpretation which representing alone can claim as "knowing" vis-à-vis the "deed."

The difficulty of proceeding from within such a re-presenting (appearing [*Anscheinen*]) of the world, in order to make Da-sein experienceable and manifest, appears unsurpassable, especially since the presupposition for everything—the power to question and the will to clarity—must be dispensed with. But how can the highest question concerning being become a question in this wasteland!

194. Man and Da-sein

Why is Da-sein the ground and abground for historical man? Why not a direct alteration of man, and why should he then not continue to be the way he is? How is he then? Can that be established? From where?

What appraisal according to what measures?

In the history of the truth of being Dasein is the essential *case of the between* [*Zwischenfall*], i.e., the case of falling-into that "between" [*Zwischen*] into which man must be displaced, in order above all to be him*self*.

As trajectory and domain of owning-to [*Zu-eignung*] and of the origin of the "to" [*zu*] and the "self" [*sich*], selfhood is the ground for belongingness to be-ing, which selfhood includes in itself the (inabiding) owning-over-to [*Über-eignung*]. Owning-over-to occurs only where there is beforehand and steadily an owning-to, but both from within the en-ownment of enowning.

But belongingness to being holds sway only because being in its uniqueness needs Da-sein and, grounded therein and grounding it, needs man. No truth holds sway otherwise.

Otherwise only the nothing reigns, in the most insidious form of the proximity of what is "actual" and "alive," i.e., of the proximity of what *is not* [*das Unseiende*].

Grasped as the being of man, Da-sein is already in *fore-grasping*. The question for its truth remains this: How does man, becoming more being, place himself back into Da-sein, thus grounding it, in order thereby to stand out into the truth of be-ing? But this self-placing and its steadfastness is grounded in *enownment*. Thus one must ask: In which history must man stand, in order to belong to en-ownment?

For this, must he not be thrown ahead into the t/here [*Da*]—an event which becomes manifest to him as thrownness?

Thrownness will be experienced above all from within the truth of be-ing. In the first pre-liminary interpretation *(Being and Time)* thrownness still remains misunderstandable in the sense of man's accidentally appearing among other beings.

From this juncture, to what power are earth and body kindled? Humanness and "life."

From where else does the thrust come to think all the way out into Da-sein other than from the essential sway of be-ing itself?

195. Da-sein and Man

Who is man? The one whom be-ing needs, to sustain the essential swaying of the truth of be-ing.

But as so needed, man "is" only man insofar as he is grounded in Da-sein, i.e., insofar as he himself becomes founder of Da-*sein*, in creating.

But be-ing is simultaneously grasped here as *en-owning*. Both belong together: grounding back into Da-sein and the truth of be-ing as enowning.

We comprehend nothing of the direction of the questioning which is enopened here if we, unawares, take random ideas of man and of "beings as such" as our foundation, instead of putting into question at

one and the same time "man" and be-ing (not only the being of man) —
and keeping them in question.

196. Da-sein and the People*

It is only from Da-sein that what is ownmost to a people can be grasped and
that means at the same time knowing that the people can never be goal
and purpose and that such an opinion is only a "popular" extension of
the "liberal" thought of the "I" and of the economic idea of the preservation of "life."

What is ownmost to a people is, however, its "voice." This *voice* does
not speak in a so-called immediate outpouring of the common, natural,
unspoiled and uneducated "man." For the "man" thus called-up as witness is already very *spoiled* and no longer functions within the originary
relations to beings. The *voice* of the people seldom speaks and only in
the few — and can it still be made *at all* to resonate?

197. Da-sein — Ownhood — Selfhood**

Self-being is the essential swaying of Da-sein, and the self-being of man
is above all achieved from within the inabiding in Da-sein.

One is used to grasping the "self" initially in the relation of the I to
"itself." This relation is taken as a representing one. Then finally the
self-sameness of representing and the represented is grasped as what is
ownmost to the "self." But what is ownmost to self can never be obtained in this way, or correspondingly modified ways.

For, first of all what is ownmost to self is not a property of extant
man and only seemingly given with the *consciousness of the I.* Whence
this illusion comes can be clarified only in terms of what is ownmost to
the self.

As essential swaying of Da-sein, selfhood springs forth from the origin
of Da-sein. And the origin of the self is *own-hood* [*Eigen-tum*], [as in
"own-dom"] when this word is taken in the same way as the word
king-dom [*Fürsten-tum*]. Mastery of owning [*Eignung*] in enowning. Owning is both owning-to and owning-over-to. Insofar as Da-sein is
owned-to *itself* as belonging to enowning, it comes to *itself,* but never in
such a manner as if the self were already an extant stock that has just not
yet been reached. Rather Da-sein first comes to itself when owning-to
the belongingness becomes at the same time owning-over-to enowning.
Da-*sein* means steadfastness of the t/here [*Da*]. The own-hood as mastery
of owning occurs in the joinedness of owning-to and owning-over-to.

---

* Cf. The Ones to Come.
** Cf. Preview, 16: Philosophy (mindfulness as self-mindfulness).

Inabiding in this occurrence of own-hood initially enables man to come to "himself" historically and to be with-himself. And this *with-himself* provides above all the sufficient ground for truly taking over the *"for another."* But coming-to-oneself is also never a prior, detached I-representation. It is rather taking over the belongingness to the truth of being, leaping into the t/here [*Da*]. Ownhood as ground of selfhood grounds Da-sein. But ownhood itself is in turn the steadfastness of the turning in enowning.

Ownhood is thus at the same time the ground of reservedness, with Da-sein as measure.

The *retro-relation* [*Rückbezug*] that is named in the "itself," to "itself," with "itself," for "itself," has what is its ownmost in the *owning*.

Now, insofar as man, even in the abandonment by being, still stands in the open of what is precisely *not* ownmost to a being, the possibility is given to him at all time to *be* for "himself" and to come back "to himself." But "oneself" [*sich*] and the self [*Selbst*] that is determined by it as "only-self" remains empty, fulfilling itself only by what one comes upon and is extant and by what one happens to pursue. To-oneself [*zu-sich*] has no decision-character and is without knowing awareness of confinement within the occurrence of Da-sein.

Selfhood is more originary than any I and you and we. These are primarily gathered as such in the *self*, thus each becoming each "itself."

Conversely, dispersion of the I, you, and we and the crumbling and leveling off of these are not merely a failing of man but rather the occurrence of powerlessness in sustaining and knowing *ownhood*, abandonment by being.

Self-being — with that we always mean primarily: doing and letting and disposing by oneself. But "by oneself" is a deceptive foreground. By oneself can mean mere "willfulness," which is deprived of all owning-to and owning-over-to from out of enowning.

The range in which the self resonates follows the originariness of ownhood and thus follows the truth of be-ing.

Pushed out of truth of being and tumbling in abandonment by being, we know little enough of what is ownmost to the self and of the pathways leading to genuine knowing. For the priority of the "I" consciousness is all too stubborn, especially since it can hide in various shapes. The most dangerous shapes are those in which the worldless "I" has seemingly surrendered and dedicated itself to an other that is "greater" than itself and to which it is referred piece by piece and limb by limb. In the dissolution of the "I" in "life" as a people, an overcoming of the "I" is begun, at the cost of surrendering the first condition of such an overcoming, namely, becoming mindful of self-being and of what is ownmost to it, which is determined by owning-to and owning-over-to.

*Selfhood is the enquivering of the counter-turning of the strife in the cleavage,
an enquivering which is gotten hold of from within enownment and sustains it.*

198. Grounding of Da-sein as En-grounding*

Da-sein never lets itself be demonstrated and described as something
extant. It is to be obtained only hermeneutically, i.e., however, according to *Being and Time,* in the thrown projecting-open. Hence, not arbitrarily. Da-sein is something totally non-ordinary; it is *destined* far in
advance of all knowledge of man.

The t/here [*Da*] is the open between [*Zwischen*] that lights up and
shelters—between earth and world, the midpoint of their strife and
thus the site for the most intimate belongingness, and thus the ground
for the "to-oneself," the *self,* and selfhood. The *self* is never "I." The
with-itself of the self holds sway as inabiding in the taking-over of
en-ownment. Selfhood is belongingness to the intimacy of the strife as
enstrifing of enownment.

No "we" and "you" and no "I" and "thou," no *community* setting itself
up by itself, ever reaches the self; rather it only misses the self and continues to be excluded from the self, unless it grounds itself first of all on
Da-sein.

With the grounding of Da-*sein* all relationship to a being is transformed, and the truth of be-ing is first experienced.

199. Transcendence and Da-sein and Be-ing**

Even when "transcendence" is grasped differently than up to now,
namely as *surpassing* and not as the *super-sensible* as a being, even then
this determination all too easily dissembles what is ownmost to Dasein.
For, even in this way, transcendence still presupposes an *under and
this-side* [*Unten und Diesseits*] and is in danger of still being misinterpreted after all as the action of an "I" and subject. And finally even this
concept of transcendence continues to be stuck in Platonism (cf. *Vom
Wesen des Grundes*).

Inceptually Da-*sein* stands in the grounding of enowning, engrounds
the truth of *being,* and does not go from *a being* over to its being. Rather,
the engrounding of enowning occurs as sheltering of truth in and as a
being; and thus, if a comparison were at all possible—and it is not—the
relationship is the other way around.

A being as such is above all sheltered in be-ing, in such a manner of
course that a being can immediately be abandoned by be-ing and continue to exist only as semblance—ὄν as ἰδέα and whatever follows
upon and from that.

---

* Letting *ground* hold sway; enowning [as] ground.
** Cf. Playing-Forth, 110: ἰδέα, Platonism, and Idealism.

200. Da-sein

Da-sein is to be taken as time-space, not in the sense of the usual concepts of time and space but as the site for the moment of the grounding of the truth of be-ing.

The *site for the moment* springs forth from the aloneness of the great stillness, in which enownment becomes truth.

When and how was the site for the moment of the truth of be-ing last inquired in thinking and when and how was its grounding prepared for—from the ground up and by putting aside everything hitherto familiar and incidental?

What does mindfulness of the basic metaphysical positions within the history of answering the guiding-question do for answering *this* question?

Time-space is to be unfolded in its essential sway as *site for the moment of* enowning. But "moment" is never merely the tiny remainder of "time" that can barely be snatched up.

201. Da-sein and Being-Away

But *being-away* can also be meant in another and no less essential sense. For if Da-sein is experienced as the creating ground of humanness and it thereby is brought to knowing awareness that Da-*sein* is only *moment* and history, then from this perspective the usual humanness must be determined as being-away. It [humanness] is "away" *from* the steadfastness of the t/here [*Da*] and completely with *beings as extant* (forgottenness of being). Man is the *away*.

Being-away is the *more originary* title for Da-sein's *disownedness* [*Uneigentlichkeit*].

Being-away [is] this manner of *pursuing* the extant as seen from the stance of the t/here [*Da*] and belonging to it.

But *besides, humanness* must now be grounded precisely as that which in turn preserves and unfolds *Da-sein* and which prepares for and is in contention with the creating ones.

202. Da-sein
(Being-Away)

Man "is" the t/here [*Da*] only as historical, i.e., as history-grounding and inabiding in the t/here [*Da*] in the manner of sheltering the truth in a being.

Da-*sein* is to be sustained solely by *inabiding* in the highest creating— and that means at the same time the en-during traversal of the widest removals-unto.

What belongs to the t/here [*Da*] as its utmost is that shelteredness-concealedness in the open that is ownmost to the t/here [*Da*], the *away*, being-*away* as constant *possibility;* man knows being-away in the various shapes of death. But wherever Da-sein is to be grasped primarily, *death* must be determined as the utmost possibility of the t/here [*Da*]. If *here* one speaks of "end" and if before all else and in all keenness Da-sein is differentiated from every manner of being-extant, then "end" here can never mean the mere ceasing and disappearing of an extant. If time *as* temporality is removal-unto, then "end" here means a "no" and an "otherwise" of this removal-unto, a total displacing of the t/here [*Da*] as such, into the "away."

And away again does not mean the "away from [*Fort*]" of mere absence of something that was formerly extant but is the totally other of the t/here [*Da*], totally concealed from us, but *in this* shelteredness-concealedness belonging essentially to the t/here [*Da*] and needing to be sustained along-with the inabiding of Da-*sein*.

As the utmost of the t/here [*Da*], death is at the same time the core of its possibly total transformation. And therein lies at the same time the allusion to the deepest sway of the nothing. Only the common understanding, which sticks to what is extant as what alone is a being, also thinks the nothing solely in a trivial [*gemein*] fashion. This understanding surmises nothing of the core relation between the away and the displacement of all beings in their belongingness to the t/here [*Da*]. What here as ownmost shelteredness-concealedness advances into the t/here [*Da*] — the reciprocal relation of the t/here [*Da*] to the away that is turned toward the t/here [*Da*] — is the mirroring of the turning in the essential sway of being itself. The more originarily being is experienced in its truth, the deeper is the *nothing* as the abground at the edge of the ground.

It is of course convenient to figure out for oneself what is said about death according to the unexamined quotidian ideas of "end" and of "nothing," instead of, on the other hand, learning to surmise how, with inclusion of death in the t/here [*Da*] — inabiding and removal-unto as measure of the inclusion — what is ownmost to "end" and to "nothing" must be transformed.

The intimacy of being has fury [*Ingrimm*] as its ownmost and the strife is always also a maze [*Wirrnis*]. And at any time both can get lost in the desolateness of what is indifferent and forgotten.

Running ahead into death is not will-to-nothing in the trivial sense but on the contrary: the highest Da-*sein*, which draws the shelteredness-concealedness of the t/here [*Da*] into the inabiding of sustaining truth.

203. Projecting-Open and Da-sein*

Projecting-open is the between [*Zwischen*] in whose openness a being and beingness become differentiable, so much so that at first only a

---

* Cf. Preview: inceptual thinking; cf. Preview, 17: Philosophy's Necessity.

being *itself* is experienceable (i.e., a being as sheltered-concealed as such and thus with respect to its beingness). Merely going over to essence as ἰδέα mistakes the projecting-open, as well as the appeal to the necessary pre-givenness of a "being."

But how the projecting-open and its essential swaying as Da-sein continue to be covered over by the predominance of *re-presenting*, how one comes to the subject-object-relation and to the I-posit-before-"consciousness," and how then *on the contrary* "life" is stressed—this reaction in the end in Nietzsche is the clearest proof for the *lack* of originariness in his questioning.

Projecting-open is not to be "explained" but rather is to be transmuted in its ground and abground and in that direction to dis-place humanness into *Da-sein* and so to show humanness the other beginning of its history.

c) The Essential Sway of Truth*

204. The Essential Sway of Truth

Are we here not asking about the *truth of truth,* and in so asking do we not begin an empty advance into emptiness?

Projecting-open is what grounds essential sway. But what is at stake here is the throw of the domain of projecting-open itself and thereby the originary taking over of thrownness, of that necessity of belongingness to a being itself, which springs forth along with the distress of the projecting-open and this in the manner of thrownness into the "midst" [*das Inmitten*].

If truth here means *clearing* of be-ing as openness of the midst of beings, then one cannot even inquire into the truth of this truth unless one means the *correctness* of the projecting-open—but that misses in manifold ways what is essential. For, on the one hand, one cannot inquire into the "correctness" of a projecting-open at all—and certainly not into the correctness of *that* projecting-open through which on the whole the clearing as such is grounded. On the other hand, however, "correctness" is a "type" of truth that as its consequence *lags* behind the originary essential sway and therefore already does not suffice for grasping originary truth.

---

* Cf. Preview, 5: For the Few and the Rare, p. 9; Preview, 9: A Glance; the separate treatise *Wahrheitsfrage als Vor-frage* [GA 73]; *Die* ἀλήθεια. *Die Erinnerung in den ersten Anfang* [GA 73]; *Da-sein* [GA 73]; *Laufende Anmerkungen zu "Sein und Zeit,"* §44 [GA 82], pp. 103–122; *Vom Wesen der Wahrheit,* lecture 1930; *Vom Wesen des Grundes I,* in: *Wegmarken* (GA 9), Heidegger's personal copy and notes; Frankfurt lectures 1936: *"Der Ursprung des Kunstwerkes,"* in: *Holzwege* (GA 5), especially pp. 25ff.; lecture course WS 1937/38, *Grundfragen der Philosophie. Ausgewählte "Probleme" der "Logik,"* fundamentals for the question of truth (GA 45, pp. 27ff.) [trans. R. Rojcewicz and A. Schuwer, *Basic Questions of Philosophy: Selected "Problems" of "Logic"*].

Is then the projecting-open pure caprice? No, it is the utmost necessity, but of course not a necessity in the sense of a logical conclusion which could be made clear through propositions.

The necessity of *distress*. Whose? Of be-ing itself, which must free up its first beginning through the other beginning—and thus overcome the first beginning.

In the usual horizon of "logic" and of dominant thinking, projecting-open the grounding of truth remains pure caprice—and this alone also clears the way for an infinite, seemingly thorough inquiry back into the truth of the truth of the truth of, etc. Here one takes truth as an object of calculation and reckoning and uses as measure the claim for ultimate intelligibility of an everyday machinational understanding. And here caprice does indeed come to the fore. For this claim has no necessity because it lacks distress, since it deduces its seeming legitimacy from the lack of distress of what is self-evident, assuming that this claim is still capable at all of questions of legitimacy regarding itself, since of course such capability lies far from anything self-evident.

And what is more self-evident than "logic"?

But the essential projecting-open of the t/here [Da] *is the unprotected execution of the thrownness of projecting-open itself, which first emerges in the throw.*

205. The Open*

From the perspective of correctness, [the open] is indicated only as condition and is thus not ensprung in itself.

The open:

as the *free* of the keenness of creating,

as what is *unprotected* in the execution of thrownness; both in themselves belonging together as the *clearing of self-sheltering-concealing*.

The *t/here* [*Da*] as en-owned in enowning.

This free [reigns] over against beings. [It is] what is unprotected by beings. [It is] the free-play of time-space of *chaos* and of *hints*. What belongs to be-ing.

206. From ἀλήθεια to Da-sein**

1. [It is] the critical return from correctness to openness.
2. The openness [is] above all the essential amplitude of ἀλήθεια, which in this respect [is] still undetermined.
3. This essential amplitude determines the "place" (time-space) of the openness: the lit up "in the midst" of beings.

---

*Truth and Da-sein.
**Cf. the question of truth in the lecture course WS 1937/38, *Grundfragen der Philosophie. Ausgewählte "Probleme" der "Logik"* (GA 45) [trans. R. Rojcewicz and A. Schuwer, *Basic Questions of Philosophy: Selected "Problems" of "Logic"*].

4. Thus truth [is] *definitively disengaged from all beings* in every manner of interpretation, be it as φύσις, ἰδέα, *perceptum*, object, as what is known, what is thought.

5. But now more than ever [it is] a question of truth's own essential swaying, which is determinable only from within the essential sway—and this is determinable by be-ing.

6. But the originary essential sway [is] clearing of self-sheltering-concealing; that is, truth is originary truth of be-ing (enowning).

7. This *clearing* holds sway and *is* in attuned and creating yielding [*Ertragsamkeit*]; that is, truth "is" as grounding of the t/here [*Da*] and as *Da-sein*.

8. Da-sein [is] the ground of man.

9. But with that one asks anew: Who is man?

207. From ἀλήθεια to Da-sein

In accord with what is its ownmost and inceptually grasped as the basic character of φύσις, ἀλήθεια defies every question concerning the relation to the other—for example, to thinking. This relation can only be inquired into when the inceptual essential sway of ἀλήθεια has already been given up for the sake of correctness.

On the other hand, ἀλήθεια demands a more originary inquiry into its own essential sway (whence and why *sheltering-concealing* [*Verbergung*] and disclosure [*Entbergung*]?). But for this questioning it is necessary above all to grasp ἀλήθεια in its essential amplitude as the openness of a being. At the same time this amplitude indicates the place that is required by the openness of a being itself for that openness as the lit up "in the midst" of beings.

But in this way ἀλήθεια is so decisively disengaged from any beings that now the question concerning its own be-ing, determined by ἀλήθεια itself and by its essential swaying, becomes unavoidable.

But the essential swaying of originary truth can be experienced only if this lit up "in the midst," which grounds itself and determines time-space—is ensprung in that *"from where"* and "for which" it is clearing, namely, for the *self-sheltering-concealing*. But self-sheltering-concealing is the fundamental teaching of the first beginning and its history (of metaphysics as such). Self-sheltering-concealing is an essential characteristic of *be-ing*—precisely insofar as be-ing needs truth and thus en-owns Da-sein and is thus in itself originarily: enowning.

Now the essential sway of truth has been originarily transformed into Da-sein; and now the question no longer makes any sense, whether and how "thinking" (which inceptually and derivatively belongs only to ἀλήθεια and ὁμοίωσις) could enact and take over the "unconcealment." For thinking itself in its possibility is now completely delivered over to the lit up "in the midst."

For the essential swaying of the t/here [Da] (of the clearing for self-sheltering-concealing) can be determined only from out of itself; Da-*sein* can be grounded only out of the lit up relation of the t/here [Da] to the self-sheltering-concealing as be-ing.

But then, on the basis of the ground (which will be clarified later), no "faculty" of hitherto existing man *(animal rationale)* is sufficient. Da-sein grounds itself and holds sway in attuned, creating yielding and thus itself above all becomes the ground and founder of man, who now faces anew the question of who he is. This question inquires into man more originarily as the guardian of the stillness of the passing of the last god.

208. Truth

How could truth be for us that last remainder of the utmost disintegration of the Platonic ἀλήθεια (ἰδέα), the legitimacy of correctnesses in themselves as [their] ideal, i.e., the greatest of all instances of indifference and powerlessness?

As enowning of what is true, truth is the cleavage that holds to abground—cleavage in which a being is disjoined and must stand in strife.

Truth for us is also not what is fixed, that suspicious descendant of validities in themselves. But it is also not mere opposition, the crude and continued flux of all opinions. It is the midpoint that holds to abground that enquivers in the passing of god and is thus the sustained ground for the grounding of creating Da-sein.

Truth is the great despiser of everything "true," for this immediately forgets the truth, the secure kindling of the simpleness of the unique as kindling of what is always essential.

209. ἀλήθεια—Openness and Clearing of Self-Sheltering-Concealing

Seen in broad outline, these are various names for the same thing; and nonetheless a crucial question is hidden behind these namings.

I. Even ἀλήθεια and ἀλήθεια are not the same. Already here one must ask how ἀλήθεια was experienced inceptually, how far its determinedness reached, whether the first determination was ever reached at all by the Platonic ζυγόν and thus whether the essential delimitation by which understanding of being was pre-delineated (φύσις) was also already definitively established, namely the delimitation to what has the character of a look [*Anblickhafte*] and later to what has the character of ob-ject for the one perceiving [*Vernehmenden*].

ἀλήθεια itself is forced into a yoke; as "brightness [*Helle*]" it concerns the unconcealedness of a being as such *and* the passageway for perceiving—and thus deals only with the domain of the *respective sides* of a being and the soul *turned to each other.* Nay, it first determines this domain as such, indeed without letting its own be-ing and ground become questionable.

And because ἀλήθεια thus becomes φῶς and is interpreted according to φῶς, the character of the *α-privativum* gets lost; and the question of *shelteredness-concealedness* and sheltering-concealing, of their source and ground, is not raised. Because only what is "positive," as it were, about unconcealedness is accounted for, namely, what is freely accessible and grants access, therefore ἀλήθεια in this respect also loses its originary depth and abground-dimension, assuming that thinking ever inquired into ἀλήθεια at all in this respect. And nothing indicates any such thing, unless we must assume that the breadth and indeterminacy of ἀλήθεια in *pre*-Platonic usage also required a correspondingly indeterminate depth.

With Plato ἀλήθεια becomes *accessibility,* in the twofold sense of a being's standing detached as such and of the passageway for perceiving. And if ἀλήθεια is seen solely from the "side" of a being as such, then this accessibility can also be called *manifestness*—and perceiving can be called *rendering manifest.*

In all cases ἀλήθεια continues to denote unconcealedness of *a being,* never of be-ing—simply because in this inceptual interpretation ἀλήθεια itself makes up *beingness,* (φύσις, emerging), ἰδέα, and having-been-seen [*Gesichtetheit*].

In going back to the first beginning, what is thus lost, such that the question of shelteredness-concealedness and of sheltering-concealing as such is not asked?

ἀλήθεια continues to be fixed in terms of accessibility and manifestness (δηλούμενον); and, disregarding sheltering-concealing in particular, what remains unasked therein is *openness as such.*

If, therefore, the name ἀλήθεια can still be claimed, then, in spite of a deeper historical connection, one must nevertheless look at and ponder the other [*das Andere*].

II. *Openness* is:

1. originarily the *multiple-onefold*—not only that "between" [*Zwischen*] for what is perceivable and for perceiving (ζυγόν) and not only what is several and various. Rather, openness must be questioned as this *onefold.*

2. not only perceiving and knowing, but every kind of comportment and stance and especially that which we call *attuning*—all belong to openness, which is not a state, but rather an occurrence.

3. the open as what is enopened and self-opening, *the enclosing, the dis-closing* [*Ent-schließung*].

210. On the History of the Essential Sway of Truth

Ever since Plato ἀλήθεια is experienced as the *brightness* [*die Helle*] in which a being as such stands, a being's *having been seen* in its presence (ἀλήθεια καί ὄν). At the same time [it is] the brightness in which νοεῖν first sees. Thus [it is] the brightness which connects ὄν ἡ ὄν and νοεῖν; [it is] the ζυγόν.

ἀλήθεια as ζυγόν now spans the relation of *one who perceives to what is encounterable,* and thus ἀλήθεια itself is harnessed to the "yoke" of correctness.

See Aristotle: ἀληθεύειν τῆς ψυχῆς. ἀλήθεια becomes *accessibility,* a being's standing detached as such, *passageway* for perceiving.

Thus the stages [in the history of truth] *are:*

From ἀλήθεια (as φῶς) to ζυγόν.

From ζυγόν to ὁμοίωσις.

From ὁμοίωσις to *veritas* as *rectitudo.* Here truth, i.e., correctness of the *assertion,* is simultaneously grasped in terms of the assertion as συμ-πλοκή, *connexio* (Leibniz).

From *rectitudo* to *certitudo,* being-certain of existing-together *(connexio?).*

From *certitudo* to validity as objectness.

From validity to legitimacy.

Truth is grasped by starting with ζυγόν, but in such a way *that thereby* ἀλήθεια is claimed as *unconcealedness* of a being as such and as the viewing domain [*Sichtbereich*] for enseeing and engrasping. That is to say: In that it comes down to setting correctness, ἀλήθεια is laid out as the ground of correctness in that limited double sense and in such a way that the ground becomes intelligible as laid out on the groundedness of what is set (on this ground). Therefore in the Greek sense ὁμοίωσις *is* still ἀλήθεια, rests on this ground, holds sway in it as essential sway, and thus can and must in addition also be so named.

But later ἀλήθεια as such is lost. What remains as the first and last thing is only directing oneself to, *rectitudo;* and within this determination an explanation of "correctness" must be sought in terms of the respective conceptions of man (as soul) and of beings—unless this correctness is simply taken for granted.

211. ἀλήθεια:
The Crisis of Its History in Plato and Aristotle, the Last Emanation and Total Collapse

1. ἀλήθεια καί ὄν—unconcealedness and indeed of a being as such, in the Platonic sense of ἰδέα; ἀλήθεια [is] always on the side of ὄν (cf. passages in Plato, *Republic,* Book VI, at the end.)

2. The lighting up of a being as such; shining seen in orientation to a being, brightness in which a being holds sway. Brightness seen in orientation to a being, *insofar as this* [is] *as* ἰδέα (at the same time from the α-, the "*anti*").

3. From there, whither the shining? Where else than toward perceiving, and this for its part [occurs] in encountering a being, a *perceiving*

which is possible only in the brightness, *all the way through it.* Thus *brightness,* i.e., the ἰδέα itself as having-been-seen, is the *yoke,* ζυγόν, although, characteristically, this is never expressed.

4. But the yoke, or truth grasped as the yoke, is the preform for truth as correctness, insofar as the yoke is itself grasped as *what ties-together* [*Verknüpfende*] and not grasped and engrounded as the ground for the agreement [*Übereinkommen*]; that is, ἀλήθεια actually gets lost. What remains is only the memory of the image of "light" that is necessary for "seeing" (cf. *lumen* [*naturale*] in the Middle Ages!).

Plato grasps ἀλήθεια as ζυγόν. But ἀλήθεια can no longer be comprehended from the point of view of ζυγόν; whereas the opposite is possible. The step toward ὁμοίωσις is taken. Interpretation of ζυγόν as ἀλήθεια is correct, but one has to know that with this interpretation ἀλήθεια is laid out in a certain respect and that actual inquiring into it is henceforth cut off.

5. And what is said in 4 is unavoidable, because 2 is the case, because ἀλήθεια in the true Greek sense [is] always only [experienced] in orientation to a being and its constant presence—and at best as the *between* [*Zwischen*].

However, as history shows, that is not sufficient. Unconcealedness must be engrounded and grounded as the openness of a being in the whole and the openness as such of self-sheltering-concealing (of being) and this as Da-sein.

212. Truth as Certainty

Insofar as *ratio* here is not immediately opposed to *fides,* but, in competing with *fides,* wants to rely on itself, what is left to *ratio* (to re-presenting) is only *self-referentiality,* so that *ratio* possess itself in its own way; and this re-presenting of the *"I-re-present"* is *certainty,* is the knowing that as such is a *known* knowing.

However, in this manner *ratio* degrades *itself,* goes underneath its own "niveau," which inceptually consisted in directly perceiving beingness in the whole.

Degraded thus, reason manages merely to achieve the *appearance* of a *mastery* (on the basis of self-deprecation). This illusionary mastery must one day shatter, and current centuries are accomplishing this shattering—though necessarily with the continual intensification of "reasonableness" [*Vernünftigkeit*] as a "principle" of machination.

But as soon as reason is degraded, it becomes more graspable for itself, so much so that it now takes the measure of understandability and intelligibility from this very success. Now this intelligibility becomes the measure for what is—and can be—valid and that now means what dares to be and be called a being.

Being itself is now all the more graspable, more familiar, without any estrangement.

What is established in Plato, especially as priority of beingness as laid out in terms of τέχνη, is now sharpened to such an extent—and raised to the level of exclusivity—that the fundamental condition is created for a human epoch in which "technicity"—the *priority* of the machinational, of the rules for measuring and of procedure vis-à-vis what is absorbed and affected by it—necessarily assumes mastery. The self-evident character of be-ing and truth as certainty is now without limits. Thus be-ing's ability to be *forgotten* becomes the principle, and the forgottenness of being that commences in the beginning spreads out and overshadows all human comportment.

Denial of all history emerges as the reversing of all events into *what is produceable* and institutable—which in the end displays itself by proving to be "providence" and "fate"—totally non-relationally and only confessionally, here and there.

But certainty as *I*-certainty intensifies the interpretation of man as *animal rationale*. The consequence of this process is "personality," of which many today still believe—and want to make believe—that it presents the overcoming of attachment to the I [*Ichhaftigkeit*], whereas "personality" can only be the disguise of that attachment.

But what does it mean that Descartes still attempts to justify certainty itself as *lumen naturale* from the viewpoint of the highest being as *creatum* of the *creator*?

What shape does this connection take later? The doctrine of postulates in Kant! The *absoluteness* of the I and of consciousness in German Idealism!

All of these are only more deeply laid, subsequent forms of the Cartesian course of thought—*ego, ens finitum, causatum ab ente infinito*—forms based on the *transcendental*.

In this way the inceptually pre-determined *humanizing* of being and its truth (I—certainty of reason) is in the end enhanced into the *absolute* and *thus* seemingly overcome. And yet, everything is the opposite of an overcoming, namely deepest entanglement in the forgottenness of being (cf. Playing-Forth, 90 and 91: From the First to the Other Beginning).

And even that era that comes after the middle of the nineteenth century has no clue whatsoever of this effort of metaphysics but sinks into the technicity of "theory of knowledge" and appeals, not totally without justification, to Plato.

[Add to that] neo-Kantianism, which philosophies of "life" and of "existence" also affirm, because both—e.g., Dilthey as well as Jaspers—continue to have no inkling of what has *actually* occurred in Western metaphysics and what must be prepared for as necessity for the other beginning.

213. What the Question of Truth Is About

1. Not about a mere alteration of the concept,
2. not about a more originary insight into essence,
3. but about the *leap-into* the essential swaying of truth.
4. And, consequently, about a transformation of *humanness* in the sense of *dis-placing* its site among beings.
5. And therefore above all about a more originary honoring and empowering of be-ing itself as *enowning*.
6. And thus above all about the grounding of humanness in *Da-sein* as the ground of the truth of be-ing that is necessitated by be-ing itself.

214. The Essential Sway of Truth
(Openness)

By recalling the beginning (ἀλήθεια) as well as by being mindful of the ground of the possibility of correctness *(adaequatio)*, we come across the same thing: *the openness of the open.* This is of course only an initial indication of the essential sway, which is determined more essentially as *the clearing for self-sheltering-concealing.*

But openness already offers enough of a puzzle, even if we totally disregard the manner of its essential swaying.

Openness, is that not the *emptiest of the empty*? (Cf. truth and abground.) So it seems, if we attempt to take it for itself—like a thing, as it were.

But the open, which hides itself and in which beings—and indeed not only as the nearest handy things—always stand, is in fact something like a *hollow medium*, e.g., that of a jug. But here we recognize that it is not a random emptiness that is merely enclosed by the walls and left unfilled by "things," but the other way around: the hollow medium is the determining framing that sustains the walling of the walls and their edges. These are merely the efflux of that originary open which lets its openness hold sway by calling forth such a walling (the form of the container) around and unto itself. In this way the essential swaying of the open radiates back into the enclosure.

We must understand the essential sway of the openness of the t/here [*Da*] in a similar way, only more essentially and richer. Its encircling walling is indeed nothing thingly or extant, nay not a being at all and itself not a being but is rather of being itself, the enquivering of enowning in the hinting of self-sheltering-concealing.

What is experienced in ἀλήθεια, un-concealment, is *being-sheltered* and the partial overcoming and eliminating of the same. But even *this*—that along with eliminating (taking-away: α-*privativum*) precisely *the open*, in which everything unconcealed stands, must *hold sway*—is not expressly pursued and grounded. Or do we here have to ponder the idea of the *light* and brightness in its relation to unconcealing as a perceiving and "seeing"? Certainly (cf. interpretation of the parable of the cave*). Something allegorical is shown here; and even the earlier allusion to the jug is still an allegory. Do we then not ever advance beyond the allegorical? Yes and no; for, conversely, the *most sensory* language and construction is precisely never only "sensory" but rather is *first and foremost* understood—an understanding that is not something "added."

But how little even the guiding idea of the light was capable of holding onto that open and its openness and of raising it to the level of knowing awareness becomes manifest since the very "clearing" and "what is cleared" [*Gelichtete*] were not grasped. Rather, the representation unfolded in the direction of shining of fire, and of sparking, whereby then soon only a causal relationship with illuminating continued to set the measure—until finally everything slid downwards into the indeterminacy of "consciousness" and of *perceptio*.

As little as *the open* and openness were attended to in their essential swaying (earlier the Greeks were assigned something else entirely), just as little the essential swaying of *shelteredness-concealedness—sheltering-concealing* became clear and was assigned to basic experience. Here, too, in a genuinely Greek manner, what is sheltered and concealed turned into *what is absent;* and the occurrence of sheltering-concealing was lost and along with it the necessity of expressly grounding it—and finally of grasping it in its inner connection with the essential swaying of openness and eventually and above all of grounding this onefold also as primal-ownmost [*ureigenes*] essential sway.

To attempt that is to name and unfold *Da-sein*. This can occur only by starting from "man"; and to this extent the first steps in grounding Da-sein "of" man, in grounding Da-sein "in" man and man in Da-sein, are very ambiguous and clumsy, especially when—as is the case up to now—there is no will to grasp the unfolded inquiry in its own terms and out of its basic intention unto the truth of be-ing and when every effort is made merely to reduce what is decisive to what has been up to now, to explain it in terms of the heretofore and thus to eliminate it.

That is why the path of a mindful deliberation on correctness and on the *ground of the possibility of correctness* is also at first not very convincing (cf. lecture on truth, 1930), because one does not get rid of the representations of a human-thing (subject, person, and the like) and accounts for everything only as "lived-experiences" of man and these experiences in turn as events in man himself.

This mindfulness, too, can only indicate that something necessary is not yet understood and grasped. *Da-sein* itself is attained only by dis-

---

* Lecture course WS 1931/32, *Vom Wesen der Wahrheit. Zu Platons Höhlengleichnis und Theätet* (GA 34).

placing humanness in the whole, and that means by being mindful of the distress of being as such and of its truth.

215. The Essential Swaying of Truth

A deciding question is whether the essential swaying of truth as clearing for self-sheltering-concealing is grounded on Da-sein, or whether this essential swaying of truth itself is the ground for Da-sein—or whether both are true? And what does "ground" mean in each case?

These questions are decidable only if what is shown as ownmost to truth is grasped as the truth of be-ing and thus in terms of enowning.

What does it mean to be placed before *self-sheltering-concealing*, re-fusal, hesitation, and to be steadfast in their *open*? [It means] *reservedness* and thus grounding-attunement: startled dismay, reservedness, deep awe. Such [is] gifted only to man—whenever and however.

216. Approaching the Question of Truth

Because the question of truth is long since no longer a question, approaching the question of truth now seems to be completely arbitrary. And yet the opposite follows from this situation: that the approach has its own unique determination, namely in distress, which is so deeply rooted that it is *no* distress for everyone, that we do not at all experience and grasp the question concerning the truth of the true as a question in its necessity.

Rather, the growing uprooting pushes either into the crudest dictatorship of opinion or into indifference or into the powerless reliance on the heretofore.

217. The Essential Sway of Truth

What belongs most intrinsically to this essential sway is that it is historical. History of truth, of shining, and of transformation and grounding of its essential sway, has only rare moments that lie far from one another.

This essential sway seems for a long time hardened (cf. the long history of truth as correctness: ὁμοίωσις, *adaequatio*), because only the true—determined by this essential sway—is sought and pursued. And so, on the basis of this constancy which is at a standstill, the illusion arises that the essential sway of truth is even "eternal," especially when one imagines "eternity" as mere continuity.

Do we stand at the end of a long period of such hardening of the essential sway of truth—and then before the gate of a new moment of its hidden history?

The wording "above all truth is sheltering that lights up" means that a clearing is grounded for self-sheltering (cf. ab-ground): self-sheltering-concealing of be-ing in the clearing of the t/here [*Da*]. Be-ing holds sway in self-sheltering-concealing. Enowning is never open and obvious, like a being, like what is present (cf. Leap, Be-ing).

En-ownment in its turning [*Kehre*] is made up neither solely of the call nor solely of the belongingness, is in neither of the two and yet resonates deeply in both. And the enquivering of this resonance in the turning of enowning is the most hidden essential sway of be-ing. This sheltering-concealing needs the deepest clearing: Be-ing "needs" Da-sein.

Truth never "is" but rather holds sway. For truth is truth of be-ing, which "merely" holds sway. Thus everything else that belongs to truth also holds sway—time-space and consequently "space" and "time."

The t/here [*Da*] holds sway; and, as that which holds sway, it must be simultaneously taken over in a being: Da-sein. Therefore, the inabiding sustaining of the essential swaying of the truth of be-ing. This twofoldness [*Zwiespältigkeit*] [is] the riddle. Therefore Da-sein [is] the "between" [*das Zwischen*] between *be-ing and a being* (cf. Grounding, 227: On the Essential Sway of Truth, no. 13, p. 248).

Because this essential sway is historical (cf. p. 239), therefore any "truth" in the sense of the true is historically all the more only a true, if it has already grown back into a ground and thereby has turned at once into a force which works ahead.

Wherever truth is hidden in the shape of "reason" [*Vernunft*] and of the "reasonable" [*das Vernünftige*] what is at work there is what is precisely not ownmost to truth, i.e., that destructive power of what is valid for everyone, whereby everyone is arbitrarily legitimized and whereby the satisfaction arises that no one has anything essential over anyone else.

It is this "magic" of universal validity that has established the domination of the interpretation of truth as correctness and has made it almost unshakeable.

In the end this is manifest in that, even where one believes to grasp something of what is historically ownmost to truth, even there only a superficial "historicism" emerges, one that assumes that truth is not eternally valid but only "for a time." But this opinion is merely a "quantitative" delimiting of universal validity and, in order to attain something like such a validity, needs the assumption that truth is correctness and validity.

The superficiality of this "thinking" is then enhanced even further when one finally attempts to balance both, the eternal validity in itself with the temporally limited.

218. The Announcement of the Essential Swaying of Truth

When we say that truth is clearing for sheltering-concealing, then the essential swaying is thereby merely announced in that the essential sway is named. But at the same time this naming should indicate that the interpretation of the essential swaying of truth remembers ἀλήθεια

—remembering, not the merely literal translation of the word, in whose domain then the conventional view again falls, but rather ἀλήθεια as the name for the first shining forth of truth itself and indeed necessarily in unison with the inceptual naming of a being as φύσις.

But the announcement of the essential sway must be aware that the clearing for sheltering-concealing must be unfolded with regard to time-space (ab-ground) as well as with regard to strife and sheltering.

219. The Jointure of the Question of Truth

Truth is what is originarily true.
What is true is the most-being.

More-being than any being is be-ing itself. The most-being "is" no longer but rather holds sway as essential swaying (enowning).

Be-ing holds sway as enowning.

The essential sway of truth is the sheltering-concealing of enowning that lights up.

The sheltering-concealing that lights up holds sway as grounding of Da-sein; but grounding is ambiguous.

The grounding of Da-sein occurs as sheltering truth in what is true, which in this way first becomes what it is.

What is true lets a being be a being.

When a being thus stands in the t/here [Da], it becomes re-present-able. The possibility and necessity of what is correct is grounded.

Correctness is an unavoidable offshoot of truth.

Therefore, where correctness pre-determines the "idea" of truth, all ways to its origin are blocked.

220. The Question of Truth

As the jointure of truth is enjoined, it continues to be a disposal of the history of being over us, to the extent that we still have the strength to assert ourselves in its stream.

The question of truth in the designated sense—and only in that sense—is for us *the* preliminary question through which we must first go.

Only in this way is grounded a domain of decision for essential mindfulness. (Cf. the separate elaboration of the question of truth as preliminary question in the direction of time-space.)

The question of truth is the question of the essential swaying of truth. Truth itself is that wherein what is true has its ground.

Ground here [means]: 1. that wherein [what is true is] sheltered, whither [it is] kept back;
2. whereby [it] makes necessary;
3. wherefrom [it] towers up.

What is true [is]: what stands in truth and so becomes a being or a not-being.

Truth [is]:   the clearing for sheltering-concealing (truth as un-truth), strifing in itself and nihilating and the originary intimacy (cf. Grounding and the Frankfurt Lectures*), and this because

Truth [is]:   truth of be-ing as enowning.

What is true and to be what is true simultaneously [include] within themselves the untrue, the *dissembled* and its variants.

The essential swaying of truth.

221. Truth as Essential Swaying of Be-ing**

Truth is clearing for self-sheltering (that is, enowning; hesitating refusal as fullness, fruit and gifting). But truth [is] not simply clearing but rather the very clearing for self-sheltering.

Be-ing: enowning, nihilating in the counter-resonance, and thus *strifing*. The origin of the strife—be-ing or not-being.

Truth: ground as abground. Ground [is] not the wherefrom but the whereunto, as what belongs. Abground: as time-space of the strife; strife as strife of earth and world, because [it is] relation of truth *to* a being!

The *first* (inceptual) *sheltering* [is] the question and decision. The question of truth (mindfulness) and its essential sway [is] to be put up for decision. Origin and necessity of decision (of the question). The question [is]: Do we have to ask (essentially), and if so, why? The question and *faith.*

222. Truth

Only when we stand in the clearing do we experience self-sheltering-concealing.

Truth is never a "system" joined together from propositions, to which one could appeal.

Truth is the ground as what takes back and towers up, ground that towers above the sheltered without eliminating it, the attuning that attunes as this ground. For this ground is enowning itself as essential swaying of be-ing.

Enowning bears truth = truth towers up through enowning.

The Question of Truth

The question of truth sounds very pretentious and creates the illusion that in spite of questioning one knows what the true is.

And yet, questioning here is no mere *prelude* in order to display something that is without question, as though that had been achieved. Questioning is here beginning and end.

---

* *Der Ursprung des Kunstwerkes,* in: *Holzwege* (GA 5).
** Cf. Preview, 9: A Glance.

And "truth" is meant as what is question-worthy in what is own-most to the true, something very provisional and peripheral for anyone who wants to grasp and possess the true directly.

And if there were to be a way out here, then philosophy would have to hide the question of truth in a different-sounding and seemingly harmless question, in order to avoid the illusion that here great procla-mations were promised.

223. What Is Ownmost to Truth
(What Is *Not* Its Ownmost)

If truth holds sway as clearing of what is sheltered and concealed, and if, corresponding to the not-character of being, what is *not its ownmost* belongs to it, then must not reversing what is ownmost spread itself out in what is ownmost, i.e., must not the dissembling of clearing as sem-blance of what is ownmost thus be exaggerated to the utmost and most superficial degree, thereby becoming an exhibition, play-acting? *Stage*— the shaping of the actual as task for the stage-designer!

If from time to time the theatrical comes to power, how is it then with the ownmost? Must it then not ground as ground in a shel-tered-concealed manner and in stillness, so much so that one hardly knows about it? But how is it *then* still ground? When seen in terms of the general [*das Allgemeine*]? But is not the essential sway of being the uniqueness and seldomness of strangeness? What is actually *not* the ownmost of truth [is] characterized in the lectures on truth as *errancy*. This determination [is] still more originary in the nihilating of the t/here [*Da*].

On the other hand, the utmost of "not ownmost" [is] still [manifest], in the very *illusion* of exhibiting.

A twofold significance of what is *not* ownmost [*Un-wesen*].

224. The Essential Sway of Truth

How little do we know about gods and yet how important is their essential swaying and dis-swaying [*Verwesung*] in the openness of the shelterings of the t/here [*Da*], in *truth?*

But *then*, what must the experience of the essential sway of truth itself say to us about enowning? And how are we capable of being rightly and thoroughly reticent about this saying?

Truth is the primarily true, indeed it is true as what lights up, is shel-tered-concealed and belongs to be-ing. The essential sway of truth lies in holding sway as the true of be-ing and so in becoming the origin for sheltering the true in a being, whereby this first becomes a being.

The preliminary question concerning truth is at the same time the grounding-question of be-ing, which as enowning holds sway as truth.

225. The Essential Sway of Truth

The essential sway of truth is *the clearing for self-sheltering-concealing.* This intimate strifing of the essential sway of truth shows that truth is originarily and essentially the truth of be-ing (enowning).

Nevertheless the question continues to be whether we experience this essential sway of truth essentially enough, whether in every relation to a being we take over that self-sheltering and thus the hesitating refusal—each time in its own way as en-ownment—and own ourselves over [*über-eignen*] to it. Owning-over-to occurs only such that we effect, produce, create, protect, and in each case let a being function, according to the call that belongs to it, in order thus to ground the clearing so that it does not become an emptiness in which everything seems to be equally "understandable" and controllable.

The self-sheltering soars through the clearing. And only when this occurs, when the strifing in its intimacy thoroughly dominates the t/ here [*Da*], can we succeed in moving out of the undetermined—and as such not at all grasped—domain of re-presentation and live-experience and succeed in attempting the inabiding of Da-*sein.*

Only when self-sheltering thoroughly dominates all interswaying regions of what is begotten and created and acted upon and sacrificed, when it determines the clearing and thus at the same time sways counter to what is closed off within this clearing, only then does *world* arise and along with it (out of the "simultaneity" of be-ing and a being) *earth* emerge. Now for a moment there is *history* [*Geschichte*].

Therefore, truth is never only clearing, but also holds sway as sheltering-concealing, equally originarily and intimately along with clearing. Both, clearing and sheltering-concealing, are not two but rather the essential swaying of the one, of truth itself. In that truth holds sway and *becomes* truth, enowning becomes truth. "Enowning enowns" says nothing other than: It and only it *becomes* truth, becomes that which belongs to enowning, so that quite essentially truth is truth of be-ing.

Any inquiry into truth that does not think that far ahead thinks too short.

Even that totally different, medieval interpretation of *verum* as determination of *ens* (beings), which moves in the domain of the guiding-question (of metaphysics) and is additionally uprooted from its nearest Greek terrain, is still a semblance of this intimacy of truth and be-ing. But one should not mix up this inquiry into enowning with that totally different relationship of beings *(ens)* that is built entirely on truth as correctness of representing *(intellectus)* with being re-presented in the *intellectus divinus,* a relationship that continues to be correct only under the assumption that, *Deus creator* excepted, *omne ens* is *ens creatum*—whereby, seen "ontologically," *Deus* too is grasped in terms of *creatio,* which proves how crucial the story of creation in the Old Testament is for this kind of "philosophy." But insight into this connection is all the more essential since this connection still continues to be maintained everywhere in modern metaphysics—even where the medieval orientation to the "legacy of faith" of the Church has long since and in principle been given up. It is precisely the many variations of the domination of "Christian" thinking in the post- and *anti*-Christian epoch that impedes every attempt to get away from this foundation and—inceptually from within a more originary experience—to think the basic relation of be-ing and truth.

226. Clearing of Sheltering-Concealing and ἀλήϑεια

ἀ-λήϑεια means unconcealment and the unconcealed itself. This already shows that concealing itself is only experienced as what is to be *abolished*, what must be taken away (ἀ-).

And therefore questioning does not aim at concealing itself and its ground; and therefore also, inversely, what is unconcealed as such becomes important; again, not *unconcealing* and this even as *clearing*, in which concealing itself now comes into the open at all. In this way concealing is not canceled but is rather first graspable in its essential sway.

Truth as clearing for concealing is thus an essentially different projecting-open than ἀλήϑεια, although this projecting-open belongs to the remembering of ἀλήϑεια and this remembering belongs to that projecting-open (cf. p. 246).

Clearing for concealing as originary-onefold essential sway is the abground of ground, as which the t/here [*Da*] holds sway.

The perplexing formulation "truth is un-truth" is too misconstruable to be able to indicate, with any certainty, the right path. But it should still indicate the strangeness that lies in the new essential projecting-open—*the clearing for sheltering-concealing,* and this as essential swaying in enowning.

What inabiding reservedness of Da-sein is thus claimed according to rank, if *this* essential sway of truth, as what is originarily true, is to be raised to knowing awareness?

The origin of *errancy* and the power and possibility of abandonment by being, concealing and dis-sembling, domination of the unground—all of this now becomes all the more clear.

Mere allusion to ἀλήϑεια, for the sake of explaining the essential sway of truth that is foundational here, does not help much, because in ἀλήϑεια the occurrence of unconcealing and sheltering-concealing is precisely *not* experienced and grasped as ground—because questioning continues to be determined from the perspective of φύσις, and a being as a being.

But it is different with clearing for sheltering-concealing. Here we stand in the *essential swaying of truth,* and this is the *truth of be-ing.* Clearing for sheltering-concealing is now the resounding of the counter-resonance of the turning of enowning.

*

But the attempts heretofore, in *Being and Time* and subsequent writings, to enforce *this* essential sway of truth as ground for Da-sein—rather than the correctness of representation and assertion—had to remain inadequate, because they were always still enacted *defensively* and thus always had what was to be warded off as their aim—thus making it impossible to know the essential sway of truth from the ground up, from the ground as which the essential sway itself holds sway. For this to succeed, it is no longer necessary to hold back the saying of the essential sway of be-ing—holding it back, again based on the notion that, in spite of the insight into the necessity for a projecting-open that protrudes, a way to the truth of be-ing could in the end still be paved by proceeding step by step from the heretofore. For this proceeding from the heretofore must always fail.

And regardless of how strong the new danger is that now enowning instantly becomes merely a name and a handy concept, from which something else could be "deduced," one must still speak of enowning—but again, not as isolated in a "speculative" discussion, but rather in the pressing mindfulness, held in the distress of the abandonment by being.

*

The clearing of sheltering-concealing does not mean lifting the sheltered up, setting it free, and transforming it into what is unsheltered and unconcealed but rather means merely grounding the ground that holds to abground and is the ground for *sheltering* (the hesitating refusal).

In my attempts up to now to project-open this essential sway of truth and in my efforts to be understood, I was always primarily concerned with elucidating the ways of clearing and the modifications of sheltering-concealing and their essential belonging together (cf., e.g., the lecture on truth from 1930).

When it came to such determinations as "Da-sein is simultaneously in truth and untruth," people immediately took this statement in a moral sense and as expressing a worldview, without grasping what is deciding in philosophical mindfulness—the essential swaying of "simultaneously" as the grounding sway of truth—without originally grasping un-truth in the sense of *sheltering-concealing* (and not in the sense of falseness, for example).

*

What does it mean, to "stand" in the clearing of sheltering-conceal-ing and to sustain it? It means *grounding-attunement of reservedness, the outstanding and historical one-timeness of this inabiding*, that here above all "what is true" is decided. What *steadfastness* does this inabiding have? Or put in another way: Who is capable—and when and how—of *being* Da-*sein*?

For preparing this being, what can inceptual mindfulness accomplish in thinking saying?

Why must in this moment this "now"—and that means the *inquiring knowing*—provide the thrust?

To what extent does the poet Hölderlin, who has already gone ahead of us, become *now* our necessity, in his most unique poetic experience [*Dichtertum*] and work?

227. On the Essential Sway of Truth*

1. *Does truth hold sway—and why?* Because only in this way [is there] essential swaying of be-ing. Why be-ing?
2. The essential sway of truth grounds the necessity of the *Why* and thus of questioning.
   The question of truth occurs for the sake of be-ing, which needs our belongingness as founders of Dasein.
3. The first question (1) is in itself the essential determination of truth.
4. How one is to approach the question of truth.
   Proceeding from the *essential* ambiguity: "truth" meant as "what is true," but what is true is truth as sheltering-concealing of enown-ing, which lights up.
   At the beginning what is lit up is a brightness, but without shine and radiance. Sheltering-concealing itself is that much brighter and shines through the depth of shelteredness-concealedness.
5. How the prolonged, traditional concept of truth as correctness not only initially guides the question but also suggests that the answer to the question needs to be measured by a correctness and thus that what is ownmost to truth could be read off something already given, which renders this ownmost accessible.
6. To unfold what is ownmost to truth above all as lighting-up of shel-tering-concealing (dissembling and hiding).
7. Truth as ground of time-space but therefore also essentially deter-minable in terms of this time-space.

---

* Cf. 1930 lecture *Vom Wesen der Wahrheit; Laufende Anmerkungen zu "Sein und Zeit,"* §44 [GA 82].

8. Time-space as the site for the moment from within the turning of enowning.
9. Truth and the necessity of *sheltering*.
10. Sheltering as strifing of the strife of world and earth.
11. The historically necessary paths of *sheltering*.
12. How a being first becomes *a being* in sheltering (cf. Leap, 152: The Stages of Be-ing).
13. How, by mindfully traversing the preceding way, the domain is first unfolded in which occurs—and which occurs *as*—the "differentiation" of be-ing and a being (cf. Leap, 151: Being and a Being). Da-sein holding sway as the "between."

*

In the face of the growing desolation and misshaping of philosophy, something lasting and essential would be gained if one succeeded in asking the question of truth in the right way and out of its necessity.

Its necessity arises from the distress of the abandonment by being. The right way of asking the question is *crossing* to the originary essential sway by clarifying the *starting point,* the dominant concept of correctness. At the same time one must understand that, with the truth in the turning, the truth of the *essential sway* and the truth of the essential swaying is first determined—and therefore from the *outset* one cannot strive for and demand a concept of "essence" in the sense of a correct, generically determined coming together of the most general properties immediately accessible to every man. Rather, [one can strive for] something higher with which the already long dominant uprooting of the question of truth can immediately be measured. From this perspective—and that means experienced necessarily historically—truth means being-displaced into transference.

That in a certain sense this transference always goes on, ever since and when man is historical, and that nevertheless this transference continues to be hidden, this essentially rests in the domination of correctness. Corresponding to correctness, man finds himself standing immediately and only in an over-against (ψυχή—ἀντικείμενον, *cogito—cogitatum,* consciousness—the known). He stakes his claims and awaits their fulfillments out of this over-against. Everything with which man believes to have come to an understanding is reflected in this over-against. The domination of "transcendence" too belongs there (cf. Playing-Forth, 110: ἰδέα, Platonism, and Idealism).

Here is the most profound reason for hiddenness and dissembling of Da-sein. For, despite all opposition to the "I," what is more clear and unquestionable than that "I" and "we" are over against objects—whereby "we" and "I" are above all the unquestioned ones, which one can safely leave behind.

Therefore, even only within this basic stance, one does not dare to become mindful to the extent that one sees that "we" have no longer "contributed" anything that, in copying and reproducing, could be true.

If we would allow even that much, then the question would already have to have come up, whether *correctness,* as what is ownmost to truth, can ground and determine the seeking and the claiming of what is true — *a correctness* which first grounds (rather than presupposes) — such a re-presenting of beings and of one who represents.

Additionally, such a correctness would never lead out of the distress of the abandonment by being but rather would only confirm and require it anew, in hidden fashion.

But what does it mean that now essential projecting-open of truth as the sheltering-concealing that lights up must be ventured and that dis-placing of man into Da-sein must be prepared?

Dis-placed *out of* that situation in which we find ourselves, namely the gigantic emptiness and desolation, without measures and above all without the will to inquire into measures, pressured into what has become unrecognizable while being handed down to us. But desolation is the hidden abandonment by being.

228. The Essential Sway of Truth Is Un-truth*

This statement — deliberately formulated as self-contradictory — is to state that what has the *character of nothing* belongs to truth but by no means only as a lack, rather as what withstands, that self-sheltering-concealing that comes into the clearing as such.

Thereby the originary relation of truth to be-ing as enowning is grasped.

Nevertheless, that statement is risky in its intention of bringing the strange essential sway of truth nearer by such estrangement.

Understood completely originarily, there lies in that statement the most essential insight into — and at the same time the allusion of — the inner intimacy and contentiousness in be-ing itself as enowning.

229. Truth and Da-sein

The clearing for self-sheltering-concealing lights up in the projecting-open. The throwing of the projecting-open occurs as Da-sein, and the thrower of this throwing is in each case that self-being in which man becomes inabiding.

Every projecting-opening includes what is transferred into its clearing and is thus relinquished, in a retro-relation to the thrower, and conversely: the thrower first becomes who it *itself* is by seizing that inclusion.

It is never the case that what is transferred into projecting-opening is purely and simply an in-itself or that the thrower is ever capable of

---

* Cf. Frankfurt lectures, *Der Ursprung des Kunstwerkes,* in: *Holzwege* (GA 5, pp. 36ff., especially pp. 40f.).

putting itself up purely for itself. Rather, this strife, which is about each turning against each—inclusively and reflexively—is the consequence of the intimacy which holds sway in what is ownmost to truth as clearing of self-sheltering. With a merely external dialectic of subject-object-relation, nothing at all is grasped here. Rather, this relation itself, grounded on correctness as an offspring of truth, has its source in what is ownmost to truth.

Of course, this origin of the strife and the strife itself must now be shown. To that end, it is not enough merely to consider the clearing and its inauguration by projecting-opening. Rather one must above all consider that clearing holds the *self-sheltering* into the open and lets the charming-moving-unto—as determining and as originating there—thoroughly attune the self-being of the thrower. Only in this way does owning-over [*Über-eignung*] to being and, within this owning-over, owning-to [*Zueignung*] the thrower itself occur, whereby the thrower in turn first comes to stand in the clearing (of self-sheltering) and becomes inabiding in the t/here [*Da*].

The more prevailingly be-ing belongs to Da-sein and Dasein belongs to be-ing, the more originary is the over-against of each to the other in not-letting-each-other-free [*das Gegeneinander des Sich-nicht-frei-lassens*].

The thrower must take over the inclusion; and thus does thrownness first become effective, insofar as it becomes manifest that the thrower itself belongs to what is enopened and freed up through the clearing.

230. Truth and Correctness

The priority of *correctness* justifies and obviously demands explanation in the sense of deducing beings as producible from other beings ("mathesis" and "mechanics" in the broadest sense).

Where this explaining fails, one turns to the inexplicable or claims consistently that what is not explainable is *not-being.*

But the inexplicable (the "transcendent") is thus only the offspring of the mania for explanation and, instead of being something higher, is itself a lowering.

But the hidden reason for this whole enterprise lies in the priority and claim of correctness; and this priority in turn lies in the asthenia for what is ownmost to truth itself, i.e., asthenia for *knowing* what supports or hems in all ever-so-sincere efforts regarding what is true.

231. How Truth, ἀλήθεια, Becomes Correctness

Truth, ἀλήθεια, hardly resonates [in correctness]—powerful, but not grounded and also not actually grounding.

Correctness gives priority to ψυχή and thereafter to the subject-object-relation. Because the domination of correctness already has a long history, its source and the possibility of something other than correctness can be brought to view only slowly and with difficulty. With ψυχή the λόγος already is given originarily as gathering and thereafter as speaking and saying.

That assertion becomes *the* locus of "truth" contributes to what is most estranging in its history, even though for us it counts as familiar.

But, apart from grasping the essential swaying itself, that is the reason why it is all the more difficult originarily to seek further and to preserve truth and what is true anywhere where we do not even suspect it.

This uprooting of truth goes along with the concealing of the essential sway of be-ing.

To what extent [is] "correctness" essential, from the perspective of establishing and sheltering (language)?

232. The Question of Truth as Historically Mindful Deliberation

What is meant here is not historical reporting about opinions and doctrines that were put together with regard to the "concept" of truth.

Philosophy in the other beginning is essentially historical, and in this respect a more originary kind of remembering the history of the first beginning must now ensue.

The question is: What fundamental movements of the essential sway of truth and its conditions for interpretation carried—and will carry—Western history?

The two outstanding basic positions in this history are marked by Plato and Nietzsche.

And Plato (cf. interpretation of the simile of the cave*) is indeed that thinker in whom—in the crossing to truth of assertion—a last shining of ἀλήθεια still becomes manifest (cf. also Aristotle, Metaphysics, Θ, IV).

And [it is] Nietzsche in whom Western tradition is gathered in the modern and above all positivistic variation of the nineteenth century and with whom "truth" is simultaneously brought into essential opposition to art and thereby into its belonging to art—both of them as fundamental modes of will to power, as the essence of beings *(essentia)* whose *existentia* is called the eternal return of the same.

233. Enjoining the Interpretation of the Simile of the Cave (1931/32 and 1933/34) to the Question of Truth

1. Why is this interpretation historically essential? Because still here, by an extended mindfulness, it becomes manifest how ἀλήθεια continues essentially to carry and guide the Greek questioning of ὄν while *at the same time* ἀλήθεια collapses precisely *through this questioning*, i.e., by setting up ἰδέα.

---

* Lecture course WS 1931/32, *Vom Wesen der Wahrheit. Zu Platons Höhlengleichnis und Theätet* (GA 34).

2. Looking further back, it becomes manifest at the same time that the collapse is not one of something established and expressly grounded at all. Neither the one nor the other was accomplished in inceptual Greek thinking, in spite of the πόλεμος-statement of Heraclitus and the fragment of Parmenides. And yet, everywhere in thinking and poetizing (tragedy and Pindar), ἀλήθεια is important.

3. Only when this is experienced and worked out can it be shown in what way then—and in a certain sense necessarily—a remainder and a semblance of ἀλήθεια must be preserved, since precisely truth as correctness must be sheltered in what is already open (cf. on correctness). That toward which re-presenting is directed must be open, as well as that for which the adequacy is to be manifest (cf. correctness and subject-object-relation; Da-sein and re-presenting).

4. If we prospectively and retrospectively survey the history of ἀλήθεια from the simile of the cave, which holds such a key position, then we can indirectly reckon what it means to install, in thinking, truth as ἀλήθεια and to unfold and ground it in its essential sway—what it means that this not only did not occur in metaphysics heretofore, but also did not—and *could not*—occur in the first beginning.

5. The essential grounding of truth as disclosing the first shining in ἀλήθεια, then, does not mean merely taking over the word and its appropriate translation as "unconcealment." Rather, what counts is to experience the essential sway of truth as the clearing for self-sheltering-concealing.

   The sheltering-concealing that lights up has to be grounded as Da-sein.

   The self-sheltering-concealing has to come into knowing-awareness as the essential swaying of be-ing itself as enowning.

   The most profound relation of be-ing and Dasein in its turning becomes manifest as that which necessitates the grounding-question and compels one to go beyond the guiding-question and thus beyond all metaphysics—*beyond* indeed into the *temporal-spatiality* of the t/here [*Da*].

6. But now because, in accord with the long history and confused tradition, in which many things have gotten mixed up, "truth" itself and its concept are no longer put into question in any kind of clear and necessary inquiry. The interpretations of the history of the concept of truth—and those of the simile of the cave in particular—are frayed and depend on what earlier was itself seized from Platonism and the doctrine of judgment. Lacking are all basic positions for a projecting-open of that which is being said and of what goes on in this simile of the cave.

   Therefore it is necessary to put forth, initially and in general, a consistent interpretation of the simile of the cave—one that origi- nates in the question of truth—and to make it effective as an intro- duction into the domain of the question of truth and as a lead into the necessity of this question—with all the reservations that go along with such unmediated attempts. For, the ground and per- spective for projecting-open the interpretation and its stages remain undiscussed and presupposed and appear as coercive and arbitrary.

234. The Question Concerning Truth (Nietzsche)

The last and most passionate one to inquire into truth is Nietzsche. For on the one hand he proceeds from "our not having the truth" (XI, 159)[1] and on the other hand he still asks what truth is—nay, even what it is worth (VII, 471).[2]

And yet, Nietzsche does not inquire originarily into truth. For, with this word he almost always means "what is true"; and whenever he asks about the essence of what is true, this is entangled in the tradition and does not come from an originary mindfulness such that this mind- fulness is immediately grasped as the essential decision also about "what is true."

Of course, when we inquire more originarily, then this never guaran- tees a more certain answer—on the contrary, only a higher question- worthiness of what is ownmost to truth. And we need this question- worthiness, for otherwise what is true will continue to make no difference.

But by being mindful of "truth," Nietzsche does not come clear, because he

1. relates truth to "life" ("biological" and idealistic) as securing its existence. "Life" is taken simply as fundamental actuality, and the general character of becoming is attributed to it.

2. At the same time, however, Nietzsche grasps "being" as what is "constant" entirely in the sense of the oldest Platonic tradition; con- sidered as coming from and unto life, this constant *as* constant is what is agreed upon and thus in each case "true."

3. Additionally, this concept of truth, directed to "life" and determined by the traditional concept of being, is completely in the trajectory of what has been handed down, insofar as truth is a determination and a result of thinking and re-presenting. This common opinion begins with Aristotle.

All of this, which has come down to us unquestioned, hinders an originary questioning of what is ownmost to truth.

[1] F. Nietzsche, *Nachgelassene Werke. Unveröffentlichtes aus der Zeit des Menschlichen, Allzu- menschlichen und der Morgenröte* (1875/76–1880/81), in: *Nietzsche's Werke (Großoktavaus- gabe)* (Leipzig: Kröner, 1919), XI, 159.

[2] F. Nietzsche, *Zur Genealogie der Moral*, in: *Nietzsche's Werke (Großoktavausgabe)* (Stuttgart: Kröner, 1921), VII, 471.

Of course, insofar as this is central to Nietzsche's last thoughts (cf. his statement on the relation of truth (of knowing) and of art; cf. the doctrine of the perspectives of the drives), everything gains a new vitality—which should not, however, delude us as to the instability of the foundation, especially not when one considers that Nietzsche in his own way *does* want to overcome Platonism.

Indeed it now does look as if, in spite of everything, Nietzsche has again drawn what is ownmost to truth into "life." But did he arrive at clarity about the truth of this departure from "life" and thus of the will to power and of the eternal return of the same? In his own way, yes; for he understands these projecting-openings of beings as an experimenting that we do with "truth." This philosophy is to be securing the constancy of "life" as such, so much so that this philosophy directly renders life free in its unsurpassable possibilities. And presumably herein lies a step in Nietzsche's thinking whose scope we do not yet estimate, because we are too close to him and are therefore compelled to see everything still too much within *that* horizon ("of life") which Nietzsche wanted basically to overcome. It thus becomes all the more necessary for us to inquire more originarily—and *not* to fall into the false opinion that Nietzsche's inquiry is thus "finished."

What weighs Nietzsche's ownmost thinking down so much and almost blocks it is the insight that the essential swaying of truth means: Da-sein, i.e., standing in the midst of the clearing of self-sheltering-concealing and obtaining from that clearing the ground and strength for humanness. For, in spite of appeals to "perspectivism," "truth" remains *wrapped up in* "life" and life itself remains—almost like a thing—a center of will and force, which wills its intensification and heightening.

If I see it correctly, that standing out which advances into the unknown—which was for Nietzsche certainly a fundamental experience—could not become for him the grounded midpoint of his inquiry—because he was stuck in the above-mentioned (p. 253) threefold entanglement in what is handed down.

And so it happens that, initially and for a long time yet, Nietzsche is not grasped in terms of his most hidden thinking-will but is relegated to the usual perspectives of the dominant thinking and worldviews of the nineteenth century in order to find what is Nietzsche's own and what is "new" to him—and to make that useful—and distinguished from that dominant thinking and worldview, with the help of those perspectives.

Indeed, the manner in which the debate with Nietzsche masters or does not master his understanding of "truth" must become a cornerstone for the decision of whether we help his actual philosophy to its future (without becoming "Nietzscheans") or whether we classify him within [the discipline of] history.

Nietzsche appears to inquire most profoundly into what is ownmost to truth when he takes up the question "What does all will to truth mean?" and when he designates knowing this question as "our problem" (VII, 482).[3] His solution is that will to truth is a will to an illusion, and this necessarily as will to power, securing of life's constancy—and this will is at its utmost in art, for which reason art has more value than truth. But will to "truth" is consequently ambiguous: This will as determined is a will against [*Widerwille*] life; and as will to illusion—as transfiguration—it is heightening of life. Nietzsche's question is: What does this will want with us?

And yet, this question and this knowing of this question is also not originary (completely disregarding the departure from "life" and the interpretation of "being"), because to Nietzsche what truth is is a question that is settled; and to him his interpretation of the ownmost (cf. pp. 253f.) is sufficiently grounded, so that he can immediately take up the seemingly keener and more originary question (because it refers to "will to power").

And yet what is truth and, above all, how do we know what truth is? Does not the *question* of what truth is already presuppose truth? And what is that for a presupposition? And how do we obtain this presupposition?

For Nietzsche truth is a condition for life, a condition that is itself *against* life. Accordingly life needs "what is against it" (What announces itself here? The relation to "a being" as such, a relation that is not experienced from the ground up and not freed up and not grounded upon representing and thinking?).

But because "life" is already *the* actuality in the sense of the most ambiguous idealism, which has sold out to positivism, truth must be established and drawn into life in advance, as mere condition. Therefore, the final and seemingly originary question is simply that of truth's "value": In what sense is it the condition for "life"—in a degrading, stagnating, co-securing, or heightening sense?

But how do we ever arrive at the criterion of "value" for life? Does this life itself require decisions about its conditions? *Which* life? And if life requires such decisions, then the question is how conditions themselves— and decisions about them—belong to "life" and what "life" *then* means.

When will to power means a willing that wills-to-go-beyond-itself and in this way to come-to-it*self*, then truth proves to be the condition for will to power—of course, truth understood differently from Nietzsche. The beyond-itself requires the openness of time-space, if it is not simply a quantitative intensification but rather enopening and grounding.

---

[3] F. Nietzsche, *Zur Genealogie der Moral, op. cit.,* 482.

Seen in this manner, truth as will to truth is not only *one* condition for *life* but the ground of its *essentia* as will to power.

Indeed, the entire ambiguity of "life" becomes manifest here; and the question remains whether and how an ordering of ranks can be set up here, in correspondence to Leibniz's doctrine of monads.

235. Truth and Genuineness*

We call true gold "genuine gold"; we call the genuine German the "true German." Genuine is what corresponds to and suffices for what is true, and true here is meant as *what is actual*, respectively, what is *fitting*.

Therefore, genuineness contains correspondence, and thus correctness.

What is genuine, however, is not simply what merely "agrees with" what is fitting, for example, something like a proposition. A proposition is correct, but not genuine—or is it? An ungenuine proposition that does not stem from Aristotle can still be correct—and conversely, an incorrect one can be *genuine*. Thus genuineness says something other than *correctness*, if this term is to be kept for the corresponding of an utterance [*Ausspruch*] to the matter that is addressed.

But, for example, a piece of gold is genuine. A "genuine Dürer," but also a "genuine" phrase of Schiller's. Here "genuine" once again means something else—not at all what is not falsified and stems solely from Dürer or Schiller but rather fitting precisely him and only him, *essentially fitting*. We also speak of what is genuine when we say of a man that he is "genuine" in his dealings.

The genuine is not only what is fitting and appropriate, thus corresponding to what is already existing, but at the same time: the *fittingness* in setting up a measure, genuine in unfolding, true to the origin in staying in *originariness*.

But what does "originariness" mean here? *What* is determined by it? Man, *humanness!* (Inabiding of Da-sein!)

Genuineness is also more essential than *honesty*. Honesty always has to do only with unfolding what is already given and *accessible* (consider the *genuine* and the *plain* and the *simple*).

Genuineness means creative strength for preserving what is given along with [*Mitgegebenen*], creative strength for effecting what is given as a task [*Aufgegebenen*]. Genuineness of the heart [*Gemüt*], of courage, of the attuned-knowing persevering will. Essential patience [is] utmost courage.

Genuineness and *reservedness*—the latter still more originary.

---

* echt; êhaft—gesetzmäßig, filius legitimus; "Ehe" [genuine; held by law—according to law, legitimate son; marriage—Ehe from Old High German ewa: "eternal law"].

236. Truth

Why is there truth? *Is* there truth, and how? If there were no truth, what would be the basis for even the possibility of the Why? Does the Why-question already confirm truth in its existence, that it must somehow be? Questioning as seeking the ground from within and on the basis of which truth is supposed to be. But whence the questioning? Does it not have as its basis man's breaking through an open that opens itself in order to shelter and conceal? And is this, the sheltering that lights up, not what is ownmost to truth? But whence and how does that breakthrough of man into that "other" occur—the "other" that he believes himself to be, what appears to him as his region, and what he nonetheless is not actually, what is rather denied him and dissembled, of which only a shining remains for him (Da-sein)?

But on what is grounded the determination of what is ownmost to truth as the sheltering that lights up? On a hold to ἀλήθεια. But who has ever decisively thought through ἀλήθεια? And from where does the right come for ἀλήθεια as what is handed down to us and simultaneously forgotten? How do we gain a foothold in what is ownmost to truth, without whose foothold everything "that is true" remains only a betrayal? Nothing is gained here by fleeing into the living actuality of a very questionable "life."

This suggests trying to see whether, in the question, Why is truth? truth lets itself be unfolded as the ground of the Why and thus be determined in what is ownmost to it.

But the question nevertheless already seems to be caught—indeterminately and confusingly and ordinarily enough—in a knowing of [*um*] "truth" in order again to question whether appealing to such knowing and opinionating is supportable.

Where are we then staggering, when we let go of appearance and what is common?

How would it be if nonetheless we came into the nearness of enowning, which might be obscured in its essential sway but still shows that a between [*Zwischen*] holds sway, between us and be-ing, and that this between itself belongs to the essential swaying of be-ing?

237. Faith and Truth

What is meant here is not the particular form of belonging to a "confession" but rather what is ownmost to faith, grasped from within what is ownmost to truth.

Faith means holding-for-true. In this sense it means appropriating what is "true," no matter how it is given and can be taken over. In this broad sense it means agreement.

Holding-for-true changes according to what is true (and finally and foremost according to truth and what is its ownmost).

But faith—especially in its open or tacit opposition to knowing—means holding-for-true that which withdraws from knowing in the sense of an explaining intuiting [*erklärende Einsichtnahme*] (even "believing" a report whose "truth" cannot be demonstrated but is vouched for by reporters and witnesses). Even here it becomes clear that in its essentiality this faith depends on the specific manner of knowing that is set against it.

Faith: holding-for-true what is completely withdrawn from any knowing. But what does knowing mean here? What is actual knowing? It is the knowing that knows what is ownmost to truth and accordingly determines it primarily in the turning [*die Kehre*] from within this ownmost.

If what is ownmost to truth is the clearing for the self-sheltering-concealing of be-ing, then knowing-awareness is holding oneself in this clearing of sheltering-concealing and thus is the basic relation to the self-sheltering-concealing of be-ing and to be-ing itself.

Then this knowing-awareness is not a mere holding-for-true something that is true or something that is outstandingly true but rather is originarily *holding oneself within the essential sway of truth.*

This knowing-awareness, essential knowing, is then more originary than any faith, which always refers to something that is true and therefore, if it ever wants to get out of total blindness, must necessarily *know* what true and something true means to it!

Essential knowing is a *holding oneself* within the ownmost [*Wesen*]. This is to say that essential knowing is not a mere representation of an encounter but rather is persevering within the break-through of a projecting-opening which, through enopening, comes to know the very abground that sustains it.

Thus, if one takes "knowing" in the heretofore sense of representation and possession of representation, then of course essential knowing is not a "knowing" but a "faith." However, this word then has an entirely different meaning, no longer that of holding-for-true, whereby truth is already known—even if confusedly—but rather that of holding-oneself-in-truth. And this holding oneself, having the character of a *projecting-open*, is always a questioning, nay *the* originary questioning as such by which man exposes himself to truth and puts what is ownmost up for decision.

Those who question in this manner are the originary and actual believers, i.e., those who take *truth* itself—and not only what is true—seriously and from the ground up, who put to decision whether what is ownmost to truth holds sway and whether this essential swaying itself carries and guides us, the knowing ones, the believing ones, the acting ones, the creating ones—in short, the historical ones.

This originary believing, of course, has nothing in common with accepting that which offers immediate support and renders courage superfluous. Rather, this believing is persevering in the utmost deciding. This alone can once again bring our history to a grounded ground.

For this originary believing is also not a self-seeking grabbing of a self-made security, insofar as, as questioning, it exposes itself precisely to the essential swaying of being and experiences the *necessity* of what is of ab-ground.

d) Time-Space as Ab-ground

238. Time-Space

In what way of questioning is the so-named [time-space] embarked upon?

Time-space as arising from and belonging to the essential sway of truth, as the grounded jointure of removal- and charming-moving-unto, (joining) of the t/here [*Da*]. (Not yet "the parameter" for representing the thing, not yet the mere in itself flux of succession.)

The site for the moment and the strife of world and earth. The strife and sheltering of the truth of enowning.

Time-space and "facticity" of Dasein (cf. *Laufende Anmerkungen zu "Sein und Zeit"* [GA 82], I , *Kapitel* 5!). The inbetween [*das Inzwischen*] of the turning and indeed as, historically, specifically inabiding! It is determined as the now and the here! The *uniqueness* of Da-sein. Hence the uniqueness of knowing standing-steadfast of what is assigned [*Aufgegebenes*] *and* what is given along with [*Mitgegebenes*].

Time — Eternity — Moment

The eternal is not what ceaselessly lasts [*Fort-währende*], but rather that which can withdraw in the moment, in order to return once again. That which can return, not as the *same* but as what transforms unto the new, the one-only, be-ing, such that in this manifestness it is at first not recognized as the same.

Then what does *eternalization* [*Ver-ewigung*] mean?

239. Time-Space*
(Preparatory Consideration)

Space and time, each represented for itself and in the usual connection, themselves arise from time-space, which is more originary than they themselves and their calculatively represented connection. But time-

---

* Cf. Playing-Forth, 108: The Basic Metaphysical Positions within the History of the Guiding-Question and the Interpretation of Time-Space That Belongs to Each of Them (i.e., on space and time); cf. lecture course WS 1935/36, *Die Frage nach dem Ding. Zu Kants Lehre von den transzendentalen Grundsätzen* (GA 41, pp. 14ff.).

space belongs to truth in the sense of the essential enswaying of being as enowning. (At this juncture we need to understand why the point of reference of *Being and Time* shows the way in the crossing.) But the question is how and as what time-space belongs to truth. What truth itself is cannot be sufficiently said in advance for itself but rather merely in grasping time-space.

Time-space is the enowned encleavage of the turning trajectories [*Kehrungsbahnen*] of enowning, of the turning between belongingness and the call, between abandonment by being and enbeckoning (the enquivering of the resonance of be-ing itself!). Nearness and remoteness, emptiness and gifting, fervor and dawdling—all of this dare not be grasped temporally-spatially in terms of the usual representations of time and space but the other way around: within them lies the hidden essential sway of time-space.

But how should this be made accessible to the usual representing of today? For this there are various preparatory ways to go. Indeed, the safest way to go seems to be simply to abandon the heretofore domain of representation of space and time and their conceptual comprehension and to begin anew. But that is not possible, because we are not dealing at all with altering representation and the direction of representation but rather with dis-placing human being into Da-sein. Questioning and thinking must indeed be inceptual, but precisely in the crossing (cf. Playing-Forth).

Being mindful of the descent out of the history [*Geschichte*] of the first beginning (being as beingness—constant presence) is unavoidable. We need to show how it happens that space and time become framing representations (*ordo*-concept) ("forms of intuition") for "mathematical" calculation and why these concepts of space and time dominate all thinking, even and precisely where one speaks of "time as lived-experience" (Bergson among others).

To this end Aristotle's interpretation of τόπος and χρόνος in *Physics* Δ is necessary—and this naturally within the framework of the entire basic position of the *Physics*.

That will show how here the "framing" representation is not—and cannot be—reached at all, since this presupposes the emergence of the "mathematical" in the modern sense. And this, i.e., the corresponding interpretation of space and time, is again possible only after the foundation of this interpretation, the Greek experience of beingness, is lost and then immediately replaced by the Christian interpretation of beings, while keeping the "results" of Aristotle. The disempowering of οὐσία and the emergence of *substantia* have long since been prepared for.

This is what nominalism then accomplishes.

But how with regard to time and space is a metaphysical interpretation still retained and attempted anew, precisely in modernity—space as *sensorium Dei*.

The ambiguity of space and time in Leibniz, their origin unclear, in Kant both simply attributed to human subject!

But of course all of this without any inkling of time-space.

Why and under what presuppositions is the breaking apart of space and time historically necessary?

Once enacted, is there a way out of the breaking-up, back into an other origin? It seems so. For, by retaining the familiar representations of space and time, it always seems as if something "metaphysical" is piled onto these empty forms of *order* (what order?). But the question is still about the legitimacy and source of these empty forms, whose truth is not yet demonstrated on the basis of their correctness and usefulness in the field of *calculation;* the opposite is hereby shown.

On the other hand the return to their source does not lead to the essential origin, to "truth," even if τόπος (spatializing) and χρόνος (which belongs to ψυχή) refer back to φύσις. For this there is no need at all for "mythical representations." For these "mythical representations" are in the end and above all to be grasped as pre-inceptual for the first beginning. If one begins with these representations, then at most one comes to the "triviality" that what is here "irrationally" experienced will later be placed in the light of *ratio.*

But where is the pathway to an initial anticipatory and in fact transitional mindfulness of time-space? In Da-sein's site for the moment. And what about this site, where we are so removed from Da-sein?

Can one attempt to proceed from the question of "unity" of "space and time" according to the usual representation? (Cf. lecture course text of WS 1935/36, introduction). Whence and why and how are both space and time together, for so long? What is the basic experience, one that would not be mastered? (the t/here [*Da*]!). Only superficially, in accordance with the guiding beingness? But how [is] the "and" [meant] for both? Has there ever been an inquiry into that, and *can* there be?

The "and" is in truth the ground of what is ownmost to both, the displacing into the encompassing open—an open which builds presencing and stability [*Bestand*], but without becoming experienceable and groundable. Consider the simultaneous collapse of ἀλήθεια and the ensuing modification into ὁμοίωσις (correctness).

For, the projecting-open that does the experiencing does not occur here in the direction of representing a general essence (γένος) but rather in the originary-historical entry into the site for the moment of Da-sein. To what extent [does] this [occur] in Greek tragedy?

The *site for the moment*, uniqueness and onset of the brightest removal-unto the domain of the hint, out of the gentle charming-moving-unto the self-refusing-hesitating, nearness and remoteness in decision, the "where" and the "when" of being-history, lights up and shelters itself from within enownment of the grounding-attunement of *reservedness*—this and the basic experience of the t/here [*Da*] and thus of time-space.

Now, of course, referring representations of space and time back to attunement seems to be not only a metaphysical aligning of these empty forms, but also at the same time a new "subjectivizing."

But in this regard the following needs to be said:

Because Da-sein is essentially selfhood (ownhood) and because for its part selfhood is the ground of the I and the we and of all lower and higher "subjectivity," therefore the unfolding of time-space out of the site for the moment is not a subjectivizing, but rather its overcoming, if not already a fundamental discarding in advance.

This origin of time-space corresponds to the uniqueness of be-ing as enowning.

The origin brings itself into its open only in and through the occurrence of sheltering truth in accord with the path of sheltering that is in each case necessary.

Time-space as essential swaying of truth (essential swaying of the ground that holds to abground) first comes to knowing-awareness in the enactment of the other beginning. But before that it continues to be concealed—and necessarily so—in the shape of the ungrasped but accustomed way of naming "space" and "time" together.

From where does the priority of the emptiness of space and time originate, of their directly re-presented stretching, of their dimension of quantifiability and calculability?

Everything goes back to the basic Greek experience of the οὐσία, in which space and time are re-presented directly, nay are even *that* in φύσις which thrusts itself forth as *re-presentable in this manner* (regarding time, consider, therefore, the priority of the νῦν).

πέρας and περιέχον are established along with presence. This approach and its interpretation continue, drawing no return to something more originary—which is possible only from within the question *of truth of being.* By contrast, in Aristotle, ποῦ and ποτέ are categories, determinations of beingness, οὐσία!

Regardless of what is then added to this by neo-Platonism, Augustine, and the Middle Ages—by the Christian belief of eternity and of *summum ens*—the basic approach remains and is the foundation for the *mathesis* that prevails in Descartes as the essential guiding-thread for determining beingness. Thus calculability and along with it pure mechanism prevail all the more; and space and time solidify themselves in this interpretation, as stubbornly and as self-evidently as the representation of beingness.

The question concerning their unifying, originary, and completely different essential sway is totally strange, unintelligible, and as such arbitrary.

240. Time and Space: Their "Actuality" and "Source"

"Time" has as little to do with the I as space has to do with the thing; and even more, neither is space "objective" nor is time "subjective."

Belonging to what is ownmost to truth, both are originarily one in time-space, both render the grounding of the t/here [*Da*] — a grounding that holds to abground — a t/here [*Da*] through which selfhood and all that is true about a being is first grounded.

What is bewildering about inquiring into the "actuality" and the "source" of space and time is what distinguishes the horizon within which the guiding-question What is a being? moves in general. See time-space as abground.

241. Space and Time — Time-Space

Space is fundamentally different from time. That in certain respects space is represented as *ordo* and as the encompassing confines of what is extant together indicates that space, when represented in this manner, becomes re-presentable in a making-present (in a certain temporality). But that says nothing about what space itself is. There is no reason to trace it back to "time," because the re-presenting of space is a temporalizing. Rather, both are not only different in the number of usually meant "dimensions," but from the ground up each has what is ownmost to it — and only by virtue of this utmost difference do they refer to their origin, time-space. The more purely what is own-ownmost to each is preserved and the deeper the origin lies, the more successful is the grasping of their essential sway as time-space, which belongs to what is ownmost to truth as clearing ground for sheltering-concealing.

1. As little as the ordinary representation of "timespace" [*Zeitraum/* span of time] accurately grasps what is meant by time-space, nay could even be a starting point for the pathway to the essential sway of time-space,
2. just as little is time-space simply a coupling of space and time in the sense that time, taken as the (t) of calculation, becomes the fourth parameter and thus the four-dimensional "space" of *physics* is established. Here space and time are merely strung together, after both have been leveled off in advance unto the same of what is countable and what makes counting possible.
3. But time-space is also merely a coupling in another, somehow conceivable sense, for example, in the sense that every historical event is "somewhen" and "somewhere" and thus might be temporally and spatially determined.

Rather, the onefold of time and space is the onefold of origin; and this origin is to be pursued only when

1. what is ownmost to each is elucidated as belonging to each and
2. what is ownmost to each is in itself brought into a sharper focus over against the other in its utmost separation and
3. what is ownmost to each is in itself grasped as arising from something originary; and
4. this that is originary is the common root of both as an other to them

but nonetheless such that, as root, it needs both of them as "stems," in order to be a root-grounding ground (what is ownmost to truth).

The interpretation of space and time from within time-space does not intend to demonstrate as "false" the heretofore knowing of space and time. On the contrary, this knowing will be above all relegated to the naturally limited sphere of its accuracy, thus making clear that, considering the essential sway, space and time are as inexhaustible as be-ing itself.

The Ordinary and Now Age-Old Representation of "Timespace" [Span of Time]

What is meant by timespace [*Zeitraum*/span of time] is a determination of time itself and only of time—and not that grounding essential sway that is originarily a one for time and space, as in the word *time-space* [*Zeit-Raum*].

Timespace means a span of "time" which goes from now to then, from then to today, etc.—a "span of time" of a hundred years. Time is represented here as spacious [*geräumig*], insofar as it is a ratio for measuring and encompassing something, a from . . . to, a something measured. Not even figuratively does "timespace" mean that openness of time which belongs to its removals-unto and which is, of course, not "spatial." Thus the ordinary concept of "time" is also represented in the word *timespace* [*Zeitraum*].

One could expect an elucidation of time-space by observing the history of representations of space and time.

But all of these historical expositions, frequently attempted since the nineteenth century, are blind and useless and without real philosophical questioning, apart from the fact that they merely pick the "passages" out of each respective context of inquiry and line them up.

History of these "representations" is the history of the truth of be-ing and can be fruitfully brought into a sharper philosophical focus only along with the history of the guiding-question. Everything else is scholarly pretense, merely misleading even more to the superficiality of collecting and comparing passages.

242. Time-Space as Ab-ground

Ab-ground is the originary essential swaying of ground. Ground is what is ownmost to truth. If time-space is thus grasped as ab-ground and if, in and through turning [*kehrig*], ab-ground is grasped more definitely from within time-space, then the relation-in-turning [*der kehrige Bezug*], and the belongingness of time-space to what is ownmost to truth is thereby enopened.

Abground is the *originary onefold* of space and time, that unifying onefold that above all lets them go apart into their separatedness.

But ab-ground is also beforehand the originary essential sway of ground, of its grounding, of *what is ownmost to truth.*

What is ab-ground? What is *its* manner of grounding? Ab-ground is the staying-away of ground.

And what is ground? It is the self-concealing-receiving, because it is a sustaining—and this as towering-through of what is to be grounded. Ground is self-sheltering-concealing in sustaining that towers-through.

Ab-ground, staying-away, as ground in self-sheltering-concealing, it is a self-sheltering-concealing in the manner of not-granting the ground. However, not-granting is not nothing but rather an outstanding originary manner of letting *be* unfulfilled, of letting *be* empty—thus an outstanding manner of enopening.

However, as essential swaying of ground, ab-ground is not a mere self-refusing as simply pulling back and going away. *Ab*-ground is ab-*ground.* By refusing itself, ground brings into the open in an outstanding manner, namely into that initial openness of *that* emptiness, which is thus already a definite one. Insofar as ground nonetheless also and simply grounds in ab-ground and yet does not actually ground, it is hesitating.

Ab-ground is the hesitating refusal of ground. In refusal, originary emptiness opens, originary *clearing* occurs; but the clearing is at the same time such that the hesitating manifests in it.

Ab-ground is the primarily essential [*erstwesentliche*] *sheltering that lights up,* is the essential swaying of truth.

But since truth is the sheltering of be-ing that lights up, it is, as ab-ground, already beforehand ground which grounds only as a sustaining that lets enowning tower-through. For hesitating refusal is the hint by which Da-*sein*—that is the steadfastness of the sheltering that lights up—is beckoned; and that is the resonance of the turning between "the call" and belongingness, en-*ownment*, be-ing itself.

Truth grounds as truth of enowning. Thus, grasped from within truth as ground, this enowning is the *ur-ground.* As self-sheltering-concealing ur-ground opens only in ab-ground. However, abground is totally dissembled by un-ground (see below).

The ur-ground that grounds is *be-ing,* but always holding sway in its truth.

The more thoroughly the ground (what is ownmost to truth) is engrounded [*ergründet*], the more essentially be-ing holds sway.

But engrounding [*Ergründung*] of ground must venture the leap into ab-ground and must enfathom and withstand the ab-ground.

As staying-away of ground in the sense just mentioned, ab-ground is the primary clearing for what is open as "emptiness."

But which emptiness is meant here? Not what is unoccupied in the forms of ordering and confines for what of space and time is calculable and extant, not the absence of the extant within absence, but rather the emptiness of time-space, the originary gaping open in hesitating self-refusal. Yet, must this hesitating self-refusal not thrust upon a claim, a seeking, an intending-to-go-to [*Hinwollen*], so that it can be a self-refusal? Certainly, but both always hold sway as enowning; and now the only thing that matters is to determine what is ownmost to emptiness itself—that is to say, to think the ab-groundness of abground, i.e., how ab-ground grounds. Actually, that is always to be thought only from within the ur-ground, from enowning, and in enacting the leap into its resonating turning.

As staying away of ground, ab-ground should be the essential sway-ing of truth (of the sheltering that lights up). Staying away of ground—is that not the *absence* of truth? But hesitating self-refusal is exactly clearing for sheltering-concealing and thus presencing of truth. Cer-tainly, "presencing," but not in the manner in which what is extant is present but rather the essential swaying of that which above all grounds presence and absence of a being—and not only that.

"Staying away" as (hesitating) self-refusal of ground is essential swaying of ground as ab-ground. Ground needs ab-ground. And the lightening [*das Lichten*] that occurs in self-refusing is not a mere gaping and yawning open (χάος—vis-à-vis φύσις), but the tuning enjoining of the essential *dis-placings* of merely *what* is lit up, which lets self-shelter-ing enter into it.

And this is so because truth as sheltering that lights up is truth of be-ing as enowning, is enownment that resonates back and forth, which grounds itself in truth (in the essential swaying of the t/here [*Da*]) and gains for itself in truth—and only in it—the clearing for its self-sheltering-concealing.

Enowning attunes—through and through—the essential swaying of truth. The openness of clearing of sheltering-concealing is thus origi-narily not a mere emptiness of not-being-occupied, but rather the attuned and attuning emptiness of the ab-ground, which in accordance with the attuning hint of enowning is an attuned—and that means here an enjoined—ab-ground.

"Emptiness" is also not the mere not-satisfying of an expectation and a wish. It *is* only as Da-*sein*, i.e., as reservedness (cf. Preview, 13: Reserv-edness), as holding back in the face of hesitating refusal, whereby time-space grounds itself as the site for the moment of deciding.

Moreover, "emptiness" is actually the fullness of what is still-unde-cided, what is to be decided, what holds to ab-ground, what points to ground, to the truth of being.

"Emptiness" is the fulfilled distress of the abandonment by being, but this already shifted into what is open and thereby related to the uniqueness of be-ing and its inexhaustibility.

"Emptiness" is not what is given along with a neediness, *its* distress, but rather the distress of reservedness, which in itself is the project-ing-open that breaks out, is the grounding-attunement of the most originary belongingness.

It is, therefore, not appropriate to call "emptiness" that which opens itself in en-ownment of reservedness of hesitating refusal; such naming is still too much determined by the barely surmountable orientation to space as the space of things and to time as the time of flux.

What opens itself for sheltering-concealing is originarily the remote-ness of undecidability whether god moves away from or toward us. That is to say: In this remoteness and its undecidability is manifest the shelter-ing-concealing of that which we, following this enopening, call god.

This "remoteness" of undecidability is prior to any isolated "space" and any distinct lapsing of time. It also holds sway prior to any dimen-sionality. Such [determinations] arise only out of the sheltering of truth and thus of time-space in a being—and indeed initially in what is extant as, and turns into, a thing.

Only when something extant is held onto and fixed does the flow of "time" that flows by the extant arise, only then does the "space" that encompasses the extant arise.

As the primary essential swaying of ground, ab-ground grounds (lets the ground hold sway as ground) in the manner of temporalizing and spatializing.

However, here is the critical juncture for the proper understanding of ab-ground. Temporalizing and spatializing cannot be grasped according to familiar representations of space and time. Rather, conversely, these representations must receive their determination from within their ori-gin in the primarily and essentially temporalizing and spatializing.

Whence do temporalizing and spatializing have their onefold origin and separatedness? Of what kind is the originary onefold that it is thrown apart into this separation? And in what sense are the parted ones here merely a one as the essential swaying of ab-groundness? Here we are not dealing with some kind of "dialectic" but solely with the essential swaying of ground (thus of truth) itself.

Again and again the jointure of this essential swaying must be put into projecting-opening: What is ownmost to truth is the sheltering that lights up. This takes up enowning and, bearing it, lets its resonance soar through the open. Bearing and letting soar, truth is the ground of be-ing. "Ground" is not more originary than be-ing but rather is origin as that which lets this, enowning, arise.

However, truth as ground grounds originarily as ab-ground. And this itself grounds as the onefold of temporalizing and spatializing. Thus these have what is ownmost to them from within that whence ground is ground, from within enowning.

Hint is hesitating self-refusal. Self-refusal creates not only the *empti-ness* of deprivation and awaiting but also, along with these, the empti-ness as an emptiness that is in itself removing-unto, removing unto futurality and thus at the same time breaking open what has been, which bounces back from what is to come and makes up the present as moving into abandonment, but as remembering-awaiting.

But because this abandonment is originarily remembering-expecting (belongingness to being and the call of be-ing), it is in itself no mere sinking and dying away in a not-having, but conversely, it is the present that aims at and is solely carried out into decision: *moment*. The remov-als-unto are shifted into this moment, and this moment itself holds sway only as the gathering of removals-unto.

The *remembering awaiting* (remembering a concealed belongingness to be-ing, awaiting a call of be-ing) puts to decision the whether or not of the onset of be-ing. More clearly: Temporalizing as this joining of (the hesitating) self-refusal grounds the domain of decision, in accord with the ab-ground. However, with the removal-unto what does not grant itself (that is after all what is ownmost to temporalizing), every-thing would already be decided. But what does not grant itself refuses itself hesitatingly; in this manner it grants the possibility of gifting and enownment. Self-refusal enjoins the removal-unto [*Entrückung*] of temporalizing; as *hesitating*, it is at the same time the most originary *charming-moving-unto* [*Berückung*]. This charming-moving-unto is the *encircling hold* [*Umhalt*] in which the moment and thus temporalizing is held (How [is] the *originary* ab-ground [to be thought]? [As] "empti-ness"? Neither emptiness nor fullness). This charming moving-unto admits the possibility of gifting as a swaying possibility and spatializes this possibility. Charming-moving-unto is the spatializing of enowning. Because of charming-moving-unto, abandonment is an abandonment that is firmly in place, one which has to be with*stood*.

"Staying-away" of ground, its ab-groundness, is *attuned* from within hesitating self-refusal; it is above all temporalizing and spatializing, removing-unto and charming-moving-unto. Spatializing grounds and is the site for the moment. As the onefold of originary temporalizing and spatializing, time-space is itself originarily the site for the moment; and this site is the temporality-spatiality of the openness of sheltering-concealing, i.e., of the t/here [*Da*]—a temporality-spatiality that is essential and holds to abground.

Thus from where comes the separatedness in temporalizing and spa-tializing? From the removal-unto and the charming-moving-unto, which are fundamentally different and demand each other from within the onefold of *hesitating refusal*. From where comes the separation of removal-unto and charming-moving-unto? From the hesitating refusal; and this is the *enhinting* as the inceptual essential sway of enowning, inceptual in the other beginning. This essential sway of be-ing is unique and once only, thus sufficing for the innermost essential sway of be-ing; φύσις too is unique and once only.

If that temporalizing and that spatializing [are] the originary essential sway of time and of space, then their source—inhering in ab-ground and grounding the ab-ground—are made manifest from out of the essential sway of being. Time and space (originarily) "are" not, but hold sway.

However, hesitating refusal itself has this originarily unifying joining of not-granting *and* hesitating from the *hint*. This hint is the self-enopening of what shelters and conceals itself as such and indeed the self-enopening for and as en-ownment, as call to belongingness to enowning itself, i.e., to the grounding of Da-sein as the domain of decision for be-ing.

But this *hint* comes to hint only in the echo of be-ing out of the distress of abandonment by being and only means further that enowning opens up neither from within the call nor from within a belongingness but only from within the "between" [*Zwischen*] that resonates both. And it means further that the projecting-open of the origin of time-space as the originary onefold is enactable from within the ab-ground of the ground (the net, cf. Leap, 142: The Essential Sway of Be-ing).

Space is rendering ab-ground that charms-moves unto the encircling hold.

Time is rendering ab-ground that removes unto the gathering.

Charming-moving-unto is the encircling hold of gathering that holds to abground.

Removal-unto is gathering unto the encircling hold that holds to abground.

When removal-unto proves to be gathering and charming-moving-unto proves to be encircling hold, then there is each time therein a counter-turning [*Gegenwendiges*]. For, removal-unto appears to be dispersal, and charming-moving-unto appears to be estranging. This counter-turning is indeed what is essential and indicates the originary referral of both to each other, on the basis of their separatedness.

Time spatializes [*räumt ein*], never charms-moves-unto.

Space temporalizes [*zeitigt ein*], never removes-unto.

But time and space also have nothing in common as a unity; rather what they have is what brings them to a one, that which lets them spring forth *into* that inseparable referral, time-space, the ground's holding to ab-ground: the essential swaying of truth. However, this springing forth is not a tearing-away but the opposite: Time-space is only the prevailing unfolding of the essential swaying of truth.

Thus rendering ab-ground of ground is not exhausted in what is its ownmost but only made clear as the grounding of the t/here [*Da*].

Time-space is the charming-moving-removing-unto gathering encircling hold, is the ab-ground that is so enjoined and correspondingly attuned, whose essential swaying becomes historical in the grounding of the "t/here" [Da] through Da-sein (its essential trajectories of sheltering truth).

In this originary essential sway, time-space still has nothing of what is commonly known as "time" and "space" in themselves, and yet time-space contains in itself the unfolding unto these—and indeed in a far greater richness than could ever ensue from the mathematization of space and time.

How is it that time-space becomes "space and time"?

Asked in this way, the question is still too ambiguous and misconstruable.

The following distinctions have to be made in advance:

1. the enduring history of τόπος and χρόνος in the interpretation of beings as φύσις on the basis of the ununfolded ἀλήθεια (cf. Grounding, 241: Space and Time—Time-Space, pp. 264f.);
2. the unfolding of space and time out of the expressly and originarily grasped time-space as ab-ground of ground within the thinking of the other beginning;
3. the empowering of *time-space* as essential swaying of truth within the future grounding of Dasein by sheltering the truth of enowning into a being that hereby has been reshaped;
4. the actual clarification, resolution, or elimination of the difficulties which for a long time beset what is known as space and time in the heretofore history of thinking—for example, the question concerning the "actuality" of space and of time; their "infinity"; their relation to "things." All these questions remain not only unanswerable but also initially unaskable, as long as space and time are not grasped from within time-space, i.e., as long as the question of *what is ownmost to truth* is not asked from the ground up as the question that leads ahead into the grounding-question of philosophy (How does be-ing hold sway?).

The connection of time-space to space and time and the unfolding of space and time from within time-space can best be elucidated in advance and in part if we attempt to take space and time themselves out of the heretofore interpretation, while still trying—in the direction of this interpretation—to grasp them in their pre-mathematical form. (Cf. *Being and Time*, on the spatiality of Da-sein and on temporality as historicity.)

However, what is crucial is the question: How is it that space and time *allow for* mathematization? The answer lies in being mindful of that occurrence whereby the ab-ground—barely begun to be engrounded—is already buried under the un-ground (cf. the *first* beginning).

The encircling hold of charming-moving-unto has the unclosed expanse of the hidden possibilities of the hint.

The gathering of removal-unto has the unmeasured and measure-repugnant remoteness of what is allotted and given along with [*Mitgegebene*] as a task [*Aufgegebene*].

The open of the ab-ground is not groundless. Ab-ground is not—like a groundlessness—the no to every ground but rather the yes to the ground in its hidden expanse and remoteness.

Ab-ground is thus the in-itself temporalizing-spatializing-counter resonating site for the moment of the "between," [*Zwischen*] as which Da-sein must be grounded.

Ab-ground is as little "negative" as the hesitating refusal; taken directly (in a "logical" sense), both *do* contain a "no"; and yet, hesitating refusal is the first and utmost shining of the hint.

Grasped more originarily, a "not" *does* hold sway in hesitating refusal. However, this is the originary "not" that belongs to be-ing itself and thereby to enowning.

The other way, from "space" and from "time" (cf. above pp. 270f. and section 241: Space and Time—Time-Space):

The other way is most securely to be taken in such manner as to interpret and make manifest the spatiality and temporality of the thing, of the tool, of the work, of machination, and of all beings—all as sheltering of truth. Projecting this interpretation open is implicitly determined by the knowing-awareness of time-space as ab-ground. But proceeding from the thing, the interpretation itself must awaken new experiences. The suggestion that we may be dealing with a self-evident description in itself is not dangerous, because this way of interpretation intends to work out space and time in the direction of time-space. The way that begins here and the way that begins with a being have to come together. Following the way that begins with a "being" (but already shifted into the open of the strife of earth and world) then offers the opportunity for enjoining the heretofore discussion of space and time with the inceptual encounter (cf. Playing-Forth).

e) The Essential Swaying of Truth as Sheltering

243. Sheltering

Leaving completely out of consideration that truth is never extant, sheltering is not a subsequent housing of the truth as extant in itself within a being.

Sheltering belongs to the essential swaying of truth. This truth *is* not essential swaying if it never holds sway in sheltering.

Therefore, when by way of indicating "what is ownmost" to truth is called clearing for self-sheltering, then this happens only in order first to unfold the essential swaying of truth. The clearing must ground itself into its open. Clearing needs that which keeps it in openness, and that

is in each case a different being (thing—tool—work). But this sheltering of what is open must at the same time and in advance be such that
the openness comes to be in such a way that self-sheltering and thereby
be-ing holds sway in it.

Thus it must be possible—with, of course, the corresponding leap
ahead into be-ing—to find the way from "a being" to the essential
swaying of truth and in this way to make manifest the *sheltering* as
belonging to truth. But where should this way begin? For that, do we
not have first to grasp today's relations to a being, as we reside within it,
i.e., put what is most ordinary before our eyes? And this is exactly what
is most difficult, because it cannot even be carried out without a shock,
and that is to say: without a displacing of the basic relation to be-ing
itself and to truth (cf. Preview, 5: For the Few and the Rare, on philosophical knowledge, pp. 9f.).

It must be shown in which truth a being stands—and how it respectively stands in this truth. It must become clear how here world and
earth are in strife and how this strife and thereby earth and world
themselves unconceal and conceal. But this nearest self-sheltering-concealing is only the preliminary shining of ab-ground and thus of the
truth of enowning. But truth sways in the fullest and richest clearing of
the remotest self-sheltering-concealing and only in the manner of sheltering, according to all ways and manners that belong to this sheltering
and that historically bear and guide the inabiding sustaining of Da-sein
and so make up being-a-people.

Sheltering also definitely and always shifts the self-sheltering-concealing into what is open, in the same way in which it is itself perme-
ated by the *clearing* of self-sheltering-concealing (for demonstration of
this interconnection, see the Frankfurt lectures, 1936*).

Therefore, from the start this projecting-opening of what is ownmost
to truth leaves no room for a still plausible reinterpretation of the Platonic relationship. For sheltering of truth in a being—does that not
remind one all too clearly of the shaping of "idea," of εἶδος into ὕλη?
However, even the phrase "sheltering of truth into a being" is misleading, as if truth could ever beforehand already be for itself "truth."

Truth holds sway always already and only as Da-sein and thereby as
the strifing of the strife. (On the origin of the differentiation of εἶδος-
ὕλη, see also the above-named lectures.)

However, understanding the prevailing interconnections here requires
that one frees oneself, from the ground up, from the simple way of think-
ing-re-presenting what is present (from being as presence and truth as
approximation to what is present) and that one fixes thinking's glance in

---

* *Der Ursprung des Kunstwerkes*, in: *Holzwege* (GA 5).

such a way that this glance traverses above all the whole essential swaying of truth.

244. Truth and Sheltering*

Whence does sheltering have its distress and necessity? From within the self-sheltering-concealing. In order not to eliminate this, but rather to preserve it, this *occurrence* needs to be sheltered. The occurrence is transformed and preserved (why) in the strife of *earth and world.* The strifing of the strife puts truth into work—into tool—experiences truth as thing, accomplishes truth in deed and sacrifice.

However, there must always be preservation of self-sheltering-concealing. For only in this manner does the history that is grounded in terms of Dasein remain in enownment and thus belong to be-ing.

245. Truth and Sheltering**

Projecting-opening and executing belong, each in its own way, to any sheltering of truth into a being.

Every *projecting-opening* is storm, bliss, verve, moment. Every *execution* is releasement, perseverance, renunciation (grasped in terms of ownedness; and the form of disownedness that belongs to it; what is precisely *not* ownmost?). Neither of the two occurs without co-attuning by the other, and both always occur out of the ground of the necessity of a sheltering.

Sheltering truth as growing back into the closedness of earth. This growing-back is never accomplished in mere re-presentings and feelings but always in procuring, manufacturing, laboring—in short, in letting worlding of a world occur, supposing that this does not deviate into mere occupation.

Increasing utilization of technicity not only develops technicity itself but also immeasurably and unceasingly increases its power, if there is not a *still* greater and more essential mindfulness of the grounding of Da-sein as a necessity which demands stillness and long-lasting preparedness for the hesitating suddenness of moments.

246. Sheltering of Truth in What Is True

Sheltering is basically preserving enowning by strifing of strife.

Preserving self-sheltering-concealing (hesitating refusal) is no mere preserving of a given but a binding that projects-open into what is open, bestrifing the *strife,* in whose steadfastness belongingness to enowning is enstrifed.

---

* Cf. Preview, 21: Inceptual Thinking (Projecting-Open).
** Cf. Preview, 35 and 39: Enowning.

Thus truth holds sway as the true that is always sheltered. But what is true is only what it is as the un-true, non-being and un-grounded at the same time.

Making sheltering of truth accessible out of its nearest manner of *caring-for,* corresponding to space and time.

247. Grounding Da-sein and
Trajectories of Sheltering Truth

Taken from this domain and therefore belonging here [is] the specific question concerning the "origin of the work of art" (cf. the Freiburg and Frankfurt lectures*).

The Machine and Machination (Technicity)

The machine, what is its ownmost, the service that it demands, the uprooting that it brings. "Industry" (operations); industrial workers, torn from homeland and history, exploited for profit.

Machine-training; machination and business. What recasting of man gets started here? (World—earth?) Machination and business. The large number, the gigantic, pure extension and growing leveling off and emptying. Falling necessarily victim to trash and to what is sham.

---

* *Der Ursprung des Kunstwerkes,* in: *Holzwege* (GA 5).

VI. The Ones to Come*

* Cf. *Überlegungen* V, 44f.; VII, 47f. [GA 94].

248. The Ones to Come

[The ones to come are] those strangers of like mind who are equally decided for the gifting and refusing that has been allotted to them. Mace bearers of the truth of be-ing, in which a being is uplifted to the simple mastery that prevails in every thing and every breath. The stillest witness to the stillest stillness, in which an imperceptible tug turns the truth back, out of the confusion of all calculated correctness into what is ownmost: keeping sheltered what is most sheltered, the enquivering of the passing of the decision of gods, the essential swaying of be-ing.

The ones to come: the lingering and long-hearing founders of this essential sway of truth. Those who withstand the thrust of be-ing.

The ones to come* are those of the future toward whom, as the ones who are retrospectively expected—in sacrificing reservedness—the hint and onset of distancing and nearing of the last god advances.

These ones to come need to be prepared for. Inceptual thinking serves this preparation as silent reticence of enowning. But thinking is only *one* way in which the few venture the leap into be-ing.

249. The Grounding-Attunement of the Ones to Come**

Echo and playing-forth, leap and grounding, each have their guiding-attunement, which attune originarily together from within the grounding-attunement.

But this grounding-attunement is not to be described so much as to be effected within the whole of inceptual thinking.

But this grounding-attunement can hardly be named with *one* word, unless it be with the word *reservedness*. But then this word must be taken in the whole original fullness which accrues historically to its meaning from within the enthinking of enowning.

Grounding-attunement contains being-attuned—the spirit of courage as the attuned-knowing will of enowning.

The guiding-attunements are attuned and attune to one another in accord.

The *guiding-attunement of echo* is the *shock* of disclosing be-ing's abandonment and at the same time the *deep awe* before the resonating enowning. Shock and deep awe together first let the echo be enacted in thinking.

The originary accord of the guiding-attunements is fully attuned primarily through grounding-attunement. The ones to come *are* in that

---

* Cf. Preview, 45: The "Decision."
** Cf. Preview, 5: For the Few and the Rare, pp. 9ff.

grounding-attunement; and as so attuned, they are destined by the last god. (For what is essential about attunement, see the Hölderlin lectures.*)

250. The Ones to Come

They reside in masterful knowing, as what is truthful knowing. Whoever attains this knowing-awareness does not let himself be computed and coerced. Besides, this knowing-awareness is useless and has no "value"; it does not count and cannot be directly taken as a condition for the current enterprise.

With what must knowing-awareness of those who truly know commence? With *actual historical* knowledge—that is, with knowing-awareness of the domain and with inabiding (questioning) in the domain out of which future history is decided. This historical knowledge never consists in stating and describing current circumstances and grouping of events and their fostered goals and claims. This knowing is aware of the hours of the occurrence that history actually builds.

Our hour is the epoch of going-under.

Taken in its essential sense, going-under means going along the path of the reticent preparing for those who are to come, for the moment, and for the site, in all of which the decision of the arrival and staying-away of gods falls. This going-under is the very first of the first beginning. But what is *not* ownmost to going-under takes its own course and goes another way—and is an abating, a no-longer-being-able-to-do, ceasing, after the appearance of the gigantic and massive and following the priority of establishment over against that which should fulfill it.

Those who *are going-under* in the essential sense are those who are suffused with what is coming (what is futural) and sacrifice themselves to it as its future invisible ground. They are the inabiding ones who ceaselessly expose themselves to questioning.

The epoch of going-under is knowable only to those who belong. All others must fear the going-under and therefore deny and repudiate it. For to *them* going-under is only weakness and a termination.

Those who truly go-under do not know gloomy "resignation," which no longer wills, because it wills nothing of the future; and just as little does the noisy "optimism" which in spite of all guarantee does not yet truly will, because it closes itself off from willing to go beyond itself and to acquire itself only through transformation.

Those who go-under are the ones who constantly question. Disquiet of questioning is not an empty insecurity, but the enopening and fostering of that stillness which, as gathering unto the most question-worthy

---

* Lecture course WS 1934/35, *Hölderlins Hymnen "Germanien" und "Der Rhein"* (GA 39); lecture course WS 1941/42, *Hölderlins Hymne "Andenken"* (GA 52); lecture course SS 1942, *Hölderlins Hymne "Der Ister"* (GA 53) [trans. W. McNeill and J. Davis, *Hölderlin's Hymn "The Ister"* (Bloomington: Indiana University Press, 1996)].

(enowning), awaits the simple intimacy of the call and withstands the utmost fury of the abandonment of being.

Inquiring into the essential sway of truth and into the essential swaying of be-ing—what else is it but resoluteness to utmost mindfulness? But this resoluteness grows out of the openness for what is necessary, which renders unavoidable the experience of distress of abandonment by being. But experience of this distress again depends on the magnitude of the strength for remembering—on the whole, on the masterfulness of knowing-awareness.

Questioning of this kind is the reservedness of seeking where and how the truth of being lets itself be grounded and sheltered.

Seeking is never a mere *not-yet*-having, a deprivation. Seen in this way, it is calculated only in view of the result attained. Initially and in actuality, seeking is proceeding into the domain in which truth is enopened or refused. In itself seeking is futural and a coming-into-the-nearness of being. Seeking brings the seeker first to *its self,* i.e., into the selfhood of Da-sein, in which clearing and sheltering-concealing of beings occur.

Self-being is the find that already lies *in* the seeking, the secure lighting that lights up ahead of all revering, by virtue of which alone we are open to the echo of the most unique and greatest.

251. What Is Ownmost to a People and to Da-sein[*]

A people is *only* a people when it receives its history as apportioned in the finding of its god—that god who pressures the people to go beyond itself and thus to become a being. Only then does a people avoid the danger of circling round itself and of idolizing as its *unconditioned* what are only conditions for its existence. But how should a people find god, if those do not exist who *for* its sake silently *seek* and, as these seekers, even apparently stand up *against* that which in "people" does *not yet* fit a people! These seekers themselves, however, must above all *be;* they are to be prepared for as beings. Da-sein: What is it other than *grounding* the being of *these* beings, grounding the being of the ones to come who belong to the last god?

What is ownmost to a people is grounded in the historicity of those who belong to *themselves out of* belongingness to god. From within enowning, wherein this belongingness is historically grounded, first arises the foundation for why "life" and body, procreation and sex, and lineage—said fundamentally: the earth—belong to history and in their own way again take history back into themselves, and in all of that serve only the strife of earth and world, born up by the innermost deep

---

[*] Cf. Grounding: Dasein; cf. *Überlegungen* V, 35f. [GA 94].

awe of always being unconditioned. For what is their ownmost is always near to enowning because inherently bound to strife.

252. Da-sein and the Ones to Come
Who Belong to the Last God

This god will set up the simplest but utmost opposition over its people as the paths on which this people wanders beyond itself, in order to find once again what is its ownmost and to exhaust the moment of its history.

World and earth in their *strife* will raise love and death into their utmost and will bring love and death together into fidelity to god and will withstand the maze—in the manifold mastering of the truth of beings.

The ones who are to come and belong to the last god will enstrife enowning in the strifing of this strife and, in the widest retrospect, will remind themselves of the greatest thing that is created: the enfilled onceness and uniqueness of being. Next to it the massive will release all rankings of its raving and will carry off all that is insecure and half-way, all that consoles itself merely with the heretofore. Will then the time of gods be *up* and the relapse into the mere living of beings who are *world*-poor begin, for whom earth remains only something to be exploited?

Reservedness and reticence in silence will be the innermost feast of the last god; they will achieve their own way of entrusting the simplicity of things and their own surging of the intimacy of charming-moving-unto removal-unto of their works; the sheltering of truth will leave sheltered and concealed what is most sheltered-concealed and will thus lend to it the uniquely present.

Today there are already a few of those who are to come. Their intimating and seeking is hardly recognizable to *them* themselves and to their genuine disquiet; but this disquiet is the quiet steadfastness of the cleavage. It bears a certainty that is touched by the shiest and remotest hint of the last god and is held toward the breaking-in of enowning. How this hint is preserved as hint in the reserved reticence in silence, and how such preserving always resides in taking-leave and arriving, particularly in grief *and* joy, in that grounding-attunement of the reserved ones, to whom alone the cleavage of be-ing opens and closes: fruit and falling-toward, onset *and* hint.

Those few to come count among themselves the essentially unpretentious ones, to whom no publicness belongs but who in their inner beauty gather the shining-ahead of the last god and then gift it to the few and the rare by radiating it back to them. They all ground *Da-sein*, through which the accord of the nearness of god resonates, a nearness which neither rises above itself nor fades away but has taken the steadiness of the deepest awe for the most singular space of resonance. Da-sein—shifting through all relations of remoteness and nearness (onset) of the last god.

The unfittingness of what is only a being, the not-being in the whole, and the seldomness of being—this is why one seeks gods *among* beings. If one seeks and does not find and therefore is coerced into the constrained machinations, [then there is] no freedom for reserved waiting for and being-able-to-await an encounter and a hint. Considering the nobility of the joining and the vigor of the trust in the hint and the unfurling fury of the frightful, let Da-sein be the *innermost order,* out of which *strifing* above all obtains its law. The strifing outshines whatever is encountered and above all allows us to experience the simpleness of what is essential. Order is the simplest self-showing and is easily falsely seen as something "next to" and "above" the appearances, i.e., *not* seen.

The ones who are to come are those who inabide in the spirit of reservedness within grounded Da-sein and the only ones to whom being (the leap) comes as enowning, enowns them, and empowers them for sheltering its truth.

Hölderlin [is] their poet who comes from afar and therefore the poet most futural of the ones to come. Hölderlin is the most futural of the ones to come because he comes from the farthest away; and coming from so far away, he *traverses* and transforms what is the greatest.

VII. The Last God

> The totally other over against gods
> who have been, especially over against
> the Christian God.

253. The Last

The last is that which not only needs the longest fore-runnership but also itself *is:* not the ceasing, but the deepest beginning, which reaches out the furthest and catches up with itself with the greatest of difficulty.

Therefore, the "last" withdraws from all calculation and therefore must be able to bear the burden of the loudest and most frequent misinterpretation. Otherwise, how could it continue to be "the surpassing" [*das Überholende*]?

Given that as yet we barely grasp "death" in its utmost, how are we then ever going to be primed for the rare hint of the last god?

254. Refusal

We move into the time-space of decision of the flight and arrival of gods. But how does this happen? Will one or the other become a future occurrence, must one or the other determine the growing awaiting? Or is decision the enopening of a completely other time-space for a—nay, *the* first—grounded truth of be-ing, enowning?

What if that domain of decision as a whole, flight or arrival of gods, were itself the end? What if, beyond that, be-ing in its truth would have to be grasped for the first time as enownment, as that which enowns what we call *refusal?*

That is neither flight nor arrival, and also not flight *and* arrival, but rather something originary, the fullness of granting be-ing in refusal. Herein is grounded the origin of the future style, i.e., of reservedness in the truth of be-ing.

Refusal is the highest nobility of gifting and the basic thrust of self-sheltering-concealing, revelation [*Offenbarkeit*] *of which* makes up the originary essential sway of the truth of be-ing. Only thus does be-ing become estranging itself, the stillness of the passing of the last god.

But Da-sein is enowned in be-ing as the grounding of the guardianship of this stillness.

Flight and arrival of gods now together move into what has been and are withdrawn from what is past.

But the futural, the truth of be-ing as refusal, contains within itself the ensuring of greatness, not magnitude of empty and gigantic eternity, but of the shortest pathway.

But to this truth of be-ing, to refusal, belongs the masking of what is not-being as such, the unboundedness and dissipation of be-ing. Only now must abandonment by being remain. But unboundedness is not empty arbitrariness and disorder. On the contrary: Everything is now trapped in planned steerability and exactitude of a secure execution and an "exhaustive" control. Under the illusion of a being, *machination* takes what is not-being into the protection of a being; and thereby the unavoidably enforced desolation of man is made up for by *"lived-experience."*

As what is not ownmost, all of this must become even more necessary than before, because what is most estranging also needs what is most current and the cleavage of be-ing should not collapse under the contrived illusion of adjustments, of "happiness" and pseudo-completion; for the last god especially hates [*hasset*] all of this.

But the *last* god, is that not debasing god, nay *the* greatest blasphemy? But what if the last god has to be so named because in the end the decision about gods brings under and among gods and thus makes what is ownmost to the uniqueness of the divine being [*Gottwesen*] most prominent?

If we think calculatively here and take this "last" merely as ceasing and the end, instead of as the utmost and briefest decision about what is highest, then of course all knowing awareness of the last god is impossible. But in thinking the divine being, how should one intend to reckon, instead of being all-around mindful of the danger of what is estranging and incalculable?

255. Turning in Enowning*

Enowning has its innermost occurrence and its widest reach in the turning [*die Kehre*]. The turning that holds sway in enowning is the sheltered ground of the entire series of turnings, circles, and spheres, which are of unclear origin, remain unquestioned, and are easily taken in themselves as the "last" (consider, e.g., the turning in the jointure of the guiding-questions and the circle of under-standing).

What is this originary turning in enowning? Only the onset of be-ing as enownment of the t/here [*Da*] leads Da-*sein* to itself and thus to the enactment (sheltering) of the inabiding and grounded truth into a being which finds its site in the lit-up sheltering-concealing of the t/here [*Da*].

And *within the turning:* Only the grounding of Da-*sein*, preparing the preparedness for the charming-moving-unto removal-unto the truth of be-ing, brings what hears—and in listening belongs—to the hint of the befalling enownment.

When *through* enowning, Da-sein—as the open midpoint of the selfhood that grounds truth—is thrown unto *itself* and becomes a self, then

---

* Here enowning is seen with regard to man, who is determined as Dasein from within it [enowning].

Dasein as the sheltered possibility of grounding the essential swaying of be-ing must in return belong to enowning.

And within the turning: Enowning must need Dasein and, needing it, must place it into the call and so bring it before the passing of the last god.

Turning holds sway between the call (to the one belonging) and the belonging (of the one who is called). Turning is counter-turning [*Wider-kehre*]. *The call unto* leaping-into enownment is the grand stillness of the most sheltered and concealed self-knowing.

All language of Da-sein has its origin here and is therefore essentially stillness (cf. reservedness, enowning, truth, and language).

As counter-turning enowning "is" thus the highest mastery over the coming-toward and the flight of the gods who have been. The utmost god needs be-ing.

The *call* is befalling *and* staying-away in the mystery of enownment.

The hints of the last god are at play in the turning as onset and stay-ing-away of the arrival and flight of gods and their places of mastery.

The law of the last god is hinted at in these hints, the law of the great individuation in Da-sein, of the aloneness of the sacrifice, of the unique-ness of choosing the shortest and steepest pathway.

In the sway of hinting lies the mystery of the onefold of the innermost nearing in the utmost distancing, traversing the widest free play of the time-space of be-ing. This utmost essential swaying of be-ing requires the innermost distress of abandonment by being.

This distress must belong to [*zugehörig*] the call of the mastery of that hinting. What resounds and spreads widely from within such belonging [*Hörigkeit*] is capable of preparing the strife of earth and world, for the truth of the t/here [*Da*] — and through the t/here [*Da*] — the site above all for the moment of decision, and so for the strifing and thus for the sheltering in a being.

Whether *this call* of the utmost hinting, the most hidden enownment, nevertheless ever happens openly, or whether the distress grows silent and all mastery stays away; whether the call is still received when it occurs; whether the leaping into Da-*sein* and thus turning from within its truth still becomes history—all of that decides about the future of man. Man with his machinations might for centuries yet pillage and lay waste to the planet, the gigantic character of this driving might "develop" into something unimaginable and take on the form of a seeming rigor as the massive regulating of the desolate as such—yet the greatness of be-ing continues to be closed off, because decisions are no longer made about truth and untruth and what is their ownmost. The only thing that still counts is the reckoning of succeeding and failing of machinations. This reckoning extends itself to a presumed "eternity"—which is no eternity but rather only the endless etcetera of what is most desolately transitory.

Wherever truth of be-ing is not willed—not shifted into the will of knowing awareness and experience, i.e., into questioning—all time-space is withdrawn from the *moment*, as from the en-lightning [*Erblitzen*] of be-ing out of steadfastness of the simple and never calculable enowning.

Or else the moment still belongs only to the most alone alonenesses, to whom, however, a grounding understanding of inaugurating a history is denied.

But these moments, and they alone, can turn into the preparedness in which the turning of enowning unfolds unto and joins the truth.

And yet: Only the purest perseverance within what is uncoercively simple and essential is ripe for preparing such a preparedness, never the transitoriness of the hurrying and self-surpassing machinations.

256. The Last God*

The last god has its *essential swaying* within the hint, the onset and staying-away of the arrival as well as the flight of the gods who have been, and within their sheltered and hidden transformation. The last god is not enowning itself; rather, it needs enowning as that to which the founder of the t/here [*Dagründer*] belongs.

This hint, as enowning, places a being into the utmost abandonment by being and at the same time radiates the truth of being as the inner-most shining of that abandonment.

Within the domain of the mastery of the hint, earth and world come together anew for the simplest strife: purest closure [*Verschlossenheit*] and utmost transfiguration, the most gracious charming moving-unto and the most terrifying removal-unto. And this again and again only histor-ically in the stages and domains and degrees of sheltering truth in a being, by which alone—within the boundless but dissembled extin-guishing into not-being—a being becomes more-being.

In such essential swaying of the hint, be-ing itself comes to its *full-ness*. Fullness is preparedness for becoming a fruit and a gifting. Herein holds sway what is the *last*, the *essential end*, *required* out of the begin-ning but not carried out in it. Here the innermost finitude of be-ing reveals itself: in the hint of the last god.

In the fullness, in the vigor for the fruit and the greatness of gifting, there lies at the same time the *most hidden and most sheltered* essential sway of the *not*, as not-yet and no-longer.

It is here that the intimacy of the swaying-into [*Einwesung*] of the nihilating in be-ing is intimated. However, in accord with the essential swaying of be-ing within the play of the onset and staying-away, the *not* itself—and accordingly also the *nothing*—assumes various shapes of its

---

* Cf. Leap, 142: The Essential Sway of Be-ing; Leap, 146: Be-ing and Not-Be-ing; Pre-view, 45: The "Decision."

truth. If this is reckoned only "logically" as negating a being in the sense of what is extant (cf. the marginal notes in the personal copy of *What is Metaphysics?*) and explained superficially and literally—in other words, if the inquiry never enters the domain of the question of *be-ing*—then all objections to the question concerning nothing is futile gossip, which remains deprived of any possibility of ever penetrating the domain of decision of the question concerning the most essential finitude of be-ing.

But this domain is enterable only by virtue of preparing for a long intimating of the last god. And those of the last god who are to come are prepared *only* and above all by those who find, traverse, and build the way *back* from the experienced abandonment by being. Without the sacrifice of those who are on the way back [*die Rückwegigen*], there would not even be dawning of the possibility of the hinting of the last god. Those who are on the way back are the true forerunners [*Vorläufer*] of those who are to come.

(But those who are on the way back are also totally other than the many who only "re-act" [*die Re-aktiven*], whose "action" is consumed solely by the blind clinging to the heretofore, briefly seen by them. What has been as it reaches over into the futural, as well as the futural in its call to what has been—this has never been manifest to them.)

The last god has its most unique uniqueness and stands outside those calculating determinations meant by titles such as "mono-theism," "pan-theism," and "a-theism." "Monotheism" and all types of "theism" exist only since Judaeo-Christian "apologetics," which has metaphysics as its intellectual presupposition. With the death of this god, all theisms collapse. The multitude of gods cannot be quantified but rather is subjected to the inner richness of the grounds and abgrounds in the site for the moment of the shining and sheltering-concealing of the hint of the last god.

The last god is not the end but the other beginning of immeasurable possibilities for our history. For its sake history up to now should not terminate but rather must be brought to its end. We must bring about the transfiguration of its essential and basic positions in crossing and in preparedness.

Preparation for the appearing of the last god is the utmost venture of the truth of be-ing, by virtue of which alone man succeeds in restoring beings.

The greatest nearness of the last god is enowned when enowning as hesitating self-refusal increases in *not-granting*. This is something essentially other than mere absence. Not-granting as belonging to enowning can be experienced only out of the more originary essential sway of be-ing, as it lights up in the thinking of the other beginning.

Not-granting as nearness of the un-avertable makes Da-*sein* the one who is overcome; that is to say: not-granting does not crush Da-sein but lifts it up into grounding its freedom.

But whether man can master both, sustaining the echo of enowning as not-granting *and* enacting the crossing to grounding the freedom of a being as such — to renewing the world out of rescuing the earth — who is inclined to decide and to know? And so, those who are consumed by such a history and its grounding always remain separated from one another — summits of the most separate mountains.

The utmost remoteness of the last god in not-granting is a unique kind of nearness, a relation that dare not be distorted and abolished by any "dialectic."

But the nearness echoes in the echo of be-ing out of the experience of distress of abandonment by being. However, this experience is the first burst of the storm into Da-sein. For only when man comes from this distress does he bring to light the necessities and with these above all the freedom of belongingness to exultation of be-ing.

Only one who thinks too short, i.e., does not actually *think*, remains caught in that place where a refusal and negation exercise pressure in order to take that as an occasion for despair. But this always proves that we have not yet envisaged the full turning of be-ing, in order to find therein the measure for Da-sein.

Not-granting distresses Da-sein to itself as grounding the site for the *first* passing of god, as a god that does not-grant itself. Only from out of this moment can one assess how be-ing, as the domain of enowning of that distressing, must restore a being, in which mastery of a being the honoring of god must be enacted.

Standing in this struggle for the last god, and that means for grounding the truth of be-ing as the time-space of stillness of its passing (we are not capable of struggling for god itself), we necessarily stand in the power-domain of be-ing as enownment and thus in the utmost expanse of the sharpest maelstrom of the turning.

We must prepare the grounding of truth; and that looks as if thereby honoring and preserving the last god is already predetermined. At the same time we must know and be bound by how sheltering of truth in a being and thus the history of preserving god is required above all by god itself and by the manner in which it needs us as founders of t/here-being [*Da-seinsgründende*]. What is required is not only a table of command-ments but more originarily and essentially that god's passing demands a steadfastness from a being and thus from man in the midst of beings — a steadfastness in which a being above all withstands the passing, thus does not stop it, but rather lets it reign as passing, always in the simplic-ity of what is regained as ownmost to a being (as work, tool, thing, deed, view, and word).

Here no redemption takes place — which is basically a subduing of man—but rather a *letting-into* [*Einsetzung*] of what is more originarily ownmost (grounding of Da-sein) in be-ing itself: the recognition of the belongingness of man into be-ing through god, the admission by god that it needs be-ing, an admission that does not relinquish god or its greatness.

That belongingness to be-ing and this needing of be-ing above all reveals be-ing in its self-sheltering-concealing as that turning [*kehrige*] midpoint in which belongingness surpasses the need and the need towers over the belongingness: be-ing as en-owning, which happens out of its own turning [*kehrigen*] overflowing and so becomes the origin for the strife between god and man, between the passing of god and the history of man.

All beings, regardless of how obtrusively and uniquely and independently and persistently they might appear to the god-less and inhuman calculating and operating, are just entry into and staying-in [*Herein-stand*] enowning, in which (the entry-into and staying-in) the site for the passing of the last god and the guardianship of man seek a steadiness in order to continue to be prepared for enownment and not to ward off be-ing—what indeed the heretofore beings in the heretofore truth had exclusively to do.

Enthinking of the truth of be-ing succeeds only when, within the passing of god, the empowering of man to god's necessity becomes manifest and thus the en-ownment in the overflow of turning between human belongingness and divine needing comes into the open—in order that the self-sheltering-concealing of enownment prove to be the midpoint and enownment prove to be the midpoint of self-sheltering-concealing, in order to foster deep resonance and thus to give rise to freedom as freedom unto the ground of be-ing, as grounding of the t/here [*Da*].

The last god is the beginning of the longest history on its shortest path. Long preparation is needed for the great moment of its passing. And for preparedness for god, peoples and states are too small, i.e., already too much torn from all growth and nonetheless delivered over only to machination.

Only the great and unrevealed individuals will provide the stillness for the passing of the god and among themselves for the reticent accord of those who are prepared.

Be-ing as the most unique and most rare over against the nothing will have withdrawn from the massivity of beings; and all history, when it descends into what is its own ownmost, will serve only this withdrawal of being into its full truth. But everything public will chase after and revel in its successes and failures, in order—in conformity with its kind—*not* to have *any* inkling of what is happening. The few and their bands seek and find themselves only between this massive way of being

and what is actually sacrificed in order to intimate that something sheltered, i.e., the passing, befalls them—despite every event's incessant
straining into what is fast and at the same time completely grabbable
and exhaustively consumable. The reversal and mistaking of the claims
and the domains of claims will no longer be possible, because the truth
of be-ing itself, in the most acute non-inclusion of its cleavage, has
brought the essential possibilities to decision.

This historical moment is no "ideal-state," because an ideal-state
always runs counter to what is ownmost to history. Rather, this moment
is the enownment of that turning in which the truth of be-ing comes to
the be-ing of truth, since god needs be-ing and man as Da-sein must
have grounded the belongingness to be-ing. Then, for this moment,
be-ing as the innermost "between" is like the nothing; god overpowers
man and man surpasses god—in immediacy, as it were, and yet both
only in enowning, which is what the truth of be-ing itself is.

However, until this incalculable moment, which, incidentally, can
never be something as superficial as a "goal," there will be a long and
very relapsing and exceedingly hidden history. It is only hour by hour
and in the reservedness of care that the creating ones must prepare
themselves for guardianship within the time-space of that passing. And
thinking mindfulness of this singularity—the truth of be-ing—can be
only a pathway on which what cannot be thought in advance is nevertheless thought, i.e., transformation of the relation of man to the truth
of be-ing has begun.

With the question of be-ing, which has overcome the question of
beings and thus all "metaphysics," the torch is lit and the first attempt is
made for the long run. Where is the runner who takes up the torch and
carries it to his forerunner? All runners must be *fore*-runners; and the
later they come, the stronger *fore*-runners they must be—no followers,
who at most only "correct" and refute what is first-attempted. The
fore-runners must be *inceptual*, more and more originarily inceptual
than the ones who run "ahead" (i.e., who run behind them) and must
more simply, more richly, and unconditionally and uniquely think the
one and the same of what is to be questioned. What they take over by
taking hold of the torch cannot be what is said as "doctrine" and "system" and the like, but rather what obliges [*das Gemußte*], as that which
opens itself only to those whose origin is in the abground and who are
one of the compelled.

But what compels is solely the incalculable and unmakeable of
enowning, the truth of be-ing. Blessed is the one who dares to belong
to the unblessedness of be-ing's cleavage in order to be the one who
hears the always inceptual dialogue of the solitary ones, to whom the
last god beckons because in its passing it is enbeckoned by them.

The *last* god is not an end but rather the beginning as it resonates unto and in-itself and thus the highest shape of not-granting, since the inceptual withdraws from all holding-fast and holds sway only in towering over all of that which as what is to come is already seized within the inceptual—and is delivered up to its [the inceptual's] determining power.

The end *is* only where a being has torn itself away from the truth of be-ing and has denied every question-worthiness, and that means every differentiating, in order to comport itself in endless time within endless possibilities of what is thus torn away. The end is the unceasing *etcetera* from which from the beginning and long since the *last* as the most inceptual has withdrawn. The end never sees itself; it takes itself instead to be completion and will therefore be least of all ready and prepared either to await the *last* or to experience it.

Coming from a posture toward beings that is determined by "metaphysics," we will only slowly and with difficulty be able to know the other, namely that god no longer appears either in the "personal" or in the "lived-experience" of the masses but solely in the "space" of be-ing itself—a space which is held to abground. All heretofore "cults" and "churches" and such things cannot at all become the essential preparation for the colliding of god and man in the midpoint of be-ing. For, the truth of be-ing itself must at first be grounded, and for this assignment all creating must take on an other beginning.

How few know that god awaits the grounding of the truth of be-ing and thus awaits man's leaping-into Da-sein. Instead it seems as if man might have to and would await god. And perhaps this is the most insidious form of the most acute godlessness and numbing of the asthenia for en-suffering the enownment of *that* coming-between of the t/here [*Da-Zwischenkunft*] of be-ing, which first offers a site to a being's entry-into and staying within the truth and imparts to a being the prerogative of standing in the remotest remoteness to the passing of god, a prerogative whose imparting occurs only as history: in re-creating a being unto the ownmost of its destiny and unto freeing it from the misuse of machinations, which, turning everything upside down, exhaust a being in exploitation.

VIII. Be-ing

257. Be-ing

Here lie the boulders of a quarry, in which primal rock is broken:
  Thinking.
  Intending being.
  Being and the difference to a being.
  Projecting be-ing open.
  En-thinking of be-ing.
  Essential swaying of be-ing.
  History.
  Da-sein.
  Language and saying.
  "A being."
  The question of crossing (Why are there beings at all and not rather nothing?).
  Be-ing-history (*Überlegungen* VII [GA 95], 97ff.: Hölderlin—Nietzsche).
  The standpoint of be-ing-history.
  The incalculable (*Überlegungen* VII [GA 95], 90ff.).

258. Philosophy

At present and in the future the essential grasping of the concept of philosophy (and thereby pre-determining the conceptuality of its concept and of all its concepts) is *historical* grasping (not historical [as a discipline]). "Historical" [*geschichtlich*] here means: belonging to the essential swaying of be-ing itself, enjoined unto the distress of the truth of be-ing and thus bound into the necessity of that decision which on the whole has at its disposal what is ownmost to history and its essential swaying. Thereupon philosophy is now primarily preparation for philosophy in the manner of building the nearest forecourts in whose spatial configuration Hölderlin's word becomes hearable and is replied to by Da-*sein* and in such a reply becomes grounded as the language of future man. It is only in this way that man enters the next, steady, and narrow walkway to be-ing. The be-ing-historical uniqueness of Hölderlin must be founded beforehand; and all "literary"-historical and poetic-historical comparisons, all "aesthetic" judgments and enjoyment, all "political" evaluations—all must be overcome, so that the moments of the "creating ones" have their "time" (cf. *Überlegungen* VI [GA 94], VII [GA 95], VIII [GA 95]).

The historical destiny of philosophy culminates in the recognition of the necessity of making Hölderlin's word be heard. Being able to hear corresponds to being able to say, which speaks out of the question-worthiness of be-ing. For this is the least that must be accomplished in preparing an arena for word. (If everything would not be turned upside down by the "scientific" and "literary-historical" approach, one could say: a preparation of thinking for interpreting Hölderlin must be created. Of course, "interpretation" here does not mean "making understandable" but rather grounding the projecting-opening of the truth of his poetizing unto mindfulness and attunement, in which future Da-sein resonates.) (Cf. *Überlegungen* VI [GA 94] and VII [GA 95]: Hölderlin.)

This historically essential characterization of philosophy grasps philosophy as the *thinking of be-ing*. This thinking should never seek refuge in the shape of a being and in that shape experience all the light of what is simple out of the gathered richness of its enjoined darkness. This thinking can also never follow the dissolution into what is shapeless. In the abground of the shaping ground—this side of shape and shapelessness (which is, of course, only in a being)—this thinking must seize the resonating throw of its thrownness and carry it into the open of the projecting-opening. The thinking of be-ing, completely other than any conformity to the objective, must belong to what is to be thought itself, because be-ing does not tolerate its own truth as an addendum and something proposed but rather "is" itself the essential sway of truth. Truth itself, that clearing of self-sheltering-concealing, in whose open gods and man are enowned for their countering, enopens be-ing as history [*Geschichte*]. We must perhaps think this history if we are to prepare the arena which in its time must preserve the resonance of Hölderlin's word—a word which again names gods and man—so that this resonance attunes those grounding-attunements which appoint future man to the guardianship of gods' needfulness.

This being-historical characterization of philosophy requires an elucidation that draws upon a remembrance of the heretofore thinking (metaphysics) but at the same time puts back this thinking and what is to come, back into historical belonging-together.

The name "metaphysics" here is used without reservation for characterizing the whole history of philosophy up to now. This name is not meant as the title of a "discipline" of scholastic philosophy, nor does this name take into account the later and only partially artificial formation of this title. The name is meant to say that thinking of being takes beings in the sense of what is present and extant as its starting point and goal for ascending to being, an ascending which immediately and at once turns again into a descending into beings.

Meta-physics is justification for the "physics" of beings by way of a constant flight in the face of be-ing. "Metaphysics" is the unadmitted perplexity toward be-ing and the ground for the final abandonment of beings by being. The differentiation of a being and of being is shoved aside into the harmlessness of a difference that is merely represented (a "logical" difference), if within metaphysics this difference itself *as such* is brought to knowing awareness at all—which strictly speaking, does not and cannot happen, since metaphysical thinking dwells only *within* the difference, but in such a way that in a certain manner being itself is some kind of a being. Only the crossing into the other beginning, the first overcoming of metaphysics—by necessarily upholding the name in the crossing—raises this difference to knowing awareness and thus for the first time puts it in question, and not into just any question but rather into questioning what is most question-worthy. Regardless of how extrinsically and completely in the sense of representational thinking the difference is initially introduced as "ontological differ- ence," it is necessary to begin becoming mindful of this difference. For the originary richness and the danger of all dangers of humanness, of grounding and destroying what is its ownmost, must become manifest in this seemingly inconsiderable and harmless "ontological" differenti- ating, i.e., differentiating that sustains ontology. This differentiating covers over the space of the utmost venture of thinking that continues to be allotted to man—a covering over that stands in the foreground.

The differentiating takes what is ownmost to metaphysics together with the occurrence of what is decisive but never decided in it and also not decidable by it: This differentiating carries the concealed history of metaphysics (not the discipline of history of metaphysical doctrines) over into the history of be-ing and moves this [history, *Geschichte*] into the arena wherein the first beginning of Western thinking of being is effec- tive—a thinking which carries the name of "philosophy," whose concept changes, depending on the manner and way of inquiry into being.

259. Philosophy

Philosophy is inquiring into being. This characterization can be inter- preted in two ways. Both interpretations contain, in their onefold, what is ownmost to philosophy heretofore, as well as to future philosophy, and thus contain the directive for crossing from the one to the other.

Initially and throughout the long history between Anaximander and Nietzsche, inquiring into being is only the question concerning the being of beings. The question aims at beings as what is asked about and inquires into what *they* are. What is inquired into is determined as what is common to all beings. Being has the character of beingness. Beingness as an addendum to beings results from an inquiry that proceeds from beings and inquires *back* into beings. However, within what is asked-about and what is inquired into, beingness as what is most con- stantly present in all beings is the most-being and therefore in each case the earlier over against every definite and individual being. As soon as beingness is grasped as object of representation and re-presentation becomes putting-before-oneself with regard to the subject, being-earlier gets another ranking allotted to it and becomes the *a priori* in the order of re-presentation. But because even this re-presentation refers to the rendering-present of what is extant as such, being-earlier here also means, indeed not an ordinary-"temporal" priority, but a priority whose time-character refers to presencing. However, for the Greeks this *a priori* is not somehow "still" "objective" and after Descartes "subjective" but is neither the one nor the other. Rather, the πρότερον τῇ φύσει simply in the sense of φύσις, i.e., in the sense of being (as in the sense of presencing emerging), is itself being, just as beingness remains the most-being.

But after Descartes the *a priori* is not "subjective" but merely "objective," is the objectivity of the object, the objectness of the object in re-presentation, and is sustaining the one who re-presents. Only when *subjectum* is misconstrued as an individualized extant I-thing and re-presentation is reduced to a property that crops up—instead of continuing to be what is ownmost to *subjectum*—can what is *"a priori"* (beingness in the sense of objectness) be misunderstood subjectivistically as "merely" subjective. Whatever the magnitude of Kant's step might be, whatever again the difference between absolute idealism of post-Kantian philosophy and Kant might continue to be, and however confusingly then everything is reduced to the half and groundless character of "logical" and "biological" interpretation of the *a priori*, which in this shape reappears again in Nietzsche—all of these differences cannot hide the simple cohesion of the whole history of this inquiry into being (into beingness, in the shape of the question of what a being is). History of *this* question concerning being is the history of metaphysics, history of the thinking that thinks being as the being of a being *from out of and unto a being*. That this inquiry into being is overpowered by beings and not only in its beginning (which is the ground for the disempowering of φύσις and ἀλήθεια), that this priority of beings is carried all the way through the history of metaphysics, as essential to metaphysics—this becomes manifest most impressively at the juncture where the question of being is enacted in its purest form since the Greeks: in Kant. Positing experience as the only decisive domain of beings goes together with the discovery of the transcendental. Beingness as "the condition for the possibility" of the object of experience—and this experience itself in its turn—is conditioned by the priority of beings in offering a criterion for that which should count as being. In Kant's transcendental inquiry, a being, "nature," is indeed seen in the light of Newtonian physics but is meant metaphysically (in historical metaphysics) in the sense of φύσει ὄν and finally φύσις. However, absolute idealism seems to overcome the priority of being. For the exclusive determination of the object out of objectness (i.e., elimination of the "thing in itself") means nothing other than erecting the priority of beingness over a being. Therefore it is of course impossible to think along with Hegel's *Phenomenology of Spirit* precisely in its beginning ("sense certainty"), if the drawing of sense certainty into the actuality of absolute spirit is not already thought *beforehand* and absolutely. What does this mean other than that a being has lost its priority to being? And yet, the actual misinterpretation of idealism might lie in this interpretation. Idealism, too, holds on to the priority of a being over beingness; but idealism merely hides this relationship and awakens the opposite impression. Every objectness and every stage of it is indeed determined from out of the absolute. However, objectness as such is already, essentially — not to speak of its being-historical origin — not only related to the object but also determined *from* the object as *from* a definite interpretation of beings, based on and proceeding from beings. The objectness seems to disappear by being sublated into absolute knowledge, but it is only spread out into objectness of self-consciousness and of reason. And precisely this, that beingness is grounded in absolute subjectivity, *indicates* that *this* being, the *subjectum*, as relational midpoint of all putting-before-oneself, decides on beingness and what can belong to it, as well as on the essential forms and stages of representedness. Thus, distinguished from the Greeks, absolute idealism shows even an increased prioritization of a being over against beingness, insofar as be-ing is determined in terms of the subject and that means at the same time in terms of the object. Being-historically, this determination is only a modification of the constant presence into representedness-before-itself of the subject. Therefore, what is enacted in absolute idealism, which *seems* to resolve everything back to being, is the complete disempowering of being in favor of the uncontested and boundless supremacy of a being.

Only through the philosophical naiveté of "epistemology" and the "epistemological" interpretation of idealism could the mistaken notion arise that "idealism" is removed from actuality and that reverting to "realism" must come to the aid of idealism. But the "realism" of the nineteenth century thrives entirely on absolute idealism. There is no reverting at work but merely collapsing into the unphilosophical interpretation of idealism, whereby then of course the disempowering of being in the pursuit of beings (hidden within idealism) seems justified — a pursuit which must then rescue itself in value-thinking, where it retains so much sensibility as to recognize how even the unconditioned affirmation of the actual and of "life" (therefore of a being) still needs a trace of the *not*-being, which one is of course no longer capable of knowing as being. If "observing" the history of metaphysics perseveres in the viewpoints of "idealism" and "realism," then "idealism" always appears as a philosophically more genuine posture, insofar as in it being still comes to word over against a being. Nevertheless, it is still true that the philosophical disempowering of being occurs in "idealism" (and in realism a disempowering that is devoid of philosophy). It is necessary to know this in order not to misconstrue right away the *crossing* from metaphysics into the other manner of questioning of being.

The question of being now becomes the question of the truth of be-ing. The essential sway of truth is now inquired out of the essential swaying of be-ing and is grasped as the clearing for what shelters and conceals itself and thus as belonging to the essential sway of be-ing itself. The question of truth "of" be-ing reveals itself as the question of the be-ing "of" truth. (The genitive here is an ur-own [*ur-eigener*] one and can never be grasped by the heretofore "grammatical" genitive.) Now the questioning of be-ing no longer thinks in terms of beings but rather as en-thinking of be-ing (cf. Be-ing, 265: En-thinking of Be-ing), is necessitated by be-ing itself. En-thinking of be-ing gives rise to be-ing as the "between" [*das Zwischen*] in whose self-clearing essential swaying gods and man recognize each other, i.e., decide on their belonging-together. As this "between," be-ing "is" not an addendum to beings but rather that holding sway in whose truth what is can above all enter the preserving of a being. But this priority of the "between" dare not be misconstrued idealistically in the sense of the "*a priori*." The questioning of being in the manner of inquiring into the truth of be-ing no longer takes place on a level in which a differentiation, such as the one between idealism and realism, could obtain a possible ground. How-ever, the reservation remains, whether it is possible to think be-ing itself in its essential swaying without proceeding from a being, whether any inquiry into being must not unfailingly remain a retro-inquiry from a being. Here the long tradition of metaphysics and the habit of think-ing that has grown out of it indeed stands in the way, especially when "logic" — itself an offspring of the inceptual disempowering of being and of truth — is nevertheless considered an absolute tribunal for thinking, one that has fallen from heaven. In that case it is "logical," i.e., definitively established, that being as what is general [*das Allgemeine*] is obtained from a being, even when one attempts to secure being in its constancy, as with a being. But *be-ing*, which must be enthought in its truth, "is" not what is general and empty but rather holds sway as what is singular and has the character of an abground, in which the one-time occurrence of history is decided (cf. Be-ing, 270: The Essential Sway of Be-ing (Essential Swaying)). Of course, here one cannot remain on the level of the metaphysical question of being and from this standpoint demand a knowing that essentially includes the abandonment of this standpoint, i.e., demands spatialization of a space and temporalization of a time, both of which in the history of metaphysics were not only for-gotten or were not sufficiently thought through but rather are inacces-sible and also not necessary to this history.

Abandoning the standpoint of metaphysics means nothing other than being subordinate to a distressing that arises from a totally differ-ent distress — a distress indeed that is brought about by the history of metaphysics, so that it withdraws as the distress that it is and lets the lack of distress (with regard to being and the question of being) become the dominating state of affairs. But in truth the lack of distress is what is utmost in this distress, which becomes recognizable primarily as the abandonment of beings by being.

In crossing from the metaphysical to the future question of being, thinking and questioning must always accord with the crossing. Thus the possibility of a merely metaphysical assessment of the other questioning is excluded. But in this way the other questioning is also not proven as "absolute" truth, for the very reason that such a proof of such a "truth" goes essentially against this questioning. For this questioning is historical because in it the history of be-ing itself, as of history's ground that is unique in its being utterly of the abground, becomes enowning. Besides, thinking in the crossing always primarily accomplishes the preparation for the other questioning, and that means preparation for that humanness which in its foundership and guardianship should become strong enough and knowing enough to take on the thrust of be-ing—a thrust long since indicated but even for a longer period not-granted—and to gather into a singular moment of history the empowering of be-ing unto its essential swaying. Therefore, thinking in the crossing can also not shake off the habitude of metaphysics by a *coup de main*. Nay, for the sake of communication, thinking in the crossing must still often go in the track of metaphysical thinking while always knowing the other. And if crossing is to become history-grounding, how could thinking that is actually historical overlook that the suddenness of what is not intimated, as well as the inconspicuousness of steadily advancing beyond itself, is conserved for this thinking? And how could thinking in the crossing also not know that much, nay most exertion continually allotted to it will one day be superfluous and will fall back into what is peripheral in order to let the stream of the history of what is unique run its own one-time course? Nevertheless thinking in the crossing dare not eschew the dearth of preparatory differentiations and elucidations, as long as they only drift in the wind of a decision that comes from afar. Only the chill of the boldness of thinking and the night of errancy of questioning lend glow and light to the fire of be-ing.

Crossing in its first enactment is marked by the difference in the question of being, which is an historical difference and which differentiates the history of metaphysics from future thinking. However, the difference does not bind together in the manner of distinguishing what is past and what is to come, a bygone history and an approaching history; but rather it differentiates two fundamentally different deep draws of Western history. That the history of metaphysics is at its end (with Nietzsche) in no way means that from now on metaphysical thinking (and that means at the same time rational logical thinking) has been eradicated. On the contrary: This metaphysical thinking now transfers its established habitude into the arenas of worldviews and of the growing scientification of daily operations in the same way that it already settles itself in the shaping of Christianity and, with Christianity, crosses over into the forms of its "secularization," wherein this thinking encounters itself again in the shape which it has assumed through its Christianization (which already begins with Plato). History of metaphysics does not stop because it now crosses over into, nay first enopens, what is without history [*das Geschichtslose*]. On the other hand, being-historical thinking of the other questioning does not now somehow just enter the light of day. Being-historical thinking remains sheltered in its own depth, but now no longer by concealing its enclosedness in the unerupted origin, as it has been since the first beginning of Western thinking and throughout the history of metaphysics, but rather in the clarity of a severe darkness of a depth that knows itself and has arisen into mindfulness.

History of metaphysical and of being-historical thinking is enowned especially in their various epochs according to various degrees of power in the priority of being over beings, of beings over being, of the confusion of both, of the extinction of any priority in the epoch of the calculative intelligibility of everything. We know the future of being-history, namely that, if it wants to remain history, be-ing itself must enown thinking to itself. But no one knows the shape of coming beings. Only this one thing may be certain: Any enthinking of be-ing and any creating out of the truth of be-ing—without the already protective appeal [*Zuspruch*] of beings—needs strengths of questioning and of saying, of throwing and of sustaining, that are other than what the history of metaphysics could ever bring forth. For these other strengths, in accord with what is their ownmost, must still draw into thinking the questioning dialogue with the first beginning and its history—a beginning that arises in bright depths—and must be equipped to become, *along with* those who are the most solitary in the first thinking, even more solitary of that ab-ground, which not only sustains all grounds in the other beginning but also permeates them. What remains for the merely subsequent object of historical erudition and research and in the end for merely academic instruction—history of metaphysical thinking in its "works"—must first *become history* [*Geschichte*], in which everything draws together unto its uniqueness and, as a lighted moment [*Lichtblick*] of thinking, emits a truth of be-ing in its own untraversed space. Because here a greatness of thinking Dasein is required by be-ing itself—a greatness whose shape we hardly surmise in the poetic Dasein of Hölderlin and in the dreadful wanderings of Nietzsche—and because this greatness alone continues to be in the space of being-historical thinking—for which reason even the talk of greatness continues to be too small—*therefore* preparation for such thinkers must summon all inexorability and move within the clearest differentiations. For only such differentiations furnish the courage for inabiding in the domain of the thrust of what is most question-worthy—that which is needed by gods and forgotten by man and which we call be-ing.

The difference in the question of being can be stated formally by two titles. The one reads: "being and thinking"; the other, "being and time." In the first title, being is understood as the beingness of a being; in the other, as the being whose truth is inquired. In the first, "thinking" means the guiding-thread along which a being is questioned unto its beingness: the representing assertion. In the other, "time" means the first indication of the essential sway of truth in the sense of the clearing of the free-play—a clearing which is open as removals-unto—in which be-ing is sheltered and, sheltering, first expressly gifts itself in its truth. Accordingly, both titles in their relationship are not at all to be interpreted as if "thinking" in the first title were merely replaced by "time" in the second, as if the same question of beingness of a being now is enacted with the guiding-thread of time rather than of asserting representation, whereby then "time" is still directly thought according to its usual concept. Rather, the "role" of thinking and that of "time" is in each case fundamentally different; in each of the two titles determination of thinking and time lends a specific unequivocality to the "and." But at the same time, by inquiring into being in the sense of the title "being and time," a possibility is created for grasping, more originarily, i.e., being-historically, the history of the question of being in the sense of the title "being and thinking," and to render manifest the truth of being—necessarily uninquired in the history of metaphysics—at first in the time-character of being, by means of alluding to the reigning of presencing and constancy in the essential sway of φύσις, of ἰδέα, and of οὐσία. Being-historically, this allusion is all the more deciding, insofar as in the further history of the question of being the time-character of beingness is more and more covered over, so that the attempt to couple being (and the timelessness of the categories and values) with "time"—no matter how—immediately comes up against the resistance that has its strength, of course, only in the blindness of not-wanting-to-inquire. Since, on the basis of not grasping the question of the truth (of "the meaning") of be-ing, the "time"-character of being itself continues to be completely estranging, one seeks to redeem oneself by equating being with Dasein, which of course now, because it somehow designates humanness, is understandable in its "temporality." But in this way everything falls out of the trajectory of the question of being and immediately shows that by itself a title is capable of nothing if exertion and knowing are lacking for interpreting it, at least in its intention. However, this knowing can never be communicated and disseminated like the knowledge of what is extant. Those who bring it to one another must already go in the crossing in that they, intimating decisions, come unto one another and yet do not meet. For scattered individuals are needed in order for decision to ripen.

But these individuals still bring along what *has been* of the hidden being-history, that detour [*Umweg*] through beings—however it might appear—which metaphysics had to take in order *not* to reach being and so to come to an end that is strong enough for the distress for another beginning, which at the same time helps in returning to the originariness of the first beginning and transforms what is past into something that is not lost.

However, the detour is not a detour in the sense of having missed a direct access and a shorter way to be-ing. Nay, the detour first leads to the distress of not-granting and to the necessity of lifting up to decision *that* which first-ever-inceptually was only the hint of a gift (φύσις, ἀλήθεια), which did not let itself be grasped and preserved.

To the genuine crossing belongs especially the courage for the old and the freedom for the new. But what is old is not the antiquated, which unavoidably obtrudes as soon as what is inceptually great—which as a consequence of its primary inceptuality is unmatched in its greatness—falls into a *historical* [*historisch*] tradition and denial. The old, i.e., that which nothing younger can ever surpass in essentiality, manifests itself only to *historical* [*geschichtlich*] encounter and to *historically* mindful deliberation. But the new is not the "modern," i.e., that which in the dominance of today obtains legitimacy and favor and remains, unbeknownst to itself, the hidden enemy of everything that pertains to decision.

Here the new means the freshness of originariness of recommencing, what ventures out into the hidden future of the first beginning and thus cannot be "new" at all but rather must be *older* than the old.

The thinkers in the crossing, who are essentially ambiguous, must nonetheless explicitly know that their questioning and saying is *not intelligible* for today, whose duration is incalculable. And that, not just because those of today are not smart enough and not informed enough for what is said but rather because intelligibility already means destruction of their thinking. For intelligibility forces everything back into the sphere of the heretofore representing. The mandate of those in the crossing is to turn those who so "ardently" wish for what is "intelligible" into those who do not understand and are not yet informed, who do not know the whereunto because those in the crossing have accomplished what is first necessary: not to expect truth from a being without falling prey to doubt and despair. Those who are not yet informed, who have not yet secured the agreement over everything but rather have preserved in questioning what is foremost and unique, namely be-ing, are the inceptual wanderers, who come from furthest away and therefore carry within themselves the highest future.

Those in the crossing must in the end know what is mistaken by all urging for intelligibility: that every thinking of being, all philosophy, can *never* be confirmed by "facts," i.e., by beings. Making itself intelligible is suicide for philosophy. Those who idolize "facts" never notice that their idols only shine in a borrowed shine. They are also meant not to notice this; for thereupon they would have to be at a loss and therefore useless. But idolizers and idols are used wherever gods are in flight and so announce *their* nearness.

Philosophy's *deliverance* [*Loslösung*] from entanglements in laying the foundation of science, in interpreting culture, in providing service to worldview, in metaphysics as what is foremost and ownmost to philosophy that degenerates into what is precisely *not* ownmost to philosophy—all of this simply *follows* the other beginning and is to be truly mastered only as *such* a following. The other beginning is the more originary taking over of what is ownmost and concealed to philosophy, its ownmost which arises from the essential sway of be-ing and, in accordance with the respective purity of the origin, remains closer to the essential decision of the thinking "of" be-ing.

What above all follows the deliverance is the necessary re-habituating within representing of that which philosophy simply is in the ever present sphere of *everyday* opinion. Philosophy then is no longer a thought-structure but rather the seemingly accidentally broken blocks of a quarry in which ur-rock is broken and the crushers and crowbars remain invisible. Who is capable of knowing whether the blocks are sealed shapes, or disjointed supports for an invisible bridge?

Philosophy in the other beginning questions in the manner of inquiring into the truth of *be-ing.* Seen from within the horizon of what has explicitly become differentiation of beings and being and reckoned within a historical [*historisch*] comparison to metaphysics and its proceeding from *beings,* questioning within the other beginning (questioning as be-ing-historical thinking) may seem to be a simple—and that means here a crude—*reversing* [*Umkehrung*]. But it is precisely be-ing-historical thinking which knows what is ownmost to mere reversing, knows that in reversing the most ruthless and insidious enslaving prevails; that reversing overcomes nothing but merely empowers the reversed and provides it with what it hitherto lacked, namely, consolidation and completion.

Be-ing-historical inquiring into be-ing is not reversing metaphysics but rather de-cision as projecting-opening of the ground of that differentiation in which the reversing must also maintain itself. With such a projecting-opening, this inquiry moves completely out of that differentiation of beings and being; and it therefore now also writes being as "be-ing." This should indicate that being here is no longer thought metaphysically.

Be-ing-historical thinking—out of its necessity for interpreting ahead—can be made question-*worthy* in four ways:

1. Within the perspective of gods.
2. Within the perspective of man.
3. In looking back at the history of metaphysics.
4. As thinking "of" be-ing.

These four perspectives can only *seemingly* be pursued in isolation from one another.

Re 1. Grasping the thinking of be-ing from within the perspective of gods appears forthwith as arbitrary and "fantastic," insofar as, on the one hand, we proceed quite directly from the divine [*das Gott-hafte*], as if that is "given"—as if everyone agrees with everyone about the divine—but even more strange, insofar as, on the other hand, we proceed from "gods" and set a "polytheism" as the "starting point" of "philosophy." But the talk of "gods" here does not indicate the decided assertion on the extantness of a plurality over against a singular but is rather meant as the allusion to the undecidability of the being of gods, whether of one single god or of many gods. This undecidability holds within itself what is question-worthy, namely, whether anything at all like being dare be attributed to gods without destroying everything that is divine. The undecidability concerning which god and whether a god can, in utmost distress, once again arise, from which way of being of man and in what way—this is what is named with the name "gods." However, this unde-cidability is not merely re-presented as empty possibility for decisions but rather is grasped in advance as *the* decision out of which decidedness or complete lack of decision takes its origin. The fore-thinking as holding out into this decision of such undecidability does not presuppose some gods or other as extant but rather ventures into the realm of what is worthy of questioning, for which the answer can only come from what is question-worthy itself, but never from the one who asks questions.

Insofar as in such fore-thinking be-ing is not in advance attributed to "gods," all assertion about "being" and "essence" of gods not only does not say anything about them—and that means about that which is to be decided—but also simulates something objective, against which all thinking comes to nought because it is immediately forced into devious paths. (Considered according to *metaphysics*, god must be represented as the most-being, as the first ground and cause of beings, as the un-con-ditioned, in-finite, absolute. None of these determinations arises from the divine-character of god but rather from what is ownmost to a being as such, insofar as this is thought as what is constantly present, as what is objective and simply in itself and is thus, in re-presenting explaining, attributed as what is most clear to god as ob-ject.)

Not attributing being to "gods" initially means only that being does not stand "over" gods and that gods do not stand "over" being. But gods *do need* be-ing, which saying already thinks the essential sway "of" be-ing. "Gods" do not need be-ing as their ownhood, wherein they themselves take a stance. "Gods" need be-ing in order through be-ing—which does not belong to gods—nevertheless to belong to themselves. Be-ing is needed by gods: it is their need. And the needfulness of be-ing names its essential swaying—what is needed by "gods" but is never causable and conditionable. That "gods" need be-ing moves them into the ab-ground (into freedom) and expresses the breakdown of any proving and demonstrating of every sort. And as impenetrable as the needfulness of be-ing must remain for thinking, it still offers a first hold for thinking "gods" as those who need be-ing. We thereby accomplish the first steps in the history of be-ing, and thus be-ing-historical thinking commences. And any effort at wanting to force what is said in this beginning into a familiar intelligibility is futile and above all against the nature of such thinking. But when be-ing is the needfulness of god, when be-ing itself finds its truth only in en-thinking, and when this thinking is philosophy (in the other beginning), then "gods" need be-ing-historical thinking, i.e., philosophy. "Gods" need philosophy, not as if *they themselves* must philosophize for the sake of their godding, but rather philosophy must be *if* "gods" are again to come into decision and if history is to obtain its ownmost ground. Within the perspective of gods be-ing-historical thinking is determined as that thinking of be-ing that understands the abground of needfulness of and by be-ing as primary and never seeks the essential sway of be-ing in the divine itself as what is supposedly the most-being. Be-ing-historical thinking is outside any theology and also knows no atheism, in the sense of a worldview or a doctrine structured in some other way.

To understand the abground of needfulness for be-ing means being transferred into the necessity of grounding the truth for be-ing and not resisting the essential consequences of this necessity but rather thinking unto them and thus knowing that, without succumbing to the claim of "absoluteness," all thinking of be-ing is by that necessity withdrawn from any merely human contrivance.

But understanding be-ing-historical thinking from within the perspective of gods is "the same" as attempting to indicate what is ownmost to this thinking from within the perspective of man.

Re 2. What here counts just as well is that no existing and familiar conception of man can serve as a starting point, because the first thing that the necessity of thinking in relation to needfulness requires must be accomplished by an essential transformation of man heretofore. Why?

If we think human beings decidedly enough, even within the centuries-old familiar definition as *animal rationale*, then we cannot avoid thinking the relation to being that has long since become insipid and empty—the one that is still meant in the "reasoning character" [*Vernünf-*

tigkeit] of this living-being. In the rapidly growing helplessness vis-à-vis what is "metaphysically" ownmost to reason, one may follow the final and crucial approach of Nietzsche, rescuing oneself by "reducing" "reason" (and everything that, under other headings, revolves within the sphere of this "property" of living-being) to "life." Confirmed by the spirit of what is self-evident and readily demonstrable, one can presume to pass reason off as mere emanation of "life" and thus as an addendum; one can assist this way of thinking to become, without exception, a familiarity in what is common-to-all representing, and still nothing changes in the essential appropriateness of "reason" in the sense of receiving the being of beings. Nay, all that prioritizing of "life" itself collapses into the nothing if that which "depends" on it—like reason—does not in itself sustain and thoroughly dominate what is ownmost to man, namely that, being in the midst of beings and comporting toward them as such, he is a being, nay "the" being which modern determination grasps in the sense of *subjectum*. As much as this determination may later appeal to "life," it is still the strongest, only correspondingly more and more blind *testimony* to what is metaphysically ownmost to man, which all organizing of "life" and any arranging of "world" tries to forget and to keep within forgetfulness.

But now, if being, though unacknowledged, offers to what is ownmost to reason its ground, if it is nothing arbitrary but rather itself could in its essential swaying lay claim to man from the ground up, and if man once again were to win back, in another originariness, his own through and through used up and dissipated way of being, and if even this gaining of man's way of being would have to consist in being claimed by the essential swaying of be-ing, and if be-ing itself would need to ground the truth of its essential sway only in such transformation of man, a transformation that an originary thinking "of" be-ing is capable of venturing—*then* from within the perspective of man a transformed thinking of being is announced. But now it also becomes quite clear that this determining of philosophy from within the perspective of man never means *man* as he is in himself but rather historical man, whose history, though hidden from us, is still current and pressing within the historical [*historisch*] re-presentation.

[Re. 3 and Re. 4 are not presented in section 259.]

260. The Gigantic

[The gigantic] was determined as that through which the "quantitative" is transformed into its own "quality," a kind of magnitude. The gigantic is thus not something quantitative that begins with a relatively high number (with number and measurement)—even though it can appear superficially as "quantitative." The gigantic is grounded upon the decidedness and invariability of "calculation" and is rooted in a prolongation of subjective re-presentation unto the whole of beings. Therein lies the possibility of a kind of magnitude that is meant here in a historical sense. Magnitude here means: erecting be-ing that is rooted in a ground that is self-grounded and which gives rise to that which wants to count as a being [*seiend*]. The gigantic shows the magnitude of the self-certain *subjectum* which builds everything on its own representing and producing.

The forms in which the gigantic appears are various; above all the gigantic is not seen suddenly and overwhelmingly in each of its forms. That which claims large numbers and measures for its representability is only the *appearance* of the gigantic, which, of course, belongs to the gigantic, since it legitimizes that kind of magnitude that relies essentially on setting down and representing.

The forms of the gigantic include:

1. The gigantism of the *slowing down* of history (from the staying away of essential decisions all the way to lack of history) in the semblance of speed and steerability of "historical" [*historisch*] development and its anticipation.

2. The gigantism of the *publicness* as summation of everything homogeneous in favor of concealing the destruction and undermining of any passion for essential gathering.

3. The gigantism of the claim to *naturalness* in the semblance of what is self-evident and "logical"; the question-worthiness of being is placed totally outside questioning.

4. The gigantism of the *diminution* of beings in the whole in favor of the semblance of boundless extending of the same by virtue of unconditioned controllability. The single thing that is impossible is the word and representation of "impossible."

In all of these interrelated forms of the gigantic, the abandonment of being holds sway, and now, of course, no longer merely in the manner of staying away of question-worthiness of beings but in the shape of an established banishing of any mindfulness on the basis of the unconditioned priority of the "act" (i.e., of the calculated and always "large-scale" operation) and of "facts."

The gigantic unfolds in the calculative and thus always manifests the "quantitative," but is itself—as the unconditioned domination of representing and producing—a denial of the truth of be-ing in favor of "what belongs to reason" and what is "given," a denial that is not in control of itself and, in heightened self-certainty, is simply never aware of itself. The gigantic enacts the completion of the basic metaphysical position of man, a position which shifts into reversing its shape and interprets all "goals" and "values" ("ideals" and "ideas") as "expression" and offspring of the sheer "eternal" "life" in itself. The superficial appearances of the gigantic are to make this "origin" in "life" representable in the most pressing way possible—i.e., historically [*historisch*] establish this origin for the epoch of the gigantic—and to confirm this epoch before itself in its "vitality." Whether "values" and "goals" are set by "reason" or arise from "instinct" of the "natural" and "healthy" life in itself, in all cases what unfolds here as the midpoint of beings is the *subjectum* (man), to such an extant that *all* cultural and political forms bring the gigantic to power in the same manner and equally necessarily, pursue historical [*historisch*] calculating with history and miscalculate history as concealing the lack of goals, and inconspicuously and unconsciously secure everywhere the avoidance of essential decisions.

In the gigantic, one recognizes that any manner of "greatness" in history arises from the unspoken "metaphysical" interpretation of happening (ideals, deeds, creations, sacrifice) and therefore its ownmost actually is not historical [*geschichtlich*] but rather historical [*historisch*]. The hidden history of be-ing does not know what is calculative about "large" and "small" but rather knows "only" what pertains to be-ing in what is decided, undecided, and decisionless.

261. The Opinion about Be-ing

Be-ing—who is ever concerned with be-ing? Everyone hunts for beings.

And how can one be concerned about be-ing? Where one is still concerned, there is also that "being" about which one does *not* need to be concerned—always granting that this being-concerned has to be fundamentally capable of deciding about what *is* and what ought to be. When one finally admits that being "is" not a being, being continues to be an empty "representation," a bringing-before-oneself that brings nothing forth, a miscalculation of re-presentation which—because it is at any time, anywhere and at every opportunity possible over against any being—with regard to a being is what is most common to everything of a being's kind but is thus what is "nothing." Finally, be-ing still counts as a name that no longer names anything but is still in use as a sign for what is most indifferent of all beings.

This opinion about be-ing does not initially need to justify its correctness in any detail. Its best confirmation is offered by those attempts which perhaps still are *against* this opinion but—bound as they are within their perspective—can hardly provide fullness for this empty name. One takes a being in the sense of what is objectively extant, as what is unquestionable and intangible, with regard to which one continues to comport oneself most appropriately by continually installing the extant as straight-forwardly at-hand and taking this in a completely technical sense.

One takes a being in this manner and admits being only as what is merely still intendable in "thinking" and then proves that being is just what is most general.

But why do we not pull ourselves together in order to shake up once and for all these most common and most broadly "pre"-supposed "pre-suppositions" (that a being is something objective and that grasping be-ing is an empty opining of what is most general and its categories)? Because we hardly recognize what is needed for that: namely, shaking up this "we" of modern man, who as *"subjectum"* has become *the* refuge of those presuppositions to such an extent that the subject-character of man itself has its origin and *the* hold of its unbroken power in the admitted predominance of those presuppositions (of the understanding of being that is consolidated in Western and modern thinking). How could it ever come to a shaking up, which would have to be essentially more than merely changing an opinion about the concept of be-ing within the "subject" that otherwise continues to function, undisturbed? In looking through these "presuppositions," how clear does it become that not-being-concerned-about be-ing is correct at all times, and especially when it generously leaves dealing with being to the hair-splitting of an "ontology" that has again become academic or—what comes to the same thing—when it agrees with the opinion that declares every "ontology" to be impossible as a "rationalization" of being. For with this either-or—every time on the basis of ontology—one decides about being and about the opinion about being—so self-evidently decides that one can hardly, and rightfully so, still find here and admit "special" necessities for deciding.

Why then do we still pay even the slightest attention to this ontology-akin *not*-concerning-oneself with being, a non-concern that has the shape of ontology? Certainly not in order to discuss or even to change or refute the respective opinions and doctrines about be-ing that are put forth but rather to guide mindfulness in the direction of seeing that all ordinary opinion about being (including ontologies and anti-ontologies) has the mastery of being itself and its definite historical "truth" as its origin. (In anti-ontology the indifference toward the question of being is carried to extremes.)

But here another misunderstanding threatens: the view that one should now "demonstrate" the "anthropological" presupposition of that opinion and *with* this demonstration should regard that opinion as "refuted." However, precisely this view is only a further consequence of that opinion about being.

But "anthropology" itself belongs to that which is under the control of that interpretation of being. Thus anthropology can never be claimed as proof against that interpretation, not to mention at all that proving any such "presupposition" on which an opinion about being rests still decides nothing about the "truth" of that opinion, that after all presuppositions as such generally do not constitute an objection.

Something else matters: to recognize in not-concerning-oneself with be-ing, a necessary state in which an outstanding stage of the history of be-ing itself is hidden. Perhaps to hear, out of this most insignificant of all events within today's affairs, the echo of deciding enowning.

Mindfulness must realize that the indifference with regard to being, which is already made totally harmless and which in "ontology" finds its academically appropriate "representation," is nothing less than the utmost intensification of the power of *calculation*. What is at work here is the most indifferent and most blind denial of the incalculable.

However, mindfulness does not consider this to be a "mistake" and a "negligence" that would simply have to be reproached but rather a *history* whose "actuality" *essentially* surpasses everything that is otherwise "actual." It is for this reason that this history is recognized by only a few, and among these few is grasped only by the most rare, as the enowning that already opens itself, in which beings in the whole are put to the decision of their truth.

Events in beings—let alone modern man—are not capable of leading into the domain of the truth of be-ing. But what is more essential than beholding *the* state of Western history wherein we already reside as the deciding ones and which we do not merely somehow cover up by the lack of decision with regard to that indifferent opinion, but whose deciding potential [*Entscheidungsträchtigkeit*] we enhance to such an extent that mindfulness or lack of mindfulness is already included in the decision and can no longer count as forms of an accidental or additional observation or one that may not happen?

Here is the juncture where be-ing itself, by virtue of its history, necessitates the knowing awareness of being into the distress of a necessity for deciding and demands of this awareness that it obtain from itself clarity about what occurs in it as the "projecting-opening" of being.

262. "Projecting-Open" Be-ing and Be-ing as Projecting-Open

Thinking's leap "into" the truth of be-ing must at the same time leap into the essential sway of truth and establish itself and become inabiding in the throw of *a* single projecting-opening.

For experiencing a being and for sheltering its truth, "projecting-open" is only what is preparatory, which then passes over in proceeding to that which is erectable and preservable in the domain of the projecting-opening—and as *preserving* receives the seal of be-ing.

In thinking's knowing awareness, projecting-opening is not something preparatory *for* something else but rather the most unique and the last and thus the most rare, which holds sway unto itself as the grounded truth of be-ing.

Here projecting-opening is not something that is, as it were, merely laid "over" beings, is not a "perspective" that is only proposed for beings.

For every *per*-spective always lays claim to what is passed *through* for its point of view. And exactly this, that, in advance and deciding everything, a *deep rent* explodes that which then first announces itself into the open as a "being," that an *errancy* lights up and rends everything unto itself for the possibility of what is true—it is this that thinking's projecting-open of be-ing has to accomplish. "Accomplish"? Of course, but not as a making or a devising in the sense of an unbounded contriving.

Projecting-opening be-ing can only be thrown by be-ing itself; for that to happen, a moment must turn out well for Da-*sein,* i.e., for what be-ing as en-owning enowns.

Thinking inquiring occurs as the *acting* renunciation, which holds *before* [*zu*] itself *the* refusal and thus takes refusal into the clearing.

Whoever ever wants to face the history of be-ing and intends to experience how be-ing stays away in its own essential sphere [*Wesensraum*] and for a long time abandons this sphere to what is precisely not its ownmost—which drives the propagation of "beings" before itself, in order even to preserve what is not ownmost unto what is ownmost to which it does belong—such a one must be able to grasp above all that projecting-openings are thrown into *that* which, thanks to their clearing, again becomes a being and only tolerates be-ing as an addendum to it, an addendum that "abstraction" had devised.

According to a prevailing convention we think of these projecting-openings as forms of representation which enable the encountering of objects: Kant's transcendental condition. And we do well to practice thinking of beings as such on the basis of this interpretation of beingness as objectness. Nevertheless, this Kantian interpretation rests on the "ground" of *subjectum* and in the sphere of re-presentation. The designation of "projecting-opening" becomes "subjective" in the best sense, i.e., not as "having the character of an I," not "subjectivistically" epistemological, but rather *meta*physically as *subjectum,* as what is presupposed and taken for a ground without questioning and as unworthy of questioning. From that point on, interpretation of the Kantian thinking can undergo an essential clarification which, in this positioning of the subject, would even lead to the insight that philosophical thinking cannot by-pass the abgrounds (such as schematism and transcendental power of imagination). However, we must have already become inquisitive about other domains in order not merely to mark such a conception of Kant's as an exaggerated peculiarity but to become serious about the allusion to what holds to the abground.

We succeed in doing that at all only if we basically already read Kant no longer "subjectively" but rather reassess him in view of Da-sein.

On a historical path, this is a step for coming closer to *that* thinking which understands projecting-opening, no longer as condition for representation but rather as Da-*sein* and as the thrownness of a clearing that takes a foothold and above all grants shelteredness and thus reveals the not-granting.

Nevertheless, for people of today it continues to be difficult in every respect to experience projecting-opening as enowning from within what is ownmost to en-ownment as not-granting. Nothing else is required in this regard than keeping all distortion away from be-ing and knowing that in the sphere of human concoction this most powerful be-ing becomes the most fragile, especially since man for a long time now is accustomed to weigh the mastery of be-ing with the weights for measuring the force of beings—only to weigh thus and never to venture what is most question-worthy.

Besides, from of old we move *within* a projecting-opening of be-ing, without this projecting-opening ever becoming experienceable *as* projecting-opening. (The truth of be-ing was not a possible question.)

Holding-off of this question is the continual thrust in the history of the basic metaphysical positions, a thrust that as such not only remains in the dark for this history but also stays *away*. This is why the metaphysics of absolute idealism can "construct" itself in its own developmental history and as completion of metaphysics.

That subjectivity of the subject in the end unfolds itself into the absolute is only a dim indication of how projecting-opening constantly holds sway since the beginning of being-history and how it announces itself as not-made and not-makeable and of how it is nevertheless in the end explained in terms of the unconditioned, which also directly conditions being. With this "explanation" philosophy runs into an end. Nietzsche's revolt is only the reversal of this state.

But in the meantime beings in the shape of what is objective and extant have become ever more powerful. Be-ing is confined to the final pallor of the most abstract concept of generality, and everything "general" comes under the suspicion of being asthenic and unreal, of being what is merely "human" and therefore also "inessential." Because be-ing is set in the mask of what is most general and the most empty, it does not even deserve an explicit rebuttal in favor of beings. One has come so far as to "get along" without be-ing. This unique state of the history of man is "fortunately" hardly recognized by him, let alone grasped or even taken up into the will of history. For now he ruthlessly pursues its immediate consequences. Thereupon one now gets along even without beings and is satisfied with objects, i.e., finds all "life" and all actuality in the *pursuing* of what is objective. In one fell swoop, proceedings, arranging, mediating, and banishing, become more essential than that for which all of this happens. "Life" is swallowed up by live-experience, and this itself is intensified by *organizing* live-experience. *Organizing* live-experience is the utmost lived-experience wherein "one" comes together. Beings are now only the occasion for this organization—and what is be-ing still supposed to be at this point? But *here* the deciding point of history comes into view for mindfulness, and knowing awareness awakens and sees that, in the face of the gigantism of the lack of history, it is only by passing through utmost decidings that a history is still rescuable.

Therefore, in order to come upon be-ing itself as projecting-opening, we seek in vain for history [*Geschichte*], i.e., its transmission through history [as a discipline]. If ever a hint into be-ing's essential sway could come to us, we must then be prepared for experiencing ἀλήθεια first-ever-inceptually. But how far and indeed how definitively are we removed from that experience?

The as yet unbroken—even if through and through disturbed and unrecognizable—dominion of "metaphysics" has led to be-ing's representing itself to us only as the concomitant outcome of representation of a being *as* a being. It is from this basic Western determination (initially still genuinely as οὐσία), then, that all modifications of the interpretation of beings ensue.

Here also is the reason why we apparently continue to move within what has the character of re-presentation, even if initially within the necessity of experiencing (en-thinking) the truth of be-ing. We grasp the "ontological"—even as condition for the "ontic"—still only as an addendum to the ontic and repeat the "ontological" (projecting-open a being unto beingness) once again as a self-application unto itself: projecting-opening beingness as projecting-opening of be-ing unto its truth. When coming from the horizon of metaphysics, there is at first no other way even to make the question of being graspable as a task.

By this approach be-ing itself is apparently still made into an object, and the most decisive opposite of that is attained which the course of the question of be-ing has already opened up for itself. But *Being and Time* after all aims at demonstrating "time" as the domain for projecting-opening be-ing. Certainly, but if things had remained that way, then the question of being would never have unfolded as *question* and thus as enthinking of what is most question-worthy.

Thus at the deciding juncture it was necessary to overcome the crisis of the question of being that was necessarily initially so laid out, and above all to avoid an objectification of be-ing—on the one hand by *holding back* the "temporal" interpretation of be-ing and at the same time by attempting besides to make the truth of be-ing "visible" (freedom unto the ground in *Vom Wesen des Grundes,* and yet in the first part of this treatise the ontic-ontological schema is still thoroughly maintained). By merely thinking further along the line of the question already set forth, the crisis did not let itself be mastered. Rather, a frequent leap into the essential sway of be-ing itself had to be ventured, which at the same time required a more originary enjoining into history: The relation to the beginning, the attempt to clarify ἀλήθεια as an essential character of beingness itself, the grounding of the distinction of being and a being. Thinking became increasingly historical, i.e., the differentiation between what is a historical [*historisch*] observation and what is a systematic observation became increasingly untenable and inappropriate.

Be-ing itself announced its historical essential sway. However, there was and still continues to be a fundamental difficulty: Be-ing is to be projected open in its essential sway, but projecting-opening itself is the "essential sway" of be-ing, is projecting-opening as en-ownment.

Unfolding the question of being unto enthinking of be-ing must all the more unreservedly give up any representational approach, the more inabiding in be-ing this enthinking becomes; and this unfolding must come to know that what matters is to prepare for a historical de-cision which can be endured only historically. This is to say that the attempt at enthinking does not transgress its own historical measure and thus fall back into what has been up to now.

The juncture in the crossing must have both of these equally clear in mindfulness: what is transmitted [*das Herkömmliche*] about *projecting-opening* be-ing and then the other: be-ing as projecting-opening, whereby likewise now what is ownmost to projecting-opening should no longer get its determination from what is representational but rather from the *en-ownment character* of be-ing.

However, as soon as and insofar as the enthinking of be-ing succeeds in leaping, it determines its ownmost as "thinking" from that which being as en-owning en-owns, from Da-*sein*.

263. Every Projecting-Open Is a Thrown One

Hence no statement about what is given reaches what is true. And even less can the re-presenting self-directing to what is given make manifest what is ownmost to the true, truth; instead, it always makes manifest only correctness.

But what does "the *thrown* projecting-open" say? When and how does a projecting-open succeed?

Projecting-open says that man throws himself free of a being unto be-ing, without a being's having already been enopened as such. But here everything remains unclear. Is man then a fettered man? To a being, of course, and this only because he directly comports himself toward "being" (e.g., language), since this relation to be-ing is the very ground of a relationship in a comporting of a comportment.

By throwing himself free of "a being," man first becomes man. For only in this way does he return to a being and *is* he the one who has returned. And the question remains: How does this free-throw occur inceptually and how does this beginning ground history?

Man up to now is the one who in the free-throw has at once

returned, who in this way has traversed for the first time the *differentiation* of a being and of be-ing without himself being able to experience this differentiation and even to ground it.

But the re-turn! One must first know the manner of dwelling and the concomitant gift, as well as the manner in which in the re-turn what was before and fettering is initially met with as what a being is found or what is found as a being—which view of being man as the returner [*Zurückkehrer*] retains.

[One must know] then how this return, how the free-throw is *forgotten* and how everything becomes an extant, orderable, and producable possession, how finally man himself declares himself as such a one *(subjectum)*; how *in this way* then everything is destroyed; how a colossal disturbance runs through all human progress; how be-ing itself as machination sets itself into what is precisely not its ownmost.

And all of this [happens] because man was *not* capable of mastering the returnership [*Rückkehrerschaft*]. This "not" [is] the ground of his hitherto Western history, in which what is ownmost to history perhaps had to be sheltered; this "not" [is] hence also not a mere nothing.

Knowing being does not rest on an ἀνάμνησις as determined since Plato, but rather on a forgetting, on the forgetting of the returnership. But this forgetting is simply the consequence of not-being-able-to-retain the return. But this not-being-able-to-retain arises from not-being-able-to-hold to the ab-ground of the free-throw. But this not-being-able-to-hold is not a weakness but rather the consequence of the necessity of initially preserving being and beings in the first as yet ungraspable differentiating

Therefore all that remains is the return, i.e., retaining beingness (ἰδέα), which is a forgetting of what is enowned.

For at that time already the free-throw, as thrown free-throw, is en-owning, but as yet totally hidden (origin of history).

But how is this to be grasped more definitively, the *throwing-oneself free*? We must avoid seeking refuge now in some human "properties" and "capabilities," e.g., reason. Aside from the fact that these themselves no longer enlighten, for their part they first grow out of the unrecognized ground of determination of man as the receiving one and thus as the one who already returns from the free-throw.

So, if a prop in explaining is refused to us, how is then this very first thing, which determines what is *ownmost* to man, to be said? We must not take man as pre-given in the heretofore familiar properties and now seek the free-throw in him, but rather: throwing-oneself-free must itself first ground for us what is ownmost to man. But how?

Throwing-oneself-free, venturing the open, belonging neither to oneself nor to what is over against and yet to both—not as object and subject but knowing oneself as countering in the open—intimating that *what* throws itself free and that from which it throws itself free holds sway in the same way as the over-against.

Countering is the ground of the encounter that is here not even sought after.

Countering is rending open the "between" [*Zwischen*] unto which the over-against each other [*das Gegeneinander*] occurs as something needing an open.

But what belongs here to "man" and what is left behind? In throwing-oneself-free, he grounds himself in that which he is incapable of making but which he is capable only of venturing as possibility, in Da-*sein*.

But this of course only if he does not ever return to himself as to one who appears in the first free-throw as the over against [*das Gegenüber*], as φύσει ὄν, as a ζῷον.

What is important is the free-throw and the grounding of what is ownmost to man in the estranging of the *open*. Only now does being-history and the history of man begin. And a being? It no longer comes to its truth in a return—but then how? As preserving what is strange. And what is strange counters the en-ownment and lets god find itself in it.

Free-throw never succeeds by mere human impetus [*Antrieb*] and human make-up.

This throw is *thrown* in the resonance of en-ownment. This is to say that being strikes man and shifts him into transformation, into an initial gaining, into a prolonged loss of what is his ownmost.

This traversing of the errancy of essential sway, as history of man, is independent of all history [*Historie*].

And when gods sink within the non-grantedness of the refusal of be-ing.

264. Projecting Be-ing Open and Understanding of Being

As it is introduced in *Being and Time,* understanding of being has a transitional and ambiguous character; this corresponds to the designation of man ("human Dasein" and "Dasein *in* man").

On the one hand understanding of being—looking back, as it were, metaphysically—is grasped as the ungrounded *ground* of the transcendental and, in general, of re-presenting beingness (all the way back to ἰδέα).

On the other hand (because understanding is grasped as projecting-open and this is grasped as thrown) understanding of being indicates grounding the essential sway of truth (manifestness, clearing of the t/here [*Da*], Da-sein). To say *"understanding of being that belongs to Da-sein"* becomes *super*fluous; it says the same thing twice and even in a weakened form. For Da-sein "is" precisely grounding the truth of be-ing as enowning.

Understanding of being moves *within* the *differentiation* of beingness and a being, without as yet validating the origin of the differentiation from within the *deciding-essential sway* of be-ing.

But understanding of being is throughout just the opposite, nay even essentially other than making this understanding dependent upon human intention. How is being still to be made subjective at that place when what counts is the shattering of the subject?

265. En-thinking of Be-ing*

With the phrase "*en*-thinking of be-ing," a way—and perhaps the decisive way in crossing—is to be named by which in the future Western man takes over the essential swaying of the truth of be-ing and thus first becomes historical. To become historical means to rise out of the essential sway of be-ing and therefore to continue to belong to it. Becoming historical does *not* mean to be referred back into what is past and historically [*historisch*] ascertainable.

But now historically mindful deliberation on the history of metaphysics shows that enactment of the guiding-question throughout its entire history has thinking as its guiding-thread (beingness and thinking). This mindfulness gives rise to the insight that the predominance of *thinking* (that it became itself the guiding-thread in the form of representation of something in general) increasingly pushed the interpretation of the beingness of beings in *that* direction from which then finally the equating of being with objectness of beings (of representedness in general) had to come. And this insight reveals that thinking and its predominance (in how it handles the guiding-question and how it chooses the guiding-thread) in the end blocked every way to the question, i.e., to the possible distressing into the question of the *truth of be-ing*. And now should en-*thinking* nevertheless become the passageway into the truth of be-ing—not only thinking but also, as it were, the utmost intensification of its mastery, en-thinking, wherein, as it were, be-ing's total dependency on thinking is expressed? That is how it looks and must look, if we come from a historically mindful deliberation on the guiding-question and its guiding-thread.

But it only looks like that. In order to avoid the appearance as if more than ever the guiding-thread of the guiding-question is being claimed for the grounding-question—which would be absurd considering, the preceding discussion—we must begin with a differentiation, omission of which would continually mislead even the mindful deliberation on the history of the guiding-question and its choice of the guiding-thread.

Thinking (1) on the one hand is meant as the name of the manner of questioning and thus in general for the manner of relating the questioning relation of man to the *being* of beings. That is thinking in the sense of the basic posture of the "thinker" (the philosopher) (thinking as *inquiring into* the question of being).

---

* Cf. *Überlegungen* VII, 78ff. [GA 95].

Thinking (2) on the other hand is meant as the name for the guiding-thread which thinking (1) needs in order to occupy the sphere within which beings as such are interpreted with respect to beingness (thinking as the *guiding-thread* of that questioning).

Now, by a definite interpretation of being (as ἰδέα) the νοεῖν of Parmenides becomes the νοεῖν of διαλέγεσθαι in Plato. The λόγος of Heraclitus becomes the λόγος as assertion and becomes the guiding-thread of the "categories" (Plato: *The Sophist*). The combining of both into *ratio,* and that means the corresponding comprehension of νοῦς and λόγος, is prepared in Aristotle. With Descartes *ratio* becomes "mathematical"; this is possible only because this mathematical essence has been the focus since Plato and, as *one* possibility, is grounded in the ἀλήθεια of φύσις. Thinking (2) in the sense of assertion becomes the guiding-thread for thinking (1) of Western thinkers. And then in the end this thinking (2) also provides direction for interpretation of thinking (1) as the basic posture of philosophy. (Closely connected with this is the peculiar predominance of the thinking of thinking and what it thinks as such, i.e., of the I and "self"-consciousness in modern philosophy—a predominance that is intensified to the utmost by equating actuality (being) as absolute with thinking as the unconditioned; the unequivocal relation of being to the logic of assertion still reigns even in Nietzsche.)

If now, in preparing for the other beginning, what is *ownmost* to philosophy is maintained as *inquiring into being* (in the double sense of inquiring into the being of beings and inquiring into the truth of be-ing)—as it must be maintained, precisely because the first-ever-inceptual inquiring into being indeed arrived at *its* end and thus not at its beginning—designation of philosophizing as thinking must also continue to be preserved. But this does not decide at all about whether now the guiding-thread of thinking (1) is also thinking (2), whether something like a guiding-thread comes into play *at all,* as it does in handling of the guiding-question. Now, in crossing to the other beginning, the question of being does become the question of the truth of be-ing, such that this truth, as what is ownmost to truth, belongs to the essential swaying of be-ing itself. The choice of guiding-thread becomes superfluous, indeed is now impossible from the start. Being now no longer counts as the beingness of a being, as the *addendum* represented within the perspective of a being, an *addendum* which emerges simultaneously as the *a priori* of a being (of what is present). Rather, now be-ing holds sway in advance in its truth. That includes that now thinking (1), too, is exclusively and in advance determined by the essential sway of be-ing and not, for example, as since Plato, as the cleansed representation of a being within the perspective of a being. *Receiving* being is not determined in terms of the grasping of beingness in the sense of the κοινόν of ἰδέα but rather from within the essential swaying of be-ing itself. This swaying must originarily and inceptually arise in order, as it were, to decide by itself what must "*be*" ownmost to thinking (1) and to the thinker. This manifold "must" announce a most original [*ureigene*] necessity of a distress that can itself belong only to the essential sway of be-ing.

However, we have been confined for too long and too firmly in the tradition not to mean initially with thinking—wherever "thinking" is named—the representation of something in general and thus representation of unity according to kind as the subordinate and differentiated. Finally, when thinking is taken as thinking of being, this counts as the most general of all. Every inquiry into being stands in this semblance of inquiry into what is most general, which one can get a hold of only by grasping its peculiarities and their connections. To grasp this most general, then, only means to let it be in its indeterminacy and emptiness and to set its indeterminacy as its singular determinedness, i.e., directly to represent it.

Thus, with the accustomed concept of thinking (the "logical" concept), once again one has decided beforehand about the essential sway of be-ing, whereby similarly this essential sway is meant in advance as that which is the object of a representation.

However, we must free ourselves even from that concept of thinking in order to allow be-ing the attuning-determining power for designating what is ownmost to thinking (en-thinking). That Greek interpretation of ὄν ἧ ὄν as ἕν, that heretofore unclear priority which the onefold and unity have everywhere in thinking of being, cannot of course be deduced from logic and from the guiding-thread-role of λόγος as assertion, because this priority presupposes a definite interpretation of ὄν (ὑποκείμενον). Seen more deeply, that onefold is merely the foreground—seen from the vantage point of gathering re-presentation (λέγειν)—of the presencing as such, in which a being directly and already gathers in its what *and* that. Presence can be grasped as gathering and thus be understood as unity—and with the priority of λόγος *must* be so grasped. But by itself, unity itself is not an originary and essential determination of the being of a being. However, inceptual thinkers necessarily come upon this unity, because the truth of be-ing must remain hidden from them and their beginning and because, for grasping being at all, it is important that presencing be maintained as what is first and nearest to being's arising; hence ἕν, but always and immediately in relation to the many as those that emerge, arise (become), and those that go away, pass away (swaying-forth and swaying-away in the presencing itself: Anaximander, Heraclitus, Parmenides). In terms of the other beginning, that unshaken and never inquired determination of being (unity) can and must nevertheless become question-worthy; and then unity points back to "time" (time of time-space that holds to the abground). But then it becomes clear that with the priority of presence (present) wherein unity is grounded, something has been decided, namely, *that in what is most self-evident [presence] the most estranging decision lies hidden,* that this deciding-character belongs to the essential swaying of be-ing and hints at the respective singularity and most originary historicity of be-ing itself.

Even with an approximate awareness of the history of be-ing, we can gather that be-ing is directly never definitively sayable—and thus never only "provisionally" sayable—as that interpretation (which takes be-ing to be the most general and most empty) would feign have it.

That the essential sway of be-ing is never definitively sayable does not indicate a lack. On the contrary, it indicates that the non-definitive knowing precisely holds fast the *abground* of, and thus the essential sway of, be-ing. This holding-fast to the abground belongs to what is ownmost to Da-sein as the grounding of the truth of be-ing.

Holding-fast to the abground is simultaneously leaping into the essential swaying of be-ing, such that be-ing itself unfolds its essential power as en-owning, as the *between* [*Zwischen*] for the needfulness of god and the guardianship of man.

The en-thinking of be-ing, the naming of its essential sway, is nothing other than the venture of helping gods out into be-ing and of preparing for man the truth of what is true.

This "definition" of thinking by that which it "thinks" accomplishes the total turning away from all "logical" interpretation of thinking. For this is one of the greatest prejudices of Western philosophy, namely, that thinking must be determined "logically," i.e., with respect to *assertion.* (The "psychological" explanation of thinking is simply an appendix to the "logical" and presupposes the logical explanation, even where it aspires to replace the logical explanation; "psychological" here stands for biological-anthropological.) But the backside of that prejudice is also when one now, in *rejecting* the "logical" interpretation of thinking (that is, of the logical relation to being; cf. *What Is Metaphysics?*), is overcome with anxiety, or better, with fear—now the rigor and seriousness of thinking is endangered and everything is left to feeling and its "judgment." For whoever says and has ever proven that the *logically* meant thinking is the "rigorous" one? That would be true—if it could *ever* be true—only by presupposing that the logical interpretation of *being* could be the only one possible; and that would be even more a prejudice. With respect to the essential sway of be-ing, it is perhaps precisely "logic" that is the *least* rigorous and *least* serious procedure in determining the ownmost—only an illusion whose ownmost lies deeper *still* than the "dialectical illusion" which Kant revealed in the domain of the possible objectification of beings in the whole. With respect to the essential grounding of the truth of be-ing, "logic" itself is an illusion—although the most necessary illusion that the history of be-ing has known so far. What is ownmost to "logic" itself, which attains its utmost shape in Hegel's metaphysics, can be grasped only from within the other beginning of *thinking* be-ing. But the abgroundness of this thinking also lets the so-called rigor of logical acumen (as the form for finding the truth, and not only as the form for expressing what is found) appear as a game that cannot master itself, which then could also degenerate into philosophical erudition in which everyone, equipped with some kind of acumen, could mull around without ever being affected by be-ing and without ever intimating the meaning of the question of be-ing.

But enthinking of be-ing is now also relatively rare and perhaps is granted to us only in the coarse steps of a preparation, if the wager of this leap which is held to the abground can be called a favor.

It is *this* thinking of be-ing which is truly un-conditioned, i.e., not conditioned and determined by something that is conditioned outside itself and outside what is to be thought by it, but rather *solely* determined by what is to be thought in it, by be-ing itself, which nevertheless is not "the absolute." However, in that thinking (in the sense of en-thinking) receives its ownmost from be-ing, in that Da-sein too—whose *one* inabiding must be en-thinking—is en-owned first and only by being, *the* thinking, i.e., philosophy, has its ownmost and highest origin out of itself, out of what is to be thought in philosophy. Only now is philosophy totally unassailable by estimation and valuations which reckon with goals and advantages, i.e., mishandle philosophy, like art, as cultural achievement or in the end only as an expression of culture, and impute to philosophy what seemingly soars above philosophy but in truth remains far below it, drag what is its ownmost down into what is intelligible and, by such dragging, shove it into what is merely still tolerated and humored.

Seen in terms of such a downgrading, what a presumption it must still be to uphold an unconditioned origin for philosophy. Yet even from a higher point of view—nay from any point of view ever attempted—we attain no other essential view of philosophy which would not include the "titanic" in its view. This view remains concealed within metaphysics and throughout its history and is finally weakened to a merely epistemologically dubious trespassing of borders. However, if in crossing from metaphysics, thinking must decide to be enthinking of be-ing, then the danger of an unavoidable presumptuousness threatens to be essentially increased. Knowing this danger is of course also modified in that no sooner is that threat named than the essential threat becomes silent. This allusion belongs within the ambiguity of the crossing, in which mindfulness must continue to touch upon that which in the enactment of crossing forthwith increasingly shifts itself into a simple doing. In philosophy this ambiguity is particularly stubborn because, as thinking

questioning, philosophy must shift itself necessarily into its own knowing, precisely insofar as it is of unconditioned origin and is all the more
originarily that unconditioned origin.

In the crossing from metaphysics, to which be-ing counted as the
most general and most common, the uniqueness of be-ing will come to
essential swaying in a correspondingly unique estrangement and opac-
ity. To the thinking in the crossing, everything that belongs to being-
history has the non-ordinariness of the one-time-only and this-time-
only. Thus, wherever and whenever en-thinking of be-ing succeeds, it
reaches a rigor and keenness of historicity for the saying of which the
language is still lacking, i.e., the naming and being-able-to-hear that is
adequate to be-ing.

En-thinking of be-ing does not think up a concept but rather
achieves that deliverance [*Befreiung*] from what is only a being, a deliverance which renders thinking fit to its determination and vocation in
terms of be-ing. En-thinking exposes to that history whose "events" are
nothing other than thrusts of en-ownment itself. We can only say this
if we say: *that* this is enowned—and what is this "this"? That Hölderlin
poetizes the future poet, that he himself "is" the first to put up for decision the nearness and remoteness of gods who have been and are to
come (consider the standpoint of be-ing-history).

Who would be surprised if in crossing from metaphysics into the
enthinking of be-ing this allusion to the first "that" of be-ing-history is
assumed to be totally arbitrary and unintelligible? Nevertheless it is of
little use to rebut this assumption by explaining how all "literary-historical," "poetic-historical," and "intellectual-historical" manners of observation must be avoided. Already here the leap into be-ing and its truth
is required, the experience that with the name of *Hölderlin* that unique
putting-up-for-decision is enowned—*is* enowned, not somehow *had
been* enowned. We can try to distinguish this "event" historically in its
uniqueness by seeing it in the midst of what is still the heretofore in its
utmost intensification and richest unfolding: in the midst of the metaphysics of German Idealism and in the midst of the formation of
Goethe's world-image, in the midst of that which is separated from
Hölderlin by abysses (in "romanticism")—even if it has historically
"influenced" him, as the bearer of the name, but not as the guardian of
be-ing. But what is the use of such a rebuttal? At most it only attains a
new misunderstanding, as if *within* that history of metaphysics and of art
Hölderlin were just someone "peculiar"—whereas we are not dealing
with the "within," but also not merely with the exceptional "without,"
but rather with the nonderivable thrust of be-ing itself, which is to be
seized in its purest "that," that, *now and ever since*, that decision is situated
in the history of the West, regardless of whether it can be received by the
still ongoing epoch and whether it can or cannot be received at all.

For the first time this decision lays time-space around be-ing itself, which along with time stretches itself out of be-ing—a time which temporalizes be-ing in the originary onefold of this free play of time-space.

From now on every thinking that reads beingness from out of and off beings remains outside *that* history in which be-ing as enowning enowns thinking for itself in the shape of what accords to and belongs to Dasein. It is the calling of thinking to rescue for be-ing the uniqueness of its history—and no longer to fritter away what is ownmost to thinking into the compartmentalization of the worn-out "generality" of categories. But that is why the knowing ones know that preparation for this history of be-ing, in the sense of grounding preparedness for preserving the truth of be-ing in a being that thus first unfolds, will be a very long preparation and will be unknown for a long time yet. Those who are preparing must as yet be able to stand far apart from the founders if they want to be touched by the thrust of the refusal of be-ing—even if only from far away—and thereby to be intimaters. The saying of enthinking of be-ing remains a boldness, so that it is named a helping out into the housing of gods and into the estrangement of man (consider be-ing as enowning).

266. Be-ing and "Ontological Difference"
"Differentiation"

This differentiation *bears* the guiding-question of metaphysics: What is a being? But in enacting the guiding-question, this differentiation as such is not expressly raised to the level of knowing awareness or even held fast as something question-worthy. Does differentiation sustain the guiding-question, or does the guiding-question first enact the differentiation, though not explicitly? Obviously the latter. For differentiation appears in the horizon of the guiding-question and initially also as something final for the elucidating mindfulness of the guiding-question. But differentiation should only be something in the foreground (why?), wherein the *onset* of the grounding-question (of the truth of be-ing) can be elucidated in a leading manner.

Be-ing-question as grounding-question would have grasped nothing of what is its own question-worthiest if it had not immediately pressed for the question concerning the *origin* of the "ontological difference." Differentiation of "being" *and* "a being"—that be-ing *distinguishes itself from* a being—can have its origin only in the *essential swaying* of be-ing, if indeed a being as such is also grounded by be-ing. What is ownmost to this distinction and its ground is *the* darkness that lies enclosed in all metaphysics—all the more estranging, the more decisively metaphysics rigidifies itself in conceivability [*Denkmäßigkeit*] of beingness, especially thinking in the sense of absolute thinking. What is ownmost to this distinction and its ground is be-ing as *en-ownment*. Be-ing, as the "between"

[*Zwischen*] that lights up, moves itself into this clearing and therefore—
without ever being recognized and surmised as enownment—is, as
being, from the vantage point of representing thinking basically something differentiable and differentiated. This is already true for the
first-ever-inceptual essential swaying of be-ing as φύσις, which
emerges as ἀλήθεια but is immediately forgotten and misinterpreted as
a most-being being [*zum seiendsten Seienden*], as being the highest manner of being in favor of a being which by means of ἀλήθεια as such is
receivable. Here is at the same time the reason why the ontological difference as such does not enter into knowing awareness, because basically a differentiation is always necessary only between one being and
another being *(the highest being)*. One sees the *consequence* in the widely
disseminated confusion in using the name *be-ing* and a *being*, which
mutually and arbitrarily stand for each other, so that, although intending be-ing, one re-presents only a being and presents it as what is the
most general of all re-presenting. Being (as *ens qua ens*—*ens in commune*)
is merely the thinnest thinning of a being and itself nonetheless a being
and—because determining every being—the most-being of beings.
Even if, after the crucial naming of this differentiation in *Being and Time*,
one now strives for a more careful use of language, nothing is attained
and not at all is it proven that a knowing awareness and questioning of
be-ing has come alive. On the contrary, the danger is now increased
that being itself is taken and worked with as something extant for itself.

Generally, stressing this "differentiation" can say something in thinking only if from the very beginning it arises out of the question concerning the "meaning of be-ing," i.e., concerning its truth—if this question
is not taken as something arbitrary but rather as *the* question that historically *decides* metaphysics and decides about metaphysics and its
inquiry, if be-ing itself becomes a distress, a distress that once again
attunes for itself the "thinking" that in its destiny belongs to distress.

"Ontological difference" is a passageway that becomes unavoidable if
the necessity of asking the grounding-question out of the guiding-question is to be made manifest. And the guiding-question itself? But this
task cannot be avoided as long as any way at all must nonetheless be
secured which leads *out of* the still very inadequate tradition of *metaphysically* inquiring thinking into the necessarily unasked question of
the truth of be-ing.

But this characterization of "ontological difference" as such, and proceeding from it with the intention of overcoming metaphysics, seems
initially to effect the opposite: now the result is getting bogged down
even more in "ontology." One takes this differentiation as a doctrine
and key for ontological deliberation and forgets what is crucial, namely,
that this differentiation has the character of a passage.

One dismisses in advance every effort not to enact this differentiation *as a re-presenting* differentiation at all, in which what is differentiated is uniformly put on the same level of differentiatedness, even if it is left completely undetermined, whereas this differentiation, taken formally and said without thinking, can only be an indication that the relation to being is other than the relation to a being and that this otherness of relations [*Bezüge*] belongs to a differentiated relating-oneself [*Sichbeziehen*] to what is to be differentiated. As grounded, the relation to being is the inabiding in Da-*sein*, is standing within the truth of be-ing (as enowning).

The relation to a being is the creating preserving of the preservation of be-ing in that which, in accord with such a preserving, is put as a being into the clearing of the t/here [*Da*].

In crossing over to Da-sein within questioning the truth of be-ing, there is no other possibility but initially to transform representing to such an extent that the relation to being as projecting-open and thus as *the* character of understanding (Da-sein's understanding of being) is established. But these determinations, as crucial as they continue to be for an initial elucidation of the totally other questioning of the question of being, are nevertheless—seen in terms of the question-*worthiness* of be-ing and its essential swaying—only a first, groping step onto a very long springboard, a groping step with which hardly anything is noticed of the demand which is necessary at the end of the springboard, for the leaping-off. Nonetheless, one does not even take this step as a first one in a long "being-underway" but indeed as the last step, in order to settle oneself in what is said as a definite "doctrine" and "view" and with it to carry out all kinds of things in historical [*historisch*] respect. Or else one rejects this "doctrine" and believes thereby to have decided something about the question of being.

However, basically stressing the "ontological difference" only indicates that the attempt at a more originary question of being must be a more essential appropriation of the history of metaphysics. But to bring both of these together into one, or basically to have them already as one—commencing with the totally other *and* with the loyalty to the history of the first beginning, which essentially surpasses all heretofore *historical* [as discipline] acquisition, commencing with the equally crucial mastery and claim of the exclusionaries—is *so* estranging for the habitude of history [as discipline] and systematization [*Systematik*] that history and systematization do not even come on the idea that something like that could be required. (But what else does the "phenomenological destruction" want?)

It is for this reason that the "ontological difference" hovers in indeterminacy. It looks as if it has already been known, at least since Plato, whereas it was only enacted and, as it were, brought into usage. In Kant it is known in the concept of the "transcendental" — and *yet not* known, because on the one hand beingness is grasped as object*ness* and on the other hand it is precisely this interpretation of beingness that cuts off any *questioning of being*. But again, it looks as if the "ontological difference" is something "new" — which it cannot be and does not want to be. This difference only names that which sustains the entire history of philosophy and *as* this sustenance could never be for philosophy as metaphysics what calls for questioning and therefore for naming. Ontological difference is something transitional in crossing from the end of metaphysics to the other beginning.

That this differentiation, however, can be named as the jointure of the domain of Western metaphysics and that it must be named in this indeterminate form — this has its ground in the inceptual history of be-ing itself. That for the most general representation (thinking) being is what is most constantly present and as such is, as it were, the emptiness of the presentness [*Gegenwärtigkeit*] itself — this is enclosed in φύσις. Insofar as thinking has entered into the domination of "logic," this presentness [*Gegenwärtige*] of *everything that is present* (the extant) is made into the most general [*Allgemeinsten*] and — in spite of Aristotle's warning that it is not γένος — into the "most common" [*Generellsten*]. If we ponder *this* historical source of the ontological difference from within being-history itself, then knowing awareness of this source already compels to a near-distance [*Vorferne*] of belongingness to the truth of being, compels to the experience that we are sustained by the "ontological difference" in all humanness as relation to beings and that we continue to be exposed hereby to the power of be-ing more essentially than in any relation to any kind of "actual" — regardless of how "true to life."

And this, man's being-thoroughly-tuned by be-ing itself, must be experienced by naming the "ontological difference" — namely, at that point when the question of being itself is to be awakened as question. On the other hand, however, with respect to the overcoming of metaphysics (the historical playing-forth of the first and the other beginning), the "ontological difference" must be elucidated in its belongingness to Da-sein. Seen from that point, the ontological difference moves into the form of a — nay, *the* — "basic-structure" of Da-sein itself.

267. Be-ing*
(Enowning)

Be-ing is *en-owning*. This word names be-ing in thinking and grounds be-ing's essential swaying in its own jointure, which lets itself be indi-

---

* Cf. the *saying* "of" be-ing, pp. 333f.

cated in the manifoldness of enownings.

Enowning is:

1. *en-ownment,* namely that, in the needfulness out of which gods need be-ing, this be-ing necessitates Da-sein unto the grounding of be-ing's own truth and thus lets the "between" [*Zwischen*], the en-own-ment of Dasein by gods and owning of gods to themselves, hold sway as en-owning.

2. The enowning of en-ownment gathers within itself the *de-cision* [*Ent-scheidung*]: that freedom, as the ground that holds to abground, lets a distress emerge from out of which, as from out of the overflow of the ground, gods and man come forth into partedness.

3. En-ownment as de-cision brings to the parted ones *countering,* namely that this "toward-each-other" of the broadest needful de-cision must stand in the utmost "counter," because it bridges over the ab-ground of the needed be-ing.

4. Countering is the origin of the strife, which holds sway by setting a being free from its lostness in mere beingness. *Setting-free* distinguishes en-owning in its relation to a being as such. En-ownment of Da-sein lets Da-sein become inabiding in what is non-ordinary vis-à-vis every kind of being.

5. But setting free, grasped out of the clearing of the t/here [*Da*], is simultaneously *the withdrawal* of enowning, namely that it withdraws from any re-presenting-calculation and holds sway as refusal.

6. As richly enjoined and without image as be-ing holds sway, never-theless it rests in itself and in its *simpleness.* It is possible that the charac-ter of the "between" [*Zwischen*] (between gods and man) might mislead into taking be-ing as mere relation and as consequence and result of the relation of what is in relation. But en-owning *is* this relating—if this des-ignation is even possible—that first brings those in relation to them-selves in order to lay their needfulness and guardianship into the open of the countering-parted ones, which the ones in relation do not first take on as property but rather out of which they draw what is their ownmost. Be-ing is the distress of gods; and, as this distressing of Da-sein, it is more of an abground than anything that may be called a being and that no longer can be named by be-ing. Be-ing is needed, is the needfulness of gods, and yet is not to be derived from them. Rather it is the other way around: be-ing is superior to them, in the ab-groundness of its essential sway as ground. Be-ing enowns Da-sein and yet is not its origin. As the ground of the countering ones in it, the "between" [*Zwi-schen*] holds sway unmediated. This determines its simpleness, which is not emptiness but rather the ground of the fullness which springs forth from the countering as strife.

7. Simpleness of be-ing carries within itself the mark of *uniqueness.* It does not at all need any distinguishing or differences, not even the dif-

ference from beings. For this difference is required only if being itself is branded as a kind of being and thereby never preserved as the unique but generalized into what is most general.

8. *Uniqueness* of be-ing grounds its *aloneness,* in accordance with which it surrounds itself only with the nothing, whose neighborhood remains the most genuine and protects the aloneness most loyally. In consequence of aloneness, be-ing holds sway to "a being" continually only mediately, through the strife of world and earth.

The essential sway of be-ing is not fully thought in any of these namings, and yet it is "entirely" thought in every one; "entirely" here says: every time thinking "of" be-ing is pulled into be-ing's non-ordinariness by be-ing itself and deprived of any explanatory aid that comes from a being.

Enowning always means enowning as en-ownment, de-cision, countering, setting-free, withdrawal, simpleness, uniqueness, aloneness. The onefold of this essential swaying is non-objective and can be known only by that thinking which must venture what is non-ordinary, not as particularity of what is conspicuous, but rather as the necessity of what is most nonappearing, in which the ground that holds to abground and is the ground of gods' lacking the ground and of man's foundership is opened and *that* is allotted to be-ing which metaphysics could never know: *Da-sein.*

By remembering the old distinctions (being and becoming)—which were still prevailing, up to their end in Nietzsche—one might likewise want to take the determination of be-ing as enowning as an interpretation of being as "becoming" ("life," "movement"). Not to mention at all the unavoidable fall back into metaphysics and the dependency of representations of "movement," "life," and "becoming" from being as beingness, such an interpretation of enowning would completely turn away from enowning, since such an interpretation makes assertions about enowning as an object, instead of letting this essential swaying—and only it—speak, so that thinking remain a thinking of be-ing which does not make assertions about be-ing, but rather says in a saying that belongs to the en-said and repels all objectification and falsification—into what is static (or "what is flowing")—because with such assertions the dimension of re-presentation is immediately entered and the non-ordinariness of be-ing is denied.

The full essential swaying of be-ing in the truth of enowning allows us to realize that be-ing and only be-ing *is* and that a being is *not.* With this knowing-awareness of be-ing, thinking attains for the first time the trace of the other beginning in crossing out of metaphysics. What counts for metaphysics is that a being is and a not-being "is" also and be-ing is the most-being of beings.

In contrast to this: be-ing *is* unique, and therefore it "is" never a being and least of all the most-being. But a being *is not,* and for that very reason thinking of beingness—forgetful of be-ing—attributes to a being the beingness as the most general property. This attribution has its legitimacy in the ordinary representation; and therefore one must say, over against this representation, that be-ing holds sway—whereas a being "is."

Be-ing is. Does Parmenides not say the same: ἔστιν γὰρ εἶναι? No. For right here already εἶναι stands for ἐόν; being is here already a being which is most-being, ὄντως ὄν, which very soon becomes κοινόν, ἰδέα, καϑόλου.

Be-ing is—that is to say that be-ing alone sways the essential sway of it itself (enowning). *Be-ing holds sway*—it must be said *thus* when one is speaking in terms of metaphysics, for which what counts is: *A being "is"* (the ambiguity of thinking in the crossing).

A being is; here one is speaking out of the mostly implicit basic position of metaphysics, which lets man light upon a being as what is the nearest and lets him start with a being and go back to a being. Therefore, here the character of assertion of this sentence is different from the saying: *be-ing is.* "A being is" must be enacted as an assertion which has its correctness; directed *toward* a being, beingness is stated from it. Assertion (λόγος) here does not merely count as a subsequent expression in the language of a re-presentation, but rather assertion (ἀπό-φανσις) here is itself the fundamental form of the relation to a being as such, and thus to beingness.

With saying as measure [*sagenmäßig*], the saying "be-ing is" is completely different (cf. *Überlegungen* IV [GA 94], 1f.). We can, of course, always take the saying as a sentence and an assertion of a proposition. Then, thought metaphysically, one must conclude that be-ing thus becomes a being and consequently the most-being. However, the saying does not say anything *about* be-ing that is generally attributed to be-ing or is extant in it, but rather says be-ing itself out of itself [*das Seyn selbst aus ihm selbst*]—says that be-ing alone is master of its essential sway and for that very reason the "is" can never become something merely attributed. In this saying be-ing is said out of "is" and, as it were, is said back into "is." However, in this way simultaneously the fundamental form is characterized in which all saying "from" [*vom*] be-ing, better: every saying *of* [*des*] be-ing must maintain itself. For this saying "of" be-ing does not have be-ing as object but rather springs forth from being as its origin and therefore, when the saying of be-ing is to name the origin, it always speaks back to the origin. Therefore, every "logic" here "thinks" too short, because λόγος as assertion can no longer remain the guiding-thread for representing being. But saying is immediately pulled into the ambiguity of assertion, and thinking "of" be-ing becomes *essentially* more difficult. But that only attests to the primary nearness to the remoteness of be-ing—that be-ing "is" refusal and set-ting-free itself and must be preserved as such in enowning and thus must always be difficult, a struggle which in the utmost depths reveals itself as the play which holds to abground.

But when a being *is not*, then this says that a being continues to belong to be-ing as the *preserving* of its truth, but a being can never transfer itself into the essential swaying of be-ing. But a being as such distinguishes itself with regard to the respective belongingness to the truth of be-ing and the exclusion from its essential swaying.

Now, what becomes of the *differentiation* of a being and be-ing? Now we grasp this differentiation as the merely metaphysical—and thus already misinterpreted—foreground of a de-cision which *is* be-ing itself (see above, n. 2). This differentiation *can no longer* be read off a being by progressing to the distinct generalization of its being. Therefore, this dif-ferentiation can also not be justified somehow by the allusion that "we" (who?) must understand being so that we can experience a being *as* a being. This understanding is indeed correct, and the allusion to it can serve at any time as a first indication of being and of the differentiability of beings and be-ing. *But:* What ensues here, what is already presup-posed, the *metaphysical* thinking of beingness, cannot stand as the basic outline for grasping—be-ing-historically and in accord with Da-sein—the essential sway of be-ing and its truth in its essential swaying (cf. Be-ing, 271: Da-sein). Nevertheless, the crossing into the other begin-ning cannot be prepared in any other way than that the courage for the old (for the first-ever-inceptual) is brought to bear on the crossing and thus initially the attempt is made to drive the old itself in its own con-stitution beyond itself: a being, being, the "meaning" (truth) of being (cf. *Being and Time*). But it is important to know that from the beginning *this* more originary retrieval demands—and already gives rise to—a complete transformation of man into Da-sein, because the truth of be-ing, which is to be opened up, will bring nothing other than the more originary essential swaying *of be-ing itself*. And this means that everything is transformed and that the walkways that still led to be-ing must be broken off, because another time-space is enopened by be-ing itself, which time-space makes a new erecting and grounding of beings necessary. Nowhere with a being and only once in be-ing does the mildness of the awesome in the innermost essential sway turn to meet man and gods, each time in a different way, as a storm.

Only in be-ing does the *possible* hold sway, as be-ing's deepest cleav-age, so that it is in the shape of the possible that be-ing must first be thought in the thinking of the other beginning. (But metaphysics makes the "actual" as what is [*das Seiende*] its starting point and the goal for the determination of being.)

The possible—and even the possible pure and simple—opens out only in the attempt. The attempt must be totally governed by a fore-grasping will. As putting-itself-beyond-itself, the will *resides* in a being-beyond-itself. This residing originarily grants the free-play of time-space, into which be-ing soars: Da-sein. It holds sway as a bold venture. And only in a bold venture does man reach into the domain of de-cision. And only in the bold venture is he capable of deliberating.

That being is and therefore does not become a being; this is expressed most sharply thus: Be-ing is possibility, what is never extant and yet through en-ownment is always what grants and refuses in not- granting.

Only when thinking has ventured to think be-ing itself without falsifying it to a mere resonance of a being, only then can man become aware that a being is never sufficient for letting be-ing even be intimated.

Thus, when be-ing is thought as the "between" [*Zwischen*] into which gods are distressed, so that it is a distress for man, then gods and man cannot be taken as "given" or "extant." In the projecting-open of that thinking, god and man are taken over—each differently—as what is historical, which itself first comes into its essential swaying from out of enowning of the "between" [*Zwischen*]. But this means that each comes to its essential swaying for the struggle for what is its ownmost, for the steadfastness of deciding for one of the hidden possibilities.

"Man" and "god" are word-hulls without history if the truth of be-ing in them is not brought to language.

Be-ing holds sway as the "between" [*Zwischen*] for god and man, but in such a way that this between-space [*Zwischenraum*] first grants essential possibility for god and man—a "between" that surges over its shore and from this surging-over first lets the shore stand as shore, a shore that always belongs to the stream of en-owning, is always sheltered in the richness of the possibilities of god and man, always this side and the other side of the inexhaustible relations in whose clearing worlds are enjoined and sink away, earths are disclosed and endure destruction.

But also in this or that way be-ing must above all remain unreadable [*deutungslos*]: the bold venture against the nothing to which be-ing owns the origin.

The greatest danger for be-ing (because it always arises out of be-ing itself), a danger which belongs to be-ing as its time-space, is to make itself into "what is" [*Seiend*] and to bear confirmation by a being. History of metaphysics—metaphysics itself in the sense of the priority of a being over being—attests to this danger and to the difficulty of withstanding it. The ambiguity of differentiating a being and being attributes being to a being and feigns a separatedness that is not grounded from out of be-ing itself.

But metaphysics makes being a being [*seiend*], i.e., makes being into a being, because metaphysics sets being as "idea" as goal for a being and then subsequently attaches "culture," as it were, on this goal-setting.

But be-ing is preventing all "goals" and breakdown of every explainability.

268. Be-ing
(Differentiation)

Be-ing holds sway as the en-ownment of gods and man to their countering. The strife of world and earth arises in the clearing of the sheltering of the "between" [Zwischen], which comes forth from within and along with the countering enownment. And only in the free-play of time-space of this strife is there preserving and loss of enownment and does that which is called a being enter the open of that clearing.

Be-ing and a being cannot be distinguished immediately, because they are not at all immediately related to each other. Although a being as what is resonates only in enownment, be-ing is—in the manner of abground—remote from all beings. The attempts to represent both together—already in the manner of naming them—stems from metaphysics. Indeed, metaphysics even has its mark everywhere therein, that, regardless of how unclear and unexpressly it may be enacted, the *differentiation* of being and beings is taken to be an immediate one. Being counts as generalization of beings; with representation as measure, being is equally graspable as a being, only "more abstract." Being is, once again a being, only rarefied, as it were, and then again not, because to be what is actual continues to be reserved for a being. On the other hand, on the basis of the predominance of thinking (of representing something in κοινόν and καθόλου) being is nonetheless granted a priority as beingness, a priority which then shines forth in the respective determination of the relation of the ones being differentiated.

Being is condition for a being, which thus continues to be determined in advance already as thing (something present as extant). Being en-things [be-dingt] a being either as its cause (*summum ens*—δημιουργός) or as ground for the objectness of the thing in re-presentation (condition of possibility of experience or, generally at first, as the "earlier" by virtue of its higher constancy and presence in accord with its generality). Here, thought in a Platonic-Aristotelian manner, *en-thinging* [Bedingen] as character of being still best corresponds to its closest inceptual essence (presence and constancy); but it also does not lend itself to further explanation. Thus it always remains distorted and destroys the originariness and carefulness of Greek thinking, if one reads the cause-character of conditioning, or even the "transcendental" conditioning, *back* into the relationship of being and a being that is meant by the Greeks. But even the *later* manners of en-thinging of a being to a being as such by means of being are, of course, prefigured and required by the Greek interpretation, insofar as beingness (ἰδέα) is what is actually produced (ποιούμενον) and *therefore* what makes up and makes a being—insofar as, on the other hand and at the same time, ἰδέα is the νοούμενον, the re-presented as such, what is first seen in all representing. Metaphysics never gets beyond these manners of differentiating being and a being and of grasping their relation. Nay, it is peculiar to metaphysics to find for itself a way out by mixing up these manners of thinking and to waver back and forth between extreme positions: the unconditionality of beingness and the unconditionality of beings as such. From this point of view a singular unequivocal metaphysical significance can be attributed to the ambiguous titles "idealism" and "realism." A consequence of this metaphysical grasping of being and beings is the distribution of both into (regions) and stages—and this simultaneously contains the presupposition for unfolding the idea of system in metaphysics.

On the other hand, projecting-open be-ing as enownment is incomparable and never graspable in metaphysical concepts and ways of thinking—a projecting which experiences itself as *thrown* and keeps away from any appearance of making. Here be-ing reveals itself in that essential swaying on the basis of whose abgroundness those countered (gods and men) and those in strife (world and earth) come to their ownmost, in their originary history between be-ing and beings, and admit the common naming of be-ing and a being only as what is most question-worthy and most separated.

But in that gods and man in the distress of be-ing meet in countering, man is thrown out of his hitherto modern Western position, thrown back behind himself into fully other ranges of determinations, in which animality as little as rationality can have an essential place, even if henceforth to ascertain these properties in extant man is in a certain sense correct (whereby one must nonetheless ask who they are who find such things correct and even erect "sciences" such as biology and ethnology of race upon such correctnesses, and thus with these sciences still seemingly undergird a "worldview"—an undergirding which is always the ambition of any "worldview").

By projecting be-ing open as enowning, the ground—and with that what is ownmost to history and its essential space—is first intimated. History [*Geschichte*] is not the exclusive right of man but rather the essential sway of be-ing itself. History alone is in play in the "between" [*Zwischen*] of the countering of gods and man as the ground of the strife of world and earth; history is nothing other than enownment of this "between." History [as a discipline] therefore never attains to history [*Geschichte*]. The differentiation of be-ing and of a being is a de-cision that originates out of the essential sway of be-ing itself and one that soars further—and only *in this way* is it to be thought.

In whatever way be-ing is raised to a condition, be-ing is already lowered to the servitude of and supplementation to beings.

Thinking in the other beginning does not know the explanation of be-ing by beings and knows nothing of en-thinging beings by be-ing, an en-thinging that always also *en-things* be-ing *unto* a being, in order then again to allow being an eminence, in the form of "ideal" and "values" (ἀγαθόν is the beginning).

To be sure, according to form and in consequence of a long custom in representation by metaphysics and supported by the language and rigidification of meaning that is minted by metaphysics, all talk of be-ing *can* now be misinterpreted as the familiar relationship of condition to conditioned. This danger cannot be met directly; rather, it must be taken over along with metaphysics, as a concomitant gift of metaphysics, whose history *then* cannot be rejected when in the originary projecting-opening of be-ing what is ownmost to history first comes into play.

269. Be-ing

Man must "experience" the full non-ordinariness of be-ing over against all beings and be en-owned, by this non-ordinariness, into the truth of be-ing.

Be-ing reminds of "nothing," but least of all of a "being," whereas every kind of being reminds of and carries on that which is its kind. Beings create a custom of representation which very soon lapses into taking being as well (as the most general and thoroughly remembered, see the ἀνάμνησις of Plato, which expresses such a custom) as a being, as the "most-being."

Be-ing reminds of "nothing," and therefore "nothing" belongs to be-ing. We know little enough of this belongingness. Yet we know one of its consequences, which is perhaps only apparently as superficial as it passes itself off to be: we shun and abhor the "nothing" and believe that we must at all times avail ourselves of such a condemnation because of course the nothing is what is nothing at all. But what if the actual reason for the flight from the (misinterpreted) nothing were not the will to an affirming and to "beings" but rather the flight in the face of the non-ordinariness of being—so that in the ordinary comportment to the nothing only the ordinary comportment to be-ing is hidden, as well as the evasion of the venture of that truth by which all "ideals" and "goal-settings," "desiderata" and "resignations" come to nothing as insignificant and superfluous.

The total non-ordinariness of be-ing over against all beings then requires also the non-ordinariness of "experiencing" be-ing; the seldomness of such experiencing and knowing is thus also not surprising.

Such knowing cannot be brought about directly. Instead of arousing a false and unproductive striving for such a goal, we must attempt simply to *think* what belongs to such a knowing of what is through and through non-ordinary.

If we call be-ing what is non-ordinary, then we conceive beings of every kind and breadth as what is ordinary, even when within the sphere of beings something hitherto unknown and novel appears and overturns the heretofore; in time we always put up with it and fit beings to beings. But be-ing is that "non-ordinary" which not only never pops up within the sphere of beings but also essentially withdraws from every attempt at putting up with it.

Be-ing is the non-ordinary in the sense that it remains untouchable by any ordinariness. Thus, in order to know be-ing, we must step out of every ordinariness. And since this ordinariness is *our* share and our activity, we are never capable of such stepping-out on our own. Be-ing itself must set us out from beings and set us—who are *in the midst of* beings, and besieged by beings—free from this being besieged. Man's being besieged by beings indicates two things: Man as a being himself belongs to and among beings but at the same time he has beings *as such ones* always within the sphere of a whole (world) openly around, in front of, under, and behind himself. This "being besieged" nevertheless is not something that might be eliminated as an accidental and improper burden, since this being besieged belongs together with that which makes up man's coming-to-grips-with beings—man as a being in the midst of beings. This coming-to-grips-with is not something merely of the kind of *man's effecting* (in the sense of the "struggle for existence") but rather an essential joining of his being. Nevertheless, there is *that* setting-free from beings which does not cancel the coming-to-grips-with beings but rather grounds and thus grants to it [coming-to-grips-with] the possibilities of groundings in which man creates beyond himself.

But this setting-free is enowned only by be-ing itself, nay this be-ing is nothing other than what sets-free [*Ent-setzende*] and what calls for setting-free [*Ent-setzliche*].

Setting-free consists in the en-ownment of *Dasein* in such a way that en-ownment withdraws in the t/here [*Da*] (in the ab-ground of the unprotected and unsupported) which is thus lit up. Setting-free and withdrawal belong to be-ing as enowning. Thus nothing occurs within the sphere of beings. Be-ing remains nonappearing; but *with* a being as such it can happen that it moves into the clearing of what is non-ordinary, casts away its ordinariness, and has to put itself up for decision as to how it suffices for be-ing. But this does not mean how a being would approximate and correspond to be-ing but rather how a being preserves and loses the truth of the essential swaying of be-ing—and therein comes into what is its ownmost, which consists in such *preserving*. But the fundamental forms of this preserving are disclosure of a wholeness [*Gänze*] of worlding (world) and the self-closure vis-à-vis every projecting-opening (earth). These fundamental forms first allow the preserving to arise and are themselves strifing, a strifing which holds sway from within the intimacy of the enownment of enowning. In each case on each side of this strifing is that which we metaphysically know as the sensible and the supersensible.

But why precisely this strife of world and earth? Because in en-owning Da-sein is enowned and becomes the inabiding of man, because from the whole of beings *man* is called to guardianship of be-ing. But what about that which is strifing and in view of which we have to think of man, his "body," "soul," and "spirit" be-ing-historically?

Be-ing sets-free in that it enowns Da-sein. This setting-free is a tuning—nay, it is the originary rift of what has the character of tuning itself. The grounding-attunement of anxiety sustains the setting-free, insofar as this setting-free nihilates in the originary sense, dis-engages [*ab-setzt*] beings as such. That is, this nihilating is not a negating but rather—if it should be interpreted at all in terms of the judgmental comportment—is an affirming of beings as such, as what is dis-engaged. However, nihilating is precisely dis-engagement itself, whereby be-ing as setting-free owns itself over to the clearing of the enowned t/here [*Da*].

And again, be-ing's nihilating in withdrawal—through and through illumined by the nothing—holds be-ing sway. And only when we have freed ourselves from misinterpretation of the "nothing" in terms of beings, only when we determine "metaphysics" according to the nihilating of the "nothing," instead of, vice versa, lowering the "nothing" according to metaphysics and the priority of beings that holds therein—lowering the "nothing" to a mere negation of *determinateness* and *mediating of* beings, as in Hegel and all metaphysicians before him—only then will we have an inkling what strength of inabiding penetrates humanness from within "freeing dismay," now taken as the grounding-attunement of "experiencing" be-ing. By metaphysics—and that means simultaneously by Christianity—we are misled and accustomed to presume in "dismay"—to which anxiety belongs as the "nothing" belongs to be-ing—only what is desolate and gruesome, instead of experiencing in freeing dismay the *be*tuning into the truth of be-ing and inabidingly to know from that truth the essential swaying of be-ing.

In the first beginning wonder was the grounding-attunement, since φύσις lit up in and as ἀλήθεια. The other beginning, that of be-ing-historical thinking, is attuned and pre-tuned by freeing dismay. This opens Da-sein for the distress of lack of distress, in whose protection the abandonment of beings by being is hidden.

270. The Essential Sway of Be-ing*
(The Essential Swaying)

Essential swaying means the manner in which be-ing itself is, namely be-ing. The saying "of" be-ing.

Be-ing holds sway as the needfulness of god in the guardianship of Dasein.

This essential sway is *en-owning* as that enowning in whose *"between"* [*Zwischen*] the strife of world and earth is enstrifed, from which strife world and earth are first enstrifed to what is their ownmost (whence and how the strife?): *be-ing as the en-strifing en-ownment for the countering of gods and man.*

Be-ing is nothing "in itself" and nothing "for" a "subject." As such an "in itself" only beingness can come forth in the form of the disempowered φύσις, as ἰδέα, καθ' αὐτό, as what is re-presented and as object. All attempts that want to find "being" and its "determinations" (categories) as something extant fall prey to the utmost entanglement in the objective.

Every saying of be-ing (saying "of" be-ing, cf. Be-ing, 267: Be-ing (Enowning), pp. 333f.) must name en-owning, that *"between"* [*Zwischen*] of the "inbetweenness" [*Inzwischenschaft*] of god and Dasein, world and earth, and must lift the between-ground [*Zwischengrund*] as ab-ground up into attuning work, always decisively *interpretive of the between* [*zwischendeutig*]. This saying is never unequivocal in the sense of an apparently linear unequivocality of the ordinary way of speaking; but it is no less than this [ordinary way of thinking] merely equivocal and ambiguous. Rather this saying singularly and inabidingly names that "between" of the enstrifing enownment.

The "between" [*das Zwischen*] is the simple "bursting open" that enowns be-ing to a being, which up until then is held back from what is ownmost to it and is not yet to be named a being. This "bursting open" is the clearing for the sheltered. But the "bursting open" does not disperse, and the clearing is not a mere emptiness.

The "between" [*das Zwischen*] which bursts open *gathers* what it removes into the open of its strifing and refusing belongingness, moves *unto the ab-ground,* out of which everything (god, man, world, earth) recoils in swaying into itself and thus leaves to be-ing the unique decidedness of en-ownment. Be-ing of such essential swaying is itself unique in this essential sway. For it holds sway as that thrust that has perhaps already announced itself as the utmost possibility of decision for Western history, the possibility that be-ing itself arises from such a holding-sway as the needfulness of god, who needs the guardianship of man. This possibility is itself the origin "of" be-ing. And what here,

---

* Cf. Be-ing, 267: Be-ing (Enowning).

according to the heretofore opinion about be-ing, seems secured by the titles "most general" and "superhistorical" is thoroughly and above all what is plainly and simply historical and unique.

Considering all that is unsupported in such questioning of the truth of be-ing, on what is the presumption based that the thrust of be-ing should already have thrown a first jolt into our history? That presumption is based again on what is unique, namely that Hölderlin had to become that sayer that he is.

Be-ing is the enstrifing enownment which originarily gathers its enowned (Da-sein of man) and its refused (god) into the abground of its "between" [Zwischen], in whose clearing world and earth enstrife the belongingness of what is their ownmost to the free-play of time-space, in which what is true comes to be preserved—what as "a being" in such preserving finds itself in be-ing (in enowning) for the simpleness of its ownmost.

To say be-ing in this way does not mean to manufacture a conceptual determination but rather to prepare an attuning for the leap, from out of and in which be-ing itself as projecting-open is ensprung for the knowing awareness, which only from this truth of be-ing also receives allotted to it what is its ownmost.

Enownment and enstrifing, historical grounding and decision, uniqueness and the onefold, what has the character of the between [Zwischenhafte] and the cleavage [Geklüft]—they never name the essential sway of be-ing as properties but rather in each case the *whole* essential swaying of its essential sway. To speak of one means not only to mean the others along with, but to bring them themselves to knowing awareness in an historical onceness of their essential swaying power. Such knowing awareness does not inform of objects, nor is it calling forth and appealing to moral circumstances and attitudes, but rather it is passing on the thrust of be-ing itself, which as enowning grounds the free-play of time-space for what is true.

If naming the envisageable [*das Anschaubare*] would help any here, then one would speak of a fire that first burns out its own hearth in the enjoined hardness of a place of its flame, whose growing blaze is consumed in the light of its brightness and therein lets glow the darkness of its glow, in order as hearth-fire to protect the midpoint of the "between" [Zwischen], which becomes for gods the unintended but still necessary abode, but for humans the free of the preserving of that which, earthwise and worldly, preserves what is true and arises and disappears as a being in this freedom. Now, when that which man as historical subsequently names a being shatters on be-ing—be-ing which is the needfulness of god—then everything is thrown back into the weight of what is allowed to everything as its ownmost and so becomes a nameable of language and belongs to the reticence in which be-ing withdraws from every reckoning among beings and still lavishes its essential sway in the grounding—that is held to the abground—of the intimacy of gods and world, of earth and man.

Be-ing is the hearth-fire in the midst of the abode of gods—an abode which is simultaneously the estranging of man (the "between" [*das Zwischen*] in which he remains a (the) stranger, precisely when he is at home with beings).

How to find be-ing? Do we have to light a fire in order to find fire, or do we not have rather to be content with above all *protecting the night* so that the false days of everydayness are restrained, whose most false ones are those that believe also to know and possess the night when they light up the night and eliminate it with their borrowed light?

271. Da-sein*

[Da-sein] is what is enowned in enowning. And only by this way of being does it have what is its own of the grounding guardianship of refusal, guardianship that preserves the t/here [*Da*].

But Da-sein is en-owned as renouncing. Renouncing lets the refusal (i.e., enownment) soar into the open of its decidedness.

Such letting-soar of renouncing lifts it essentially out of any mere negating and negated. Renouncing is originary standing: unsupported in the unprotected (the inabiding of Da-*sein*).

This standing keeps up with *possibility*—not with an arbitrary possibility and not with "the" possibility in general but rather with what is ownmost to possibility. But that is enowning itself as the ability for what is most unique to en-ownment, an ability that withdraws unto the utmost. *Such* withdrawal sends the severest storm against renouncing and grants to it the nearness of the ab-ground and thus the cleavage of be-ing. This is of course the mark of Da-sein, to stand unsupported and unprotected downward into the ab-ground and therein to surpass the gods.

The *sur*passing of gods is the going-*under* into the groundership of the truth of be-ing.

But be-ing en-owns Da-sein for itself, for grounding its truth, i.e., its clearing; because without this lit up, separating-deciding [*lichtende Entscheidung*] of it itself into the needfulness of god and into the guardianship of Da-sein, be-ing would have to be consumed by the fire of its own unredeemed glow.

How can we know how often this has not already happened? If we knew that, then there would be no necessity of thinking be-ing in the uniqueness of its essential sway.

---

* Cf. Grounding.

As inabiding, Da-*sein* grounds the ab-ground that is thrown out and yet carried by be-ing in enownment, grounds it in that being as which man is. But the being of this being is itself primarily determined from Da-sein, insofar as from out of Da-sein man is transformed into the guardianship of the needfulness of gods. The man of such and primarily futural way of being "is," as a being, not originary, insofar as only be-ing *is*. However, the man who is determined in terms of Da-sein is again distinguished over against all beings, insofar as what is his ownmost is grounded on projecting-open the truth of be-ing, a grounding which surrenders him, as one who is mediately enowned, to be-ing itself. Thus man is excluded from be-ing and yet directly thrown into the truth of be-ing in such a way that the exclusion—one that belongs to being [*seinshaft*]—prevails in renouncing, with Dasein as its measure. Man is like a steady bridge in the "between" [*im Zwischen*], as which en-owning throws the need of gods to the guardianship of man, in that en-owning surrenders man to Da-*sein*. Such throwing-surrendering, from which thrownness emerges, brings into Da-sein the removal-unto be-ing, which removal appears to us in the foreground as project-ing-open the truth of be-ing and, in the foreground that is foremost and most readily still turned to metaphysics, appears as the understanding of being. However, there is nowhere here a place for the interpretation of man as "subject," neither in the sense of a subject with the character of an I nor in the sense of subject that belongs to a community. But the removal-unto is also not man's being-outside-of-himself in the form of a getting-rid-of-oneself. Rather, it grounds what is ownmost to self-hood, which is to say that man has what is his ownmost (guardianship of be-ing) as his ownhood, insofar as he grounds himself in Da-sein. But to have what is ownmost as ownhood means having inabidingly to enact the appropriating and losing the "that" and the "how" of man's being enowned (removed into be-ing). What makes up the ownmost of selfhood is to be *owned*, to be what is ownmost to the owner and ina-bidingly to sustain and not to sustain this ownedness, depending on the ab-groundness of enownment. Selfhood can be grasped neither from the "subject" nor at all from the "I" or the "personality" but rather only from inabiding [*Inständnis*] in the guardianship of belongingness to be-ing, i.e., however, according to the forth throw [*Zuwurf*] of the needfulness of gods. Selfhood is the unfolding of the ownhoodship of the ownmost. That man has what is his ownmost as his ownhood says that man's ownhood stands in constant danger of loss. And this is the resonance of en-ownment, is the surrender to be-ing.

Only in Da-sein, into which man becomes inabiding by the essential transformation in the crossing, does a preserving of be-ing succeed, into that which thus first appears as a being. When it is said in *Being and Time* that through the "existential analysis" at first only the being of non-human beings becomes determinable, that does not mean that man is what is first and initially given, according to whom as measure the rest of beings receive the formation [*Prägung*] of their being. Such an "interpretation" insinuates that man is *still* being thought, in the manner of Descartes and all his successors and mere opponents (even Nietzsche is one of them), as subject. But what counts as the next goal is not at all and no longer to begin with man as a subject [*Subjektum*], because he is beforehand grasped in terms of the question of being, and only in this way. But when nevertheless Da-sein gains a priority, then this means that man, grasped with Da-sein as measure and projecting being open, grounds what is his ownmost and the ownhoodship [*Eigentumschaft*] of what is his ownmost and is therefore—in all comportment and every relationship—held within the domain of the clearing of be-ing. But this domain is through and through not human, i.e., not determinable and not sustainable by *animal rationale* and even less by the *subjectum*. The domain is not at all a being but rather belongs to the essential swaying of be-ing. With Da-sein as measure, man is grasped as that being which, while being, can lose what is his ownmost and thus is always most uncertainly and most daringly certain of himself—but this on the basis of being surrendered to the guardianship of be-ing. The priority of Da-sein is not only the opposite of any manner of humanizing of man; this priority grounds a totally other essential history of man, one that is never graspable in terms of metaphysics and thus also not in terms of "anthropology." That does not exclude, but rather includes, that man now becomes *even more* essential for be-ing while at the same time esteemed as unimportant in the perspective of a "being."

Da-sein is the grounding of the abground of be-ing by laying claim to man as that being which is surrendered to the guardianship for the truth of be-ing. On the basis of Da-sein man is primarily transformed into that being to which the relation to be-ing allots what is deciding, which immediately indicates that the talk of a relation to be-ing expresses what is actually to be thought into its opposite. For the relation to be-ing is in truth be-ing, which as enowning shifts man into its relation. Therefore manifold misinterpretation surrounds that "relationship" which is indicated by the heading "man and be-ing" (cf. Be-ing, 272: Man; 273: History).

272. Man*

For the one who has grasped the history of man as history of *what is ownmost* to man, the question of who man is can only mean the necessity of inquiring man out of his hitherto metaphysical sphere of dwelling

---

* Cf. Be-ing, 276: Be-ing and Language, pp. 351f.; *Überlegungen* VIII [GA 95].

and inquiringly referring him into another way of being and thus overcoming this very question. This question still stands unavoidably under
the illusion of "anthropology" and in danger of an anthropological misinterpretation.

1. To what summits must we climb in order freely to have an overview of man in his essential *distress*? That what is his ownmost is his
   ownhood and that means loss, and indeed from within the essential swaying of be-ing.
   Why are such summits necessary, and what do they mean?
2. Has man willfully lost his way into what is "merely" a being or was
   he instead repelled by be-ing or was he simply suspended by be-ing
   and abandoned to self-seeking?
   (These questions move within the differentiation of being and beings.)
3. Man, the thinking animal, as extant source of passions, drives, goal-
   and value-settings, fitted out with a character, etc. This is at any
   time establishable, as what is certain of everyone's understanding,
   especially when all have agreed not to inquire any more and to let
   nothing else be than that everyone is:
   a) *as what* we encounter man.
   b) *that* we encounter him.
4. Man a one who is returned in the free-throw (thrown projecting-open); we must understand being if. . . .
5. Man the guardian of the truth of be-ing (grounding of Da-sein).
6. Man neither "subject" nor "object" of "history," but rather the one
   blown upon by history (enowning) and pulled along into be-ing,
   the one belonging to be-ing. Call of needfulness, handed over into
   guardianship.
7. Man as the *stranger* in the executed free-throw, who no longer
   returns from the ab-ground and who in this foreign land *keeps* the
   remote neighboring to be-ing.

273. History

Until now man *was* never yet historical. By contrast, he "had" and "has"
a history. However, this having-history immediately betrays the kind of
"history" that is solely meant here. History is overall determined by
what is "historical" [*das Historische*] — even where one believes that he
grasps historical actuality itself and defines it in its essence. That happens partly "ontologically" — historical actuality as actuality of becoming — and partly "epistemologically" — history as the ascertainable past.
Both interpretations are dependent on that which makes "ontology"
and "epistemology" possible, i.e., on *metaphysics*. The presuppositions
for [the discipline of] history are also to be found here.

However, if man is to *be* historical and if what is ownmost to history
is to be raised to knowing awareness, then what is ownmost to man

must become especially questionable and being must become question-worthy—for the first time question-worthy. It is only in the essential sway of be-ing itself—and that means simultaneously in its relation to man, who is equal to that relation—that history can be grounded.

Whether man indeed attains history and whether what is ownmost to history comes over beings, whether history [as a discipline] can be *destroyed*—this cannot be calculated; it is a matter for be-ing itself.

At the very beginning of elucidating this question, a major difficulty gets in the way, namely, that we are barely able to free ourselves from history [as a discipline], especially since as yet we cannot at all survey how far, in manifold hidden forms, history [as a discipline] dominates human being. It is no accident that "modernity" brings [the discipline of] history to actual dominance. This dominance already extends so far today, i.e., in the beginning of the deciding segment of modernity, that, by the conception of history [*Geschichte*] which is determined by [the discipline of] history [*Historie*], history is pushed into what is without history and that what is ownmost to history [as not a discipline] is sought there. Blood and race become the carriers of history. *Pre*history now gives history its character of validity. The manner in which man manages himself and calculates and enters into the scene and compares himself, the way in which he adjusts the past for himself as background of his presentness [*Gegenwärtigkeit*], the manner in which he stretches this present out into an eternity—all of this shows the predominance of history [as discipline].

But what is *meant* here by *history* [as a discipline]? The ascertaining explaining of the past from within the horizon of the calculative dealings of the present. Beings are hereby presupposed as what is orderable, producible, and ascertainable (ἰδέα).

Ascertaining serves a retaining which does not so much want not to let the *past* slip away as to eternalize what is *present* as *the* extant. *Eternalizing* as a striving is always the consequence of the domination of history [as discipline], is the flight from history [*Geschichte*] that is apparently prescribed for history [as discipline]. Eternalizing is not-getting-free-of-itself (as of an extant) of a present that is removed from history.

As this ascertaining, history [as discipline] is a constant comparing and bringing in the other, wherein one mirrors oneself as one who has come further—a comparing that thinks away from itself, because it does not come to terms with itself.

History [as discipline] disseminates the deception of the complete controllability of everything actual, insofar as it [history as discipline] moves along whatever is superficial and deflects the surface itself as the singularly sufficient actuality. The boundlessness of knowing that is inherent in history [as discipline]—knowing everything in all respects and by all means of presentation, the mastery over everything factual—

leads to a barring from history which, the more decisive this barring becomes, the more unrecognizable it continues to be to those who are barred.

In its pre-forms, its development into science, and in the leveling off and understandability of this science unto common calculating, history [as discipline] is thoroughly a consequence of metaphysics. But this says: [a consequence of] *history* of be-ing, of be-ing as history, whereby, however, be-ing and history remain totally hidden, nay even hold themselves back in hiddenness.

Be-ing as en-owning is history. It is from this perspective that what is own-most to history must be determined, independently of the representation of becoming and development, independently of the historical [as discipline] *observation and explanation.* Therefore, what is ownmost to history can also not be grasped if, instead of setting out from the historical (investigated) "subject," one aims at the historical "object." For what is the object of history [as discipline] supposed to be? Is "objective history" an unattainable goal? It is not at all a possible goal. In that case then there is also no "subjective" history. It belongs to the essence of history [as discipline] that it is founded on the subject-object-relationship; it is objective because it is subjective; and insofar as it is this, it must also be that. Therefore, an "opposition" between "subjective" and "objective" history makes no sense. All history [as discipline] ends in anthropological-psychological biographism.

274. A Being and Calculation

The planning-calculating makes a being always more re-presentable, accessible in every possible explanatory respect, to such an extent that for their part these controllables [*Beherrschbarkeiten*] come together and become more current and thus broaden a being into what is seemingly boundless—but only seemingly. In truth what is accomplished by the increasing widening of research (of history [as discipline] in the broadest sense) is a relocating of the gigantic into the planning itself, by what is subordinated to the planning. And in the moment when planning and calculation have become gigantic, a being in the whole begins to shrink. The "world" becomes smaller and smaller, not only in the quantitative but also in the metaphysical sense: a being as a being, i.e., as object, is in the end so dissolved into controllability that the being-character of a being disappears, as it were, and the abandonment of beings by being is completed.

The metaphysical diminishing of the "world" produces a hollowing-out of man. The relation to a being as such loses, in and with this being, all purpose; the relation as comportment of man extends itself only to itself and to its methodical [*planmäßig*] enactment. The feeling of feeling feels only feeling, feeling itself becomes the object of enjoyment. The "live-experience" attains the utmost of what is its ownmost, lived-experiences are lived. The lostness into beings is lived as capability of transforming "life" into the calculable whirlwind of empty circling around itself and of making this capability believable as something "true to life."

275. A Being

Preserving be-ing (preserving [thought of] enowning-historically). Why? So that gods come to *truth* in a being and are in themselves thoroughly attuned, and be-ing glows without extinguishing. But danger!

A being "in the whole"? Does the "whole" now still have a necessity? Does it not fall apart as the last remnant of "systematic" thinking?

How old is ὅλον in *being-history*? As old as ἕν? (The first concept by which φύσις is gathered into the steadfastness of presencing.)

"A being"—why do we understand by that primarily always what is precisely extant here and now? (Whence the priority of the *present*?) Is the way to what has the character of an object no longer a way to a being?

When "nature," a confused offshoot of φύσις, has returned to *its* beginning and no longer reaches down into a being—merely counting for those of today as producing and representing of beings? As if "nature" as object of natural science and as exploitation of technicity still somehow encounters beings—or also simply so that "philosophy" could be called upon to complement it—philosophy that has long since made itself at home only in the *objectness* of these objects (epistemologically, ontologically, i.e., in terms of representation).

But what if we rescued ourselves by going back to Goethe's view of nature and then made "earth" and "life" into a theory?

When burrowing in the irrational begins and now more than ever everything stays with what has been heretofore, nay the heretofore is now in the end confirmed without qualification? That must still come, for without it modernity would not reach its completion.

Romanticism has not yet come to its end. Romanticism attempts once again a *transfiguration* of beings, which as re-acting against the thorough explaining and calculating strives only to evolve beyond or next to this explaining and calculating. This transfiguration "calls upon" the historical renewal of "culture," urges its rootedness in the "people," and strives for communication to everyone.

This popularization of "metaphysics" brings about a vivifying of what has been up to now; what has lain fallow is again heeded and protected and brought forth for enjoyment and for elation. And in comparison with what has seemingly become old, something new seems to arise. And yet, everything moves in a lack of decision, insofar as considering be-ing a being itself remains unquestioned and, in spite of dissemination and vivification, unobtrusively vanishes and leaves behind only the objective as its glimmer.

276. Be-ing and Language*

1. Language as assertion and saying.
2. Saying of be-ing.
3. Be-ing and the origin of language. Language [as] the resonance that belongs to enowning, in which resonance enowning gifts itself as enstrifing of the strife into the strife itself (earth-world) (the consequence: using up and mere usage of language).
4. Language and *man*. Is language given along with man or man along with language? Or does the one become and be, through the other, not at all *two* different things? And why? Because both *belong* equally originarily *to* be-ing. Why [is] man "essential" for determining what is ownmost to language—man as? [As] guardian of the truth of *be-ing*.
5. *Animal rationale* and the misinterpretation of language.
6. Language and logic.
7. Language and beingness and a being.

Within the history of metaphysics (and thus generally in philosophy up to now) determination of language is guided by λόγος, whereby λόγος is taken as assertion and assertion as the binding of representations. Language takes over the asserting of beings. At the same time language—again as λόγος—is allotted to man (ζῷον λόγον ἔχον). The basic relations of language, from which "what is its ownmost" and "origin" is deduced, extend to beings as such and to man.

Depending on which interpretation of *animal rationale* and depending on which version of the interconnection of *ratio* (of the word) with beings and with the most-being *(deus)*, variations of "philosophy of language" ensue. Even when this designation is not specifically used, language as an extant object (tool: formation-capable-product and gift of the creator) enters the domain of philosophical deliberation alongside other objects (art, nature, etc.). As certainly as one may admit that this special product *indeed* does accompany all representation and thus extends itself over the entire domain of beings as a mode of expression, just as little does the observation thereby go beyond that inceptual determination of language by which it remains connected, however undetermined, to beings and to man. One has hardly attempted, out of this relation to and from language, to grasp more originarily what is ownmost to man and his relation to beings and vice versa. For this already demanded that language be set free of relation, as it were. But whither is language to be grounded, since language's being extant in itself obviously goes against all experience?

---

*Cf. Be-ing, 267: Be-ing (Enowning), pp. 333f.

If we additionally consider that "the" language in general never is, but rather that language can only be as unhistorical ("language" of the so-called primitive people) and as historical, if beyond that we estimate how unclear what is ownmost to history continues to be for us, in spite of the intelligibility of history [as discipline], then all attempts to grasp the "essence" of language immediately appear to swirl confusedly at the beginning of the way. And all historical [as discipline] gathering of heretofore views of language may be instructive, but it still cannot lead beyond the established metaphysical sphere of relations of language, to man and to beings. But this is still the first actual question: Has then—with the even historically, inceptually necessary interpretation of language in terms of λόγος and with the predelineated fitting into the metaphysical sphere of relations—the possibility of an essential determination of language been limited to the domain of metaphysical consideration? But now, if metaphysics itself is recognized, and its inquiring within its essential limitation to the question of beingness, and if the insight is gained that with this metaphysical inquiring into a being in the whole nevertheless not yet everything could be inquired—and precisely not what is the most essential thing that *is*, namely, be-ing itself and its truth—then another viewpoint opens up here: Be-ing and nothing less than its most ownmost [*eigenste*] essential swaying could actually make up that ground of language out of which language could draw its owning for determining first of all and all by itself that in relation to which language is explained metaphysically.

The first actual question, with which all philosophy of language as such (i.e., as metaphysics of language and consequently as psychology of language, etc.) comes simultaneously to naught, is the question of the relation of language to be-ing, a question that in this form, of course, does not even get to what it asks. But this relation can be elucidated by an approach which simultaneously still focuses on that domain which was always guiding in the observation of language up to this point.

According to the correctly understood and until today valid determination of man as *animal rationale*, language is given along with man—and this so certainly that, even turning it around, one can say that along with language man is first given. Language and man determine each other, mutually. Whereby does that become possible? Are both in a certain respect the same, and in which respect are they this? By virtue of their belongingness to be-ing. What does this mean: belonging to be-ing? Man as a being belongs to beings and thus is subordinate to the most general determination that he *is* and *is* such and such. However, that does not distinguish man as man but rather merely equates him as a being with all beings. But man can belong to *be-ing* (not only among beings), insofar as he draws out of this belongingness—and precisely out of it—what is most originarily his ownmost: Man understands be-ing (cf. *Being and Time*); he is the governor of projecting-open be-ing. The guardianship of the truth of be-ing makes up what is ownmost to man, grasped out of be-ing and "only" out of this. Man belongs to be-ing as the one who is enowned by be-ing itself for the grounding of the truth of be-ing. Owned in this way, man is surrendered to be-ing, and such surrender directs the preserving and grounding of this human being in that which man himself must first make for himself as his ownhood, with reference to which he must be owned or unowned into Da-sein, which is the grounding of truth itself, the ab-ground that is thrown forth and sustained by be-ing (enowning).

But how does language relate to be-ing? If we dare not account for language as a given and thus as something already determined in what is its ownmost, since it is important first to "find" what is the ownmost, and if be-ing itself is "more essential" than language, insofar as language is taken as a given (a being), then the question must be asked differently.

How does be-ing relate to language? But even in this form the question is still misconstruable, insofar as the question now appears only as the mere reversal of the foregoing relationship and language again counts as something given, with which be-ing enters into a relationship. How does be-ing relate to language? — This is to ask: How does what is ownmost to language arise in the essential swaying of be-ing? But is this not to anticipate a response that language merely arises out of be-ing? But every genuinely essential question — determined as projecting-open by what is to be projected-open — anticipates the response. What is ownmost to language can never be determined in any other way than by naming its origin. Thus, one cannot give out essential definitions of language and declare the question concerning its origin unanswerable. The question concerning the origin of course includes within it the essential determination of origin and of origination itself. But origination means: belonging to be-ing in the sense of the last formulated question: How does language sway in the essential swaying of be-ing? The preliminary observation has made clear that this relation of language to be-ing is generally not an arbitrary invention. For in truth that metaphysical double-relation (only not thought back into the origin) of language to beings as such and to man (as *animal rationale, ratio* — guiding-thread for the interpretation of beings unto beingness, i.e., being) says nothing other than that language is through and through related to being, and precisely in those respects by which metaphysics determines it. But because metaphysics is what it is only out of perplexity toward be-ing, precisely *this* relation and in the end its correct understanding can never attain to the domain of its questioning.

Language arises from be-ing and therefore belongs to it. Thus, everything once again depends on projecting-open and thinking "of" be-ing. But now we must think this be-ing in such a way that we thereby simultaneously remind ourselves of language. But how should we now grasp "language" without pregrasping the essential determination that must first be obtained? Considering all that has been indicated, apparently in such a way that language becomes experienceable in its relation to *be-ing*. But how to do this? "The" language is "our" language; "our" language, not only as mother tongue, but also as the language of our history. And thus what is finally question-worthy within the mindfulness of "the" language befalls us.

Our history—not as the historically known course of our destinies and accomplishments, but we ourselves in the moment of our relation to be-ing. For the third time we fall into the abground of this relation. And this time we know no answer. For all mindfulness of be-ing and of language is really only a thrust ahead [*Vorstoß*] in order to encounter our "standpoint" in be-ing itself and thus our history. But even when we want to grasp our language in its relation to be-ing, what is familiar in the hitherto metaphysical determination of language clings to this questioning—a determination of which one cannot simply say that it is entirely untrue, especially since it has in view, even if covered over, precisely the language in its relation to being (to beings as such and to man who represents and thinks beings). Along with the assertion-character of language (assertion taken in the broadest sense that language, the said and unsaid, means something (a being), and represents it and in representing shapes or covers it over, etc.), language is known as property and tool of man and at the same time as "work." But this interconnection of language to man counts as something so profound that even the basic determinations of man himself (again as *animal rationale*) are selected in order to characterize language. What is ownmost to man, in terms of body-soul-spirit, is found again in language: the body (word) of language, the soul of language (attunement and shade of feeling and the like), and the spirit of language (what is thought and represented) are familiar determinations of all philosophies of language. This interpretation of language, which one could call anthropological interpretation, culminates in seeing in language itself a symbol for human being. If the question-worthiness of the idea of symbols (a genuine offspring of the perplexity toward be-ing that reigns in metaphysics) is here set aside, then man would have to be grasped as that being that has what is his ownmost in his own symbol, i.e., in the possession of this symbol (λόγον ἔχον). Let it remain open how far this interpretation of language according to symbol, when thought through metaphysically, can be made to go beyond itself in being-historical thinking so that something fruitful springs up. It cannot be denied that, with what in language supports its conception as symbol for man, something is encountered that is somehow peculiar to language: the word in its *tone* and sound, the attunement of the word and the word's meaning, whereby, however, we once again think in the horizon of perspectives that arise in metaphysics, i.e., the perspectives of sensible, nonsensible, and supersensible—even when with "word" we do not mean the individual words but rather the saying and silencing of the saying of what is said and unsaid and the unsaid itself. The sound of the word can be traced back to anatomical-physiological constitutions of the human body and can be explained in its terms (phonetics—acoustics). Likewise word's attunement and word's melody and saying's feeling-stress are objects of psychological explanation; and word's meaning is the matter for logical-poetic-rhetorical analyses. The dependence of this explanation and analysis of language on the kind of conception of man is obvious.

But now, when with the overcoming of metaphysics anthropology too is overthrown, when what is ownmost to man is determined in terms of be-ing, then that anthropological explanation of language just given can no longer be determinative; it has lost its ground. But nevertheless, nay even exactly now *that* remains in full power which was singled out in language as its body, its soul, its spirit. What is that? Can we not now, correspondingly thinking in terms of being-history, proceed in such a way that we interpret what is ownmost to language from within the being-historical determination of man? No. For doing so we still remain stuck with the idea of symbol; but above all we would not be serious about the task of enseeing the origin of language from within the essential swaying of be-ing.

277. "Metaphysics" and the Origin of the Work of Art

The question of the origin of the work of art does not aim at a timelessly valid determination of what is ownmost to the work of art, which could simultaneously serve as the guiding-thread for a historically retrospective explanation of history of art. This question is most intimately connected with the task of overcoming aesthetics and that means simultaneously with overcoming a certain conception of beings as what is objectively representable. Overcoming of aesthetics again results necessarily from the historical encounter with metaphysics as such. This metaphysics comprises the basic Western position toward beings and thus also the ground for what is heretofore the ownmost of Western art and its works. Overcoming of metaphysics means freeing the priority of the question of the truth of being in the face of any "ideal," "causal," and "transcendental" and "dialectical" explanation of beings. Overcoming of metaphysics is, however, not discarding the hitherto existing philosophy but rather the leap into its first beginning, without wanting to renew this beginning— something that remains historically [*historisch*] unreal and historically [*geschichtlich*] impossible. Nevertheless, mindfulness of the first beginning (out of the pressing need for preparing for the other beginning) leads to *distinguishing* inceptual (Greek) thinking, which favors the misunderstanding that by this retrospective observation a kind of "classicism" in philosophy might be what one is striving for. But in truth, with the "retrieving" question that begins more originarily, the solitary remoteness of the first beginning opens out to everything that follows it historically. In the end the other beginning stands in a necessary and intimate but hidden relation to the first beginning, a relation which at the same time includes the complete separatedness of both in accord with their origin-character. Thus it happens that, precisely where preparatory thinking most likely reaches the sphere of the origin of the first beginning, the illusion emerges that the first beginning is only renewed and that the other beginning is only a historically [as discipline] improved interpretation of this one.

What is true in general of "metaphysics" also fits the mindfulness of the "origin of the work of art," a mindfulness which prepares a historical decision in the crossing. Here, too, for purposes of illustration, the earliness [*das Frühe*] of the first beginning can most readily be chosen, but one must simultaneously know that what sways essentially in Greek art can and will never be determined by that which we have to unfold as essential knowing about "art."

But overall here the issue is to think historically [*geschichtlich*] and that means to *be* historical [*geschichtlich*], instead of calculating historically [*historisch*]. The question of "classicism" and the overcoming of "classicistic" misinterpretation and lowering of the "classical" and likewise characterization of a history as "classical" is not a question of the place of art but rather a decision for or against history.

Epochs which through historicism know much—and soon everything—will not grasp that a moment of history that *lacks art* can be more historical and more creative than times of a widespread art business. The lack of art here does not arise from incapacity and decadence but rather from the power of knowing the essential decisions through which that must pass which up until now and seldom enough occurred as art. In the horizon of this knowing, art has lost its relation to culture; it reveals itself here only as an enowning of be-ing. *Lack of art* is grounded in knowing that the exercise of perfected capabilities—even according to the highest measures and models that have existed up to now—from out of the most perfect mastery of the rules can never be "art"; that the planned furnishing for producing such that corresponds to heretofore existing "artworks" and their "purposes" can have wide-ranging results without ever forcing, out of a distress, an originary necessity of what is ownmost to art, namely putting the truth of be-ing to a decision; that a dealing with "art" as means for an operation has already placed itself outside what is ownmost to art and thus remains precisely too blind and too weak to experience the lack of art or even to let it merely "count" in its power for preparing for history and for being allotted to be-ing. Lack of art is grounded in knowing that corroboration and approval of those who enjoy and experience [*erleben*] "art" cannot at all decide whether the object of enjoyment stems generally from the essential sphere of art or is merely an illusionary product of historical [as discipline] dexterity, sustained by dominant goal-settings.

But the knowing by which lack of art *is* already historical without being known publicly or being admitted within a constantly increasing "art-activity," this knowing itself belongs to what is peculiar to an originary en-ownment, which we call Da-sein, from within whose inabiding the destruction [*Zertrümmerung*] of the priority of beings is prepared, and along with that what is non-ordinary and unnatural about another origin of "art": the beginning of a hidden history of reticence of a countering of gods and man—a countering that is held to abground.

278. Origin of the Work of Art

I. Schinkel's proposition: "With the intention of the Greek people to leave behind for posterity everywhere mementoes of its existence and working *arose* the many-sided art-activity. . . ."[1]

1. *With the intention:* "occasionally" or "from within" that intention?
2. Is stress laid on the explanation only of the arising of the *many-sidedness* of art or [of the arising of art] itself?
3. *Art-activity:* "art" and *being-active in it* or letting *what is ownmost to art* itself first come forth as necessary?
   Being active in it, different things as "ground," as different directions and layers of grounding the "arising":
   a) essential ground (origin of what is ownmost from within the essential swaying of be-ing) see below VI.
   b) occasion, commissions, imitation.
   c) initiatives and incentives (needs and drives).
   d) conditions (natural tendency, skills).
   e) ἀγών, *self-surpassing*, but that also not as record, but δόξα.
   f) the metaphysical ground of ἀγών.
4. "Posterity," undetermined:
   a) thought according to modernity and historically [as discipline]: the West, historical education, "eternalization."
   b) thought in a Greek perspective, for one's own *people*, i.e., however, no "eternity," nothing of which posterity (randomly [so-called] or even the West) have historically a memory, "memen-

---

[1] K.F. Schinkel, *Aus Schinkels Nachlass. Reisetagebücher, Briefe und Aphorismen. Mitgeteilt von A. v. Wolzogen. Nachdruck d. Ausgabe 1862* (Mittenwald, 1981), III, 368.

toes," but rather to keep the *Greeks themselves* with themselves as their property; remaining *present* in their *presence* (δόξα) — also not "nationally," but rather metaphysically.

II. δόξα and ἰδέα, the Greek sense for *fame* and for glorification: emerging into *appearing*, i.e., *belonging together* with an actual being and co-determining it (κλέος) and thus being allotted to gods. δόξα: presentness in the presence of one's own unfolding of what is ownmost to one and belonging to this.

But:

III. *High Greek time* (Pindar and earlier) and *Plato, reverberation,* "fame" already reputation.

And above all:

IV. Even in the highest time only moments, uniqueness, not a state and a rule, not ideal.

V. *Modern* view that emphasizes activity, the accomplishing-character of the work, "genius," and correspondingly "work" as accomplishment. Finally *art in general* as means for culture-oriented politics.

VI. *The question of origin:* "the" origin [is] always historical in the sense that the essential sway is itself historical and has the character of enowning.

The ἀεί of the Greeks [is] not the historically thought duration of progressive and endless continuity but rather the steadfastness of the presence of the inexhaustible essential sway.

The Greeks were unhistorical [*unhistorisch*], and ἱστορεῖν aimed at what is present-extant and not at what is past as such.

But the Greeks were so originarily historical [*geschichtlich*] that history [*Geschichte*] itself still remained hidden from them, i.e., did not become the essential ground for the shaping of their "Dasein."

The ἀεί [is] not the presence of what is continual but rather that rendering simple that gathers into the present what is always essential (the ἕν as ὄν).

279. What about Gods?*

[Gods] not from within "religion"; not as something extant, nor as an expedient of man; rather [they come] from out of be-ing, as its decision, [they are] futural in the uniqueness of the *last one*.

Why must this decision be ventured? Because thereby the necessity of be-ing is raised to the highest question-worthiness and the freedom of man — that he relegates to the depths the fulfilling of what is his ownmost — is thrust deep into ab-groundness, because being is thus brought into the truth of the simplest intimacy of its en-ownment. And what

---

* Cf. The Last God.

"is," then? Only *then* is this question impossible, then en-owning is, for a moment, enowning. This moment is *the time of being.*

But be-ing is the needfulness of god, in which god first finds *itself.* But why god? Whence the needfulness? Because the abground is hidden? Because there is a surpassing, therefore those who are surpassed [are], nonetheless, higher? Whence the surpassing, ab-ground, ground, being? In what does the godhood of gods consist? Why be-ing? Because of gods? Why gods? Because of be-ing?

En-owning and the possibility of the *why*! Can the "why" still be made into a tribunal, before which be-ing is to be placed?

But why the *truth* of be-ing? It belongs to be-ing's essential sway!

Why a being? Because a highest being causes it to be, produces it?

But disregarding the inappropriateness of manufacturing, the highest being, *summum ens,* belongs all the more to beings. How is the "why" to be answered from there? Why a being? Why? To what extent? Grounds! Ground and origin of the "why." Each time going beyond beings. Whither? Because be-ing holds sway. Why be-ing? From within it itself. But what is it itself? The en-grounding of be-ing, of its ground, is: the "between" [*Zwischen*] of be-ing as ab-ground, the knowing awareness that is held to abground as Da-sein, Da-sein as en-owned, ground-less, held to abground.

280. The Question of Crossing

The question of crossing (why are there beings at all and not rather nothing? cf. SS 1935*) inquires into beings and [is] initially and exclusively to be unfolded thus—in order unawares to place before an essential step—the *hovering* of be-ing.

As the metaphysical asking of this question already places it into the "space" of be-ing, because this question is pushed to the utmost (difference between Middle Ages and Leibniz, Schelling), so [is] the take off [*Anlauf*] unto the leap into be-ing.

The metaphysical shape of the question: highest cause, *ens entium!* No answer, because not *asked.*

And the nothing? Its constancy? And the why? Its ground? And the question itself? As thinking "of" be-ing.

281. Language
(Its Origin)

When gods call the earth and a world resonates in the call and thus the call echoes as Da-sein of man, then language is as historical, as history-grounding word.

---

*Lecture course SS 1935, *Einführung in die Metaphysik* (GA 40).

Language and enowning. Fleeting shimmer of earth, resonance of world. *Strife,* the originary sheltering of the cleavage, because the innermost *rift.* The *open place.*

Language, whether *spoken or held in silence,* [is] the primary and broadest humanization of beings. So it seems. But *it* [is] precisely the most originary non-humanization of man as an *extant living-being* and "subject" and the heretofore—and thereby the grounding of Da-sein and of the possibility of non-humanization of beings.

Language is grounded in silence. Silence is the most sheltered measure-holding. It *holds* the measure, in that it first sets up measures. And so language is measure-setting in the most intimate and widest sense, measure-setting as essential enswaying of the jointure and its joining (enowning). And insofar as language [is] ground of Da-sein, the measuring lies in this [Da-sein] and indeed as the ground of the strife of world and earth.

Editor's Epilogue

More than fifty years after its composition and on the one-hundredth anniversary of the thinker's birthday, another major work of Martin Heidegger's, *Beiträge zur Philosophie (Vom Ereignis)* [*Contributions to Philosophy (From Enowning)*], appears herewith for the first time. With its appearance begins the publication of the volumes of the third division of the *Gesamtausgabe*.

Following the first, fundamental-ontological onset of the question of being in *Being and Time, Contributions to Philosophy (From Enowning)* is the *first, encompassing attempt* at a second, be-ing-historical, i.e., "more originary" onset and elaboration of the same question, in which the meaning of being—as the truth and the essential sway, i.e., essential swaying of be-ing—is inquired into and this essential swaying is thought as enowning. Thus the proper title "From Enowning" belongs to the "public title," "Contributions to Philosophy." Although the thinking that is enacted therein understands itself as "a projecting-open of the essential swaying of be-ing as enowning," this thinking cannot yet "join the free jointure of the truth of be-ing from out of be-ing itself." Thinking is only now on the way toward such a joining. Nevertheless, the be-ing-historical elaboration of the question of being in *Contributions to Philosophy* attains for the first time the jointure of a sixfold "outline." This "outline" is "drawn from the still unmastered ground plan of the historicity of the crossing itself," "the crossing from metaphysics into be-ing-historical thinking." Within this "outline" be-ing-historical questioning begins within the " 'echo' of be-ing in the distress of abandonment of being" and accomplishes "the mutual 'playing-forth' of the first and the other beginning," as "thinking 'leap' into be-ing," as "thinking 'grounding' of its truth" and as "thinking preparation of 'the ones to come' 'of the last god.'" A "Preview" that looks ahead to the whole of the "outline" precedes this "outline"; and *Contributions to Philosophy* ends with "Be-ing," which comes after the "outline" and is an attempt to retrospectively "grasp the whole once again." The thinking of the essential sway of be-ing as enowning thinks "the richness of the turning-relation of be-ing to Da-sein, who is enowned to be-ing." Accordingly, this thinking thinks what is ownmost to man, Da-sein, from within the turning which itself belongs to the essential sway of be-ing as enowning.

The motto guiding the *Gesamtausgabe*, "pathways, not works," is elucidated right at the beginning of *Contributions to Philosophy*. These contributions are not a "work" of the style heretofore, because be-ing-historical thinking is a thinking that is *underway,* "through which the domain of be-ing's essential swaying—completely hidden up to now—is gone through, is thus first lit up, and is attained in its ownmost enowning-character."

In a marginal note to the *Letter on Humanism* Heidegger himself points to the outstanding place that *Contributions to Philosophy* occupies on his pathway of thinking. There he notes that what is said in this text was not thought "first at the time of writing the *Letter on Humanism*" (1946) but rather rests "on traversing a pathway that began in 1936, in the 'moment' of an attempt simply to say the truth of being" (*Wegmarken, Gesamtausgabe*, volume 9, p. 313). The way that began in 1936 is the way that began with the writing of *Contributions to Philosophy* in the same year. In a second marginal note in *Letter on Humanism*, an expansion of the first marginal note, we read: "'enowning' has been since 1936 the guiding-word of my thinking" (ibid., p. 316), i.e., since the beginning of elaborating the *Contributions to Philosophy*.

The reason that this large, path-finding manuscript was not published at the beginning of the publication of the *Gesamtausgabe* but only fourteen years thereafter is Heidegger's directive for the publication of his *Gesamtausgabe*, which was particularly important to him. According to that directive, publication of the manuscripts planned for the third and fourth divisions could begin only after the lecture courses were published in the second division. He explained this decision with the remark that knowledge and appropriating study of the lecture texts are a necessary prerequisite for understanding the unpublished writings, especially those from the 1930s and the first half of the 1940s. This directive was complied with in that during the past fourteen years since publication of the *Gesamtausgabe* began in November 1975, most of the volumes of the lecture courses have now appeared or will appear in the course of the anniversary year, and that therefore only a few lecture texts remain unpublished at the present moment; but they have been assigned for editing and will appear in the near future.

Among the lecture courses of the 1930s whose study is a prerequisite for the necessary enactment of *Contributions to Philosophy*, the *Basic Questions of Philosophy: Selected "Problems" of "Logic"* (from WS 1937/38) towers above everything else. For, by unfolding in this lecture course the question of truth as the preliminary question for the grounding-question of be-ing, Heidegger communicates an essential thought process of *Contributions to Philosophy*—in lecture style, thus meeting the demands of academic teaching. Thus the study of this lecture text, which appeared in 1984 as volume 45, is the most important and immediate preparation for understanding *Contributions to Philosophy*. Especially a comparison of the text "From the First Draft" and the complete outlining of how the question of truth unfolds (both published in the appendix to volume 45) with *Contributions to Philosophy* shows how these texts emerge from *Contributions to Philosophy*, as it had just recently been worked out.

*

The manuscript of *Contributions to Philosophy* consists of altogether eight parts and has 933 pages Din A 5 in size—with only a few exceptions in smaller format—and is divided into 281 sections of varying length, each with its own title. In the lower left-hand corner on the first page of every section, there is the ordinal number; and on every page of a section with more pages there is, in the upper right-hand corner, the inner pagination of this section; and on every page of the manuscript, in the upper left-hand corner, the consecutive pagination.

In arranging the eight parts of the manuscript and correspondingly in the counting of the sections of these parts by ordinal number, "Be-ing" comes after "Preview" as the second part. At the end of the typescript of the "Table of Contents," however, a note by Heidegger, dated 8 May 1939, reads: " 'Be-ing' as Section II [Part II] is not correctly arranged; as an attempt to grasp the whole once again, it does not belong at this juncture." Therefore, following this note, the editor put the part entitled "Be-ing" at the end, i.e., after the last segment of the "outline." The fact that the part of the manuscript entitled "Be-ing" is not somehow erroneously attached to *Contributions to Philosophy* is shown unequivocally in Heidegger's handwritten remark on the title page of this part of the manuscript which indicates that this part is: "for *Contributions to Philosophy (From Enowning)*." By rearranging this part of the manuscript, whereby it no longer makes up the second part but rather the eighth part, the ordinal number changes from section 50 onward. For the "Preview" has 49 sections; the fiftieth section, in both the manuscript as well as the typescript, begins with "Be-ing," whereas now, after rearranging, section 50 begins with "Echo," the first part of the "outline."

The handwritten title page of the entire manuscript bears the inscription *Beiträge zur Philosophie (Vom Ereignis)*. Accordingly, to the title of this manuscript belongs not only the "public" title but also the "proper" title, which as such is put in parentheses by Heidegger. The title page indicates the years 1936/37 as the time of composition of the manuscript. The dates refer to the "Preview" and the six parts of the "outline." The part of the manuscript entitled "Be-ing" was composed only later, in 1938, so that the years 1936–1938 are to be viewed as the period of the genesis of the entire manuscript of *Contributions to Philosophy*.

At the behest of Martin Heidegger, the typed version of the manuscript was prepared by his brother, Fritz Heidegger, who began with the typing right after the handwritten version was completed in May 1939, at the latest. The consecutive pagination of the handwritten version appears in the upper right-hand corner of the pages of the typescript.

Since one typescript page often contains more than just the text of one handwritten page, there are often two or even three consecutive page numbers that correspond to the handwritten version. The ordinal numbers from the handwritten version are in the upper left-hand corner of the typescript of the first page of every section. The entire typescript of the handwritten version is without its own consecutive pagination. Instead, parts I through V and part VIII each have their own new pagination, and part VI (The Ones to Come) and part VII (The Last God) have on top in the middle of the typewritten page their own consecutive pagination. The Roman numerals at the beginning of the eight parts are not to be found in the handwritten version but are in the copy and the table of contents prepared by Fritz Heidegger.

Already when Fritz Heidegger prepared the typescript, the top half of manuscript page 656a, designated by him as a "scrap of paper," was diagonally ripped, whereby a segment of the text has been lost, as indicated by an {*} before the "and" on page 184.

A handwritten note by Heidegger, from 3 June 1939, indicates that the typescript has been "compared with the original." This comparison was done together with his brother in the following manner: Fritz Heidegger read his copy aloud and Martin Heidegger compared what was read aloud with his handwritten version.

*

In preparing the text for publication, the editor again compared word for word the typescript with the 933 handwritten pages. This comparison confirmed once again the great care with which Fritz Heidegger always typed his brother's manuscripts. A few omissions and misreadings, which belong to the nature of typing manuscripts and which also were not detected by Heidegger during the comparison of the typescript with the original, had to be restored and corrected by the editor. Likewise, in fourteen instances obvious slips of the pen were corrected. Peculiarities in spelling were left for the most part. The alternating spellings *"Seyn"* and *"Sein"* ["be-ing" and "being"] were left unchanged, even where the matter at hand is *"Seyn"* ["be-ing"] and not *"Sein"* ["being"] and where Heidegger here and there, apparently during the writing, did not consistently maintain the different spelling. Numerous abbreviations, which he used for referring to his own writings and manuscripts and especially for the basic words of his thinking—and which Fritz Heidegger also kept for the most part in his copy—had to be written out for publication. The few handwritten additions by Martin Heidegger that are contained in Fritz Heidegger's typescript were carried over to the copy for publication.

Since the typescript keeps intact the often incomplete punctuation of the manuscript, this incomplete punctuation was carefully examined and completed in accordance with Heidegger's directives. Fritz Heidegger reproduced in his typescript the underlinings that exist in the manuscript in most cases by interspacing, but occasionally also by underlinings. The latter apparently occurred as a subsequent correction of an interspacing that was not always observed in time. Since Martin Heidegger established italics as the exclusive method of indicating emphasis in the volumes of the *Gesamtausgabe,* everything that is interspaced or underlined in the typescript had to be uniformly set in italics for publication. The inner structuration, in print, of each section according to paragraphs corresponds to the division of paragraphs in the manuscript.

The ordinal numbers, with which the sections are counted and which, as already described, are found in each case on the first page of each section, in the lower left-hand corner, were in each case placed before the title of a section, whereas in Fritz Heidegger's typescript they stand in the upper left-hand corner of the page, and only in the table of contents do they stand before the section titles. But because many of the titles are repeated more than once, the ordinal numbers had to be added to the titles in order to be able to distinguish the sections that have the same title but are independent sections and thus to be able to avoid confusion.

All footnotes with an asterisk contain Heidegger's cross-references in the manuscript to either sections within *Contributions to Philosophy* or to his other writings and manuscripts. In the manuscript these cross-references are added to a title or are in the text. For publication the editor completed all abbreviated information in the cross-references, which Fritz Heidegger left unchanged in his typescript. Included here are: completing the titles of the parts of the manuscript with articles, completing the wording of the section titles, and adding the ordinal numbers. Only when the title of a section within a part of the manuscript came up again and again and it could not be ascertained to which section this title referred was the ordinal number not added. To the extent that other manuscripts to which Heidegger refers have already appeared in the *Gesamtausgabe* or have already been firmly assigned to volumes not yet published, the editor notes this in parentheses by indicating the volume number.

The few numbered footnotes contain bibliographical data added by the editor for quotations from other authors which Heidegger uses in the text.

Heidegger repeatedly refers to two Freiburg lectures, which have to do with still-unpublished earlier versions of published, later versions. The Freiburg lecture "Vom Wesen der Wahrheit" from 1930 is the first version of the text which was later often gone over and was published in 1943 in a separate edition under the same title—a text which in 1967 also appeared in *Wegmarken* (*Gesamtausgabe,* volume 9). The Freiburg lecture "Vom Ursprung des Kunstwerkes" (1935) gave birth to three Frankfurt lectures of 1936, "Der Ursprung des Kunstwerkes," which appeared in 1950 in *Holzwege* (*Gesamtausgabe,* volume 5). Both Freiburg lectures will be published in the third division of the *Gesamtausgabe,* in the volume *Vorträge,* which will collect all of Heidegger's lectures that remained unpublished in his lifetime.

From the remaining manuscripts mentioned in *Beiträge zur Philosophie,* there will appear in the third division: "ἀλήθεια. Die Erinnerung in den ersten Anfang"; "Entmachtung der φύσις" (1937); and "Besinnung" (1938/39). In the fourth division the following will be published: notes for the seminar in the summer semester 1937, "Nietzsches metaphysische Grundstellung. Sein und Schein"; as well as notes for the seminar in the winter semester 1937/38, "Die metaphysischen Grundstellungen des abendländischen Denkens (Metaphysik)"; and the notes for the working group of university lecturers of the faculty of natural sciences and medicine, "Die neuzeitliche Wissenschaft" (1937). Further, in the fourth division will be published: the manuscripts "Laufende Anmerkungen zu 'Sein und Zeit'" (1936); "Anmerkungen zu 'Vom Wesen des Grundes'" (1936); "Eine Auseinandersetzung mit 'Sein und Zeit'" (1936); and "Überlegungen," whose Roman numerals indicate the order of the notebooks. The reference to the "personal copy" of the treatise *Vom Wesen des Grundes* alludes to the interleaved copy of the first edition of 1929 and to the many marginal notes that are written therein—notes which have already been published in *Wegmarken* (*Gesamtausgabe,* volume 9), in the footnotes numbered with small letters.

*

The expression of gratitude that has been saved for the end of the epilogue is manifold. The first thanks go to Herr Dr. Hermann Heidegger, the testamentary literary executor, for his decision to publish, on the occasion of the one-hundredth birthday of the philosopher, *Beiträge zur Philosophie (Vom Ereignis),* a manuscript that had been guarded for many years by Martin Heidegger and that has long been awaited in philosophical circles.

However, the punctual appearance of this volume at the beginning of the anniversary year would not have been possible without the understanding and cooperation of several individuals and institutions. For the editorial work the editor needed the one-semester release from his teaching duties at the university. Due thanks are rendered to the Philosophy Faculty and to the Rectorate of the Albert-Ludwigs-Universität Freiburg as well as to the Ministry for Science and Art of Baden-Württemberg for granting an early research semester. I express my sincere thanks to the minister for Science and Art of the State of Baden-Württemberg, Herr Professor Dr. Helmut Engler; to the rectors of Freiburg University, Herr Professor Dr. Volker Schupp and Herr Professor Dr. Christoph Rüchardt; to the chancellor of the University, Herr Dr. Friedrich Wilhelm Siburg; as well as to my colleagues Herr Professor Dr. Gerold Prauss and Herr Professor Dr. Klaus Jacobi for granting and supporting the application.

I thank the present owner of the manuscript, Herr Professor Dr. Silvio Vietta, who was kind enough to make this manuscript available for photocopying.

Special thanks are due to the long-time—in the meantime retired—director of the Deutsche Literaturarchiv in Marbach, Herr Professor Dr. Dr. h.c. Bernhard Zeller, Litt. D., as well as to his successor, Herr Direktor Dr. Ulrich Ott, for creating outstanding working conditions under which the continuing edition of the *Gesamtausgabe* could be prepared. All editors owe special thanks to all the colleagues in the Deutsche Literaturarchiv Marbach, who from the beginning of the publication of the *Gesamtausgabe* have happily and in manifold ways made available the documents for the edition of the individual volumes and thus also for this volume—and thereby have decisively participated in the continuing growth of the edition. To be named here are: Herr Dr. Joachim Storck, Frau Ute Doster, Frau Inge Schimmer, Herr Winfried Feifel, Frau Ingrid Grüninger, Frau Ursula Fahrländer, Frau Elfriede Ihle, and Frau Beate Küsters.

Herr Dr. Hartmut Tietjen, with his great expertise in reading and transcribing Martin Heidegger's handwriting, was helpful and supportive in several difficult questions of deciphering, for which I thank him cordially. I cordially thank Herr Dr. Hans-Helmuth Gander for the great care with which he undertook the final reading of the proofs. My cordial thanks go to him and to Herr Dr. Franz-Karl Blust for the conscientious and careful reading of the proofs.

F.-W. von Herrmann
Freiburg i. Br., February 1988

DATE			